AF664063

Politics *of* Conversion

Politics *of* Conversion

Edited by

Devendra Swarup

Originals

Delhi

First Published 1986
This Impression Published 2017
Reproduced with permission from:
Deendayal Research Institute
7-E, Jhandewala Extension,
New Delhi 110055

ISBN 13: 978-81-8454-152-6
ISBN 10: 81-8454-152-6

Published by
Originals
A-6, 2nd, Nimri Commercial Centre,
Ashok Vihar Phase 4, Delhi 110052 (INDIA)
tel.: +91-11-27302453 fax.: +91-11-47061936
website: www.LPPindia.com e-mail: info@LPPindia.com

Printed at
Monica Enterprises
Delhi

PRINTED IN INDIA

Contents

DOCUMENTS, QUOTATIONS AND STATISTICS

Editor's Note

Why a wave of anger and concern should have surged through an entire nation four years ago when all that had happened was just the mass conversion of a small group of people to Islam in a tiny, unknown hamlet of Tamil Nadu—Meenakshipuram? In a country like India, where the vast majority of its population called Hindu believes in *Sarva Dharma Samabhava* (सर्वधर्म-समभाव) and has thought it fit to enshrine the concept of secularism as an article of faith in its Constitution, which was framed with the holocaust of Partition as its backdrop, what did it matter if a small fraction of its population preferred to change its mode of worship ? Isn't religion a matter of one's personal faith and shouldn't one be free to adopt any name or form as his object of worship if so impelled by his inner spiritual experience ? Had not the Indian *Rishis* declared centuries ago "Ultimate Reality is one, only the learned call it by different names" (एकं सद्विप्रा बहुधा वदन्ति)? Lord Krishna himself proclaimed in the Bhagvad Geeta:

यो यो यां यां तनुं भक्तः श्रद्धयार्चितुमिच्छति ।

तस्य तस्याचलां श्रद्धां तामेव विदधाम्यहम् ॥

In whatever form and whatever way a devotee chooses to worship me, in that very form do I stabilize that devotee's faith.

Bhagvad Geeta, VII, 21

'सर्व धर्म समादर भाव' has to be a natural outflow of such a grand and liberal philosophical tradition. That is why Hinduism has not developed into a bundle of a few rigid religious tenets, dogmas or precepts with a monolithic Church or hierarchical structure, i.e., an external organisation exercising monopolistic religious authority. For a Hindu, it is immaterial if a person born as Hindu believes in an impersonal *Brahman* or in a personal God, or in many gods or in no God at all. Hindu you are and Hindu you remain.

Therefore, it appears strange that the Hindu, who by virtue of his amazing breadth of vision and liberal outlook has never thought it worthwhile to seriously concern himself with either proselytisation or apostasy, should have reacted so strongly to the recent efforts at mass conversion.

One plausible explanation for this unexpected Hindu reaction may be the justifiable suspicion that if conversion has anything to do with inner faith and spiritual quest of an individual, it can take place only at an individual level and not *en-masse*. For, mass conversions cannot be brought about without organised efforts of some external agency. Therefore, to get to the roots of the present Hindu reaction we will have to probe as to which elements are interested in mass conversions in a secular India; what are their real motives; which are their target groups; and what is their *modus operandi*? What are the real impulsions and compulsions of converts at the time of conversion ? All the material collected in these pages is an attempt to find answers to such questions.

In the first article titled 'From Meenakshipuram to Puliangudi', eye-witness accounts and investigative reports by independent observers have been quoted, without any comment on our part, in order to give an authentic and clear idea of all the aspects of the recent incidents of mass conversion, its nature, agents of conversion and their techniques, social background of the converts, their basic urges and immediate compulsions etc.

A peep into this source material is sufficient to show that even in Independent India, the Hindu concept of *Sarva Dharma Samabhava* is being challenged by two well- organised religions with global ramifications, each one of which believes that it is *complete* in itself and is the *only* true path leading to human salvation and is, therefore, expansionist by nature.

This is not the first time that India has been victimised by expansionist nature of these religions. Its history is many centuries old and continuous and is full of bitter and painful memories. Unfortunately their expansion is also closely linked with foreign aggression and domination over India.

The process of conversion, which raised its ugly head in the eighth century in India, resulted in the partition of the motherland and creation of two independent and antagonistic states on Indian soil-namely, Pakistan (further divided into W. Pakistan and Bangladesh) and Bharat. The tragic partition of the country and the end of British rule in 1947 had created an illusion in the Indian mind that the chapter of aggressive and separatist politics of conversion was closed forever and now the Divided India could experiment peacefully with her age-old concern of *Sarva Dharma Samabhava*. But the new wave of mass conversion, which began at Meenakshipuram, came as a grim warning that the process of exploitation in the name of religion, which seemed to have ended with the partition of the country, was still very much alive and had got a fresh and vigorous start.

With the memories of the bloodshed in the wake of the earlier partition not yet completely faded out, a question naturally arose in Hindu mind: Will this unfortunate trend lead to another round of partition and senseless carnage? To find an answer to this question, it becomes very necessary to identify the immediate and basic factors responsible for this revival of mass conversion. A study of these documents will reveal that Islamic expansionists have selected as their target group that sector of the Hindu society which as a result of the degeneration of *Varna Vyavastha* has been suffering social discrimination and atrocities for many centuries and is now desperately searching for social and economic equality for itself.

If the Muslim expansionists are concentrating all their efforts on the socially backward sections of the Hindu society, the Christian missionaries league with British imperialism had selected millions of Indian tribals who were leading a secluded and peaceful life for centuries in hilly and forest areas, almost at the periphery of the main current of Indian nationalism. Obviously, the expansionists in both the camps, instead of approaching the spiritually and intellectually awakened individuals, have selected as their target groups only those sections of the Indian society which happen to be socially and economically backward. Quite naturally, they are allured into conversion not through an appeal to their religious consciousness, but to their social and economic needs. In the past, state patronage and money-power was freely used for the purpose, but now, bereft of political power, money-power seems to have become the main instrument of proselytisation. Many independent observers have felt that not religion but social and economic motives have played a dominant role in these mass conversions. Rather, religion seems to have lost its grip over the self- appointed leaders of these backward sections and for them the so-called religious conversion means, perhaps, nothing more than a change of clothes.

This naturally leads one to conclude that there is less of religion and more of politics behind such mass conversions. And, if separatist demands leading to the partition of the motherland and the current separatist movements in North-East India are any indications, this politics of conversion aims at numerical superiority, separatism and acquisition of political power.

Without doubt, such a politics of conversion poses a grave menace to our national ideals of secularism and democracy as well as to our national integrity. The history of Pakistan and Bangladesh since their birth proves conclusively that if India, inspire of innumerable stresses and strains, has been able to stick firmly to the path of *secularism* and *democracy* , it's entire credit goes to the Hindu ethos which pervades the vast majority of its population. If this Hindu ethos is lost, India may survive as a territorial entity but not as a nation committed to the ideals of *secularism* and *democracy*.

If India is to survive as a nation, these alarming separatist tendencies will have to be defeated. This may be possible only when the Hindu society resolutely sets its own house in order. For, it is the internal weakness of Hindu society which invites others to play their game of mass conversions. Hindu society should blame none but itself for the present sorry state of affairs. Why should it not have translated its own liberal and catholic ideal of आत्मवत् सर्वभूतेषु from a philosophical and religious plane into a social reality and thus eliminated the roots of social discrimination ? Warning came many times, but its response did not go beyond passing every time a pious resolution against untouchability and casteism. It was never followed by concerted and determined efforts. And if the Hindu society cannot reform itself, what moral right does it have to stop its depressed classes from walking out of its orbit in search of social and economic equality?

Of course, walking out of Hindu society does not automatically lead to social equality. Christian and Muslim communities in India are as much prisoners of caste system as the Hindu society. Economic and social inequality is galore in both. The recent Christian demand for extension of special privileges and concessions, which are available to Hindu Scheduled Castes under Reservation Policy, to Christian Scheduled Castes also shows that every religious group in India has its own scheduled castes or weaker sections. So, what is the fun in losing one's moorings and gain nothing in return. Therefore, the only permanent solution to the problem is that the Hindu society must reform itself down to its very roots. Hence, it becomes imperative to make an in-depth study of the Hindu response to this politics of conversion, to find out whether the present wave of Hindu resurgence and self-introspection will culminate in a total social reform or will peter out like many earlier waves.

The problem being vast and complex in nature, a collective effort is being made for its in-depth study. Various writers, representing different shades of opinion, have tried to tackle the problem from their own angles and in their own ways. The material collected in these pages can be no means claim to be exhaustive. It is only with a desire to stimulate further debate and research, on this subject, that we venture to dedicate this humble effort of ours to the collective wisdom and ethos of our Nation.

—Devendra Swarup

Meenakshipuram to Puliangudi: Events & Causes

Compilation

EVENTS

• Meenakshipuram Distt. Tirunelvelli: (19th Feb, 1981.)

INDIAN EXPRESS, New Del hi, April 13, 1981

On February 19, a function was arranged with pomp and show at Meenakshipuram. About 4,000 Muslims from neighbouring Tenkasi, Kadayanallur, Vadakari, Vavanagaram and other places participated in the conversion ceremony with their families. Mr. Sahul Haraeed, MLA, Kadyanallur, took an active part. The religious leaders of Islam also participated in large numbers.

The entire village wore a festive look. The *Salath* (prayer) started with *Fazar* (sunrise prayer), followed by *Luhar, Azar* and *Maqarib* at 1 pm, 4.30 pm. and 6.40 pm. respectively with all the congregation reciting the *kalama*.

SUNDAY, WEEKLY, Cal cut t a, 7 June, 1981

"...But on Thursday, 19 February most of the harijans woke up early and excited. It was the day they had chosen to break from the past- from their traditions and beliefs. After a bath they put on their best clothes. The women, however, stayed back in their huts, while the men, wearing unfamiliar caps, left their houses for the *maidan* at the back of the Kali temple. Some of the caps were gifts from the *Jamaat-ul-Ulema* branches at Tenkasi, the nearest railhead, and Panpoli, a neighbouring country town. But most cap-wearers had stitched the caps themselves. Some also sported well-trimmed beards–again, a new experience for many. The village, which had hardly ever been visited by any outsider, witnessed a sudden rush of visitors that day–mostly Muslim VIPs. Prominent among them were Mr. Sahul Hameed, the Muslim League MLA from Kadaynallur constituency of which Meenakshipuram is a part; Mr. A.K. Rifai, a former MP; and Mr. Abul Hasan Sahad Ali, the *Jamaat-ul-Ulema* chief for that area.

By 11.30 a.m. almost all the male harijans had turned up at the *maidan*. The *Jamat* chief took the stage. He explained how Islam treated all its followers as equals. Then he chanted the *Kalima*. Repeating after him the villagers knelt down facing west for their first prayers to Allah. In less than an hour, Sunderraj had become Sardar Mohammad, Madaswamy had become Mohammed Soaib, Jabamoni had become Jabarulla Khan, Murugesan had become Mohammed Ismail. Then, some of the visiting women went to bring the harijan women who were still in their houses. With their heads now covered they were escorted to the *maidan* where a moulvi (borrowed from the Panpoli mosque) married the wives again to their respective husbands, according to Islamic rites. Unmarried women too got new names and a religion. The conversion was now complete; more than three-fourths of the harijans of the village had abandoned the faith of generations, watched by the deities their fore-fathers had installed to protect them from the evil. A village which had no Muslim ever before had around 1,000 of them. Meenakshipuram became Rahamatnagar.

A feast followed, and the visiting Muslims shared food from the plates of the harijan converts, which was a novel experience for the harijans; they were equals at a feast! No teashop, in the past, gave them tea out of cups; they had to sip the beverage out of coconut shell or a tumbler made out of leaves. They could not draw water from the common wells or drink it from the same tap, if the caste Hindu were around.

After the feast came announcements: the villagers would get a mosque, a school which would also teach Arabic, and a burial ground where the dead could be buried with dignity. The foundation stone for the mosque was in fact, laid on 3rd March by Mr. Abdul Samad, the Muslim League MP of the area.

Report of The Parliamentary Committee on The Welfare of SC & ST Visited Meenakshipuram on 11th August, 1981.

On 19th March, 1981, the Muslims of the area and certain Muslims who had come from outside had arranged a feast and invited the Harijans for feast (*bada khana*). Those Harijans who did not want to go were dragged to that feast. The conversions followed the feast on that day. Prior to that a local M.L.A. belonging to Muslim League and a Member of Parliament belonging to the same party were seen visiting the village. They generally came after 10 P. M. and remained there for some time. It was alleged that many well-to-do muslims were putting pressure on them to get converted. They were being told that if they embraced Islam they would get social equality and respect. They would be able to marry their children in the Muslim families and also their children would be sent abroad for jobs. It was staged that they had no knowledge whether any money had been paid to those who had embraced Islam. It was also reported that a large number of Muslims from neighbouring districts and from Kerala visited Meenakshipuram regularly and exchanged greetings with the newly converted Harijans. The Study Group saw for themselves on that day that more than 100 Muslim men and women had come from outside and were present there.

- **Attiyyuttur Distt.: Ramnad (14th June, 1981)**

The village has a total population of 1650 out of which 800 are Muslims. By the efforts of the Keelkarai Muslims a total of 192 Pallas (Hindu-Harijans) out of the total of 260 were converted to Islam at a mass conversion ceremony on 14th June 1981. Sri Shahul Hameed Harakayar, leader of '*Ishadul Islam*' Palayamkottai and Moulana Moideen, a leader of the *Jamait-e-Islam*, attended the function. Pullaver Mustafa a High School teacher also attended.

- **Kooriyoor, Distt. Ramanathapuram (July 26, 1981.)**

In all 31 Harijan families of Kuriyoor village, 2 km, from here, embraced Islam yesterday reports UNI.

The development took by surprise the Hindu-leaders who gathered here for a day-long Hindu Solidarity Conference today. The Harijans, who had planned to embrace Islam in August, apparently advanced the date in view of the conference. A member of the Rameswaram Trust Board and a former police head constable were said to be among the 192 persons who became Muslims in the second instance of mass conversion of Harijans at this village recently.

The P.T.I. report adds, "Two Moulvis, Jamal Mohamed of Chinnamannur and another from Siddayan kotta from Madurai district officiated at the conversion ceremony. They distributed clothes and cash doles to the converts." At Athiyoothu and Elamanoor village also some conversions took place yesterday.

- **Thanjavur Distt.**

PATRIOT, **New Delhi 29th July, 1981**

The wave of conversion of Harijans to Islam which is sweeping some parts of Tamil Nadu has spread to Thanjavur district also. About 180 persons including a former Congress MLA had embraced Islam in nine villages in Thiruthuraipoondi–Mannargudi areas of the district, according to information.

Intensive efforts for conversion were reportedly going on in some villages in Papanasam area of the district. A large number of Islamic literature from abroad had also been reportedly received for conversion purposes. The reports said conversion of Harijans to Islam had been reported in the village of Kulamanickam, Sangenthi, Ammamoor, Mangathikudi, Kalappal, Uthamarthandapuram, Engan Vittukatti and Kallimenu villages in Thiruturaipoondi–Mannargudi area of the district.

- **Gudiyattam Taluk, (August 12 & 13, 1981).**

INDIAN EXPRESS, **New Delhi August 19, 1981**

Twenty-one Harijans in four villages in and around Peranambut block in Gudiyattam taluk here have embraced Islam in pursuit of social status and jobs. They include ten Harijans (Christians belonging to three families) from Salapettai, nine from Erukkambat, one each from Rangampettal and Peranambut Harijan colonies. The conversions took place in the mosque on August 12 and 13.

The converts are being kept in the house of one Cheri Sait, a leading beedi merchant in Peranambut. They have been given new clothes-lungies, shirts, big hankies and saris. Muslim visitors to the house hug their new brethren and teach them the Islamic way of life.

- **Mandaikkadu, Distt. Kanya Kumari (March 1, 1982.)**

Report of the HINDU MUNNANI, Kanyakumari

Mandaikkadu used to be a peaceful, small, and beautiful hamlet, situated on the coast, 20 kms from Nagercoil. It is famous for its 1000-years old Bhagavathi Amman Temple. Our Harijan brothers, especially, have always been worshipping at this temple, in great numbers. The devotees of Bhagavathi Amman have their traditional bath in the sea, followed by–dip in the AVM channel, before proceeding to the temple proper. In the month of *Maasi*, (Feb-March), the *Maasi Kodai* Festival is conducted, every year. Since 1936, the *Haindava* (Hindu) *Seva Sangam* has been organising this festival. This year the *Kodai* Festival began on the 28th February. However, the fisherwomen of Mandaikkadu were heard gossipping, as early as January, that there would be no *Kodai* this year.

The first day of March 1982 was a BLACK DAY in the 1000–year old history of the Bhagavathi Amman temple. As the temple festivities began and hundreds of pilgrims, especially women walked to the sea for a bath, there was unusual commotion and activity in Pudur village. The small posse of 25 police was stationed near the channel. Suddenly cries were heard. With a shock, the S. I. on duty turned to see ladies running in panic from the sea towards the temple–many of them with no clothes on ! He rushed to the seashore. Some men had jumped into the sea, assaulting and molesting the pilgrims –and the ladies were running, screaming in terror !

Simultaneously, two things happened. A crowd of fishermen surrounded the S. I. Murugesan, hit him with a heavy fishing hook and tried to drag him. As Murugesan twisted to free himself, he saw a mob rushing towards the line of petty shops near the temple, looting and destroying them. Murugesan escaped, collected his policemen and ran to stop the looting mob. At that time, the church bell of Pudur was rung frantically. And in an incredibly short span of time 3000 howling and gesticulating men were rushing at the tiny police party, armed with numerous weapons!

Since lathi charge proved to be ineffective, the police fired in the air. It was of no use. The mob kept attacking police, burning the shops and looting them. Ultimately order to fire was given. This is what Mr. George, Asst. Sub-Inspector has to say about that fateful night.

" ...... The Christians did not like the Hindus having bath in the sea...

Around 8.00 p. m. about 3000 persons came as a group from Mandaikkadu Pudur and attacked the devotees. They looted the shops. The 23 strong police party including myself was injured. Unable to control the 3000 strong mob, we resorted to firing." (THUGHLAK TAMIL FORTNIGHTLY, 15-3-1982). As a result, six men died and about 25 were injured.

As the horrified members of the *Haindava Seva Sangam* rushed to the spot, little did they realise the diabolical role this small but powerful group was to play in the next few, very vital, hours.

The D.I.G., Collector and other officials hurried to the spot. And immediately Mrs. Lourdammal Simon and the priests surrounded them; and for more than 4 hours,–4 vital hours when the authorities would get their first impression of what took place there–until well past midnight, none of the Hindu victims or eyewitnesses were permitted to meet and speak to the authorities !

It was only at 2-30 A. M. that the organisers of the festival could voice their grievance to the officials. All the while, Mrs. Simon and her cohorts kept continuously shouting and protesting that the Hindu pilgrims should not have their dip in the sea.

The Christian D. S. P. and Collector who are close associates of the Bishop of Kottar, refused to listen to the Hindu's pleas, (Both have since been transferred). Instead of taking immediate steps and arresting the anti-social elements, some of the regular rituals in the festival like the popular 'Elephant procession' were ordered cancelled.

As news of the ghastly incidents was being flashed by the Press to a stunned public, Bishop Arokiaswamy was busy carrying out the second phase of the diabolic plan. The corpses of the six dead, after post mortem, were kept at the police premises. Against all rules, the Archbishop was permitted to see the bodies and take possession of them. A death procession was taken out around many areas and tension was dramatically built up. The church leaders spoke of the six dead as 'Martyrs' who had died for their Religion ! It was vowed that until the six deaths were avenged with Hindu deaths, the Christians would not rest.

On the 3rd March, about one lakh Christians and muslims went in procession. All Christian institutions were ordered to close that day. Loudspeakers urged all Christians to join the procession. Communal frenzy rousing anti-Hindu slogans reverberated.

Mischief was afoot! And it took its course ! A storm of violent attacks left the Hindus stunned.

Eathamozhi was the first target. Hundreds of houses were burnt. With the help of Maharishi Mahesh Yogi Institute, many service schemes, including two sewing centres, are being run by the Vishwa Hindu Parishad. All of them were destroyed. One Hindu was kidnapped. Scores were seriously injured. Even woman and children were not spared. All the major newspapers carried reports of this savage attack.

From then onwards, Hindu population in neighbouring villages was attacked in a systematic and pre-planned manner, as the following facts indicate:

—Manavalapuram (13th March), Melamannkudy and Samadhanpurum (15th March), Colachel (16th March) Vivekanandpurum and Erayumanthurai (18th March). The nature of planning and preparations made by the Christians, can be gleaned from the following press report.

Indian Express, Delhi, 17 March, 1982.

Nagarcoil, March 16. According to reports reaching here, the police resorted to firing when they were attacked by a group of armed fishermen. The police had gone to the village to clear road blocks. The fishermen had spread glass pieces on the road and dug holes, the report said. About 25 policemen were injured in the attack and some of them were admitted to the local hospital.

The fishermen, the report said, had "cut off" the village, following a rumour that members from the other community were coming to attack them. They mistook the police to be members of the other community and attacked them with weapons. There was also heavy stone-throwing, the report said.

Christian Version

IMPRINT, Monthly, Bombay, July 1982 (Report: Kumar Raj).

Police opened fire on the night of March 1 at Mandakadu about 20 km from Nagercoil, leaving six Christian fisherman dead. The official machinery in the district is alleged to have committed a Himalayan blunder by not providing adequate protection. It is unlikely that they had not sensed danger because tensions had been mounting for the last few months following attacks and counter-attacks between religious factions. Yet, though additional police protection was sought by Fr. Sebastian Fernando on February 27 itself while the festival started the next day and the firing took place the day after, no extra police force was provided. After the firing, the State Government had no option but to transfer the District Collector and the Superintendent of Police.

The firing is said to be a sequel to the growing friction between the fishermen and the police over the use of loudspeakers and the rude behaviour of the former.

The annual 10-day Masi festival of Bhagavatiamman temple at Mandakadu commenced on February 28. People belonging to all walks of life as well as from all over the country, particularly from Kerala, started pouring into Mandakadu. It is customary that the Hindus use loudspeakers during these festive days. This year, unusually a speaker was fitted very near the Kurusadi, (shrine in the church) and another was focussed on Puthur and abusive words are said to have been uttered by some Hindu fanatics. The fishermen also paid back in the same coin. However, the real trouble started when policeman disconnected the loudspeakers of the latter on a complaint by the former.

Dr. Arokaisamy, Bishop of Kottar, charges that the firing was "unwarranted and unprovoked" and that it was not preceded by any warning. He claims that no top official who could issue an order to "fire" was present at the time. To justify the firing episode, the police themselves are said to have demolished some thatched shops and set fire to them, besides igniting a police vehicle. At least one police constable is said to have inflicted bruises on his hand after the event to substantiate the firing. Against the police evidence the entire blame fell upon the poor, defenceless fishermen. The Bishop is certain the fishermen of Puthur did not prevent the pilgrims from the ritualistic bath and never did they molest any women, as alleged. If the police opened fire to disperse two warning groups and that too near the Bhagavatiamman temple, how is it that the victims belong to only one group ? And, why were the dead bodies found lying near the Kurusadi belonging to the church of St Lucia, Puthur—a locality of Christian fishermen and not near the temple? The Kurusadi is about two furlongs away from the temple.

• **Puliangudi, Distt. Tirunelveli (June 8, 1982)**

THE STATESMAN, DELHI, 13-06-1982

Madras, June 12—The Vishva Hindu Parishad's *Gnana Ratham* launched at the holy shrine of Sri Arunachaleswarar at Tiruvannamalai in North Arcot district last Sunday by Sri Jayendra Saraswathi of Kanchi Kamakoti Peetam for the propagation of Hindu dharma in rural Tamil Nadu, ended up by spreading "Adharma" in interior Tirunelveli district resulting in the death of seven Harijans in clashes with the Thevar community and another in Police firing, and the withdrawal of the *Ratham* for the time being.

When the *Gnana Ratham* reached Puliangudi on Wednesday, some Harijan members of the *Samathuva Sahodarathuva Sangam* objected to the Thevars, who refused to accept the Harijans as equals or allow them to offer worship at their temples, to erect a welcome arch in the Harijan sector of the village.

The police intervened and prevented the Harijans from demolishing the arch. An irate Harijan mob attacked the Puliangudi police station. In the melee four constables were injured and several shops in the vicinity ransacked. The police fired in the air to disperse the crowd.

The same day, Muslims and Harijans converged in large numbers at nearby Kadayanallur village for a meeting addressed by Mr. Ibrahim Sulaiman Sait, MP, president of the Indian Union Muslim League, Mr. Rifayee and Shahul Hamed, M.L.A.

The *Gnana Ratham* went about its mission and was taken in procession by the Thevars through the main streets of Puliangudi when devotees performed *ahhishekam* and *archana* to the itinerant Lord Muruga. The police, however, withheld permission for the procession to pass through the Harijanwadi as members of the *Samathuva Sangam* objected to it.

TIMES OF INDIA, Delhi, 28th June 1982 Report By V.G, Prasad Rao.

Last year, Mr. Refayee and Mr. Shahul Hameed started the *Samathuva Sahodarathuva Sangham* (association of equality and fraternity) in Kadayanallur, 15 km from Puliangudi. Kadayanallur is Mr. Shahul Hameed's constituency. The SSS has more than 60 branches in Tiruneleveli district and has been organising regular meetings in the surrounding villages.

At a meeting organised by the SSS at Kadayanallur on June 1, the president of the Indian Union Muslim League, Mr. Ibrahim Sulaiman Sait, M.P., was reported to have called on Harijans and other depressed classes to make common cause with the Muslims to capture political power. Mr. G. Moorthy, the lone Republican Party (Gavai group) member in the state assembly, was alleged to have abused gods of the Hindu Pantheon.

Following this, there were clashes between Harijans returning from the meeting and non-Harijans. The same day, the "*Gnana Ratham*", launched on June 6 from the Tiruvannamalai temple by the Sankarcharya of Kanchi, Jayendra Saraswati Swami, arrived at Puliangudi. The Harijan community was split with some objecting to its presence and others, including the headman, welcoming the opportunity of worshipping Lord Muruga.

The Union minister of state for home, Mr. P. Venkatasubbiah, thinks the Meenakshipuram conversions are at the bottom of the trouble. Mr. R.P. Kosairam, Congress (I) M.P., who hails from the district has blamed the "provocative" speeches made at Kadayanallur. The Harijan and Muslim factions blame the RSS.

Both the Muslim League and the Dravida Kazhagam leaders have raised the RSS bogey. Mr. Suleiman Sait was said to have accused the chief minister of even siding with the RSS. There is, however, no evidence so far to show that the RSS as a body is involved in Puliangudi. The Congress (I) president, Mr. M.P. Subramaniam, who has toured the affected villages, has called for a judicial probe into the clashes.

'India Today', fortnightly, N. Delhi, July 15, 1982

But ever since the Meenakshipuram conversions, tension has been building up in these villages. Harijans, who form an estimated 50 per cent of the population in the villages around Meenakshipuram, have finally gathered courage with the support of local Muslims. They are raising their voices against the suffocating discrimination that the caste Hindus have allegedly practised against them.

The first signs of their militancy showed itself early this year when on January 10 a nebulous organisation of Muslims and Harijans called *Samuthuva Sahodarathva Sangham* (SSS)-an association for equality and brotherhood—was formed by A. Shahul Hameed, the lone Indian Union Muslim League (IUML) member in the Tamil Nadu Assembly, who was elected from Kadayanallur taluk 10 km from Puliagudi, ironically supported by the opposition front which included the DMK and the Congress (I). Hameed is the convenor of the Tirunelveli-based South India Islamic Society which was responsible for the Meenakshipuram conversion. The SSS was formed mainly to bring about greater amity between Harijans and Muslims as a first step to the former's conversion. Meanwhile the Harijans in Puliangudi organised themselves into an association called *Thhalthapattor NaIla Urimai Sangham* (Association for the Welfare of the Downtrodden) on March 24, which lent support to the SSS. Said E. Samuel, the *Sangham's* young general secretary: 'We had decided we would shed our blood to gain equality with other castes. To symbolise their militancy they designed a red and green flag. While the red stood for their blood the green was supposed to mean equality but its similarity to the green of the IUML flag was too close to be a coincidence. The *Sangham* then started mobilising Harijans in other villages and on April 4 organised a massive convention which representatives of 90 surrounding villages attended. The convention decided that all the 76 sub-castes of Harijans would put up a unified struggle for equality.....

While the loosely knit joint associations of caste Hindus claimed that their relations with the Harijans were cordial, they accused the Muslims of driving a wedge between them. Said M. Sankarapandian Pillai, a former MP and town Congress (I) president. "The alarming activities of the SSS, aimed at transforming Puliangudi into another Meenakshipuram, forced us to come together despite political differences."

Things worsened when Harijans pulled down all flags on their streets and put up their green and red banner. The Hindus retaliated by putting up yellow flags with the 'Om' symbol on top of their houses. Then on June 8 two unfortunate coincidences sparked off the riots: a meeting was organised by the SSS at Kadayanallur which was to be addressed by the president of the IUML, Suleiman Sait at 10 p.m. On the same day the *Gnana Ratham*, a mobile unite for the propagation of the Hindu religion designed by the *Vishwa Hindu Parishad* was to arrive. The mobile unit was equipped with sophisticated audio-visual equipment such as a photophene slide projector, a 16 mm film projector and pre-recorded cassettes of devotional songs and discourses.

Two contradictory versions are given by the continuities as to what caused riots. The caste Hindus maintain that the *Ratham* was prevented from going through the streets by Harijans who on the next duty damaged one of its supporting pillars. The Harijans claim that while they were attending the SSS meeting they were stoned by the Marawa community in a village called Chokampatti. The Marawas on their part claim that it was the inflammatory speech of Suleiman Sait at the SSS meeting that sparked off the violence. Asked about the real cause of the riot District Collector Nirmal Singh Hira said: "don't know. We are investigating." ....

The Secretary of the Communist Party of India Govindan Nair told newsmen in Madras last month that the conversions of Harijans had proved 'counter-productive' because of 'Hindu backlash'.

Forewarnings

Puliangudi riots could not be termed as coming "like a bolt from the blue". Their ground was being prepared for the last so many months. In fact, the following reports published in the HINDU, *Madras (6th Feb. 1982) and* INDIAN EXPRESS, *New Delhi (15th Feb. 1982) had forewarned the country in advance.* — Ed.]

THE HINDU, MADRAS Tir unel vel i, Feb. 5, 1982

After Meenakshipuram, Kadayanallur is the place to be watched. The Harijans of Kadayanallur are openly talking about embracing Islam "to improve their lot on the social plane." ....

An organisation called *Samathuva Sahodarathuva Sangham* was formed for the Kadayanallur Assembly constituency on January 10. Harijans and Muslims are equally represented in its membership as well as its executive.......

It was formed at a meeting held under the presidentship of Mr. A.K. Rafai, former MP, who is also the President of *Ishathul Islam Sabha* under whose auspices conversions took place in Meenakshipuram Its objectives have been variously stated by Harijan and Muslim leader, but both aver that it has nothing to do with conversion. When this correspondent visited Kadayanallur on January 25, Mr. Ramanathan, "Nattamai" (leader) of the Harijans in Ward Nos. 18 and 19 and Mr. John said the the *Sangam* had been formed to promote close understanding and cooperation between Harijans and Muslims in all elections.

They said Kadayanallur Panchayat Union was originally a reserve constituency for the Scheduled Castes. But later, an influential leaver of the Thevar community had it changed to the unreserved category. They also said that the major political parties like the Congress (I), AIADMK and DMK had named candidates from this community. This made Harijans sit up and think. In the Kadayanallur constituency there are 35,000 voters, of whom 1,000 are Harijans and 3,000 Muslims. If these two sections unite they would be able to win any election. Hence the decision to form the *Sangam*.

INDIAN EXPRESS, DELHI 15.2.82.

Another wave of Conversions

A year after the mass conversion of Harijans to Islam at Meenakshipuram the stage appears to have been set for a new wave of conversions in this southern Tamil Nadu district.

The anniversary celebrations were preceded by a series of village-level meetings organised by the Equality and Brotherhood Association, formed on January 10 at Kadayanallur with representatives of Muslims and Harijans.

The association was formed on the initiative of the 37 year old South India *Ishathul Islam Sabha* which claims to have arranged 7,000 conversions in Tamil Nadu since its inception. The *sabha*, with the headquarters in this district town, has branches in Madras, Thanjavur, Tiruchirapalli, Cumbum, Kilakaria and Tenkasi. It runs a college, a middle school, a girls' hostel and an orphanage. In a report circulated among its members recently, the *sabha* said: "Thousands of non-Muslims are waiting to join the holy faith of Islam but they are kept in the waiting list for want of funds."

It claimed that about 5,000 people at Puliyangudi, Vasadevanallur and Kannapatcheri near Kadayanallur and Chintamani and Ilanji near Tirunelveli had approached it expressing readiness to embrace Islam. About 1,000 people at Sivakasi in Ramanathapuram were ready for conversion. But it was being delayed due to lack of funds for clothes, food and circumcision.

The society said it had to assume responsibility for providing the converts with all facilities so that they did not turn to others for help. It had some schemes on hand and if these were implemented, "We hope many brothers from other communities will rush of their own accord to embrace our faith."

The *Sabha* noted that the area was "replete with innumerable Hindu and Christian institutions" and said a "strong and resourceful Islamic organisation was essential to carry on conversion, orientation, assimilation and rehabilitation of those eager to embrace Islam."

Sabha president A.K. Refayee said in an appeal circulated with the report that its objective was to help the neo-Muslims, from the day of conversion to the time they were settled in life. "Lead a good Muslim's life." He appealed to co-religionists all over the world to extend a helping hand to the *sabha*. It was suggested that aid be "directly made available to us and not routed through other organisations" as this would enable the *sabha* to take expeditious action. He also suggested that the converts be considered for employment in the Arab countries.

Minister for Home Affairs, Shri Zail Singh in reply to a question, informed the Lok Sabha on 19th August, 1981 that "about 2000 Harijans in Tamil Nadu have embraced Islam since February 1981. Some isolated cases of conversion of Harijans to Islam have also been reported from some other parts of the country."

• **North Arcot, South Arcot & Salem districts.**

Dina Malar, Tamil daily, 13-7-82.

The Criminal Investigation Department of Tamilnadu Government has unearthed vigorous efforts at forcible conversion in South Arcot, North

Arcot and salem Districts of Tamilnadu. The Ulundurpet Police have registered cases against 21 persons, connected with Christian Missions, who are carrying on these forcible conversions in South Arcot District. The investigation is going on.

It has been estimated that the number of people thus forcibly converted during the last few months in South Arcot district alone, runs into thousands. The District Collector Kumari Chandralekha has taken stringent measures to prevent this situation from worsening.

In general, forcible conversions into Christianity failed to click in the comparatively fertile taluks of South Arcot. Districts like Chidambaram, Cuddalore, Panruti and Kattumannarkoli. Proselytisation could proliferate only in the drought hit area of the district like Kallakkurichi, Ulundurpet, Thirunavalur and Ginge. It has been detected that an amount of Rs. 7 lakhs had found its way into Kallakkurichi alone during May last year. It is estimated that the expenditure on each prospective convert ranges from Rs. 500 to Rs. 5000.

The tribal people of Kalroyan Hills are the main target of these missionaries. Recent months have seen a Church coming up fast at Vallimalai. It has been estimated to cost Rs. 5 lakhs.

CAUSES

(a) **Social Inequality and Caste Atrocities**

INDIAN EXPRESS, N. Delhi, (13 April, 1981)

The Harijans of Meenakshipuram are different from their counterparts in the district. More than 40 per cent of them are educated, and by and large they are sufficiently rich. Ninety percent of them are registered cultivating tenants of the Thiruvaduthurai Mutt lands in the adjacent Mekkarai.

Some of the villagers are well-placed in government service. With their improved economic status and literacy rates, the Harijans demanded equal social status with other communities, specially Thevars. But they were ill-treated. They allege that separate tumblers were used for serving coffee and tea in hotels. They were not even allowed to sit in the buses when other caste Hindus were in large numbers. They were socially boycotted and persecuted.

'SUNDAY' WEEKLY, Calcutta (7 June, 1981)

...The harijans of Meenakshipuram were among the more fortunate of their kind in the country. More than 40 per cent of them were educated. Among them were two MBBS doctors, an agricultural scientist and five graduates. A number of them were well placed in government services and two of the four teachers of local primary school were harijans. Some 80 families in a community of 180 families owned land, and the biggest landholder in the village was a harijan–Chinna Madaswamy, with about 10 acres of land in his possession. Some 20 harijan houses, four of them concrete structures, had electricity. Those who did not have land or those who had marginal holdings were cultivators for the Thiruvaduthurai Mutt (temple estate) in the adjoining Mekkarai village.

With the education and a certain amount of prosperity came the urge to be at par with high caste Thevar community who, of course, were even better off, and lived in another section of the village. The temple of Karuppan marks the division–the harijans stay to the east of the temple, the Thevars to the west, segregated from each other by a ribbon of dirt track. The harijans wanted this dividing line to disappear, Thevars did not.

"We were sick of being treated like dirt," says 37 year-old Sundarraj, now Sardar Mohammed. The caste Hindus would not let a harijan carry a towel on his shoulder; this would be treated as a subtle effort to behave as a social equal. If he did he would certainly invite abuse–"*thimir pidicha pallan*" (you insolent low caste). The harijan had to carry his towel only under the armpit. Sundarraj was bitter as he talked about the humiliations harijans had to suffer. "If we have to talk to a caste Hindu, we had to bow head, fold our hands, and hold a palm on our mouth so that our saliva did not accidentally fall on the person we were talking to and pollute him." One of the oldest villagers, Madaswamy (now Mohammed Soaib), 65, cuts into the conversation and says, "They would not even let us hang our towels at the elbow; we had to hang them further down on our arm and keep the arm pressed against, the chest while walking." "Still worse is a harijan sporting a clean starched shirt; it is just not tolerated," said 16-year-old Sarvana Kumar (now Umar Faruque).

The Hindu daily, Madras (June 15, 1981)

"It is not poverty that made us to switch over to Islam", said Paramasivam, a former President of the Panchayat Board, who now calls himself Syed Sulaiman, but "the torture the select Harijans in the village were subjected to by the Police." He alleged that following the murder of two members of the Thevar community at Mekkarai village, near Meenakshipuram, the Harijans were frequently interrogated in an attempt to trace the culprits involved in the murder but still absconding.

Another convert said that most Harijans in the villages were farm workers. To reach their place of work they had to go through the village of Panpozhi inhabited by Caste Hindus who always humiliated them. His contention seemed to be that the idea of conversion was not of recent origin but was lingering in their minds for the last few years. He said that a Harijan's attempts to open a tea-stall were thwarted by caste Hindus. Another man had to close down a hair-dressing shop he was running because of threat from the upper caste Hindus.

Even among Harijans there were sub-sects. One Harijan in Ambasamudram (Tirunelveli district) said that in South Arcot and Thanjavor district, the Harijans would neither be hosts nor the guests of certain sub-sects of Harijans. In Tirunelveli itself, he added, "inter-marriage is prohibited between these groups and the *Samban* caste is supposed to be superior to others. There are instances where barbers and washermen do not serve Harijans and the Harijans have washermen of their own caste.

TIMES OF INDIA, N. Delhi (28 June 1982)

The Thevars, incidentally, are no better off than Harijans economically speaking, but they enjoy several traditional rights over them including free service.

Till some years ago, according to a custom in Puliangudi, when a Thevar died, a Harijan had to shave his head and then dig the grave for the burial of the bones and ashes of the deceased. If the Harijan happened to be a government servant, he could pay a "fine" of Rs. 25 and escape from the demeaning task. Harijans have naturally refused to observe this practice in the last few years. The Thevars have also been keeping the Harijans away from temples though these are supposed to be open to all.

INDIA TODAY fortnightly New Delhi (July 16-31, 1981)

Syed Mohammed or Sethu, a sturdy man who was wearing a new printed shirt, is the leader of the Harijans. Sethu became emotional when asked his reasons for changing his religion: "Press reports said that the riots were between Harijans and caste Hindus. Aren't we Hindus?" A relevant question but then the riots had not affected their village. "We are physically lit and educationally equal. Why are we being treated badly? Why don't the Hindus allow us to run a shop in the town ? Whenever we open one, they don't buy anything from our shops. But Muslims treat us equally. "Why not become a Christian ?" "Even among Christians here are caste problems. We have Nadar Christians, Harijan Christians and so on. Again we will be discriminated against."

PARLIAMENTARY COMMITTEE for the welfare of SC & ST

EXTRACTS FROM THE REPORT of the study tour to Tamil Nadu (August, 1981).

(52) The Study Group stated that wherever the Members had gone, they had been told that the following were the main reasons that promoted Harijans to embrace Islam:-

i. Atrocities committed by the Caste Hindus.
ii. Atrocities committed by the Police.
iii. Economic backwardness and social disability.

According to the Social Welfare Secretary Tamil Nadu Government conversion had been going on for a long time and the State Government had the statistics. In spite of economic development, the harijans had not been given social equality. A new awareness had come among the Scheduled Castes. It were not the poor among the poorest who were converting but the educated, who had taken advantage of the relaxations and benefits earmarked by the Central and State Government for these communities. The educated persons had a feeling that their social status had not changed in spite of the high education. They were now revolting against the social inequality. An intellectual revolt is taking place among them. They felt that by embracing Islam if not they, at least their children would get social status. The harijans had also a feeling that Muslims responded more to their grievances and difficulties than the Hindus.

At Meenakshipuram

The Study Group held a meeting with those Harijans who had embraced Islam. One of them stated that he had been a Member of the village Panchayat for about 12 years. Every month the Panchayat held a meeting and at those meetings he was never served drinking water. He stated that atrocities committed on them by Caste Hindus and Police were the main reasons for their conversion.

Kuriyur Visited 11.8.81

(13) Shri Govindan (he has since embraced Islam alongwith 27 other persons after the visit of the Study Group, as reported in the HINDUSTAN TIMES dated 21st August, 1981) a Harijan advocate informed the Study Group that in July, 1981 about 192 Harijans had embraced Islam. These conversions were the direct result of the riots that had taken place in Ramanathapuram in which the Harijans were subjected to atrocities and untold misery unleashed by the Caste Hindus on them. He stated that even the educated persons among the Harijans were not spared from these atrocities. His own office in Ramanathapuram was burnt along with his law books costing more than Rs. 20,000/- and his family members were injured, as he was considered to be the leader of the Harijans. He was also implicated in some criminal case.

(14) Shri S.K. V elu, another Harijan informed the Study Group that he had been the local village Panchayat President for the last 12 years. He was mercilessly beaten by the Caste Hindu and was taken to the Police Station. There too he was beaten by the Police. He attributed the Police atrocities on the Harijans as the main factor for compelling Harijans to embrace Islam.

(51) The Harijans had reached a saturation point due to the age long atrocities being committed on them, their social-unacceptability, having

been disowned by the Hindu and their utter helplessness in getting just ice from the police, denial of drinking water facilities, provision of separate utensils for them in public eating places, denial of entry in the temples, not permitted to wear *chappals* and proper and new clothes and their utter economic and social backwardness.

It had been stated that the leaders of the movement for conversions were young educated scheduled caste persons who occupied posts in Government. One of them was a doctor in Urban Municipality, another was an engineer, the third was a local fund auditor and there was a large number of teachers who had got converted to Islam. There was also a case of a temple trustee, a scheduled caste, himself getting converted. Those young educated people appear to have given the conversions an intellectual base and reasoning that it was a revolt against harassment by the caste Hindus and the traditional apathy of Hindu society. In general it had made them to turn their back to Hinduism.

(46) Conversions in Meenakshipuram, Kurayur and other villages had revealed that religion had ceased to be a matter of conviction. It had become more a matter of convenience. The most attractive feature currently popular among the educated youth of the scheduled castes had been that they would be treated at par and enjoy a common brotherhood if they embraced Islam. Moreover, in actual practice, whenever the caste Hindus committed atrocities on the scheduled castes, Muslims often helped them. It had been found by the State Government that after conversion the converts were under continuous follow up action for the purpose of religious initiation and were drawn into their religious network systematically. All the converted families were continuing to receive attention and support, both moral and economical from the entire Muslim community of the neighbouring villages and from the Muslim organisations. This was in sharp contrast to the neglect suffered by hem at the hands of Hindu religious institutions.

Sex and Crime Police

Hindustan Times, N. Delhi (23 July 1981)

Those in quest of dowry seem to have found a new way out. The latest is bigamy by changing one's religion. There is little the law of the land can do if a man change his religion from Hinduism to Islam and take on a new wife.

A number of such cases have come to the notice of a women's organisation, *Nari Raksha Samiti* which today held a demonstration in Krishna Nagar in front of the house of an alleged victim's husband.

Rajni Kanta is a lower division clerk. Married in June 1975 to a bank official, she today finds herself and her child without hearth and home.

Her husband Ramesh Khanna on Feb. 26, became a Muslim and married another Hindu girl called Neeru.

HINDUSTAN TIMES Delhi (4 June, 1982)

(UNI) – Mr. Abdul Razack (51), the husband of Mrs. Noorjahan Razack, AIADMK member of parliament was found dead in the residence of one of his three wives here, Police said today.

Mrs Noorjahan Razack in a complaint to the Police said that her husband was murdered last night by someone by administering poison to him.

Police recovered the body of Mr. Razack early today from the residence of Mr. Razack's first wife Rajalakshmi and sent it for post-mortem. A case has been registered by the police.

Mr. Razack, formerly Gupta, embraced Islam when he married Noorjahan. He had already married twice. While his first two wives are residing in the same building Mrs. Noorjahan had a separate house.

TIMES OF INDIA, Delhi (23 June, 1982)

Eve-teasing has been often the cause of clashes involving Harijans and non-Harijans in Tamil Nadu. These clashes have taken a toll of 40 lives since 1978, of them 34 Harijans.

A study of the clashes reported in the past four years shows that caste Hindus intolerance towards Harijans and growing unwillingness of Harijan youths to put up with indignities of the kind suffered by their parents lie at the root of recurring caste violence.

RSS STUDY TEAM'S REPORT

Kurayoor Village is situated 30 km from Madurai with about 500 families of Harijan Hindus and equal number of non-Harijan Hindu families. During the period from February-September, 1980, about 40 Harijan Hindu families have been converted to Islam.

Although there is age-old enmity between Thevars and Harijans, the immediate cause of conversion appears to be the initiative taken by Dr. Manoharan, a District Medical Officer of Ramnad District, and the Muslim community. According to a doctor colleague of his, Dr. Manoharan a married man, fell in love with a Muslim lady and desired to marry her. When this was resisted by his Hindu mother and wife, he became a Muslim and married the Muslim girl. His mother and first wife still remain Hindus. Dr. Manoharan obviously took shelter under the Muslim personal law to have another wife (in fact one can have three more wives !) while the first one is living, whereas the Hindu Law prohibits it.

Dr. Manoharan was converted as back as 1978 and the Kurayoor conversion took place after March 1980. Therefore, it appears more than probable that having become a Muslim for personal reasons, Dr. Manoharan has been made a pincer in the hands of the Muslims for converting the Harijans of Kurayoor Village.

H.V. Sheshadri: Warning of Meenakshipuram (p. 6)

Meenakshipuram is a small hamlet near Pampohzi village in Tenkashi, Tirunelveli District. This area bordering Kerala is notorious for inter-state smuggling and other inter-state crime gangs. Recently, the police unearthed a massive counterfeiting activity in an estate near the village. The counterfeiting was being done, according to the police, by some Christian Padris with the aid of a printing machine donated by Doulgas Charity of America. This has been established by the accused persons to the police.

A Christian family residing in Tenkashi Taluk, where Meenakshipuram is situated, is also running and orphanage aided by the Douglas Charity. The primary purpose of this orphanage is conversion of Harijans to Christianity. This orphanage abets several Harijans to create tensions between Harijans and non-harijans in several villages, so as to create among the former an atmosphere of alienation from the Hindu society, which is necessary for conversions. The family running the orphanage is also said to have made available the machinery for counterfeiting.

According to the police, printing and distribution of counterfeit currency has been going on for several years. The modus operandi is that the printing is done by the Christians and the distribution outlets are the trade channels of Muslims, The Harijans are employed to carry the counterfeit currency.

The police stumbled on the counterfeiting case quite fortuitously while investigating the murder of two non-Harijan Hindus, allegedly by some Harijans. One Thangaraj, a notorious local *goonda,* changed over to Islam and became Yusuf when he eloped with a Thevar girl. When two Thevar youths, keeping watch on him, discovered that he was a link in a big counterfeiting racket, they w'ere murdered. In the course of the investigation of the murder case, some Harijans were taken into the custody and the police used their usual methods on them. In the course of their confessions the counterfeiting activity was unearthed by the police.

Although the involvement of Muslims in the counterfeiting case was established, due to their political pull, the police did not take any action against the Muslims; but the Harijans were taken into custody and beaten up.

The Muslims found their chance of fishing in troubled waters, they told the Harijans that if they became Muslims the police would not dare touch them and that they (Muslims) would also provide enough money and business for them.

THE STATESMAN, N. Delhi (July 22, 1981)

"The security the new religion accords to converts is best demonstrated by the experience of Mr. Thankaraj, a Harijan youth of Rahamatnagar near Meenakshipuram, who eloped with a Thevar (Caste Hindu) girl of Mekkarai, seven kilometres away. To escape the wrath of Thevars, he got himself converted to Islam and took on the name Mohammed Yusuf. There is a preponderance of Muslim population in this part of Tiruneveli district, bordering on Kerala. When the Thevars caught up with Mr. Thankaraj, he hit back and broke the leg of one of his pursuers. The Police could not do him any harm as he pleaded his action was in self-defence, and it was borne out by his co-religionists. Subsequently, the police tried to book him in connection with the murder of two Thevars in a nearby estate. Thanks to the physical transformation Mr. Thankaraj has undergone following his conversion, he has been able to escape the police dragnet.

"The Thankaraj story in no small measure influenced the red of the Meenakshipuram Harijans to embrace Islam, and the Tirunelveli-based South Indian Islamic Society, engaged in proselytizations, was too happy to oblige. The police dare not enter Rahamatnagar and harass the people there. The Thevars are equally afraid of the converts for any quarrel with them is bound to take on a communal colour with repercussion elsewhere in the country.

THE STATESMAN, New Delhi (20 July 1981)

Yusuf (formerly Thangaraj) insisted that police harassment was responsible for the mass conversion. He is the principal accused in a case registered by the police in connexion with the murder of two members of the Thevar community, both watchmen in an estate in neighbouring Panpoli village, in January.

He claimed that he had been implicated in the case because he had earned the displeasure of the Thevars on two counts: first, he had married a Thevar woman. Secondly, he had exposed two Thevars who had been collecting donations and fattening themselves in the m me of the Thiruvanduthurai Adheenam, which owned most of the land in the village. The Circle Inspector of the area happened to be a Thevar.

He alleged that residents of Meenakshipuram were subjected to harassment in the wake of the murders. Harijan men and women were stripped end beaten up by Thevars. A Harijan woman's nipple was cut off. At that stage, the Harijans decided enough was enough and decided to seek refuge in Islam.

Haja Mohideen (formerly Kandaswami), a teacher of the Government high school, Panpoli, and several other converts said the harassment that followed the murder of the Thevars and the case against Yusuf were the immediate cause of the mass conversion.

"The story of police harassment and nipple-cutting is a total lie" said a police official who did not want to be identified. He said the two watchmen were murdered after they discovered that fake notes were being printed in the estate. During the investigation of the case many villagers were interrogated.

Yusuf, the prime suspect of the case, was already a Muslim, he pointed out, having converted to Islam in 1977 soon after his marriage "in the hope that Muslims will protect him from Thevars who were angry as he had eloped with a Thevar women".

He claimed that the police were a demoralized lot today. "If so much fuss is made about a simple interrogation in a murder case and if the guilty take shelter behind the facade of religion, what can we do ?" he asked. "The police are being blamed for everything" he lamented. "We are being made the scapegoats".

He argued that the fact that 12 of the 20 accused in the murder and counterfeiting cases were still Hindus disproved the claim that police harassment was responsible for the mass conversion.

He offered another theory to explain the conversion. There was a large Muslim population in the area. Muslims were landowners, traders and money-lenders. The Harijans were economically dependent on them. Conversion to Islam had been going on at a steady rate for many years. The only new thing which happened at Meenakshipuram was that a large number of persons changed faith on a single day.

India Today, N. Delhi (July 16, 1981)

While police atrocities against them was the main reason put forward by the converted Harijans, this argument is untenable in Athiyuthu where not even a single villager was arrested. Yet this village was the first to give the lead and it has the largest number of converts.

Of the 350 families who inhabit this tiny village, 17 kilometres from Ramanathapuram, 250 are Muslims. Of the remaining 100 families, 65 are Harijans. There are only 35 upper-caste Hindu families in the village. But irrespective of caste all the Hindus are poor and live in thatched huts. The Muslim community, on the other hand, appears to be flourishing. Their gaudily painted, concrete-roofed houses are in stark contrast to the dilapidated dwellings of the Hindus.

What stood out most when India today visited Athiyuthu was the beautiful marble-white mosque that is visible for miles from the village. The mosque which was built several decades ago has been freshly painted for the mass conversion ceremony. Hardly 50 metres away from it was a rundown temple dedicated to the goddess Kali.

The men of the village were mostly clothed in grubby *dhoties* and, understandably in the heat, were shirtless. The women wore faded *sarees*. Their tired faces and haggard appearance were visibly different from a group of Harijan converts who sported obviously new, black Muslim caps and decked in clean shirts and colourful *lungis*, exuded the pungent smell of oriental musk.

Politics and Money

THE HINDU, Madras (August 10, 1981)

The Constitution did not bar any one from practising or preaching any religion. But when 1,500 or 1700 persons changed their faith at one stroke he (Zail Singh) thought, it was not out of one's own conviction, but there was something else behind it "There may be a conspiracy of political motivation", he said.

Several reasons: The mass conversions might have happened due to several reasons–the offer of some inducements or the attitude of caste-Hindus towards Harijans. It might also be due to resentment against the administration that it had not rendered justice to them.

Perhaps there was some kind of allurement and side by side the caste Hindus had not treated the Harijans as their brethern. "Anything is possible. I cannot say anything just now, the matter is under investigation"

Asked whether the Government was unduly alarmed over the reports of mass conversions, Mr. Zail Singh replied that it was a matter concerning one and all–the Government, the ruling party and other political parties alike. "Because this kind of conversion is politically motivated, and this is not a good method of changing religion."

THE STATESMAN, N. Delhi (July 22, 1981)

Although it would seem a spontaneous move on the part of the Harijans a close study of the issue would bring to light a well-drawn-out programme behind these organized conversions. Meenakshipuram, the 1,300-strong Harijan village in Tiruneveli district, which was renamed Rehamatnagar when the entire population embraced Islam on February 19 last is not an isolated case. It was timed to coincide with the Sixth all-India conference of the Jammat-e-Islami Hind, held in Hyderabad after Sheikh Abdullah refused them permission, to meet in Kashmir.

The tenor of the Hyderabad conference was set by Maulana Muhammed Yusuf, *Ameer-e-Jamaat-e-Islami Hind*, in his presidential address, when he outlined the duties and responsibilities of Indian Muslims. The Maulana harped on Muslims being a distinct, separate entity, with more things in common with their co-religionists in foreign lands than their compatriots.

One of the outcomes of the Hyderabad session of the *Jammat*, attended by fraternal delegates from the Arabian Gulf countries, was a plan to raise the Muslim population of India from 80 million to 200 million in the next decade. An Islamic bank established in Kuwait and the London-based Islamic Cultural Centre would extend all support, financial and moral, for the proselytization drive.

The choice of Tirunelveli and Ramanathapuram by the proselytizers is not without significance. These two districts of Tamil Nadu are contiguous to Kerala where Islam entered as early as the 7th century. Unlike the North where conquest by Muslim imperialists was responsible for the spread of their religion, in Kerala it was the result of peaceful work by enterprising merchants and zealous missionaries. There are mosques in Kerala as old as the *Haramel Sherif* in Mecca, the Muslim holy of holies. After partition, the Kerala Muslims were the first to organize themselves politically on communal basis and succeeded in even carving out a separate Muslim majority district. Today, they wield such political clout that no party in the state could from a government without the active support and participation of the Muslim League.

This sharing of power by Muslims with non-Muslims in Kerala is unique in the history of Islam. Muslims have either ruled themselves and others or been ruled over by foreign powers. They have never before shared power with others. If the present pace of proselytization is kept up, it would not be long before a Muslim communal party could hold the balance of power in Tamil Nadu also. And what can be achieved in Tamil Nadu is equally applicable to neighbouring Karnataka and Andhra Pradesh.

Report of The Parliamentary Committee on The Welfare of SC & ST

When asked about the views of the State Government on the mass conversions, the Home Secretary, Tamil Nadu Government, said that the conversions in Tamil Nadu had taken place as long back as 1944 but the present mass conversions were very serious. The matter was of great concern to the state government and they were trying to find out what and where the things had gone wrong. He stated that Meenakshipuram, which was the recent scene of conversion, was situated among three Muslims villages and was therefore having considerable impact of Muslim culture. Harijans of that village had been working in the houses of Muslims since long and they were conversant with their customs and their minds were ready for conversion. The State Government had received information that people from outside the State were visiting the area and encouraging Harijans to embrace Islam.

In a subsequent note on 'Mass Conversion of Adi-Dravidars to Islam, in Tamil Nadu' furnished to the study group, it had been stated that conversion of Scheduled Castes to Islam was being done in an organised way.

The Times of India, N. Delhi, (July 28, 1982)

The organisation behind the conversions is the South India *Isha-Athul Islam Sabai*. It runs educational institutions and orphanages. It also looks out for "voluntary" converts to Islam. The *Sabai* has stepped up its proselytising activities in recent times and has been raising funds abroad, patrons abroad to finance "schemes and plans to help new Muslims from the day of conversion to the time they are settled in life and lead a good Muslim life." Mr. A.K. Refayee, a former M.P., is the president of the *Sabai* and his brother, Mr. A. Sahul Hameed, the lone Indian Union Muslim League member of the Tamil Nadu assembly, its general secretary.

In 37 years of functioning, the *Sabai* claims to have received into the Islamic fold 1700 "voluntary" converts from all over Tamil Nadu.

The *Sabai* says that it should be as free to carry out its activities as are the Christian missionaries in South India with their vast resources, often received from abroad.

Indian Express, N. Delhi, (June 17, 1981)

(1) "Almost all the Hindus we met claimed that money had played a big part in the conversions. A labourer in his mid-thirties in Brahmin Street said he was offered some money and some clothes, but he refused."

The Hindustan Times, New Delhi (July 18, 1981)

"The bulk of the converts in Meenakshipuram and adjoining areas belong to the lowest rungs of the social and economic ladder. It appears that the proselytizing zeal of those who triggered the conversions extends to the provision of considerable material benefits. Cash doles and agricultural pump-sets have apparently figured among the incentives. There are also rumours of a large influx of money from the Gulf Arab countries. The veracity of these reports is now being probed by the Home Ministry."

Indian Express, N. Delhi, (June 26, 1981)

"The extravagant spending on the occasion Meenakshipuram, 19th feb. 1981 and on the gifts offered to the newly-converted Harijans lent credence to the belief that monetary inducements had a role to day. A strong-willed Harijan youth, Ayyappan, resident of Meenakshipuram, proclaimed that he had spurned the offer of Rs. 500 in cash to induce him to renounce his faith...There is evidence that a few converted Harijan families are living in far greater ease and comfort than their known source of income can permit. There is no plausible explanation for this'"

THE STATESMAN, N. Delhi, (July 20, 1981)

Subramaniam, who returned to the Hindu fold last week after having embraced Islam under the name of Ashref Ali early this year, told a UNI correspondent he had received Rs. 500 on February 21, the day the mass conversion took place, and had been promised more assistance. A Police official added that wealthy Muslims from Madurai and Tiruchirapalli handed gifts, including cash to the converts.

INDIA TODAY, N. Delhi (July 16-31-1981)

Much of Singhal's worries are justified in view of the reported move, funded by the Gulf countries, to convert at least one million Harijan families into Islam every year. The London-based Islamic Cultural Centre recently circulated a report which said that 50 Harijan families had been converted to Islam simply by a grant of Rs. 400,000 for an agricultural project. The expectation was that the sword of Islam, liberally lubricated with oil from the Gulf, would cut a deep swathe across the lower strata of the Hindu society, raising the Muslim population from 80 million to 200 million at the end of the decade.

In Hyderabad, for example, a few hundred *maulvis* fan out of the city every year and scout around villages for people willing to embrace Islam. From a meager 50 such cases before Independence, the number of conversions has now gone up to 500 a year.

While police atrocities against them was the main reason put forward by the converted Harijans, this argument is untenable in Athiyuthu where not even a single villager was arrested. Yet this village was the first to give the lead and it has the largest number of converts.

Of the 350 families who inhabit this tiny village, 17 kilometres from Ramanathapuram, 250 are Muslims. Of the remaining 100 families, 65 are Harijans. There are only 35 upper-caste Hindu families in the village. But irrespective of caste, all the Hindus are poor and live in thatched huts. The Muslim community, on the other hand, appears to be flourishing. Their gaudily painted, concrete-roofed houses are in stark contrast to the dilapidated dwellings of the Hindus.

What stood out most when INDIA TODAY visited Athiyuthu was the beautiful marble-while mosque that is visible for miles from the village. The mosque which was built several decades ago has been freshly painted for the mass conversion ceremony. Hardly 50 metres away from it was a rundown temple dedicated to the goddess Kali.

The men of the village were mostly clothed in grubby *dhoties* and, understandably in the heat, were shirtless. The women wore faded *sarees*. Their tired faces and haggard appearance were visibly different from a group of Harijan converts who sported obviously new, black Muslim caps and decked in clean shirts and colourful *lungis*, exuded the pungent smell of oriental musk.

Alleged B.R. Navasakthe, president of the Ramanathpuram Ryots Sangham. "The whole thing is stage managed." The Muslims in Athiyuthu and Killakarai are said to be supporting the Harijans. There are flourishing businessmen amongst them with known business connections in the Gulf. In fact Killakarai is one of the richest villages in Ramanathampuram district and the Muslims are known to be connected with the South Indian Islamic Society, an association which is meant to promote Islam and was instrumental in converting the Tirunneveli Harijans. Concluded the official, "It is obvious that money power was the main motivating factor." Tamil Nadu Chief Minister M.G. Ramachandran had hinted at this when, in a speech in Madurai recently, he termed the conversions as "ridiculous" and said it was done by the Harijans to improve their "socio-economic conditions".

In an appeal dated February 10, the *Sabai* solicited money from its

Report of The Parliamentary Committee on The Welfare of SC & ST

It had been further stated in that note that there had been considerable mention that money had played a definite part in the conversions. It was, however, difficult to state exactly to what extent money had influenced the decisions of the various families. This was an aspect which needed further probe in much greater detail since its ramifications were likely to be of wider implications. As far as specific instances were concerned, the following might be quoted:—

(i) One of the reports stated that a donation of Rs. 20,000 was promised by a religious preacher from Saudi Arabia for building a Mosque for which he laid the foundation stone.

(ii) Three converted boys had already been sent by *Jamaith* to study Arabic.

(iii) The religious preacher from Saudi Arabia also assured that he would soon arrange to take five of the converted boys to Arabian countries for study of Islamic culture.

(iv) It had been mentioned that a busload of Muslims crossed over from Kerala and made large donations.

It was further added that enquiries made of the converts had not been successful so far in elucidating further information since the very nature of the transaction was such that both the giver and the *recipient* would be interested in suppressing the information.

The RSS Study Team Report

Killakarai is a notorious place in the South for smuggling operations. It is well known that the entire Muslim community in and around Killakarai thrives substantially on smuggling activities. This is well known to the government at the Centre and State. The Killakarai Muslims have intimate relations in and with Gulf countries. Illegal remittances of money from Gulf countries is arranged through Ceylon and Singapore. Even business firms in Madras make use of these channels to, take out or bring in money. Large involvements of Killakarai resources in these conversions is strongly suspected. In fact, the conversions in Attiyuttu village and surrounding villages in Tirunelveli are being organised and executed by Killakarai money. A substantial involvement of 'legal' foreign funds is also suspected. There has been a sudden increase in grants and remittances from Gulf countries to individuals and institutions in the sensitive districts. For instance, *Satguna Vaidyasalai* an institution run under the sole proprietorship of a single Muslim has received Rs. 1.25 crores from Libya, allegedly for running a technical school. The Government is well aware of such sudden increase in remittance from Gulf countries. However, inflow of illegal foreign money goes on unchecked.

"One Kandan of Pudduvayal village presently working in Dubai embraced Islam for monetary incentives. He came back to Bharat specifically for conversion ceremony and met his cousin Sethu in Chittrakotai village near Attiyuttu and converted his family.

Indian Express, N. Delhi (April 13, 1981)

Paramasivan, 45, a Harijan, whose name has been changed to Ashraff Ali, said he was forcibly converted. On the day of conversion he came to Meenakshipuram and his name was also included. Someone placed a cap on his head and gave him the new name. Before he could come out of the daze, everything was over and his own relatives in the crowd started calling him Ashraff. He went home only to be scolded by his family and was ostracised.

Notes:—

a. Bracketed numbers on page **XXXXX page nos. to be changed according to new page making)**, (52, 13, 14, 51,& 46) are the paragraph numbers in the original report.

b. Subheading on page 25 should be read as "Sex, crime and Police".

A Prophecy indeed!

Your insolence towards the lower classes of Hindus is being repaid by the latter running their back on you. Mohammedanism and Christianity are extending their arms to embrace them and indications are not wanting of the readiness of the lower classes of Hindus to accept the hospitality of non-Hindu religious and social systems. Why, the reason is obvious. As a

Hindu you won't touch him; you would not let him sit on the same carpet with you, you would not offer him water in your cups, you would not accept water or food touched by him; you would not let him enter your temples, in fact you would not treat him like a human being. The moment, however, he becomes a Mohammedan or a Christian, without even giving up his ancestral occupation, you are all smiles to him, you welcome him to your home; and have no objection at times to offer him drink and food in your utensils etc.

It is a deep-rooted sentiment that has so far prevented the depressed classes of Hindus from deserting Hinduism en-masse. Sentiments are, however, melting away before the matter-of-fact civilization of the West. The time does not seem to be very distant when sentiment will cease to control the desire of the depressed classes to better their social position, if it cannot be had otherwise than by a change of faith. There are circumstances and causes in the environments of these classes which are working with effect to bring about that consummation and if the Hindus want to avoid that catastrophe, it is time that they subordinated their caste pride to the exigencies of the situation and took time by the forelock.

—LALA LAJPAT RAI

(Extracts from an article published in *Modern Review, Calcutta,* July 1909)

(cf. Writings and Speeches Vol. 1, p.172)

DETAILS OF HARIJANS CONVERTED TO ISLAM

The following statement showing the details of the Harijans converted to Islam from February, 1980 to June, 1981, was submitted to the Study Group of Parliamentary Committee by the Govt. of Tamil Nadu on 13th August, 1981.

S. No.	Name of the Village	No. of Converts			Date of Conversion
		Male	Fe-male	To-tal	
Tirunelveli District					
1.	Meenakshipuram (Shencottai Ps. Limits)	–	–	1000	19.2.81
Ramanathapuram (East) Distt.					
2.	Maravaikudi (Sikkal Ps. Limits)	28	20	48	15.5.81

3.	Veeravanur (Chatrakudy Ps. Limits)	30	26	56	20.5.81
4.	Peraiyur (Peraiyur Ps. Limits)	4	–	4	–
5.	Pooseri (Mudukulathur Ps. Limits)	1	–	1	–
6.	Melamadai (Killakarai Ps. Limits)	29	17	46	29.5.81
Ramanathapuram (West) Distt.					
7.	Pattamputhur (Virudhunagar East Ps. Limits)	3	2	5	10.4.81
Madurai (North) District					
8.	Rayappanpatti	1	–	1	3.6.81
9.	Narayanarhevan Patti	4	4	8	Between 6.80 & 3.81
10.	Ernampatty	16	13	29	5.81
11.	Thimminaickenapatty	1	1	2	31.5.81
Madurai (South) District					
12.	Kurayur (Killikudi Ps. Limits)	–	–	400	Between 2.80 & 5.81
13.	Kanday (Sindupatty Ps. Limits)	60	20	93	
		Children 13			June, 81
			Total	1693	

The District-wise numbers (which had come to the notice of the R. S. S. Study Team) up to the end of July 1981 were as follows:

(1)	Ramnad	(7 Places)	678
(2)	Madurai	(2 places)	715
(3)	Tirunelveli	(1 place)	765
(4)	Tanjore	(1 place)	45
		Total	2203

1
Conversions: A Viewpoint

Dev Dutt

Reputed journalist and thinker;
Founder-editor of 'Point of View', New Delhi

LAST year Meenakshipuram, a desolate hamlet in Tirunelveli District, zoomed into headlines when 200 families of Harijans, of which 75 members were Christians, embraced Islam in an impressive ceremony wherein a number of Muslim politicians were also present. This was immediately followed by a number of similar incidents of group conversions in the villages of Ramanathapuram and Madurai. There were also reports of conversions and re-conversions, counter conversion of Hindus, Muslims and Christians in other parts of India and up to October 1981 more than 2000 conversions had taken place in Tamil Nadu alone.

It looked as if conversions had assumed the dimensions and the nature of a communal phenomenon, and the fact that it did shake various quarters and give rise to several types of reactions, made it clear that this phenomenon is also of national importance. For example, the Central Government appointed a committee to go into the issue. The intelligence agencies were asked to report. A delegation of MPs visited Meenakshipuram, made an on-the-spot study and submitted a report. The PM kept a watchful eye on these developments. The Parliament discussed it. The state government exhibited deep concern and encouraged such programmes as *Sambandham Bhojanam* in order to assuage the feelings of the Harijans. At one stage it even considered passing a bill prohibiting mass conversions. The Arya Samaj, the RSS and the Vishva Hindu Parishad took it as a red signal and swung into vigorous action. They launched a variety of programmes of reconversion, and fresh conversions, programmes of reforms in Hindu society and economic amelioration of the Harijans; the training of Harijans as *Pujaris*; a massive propaganda offensive and finally the creation of an effective organizational infrastructure to sustain these programmes. The *Mathadhipatis* came out of their cloistered world of meditation and prayers. Leaders of all castes and sects, 'touchables' and 'untouchables' gathered in Hindu Unity Conferences. Equality and harmony became the theme of all their invocations. Religious and social leaders visited the neglected brethren. They enquired after their problems and offered immediate relief. Most important of all, they refurbished their faith in ancestral *Dharma*. The backlash of Hindu community-mindedness had caught on.

Though the statistics of conversion were not so spectacular as to merit such large scale response, what seems to have upset the Hindu leaders was the sudden up-swing in the frequency and the geographical spread of conversions. They considered the spate of conversions unusual. What was once a trickle had suddenly become a torrent. The minorities too became more apprehensive specially the Christian leadership who joined issue because some of their own followers too had embraced Islam owing to caste discrimination in the churches. The leaders of Muslim public opinion also reacted sharply to the response of the Hindus. Conversions became a cheap game of numbers. Everyone was out to add more numbers to a particular religion. Perhaps the religious heads were also infected with the prevalent virus of political defection where one can join or leave a political party whenever one feels like it. In their preoccupation with numbers, the religious leaders were not worried about the methods employed to attract people.

Unintended Winners

The unintended winners in this unseemly game of conversions today are the weaker sections of Indian society. They took full advantage of the attention they got. Their attempts to win their legitimate rights through political means being frustrated, they had realized that they had to do something drastic. Conversion became a powerful weapon in their hands. It had the desired effect by demonstrating the fact that they had an alternative by adopting Islam to establish their human dignity. Conversion became a 'game.' The slum dwellers of Chetpet in Madras thought it expedient to issue a threat that if their civic rights were not met, they would change their faith.

The politicians at all levels did not miss the opportunity to fish in the troubled waters. For example, at the micro level, there were cases when in a place like Achapur, a simple village quarrel was blown up into a conversion fight. At macro level, the political parties operated in a subtle way and refrained from taking a position, a fact which was tantamount to abetment. Leaders like R. S. Gavai, speaker of the Maharashtra Legislative Council tried to exploit the climate of opinion created by conversions for political ends. He declared that 5,00,000 will embrace Buddhism, while only 15,000 people were given *deeksha* in Nagpur that too in a perfunctory manner.

II

What is the situation today? Some commentators, especially those close to Vishwa Hindu Parishad seem to be satisfied that the tide of conversions has been contained and that they have acquired the ability to discern the precise nature of the challenge posed by Meenakshipuram. But, the dragon is not only not dead but very active. Recent events have confirmed that communalism and fundamentalism have taken fresh forms and it threatens to further weaken the already fragile fabric of inter-community relations. Briefly stated, today in addition to conventional forms of antagonism such as riots, etc. the large-scale use of conversions, desecration of places of worship and aggressive competitive ways to propagate religion in public have come to stay as the most striking features of antagonism between the various religious communities in India. There are reports which indicate that the enthusiasts of conversions are still active. For example, on 15 February 1982 it was reported that several hundred Harijans in a village embraced Islam. The anniversary of the Meenakshipuram conversions was celebrated and it is reported that hundreds of Muslims and Harijans from Tirunelveli district attended it.

Warnings by the Press

Here is a detailed report published in the Hindu of 6th February 1982.

"Kadayanallur in Tirunelveli district has become a sensitive place, as a few small incidents have resulted in an estrangement between Harijans and another section of Hindus. After Meenakshipuram, Kadayanallur is the place to be watched. The Harijans of Kadayanallur are openly talking about embracing Islam to improve their lot on the social plane. An organisation called *Samathuva Sahodarathuva Sangham* was formed for the Kadayanallur Assembly constituency on January 10. Harijans and Muslims are equally represented in its membership as well as its executive. It was formed at a meeting held under the president-ship of

Mr. A. K. Rafai, former MP, who is also the president of *Ishathul Islam Sabha* under whose auspices conversions took place in Meenakshipuram. Its objectives have been variously stated by Harijan and Muslim leaders, but both aver that it has nothing to do with conversion.

When this Correspondent visited Kadayanallur on January 25, Mr. Ramanath "*Nattamai*" (leader) of the Harijans in Ward Nos. 18 and 19 and Mr. John said the *Sangham* had been formed to promote close understanding and cooperation between Harijans and Muslims in all elections. They said Kadyanallur Panchayat Union was originally a reserve constituency for the Scheduled Castes. But later, an influential leader of the Thevar community had it changed to the unreserved category. They also said that the major political parties like the Congress (I), AIADMK and DMK had named candidates from this community. This made Harijans sit up and think. In the Kadayanallur constituency there are 35,000 voters, of whom 9,000 are Harijans and 3,000 Muslims. If these two sections unite they would be able to win any election. Hence the decision to form the *Sangham*. In contrast, Mr. Shahul Hameed, MLA, asserted that *Sangham* was non-political though anyone belonging to any political party could be a member. He said one reason which hastened its formation was the "harassment" of a Harijan who had embraced Islam recently and assumed the name Rahamatullah. The convert was a teacher at the Kadayanallur Higher Secondary School......."

Here is another report published in the INDIAN EXPRESS dated 15.2.1982 "In a report circulated among its members recently, the sabha said: 'Thousands of non-Muslims are waiting to join the holy faith of Islam but they are kept in the waiting list for want of funds.' It claimed that about 5,000 people at Puliyangudi, Vasadevanallur and Kannapatcheri near Kadayanellur and Chintamani and Ilanji near Tirunelveli had approached, expressing readiness to embrace Islam. About 1,000 people at Sivakasi in Ramanathapuram were ready for conversion. But it was being delayed due to lack of funds for clothes, food and circumcision. The society said it had to assume responsibility for providing the converts with all facilities so that they did not turn to others for help. It had some schemes on hand and if these were implemented, "We hope many brothers from other communities will rush of their own accord to embrace our faith."

"The sabha noted that the area was 'replete with innumerable Hindu and Christian institutions' and said "a strong resourceful Islamic organisation was essential to carry on conversion, orientation, assimilation and rehabilitation of those eager to embrace Islam". Sabha president A.K. Refayee said in an appeal circulated with the report that its objective was to help the neo-Muslims, from the day of conversion to the time they were settled in life, "lead a good Muslims life." He appealed to co-religionists all over the world to extend a helping hand to the Sabha. It was suggested that aid be "directly made available to us and not routed through other organisations" as this would enable the Sabha to take expeditious action. He also suggested that the converts be considered for employment in the Arab countries.'

It appears that Hindu leadership chose Kanyakumari, with a preponderance of Christian and a small but fairly affluent Muslim population, for rearguard action. The growth rate of these two communities has been higher than that of Hindus who, according to the 1981 Census, constituted half its total population of 1,419,110. A publication of the Hindu Front, which describes the district as a "burning volcano" say: that unless the trend is reversed, Kanyakumari (named after the young goddess Parvathi doing penance to win over Lord Shiva) may well end up as "Kanni (Virgin) Mary" district. It may be noted that Kanyakumari district through the ages had been known for communal harmony among the people professing different faiths. Nowhere else in the country could one see the juxtaposition of shrines of all faiths, each benefitting from the festivals and fairs of the others. Strange as it may seem, this bonhomie was rudely shaken.

Further, free and secular India is a witness to a spurt of keenly competitive forms of entrepreneurial type of activity in the realm of propagation of religion. The leaders of religious communities are taking to aggressive salesmanship in the work of promoting religion by adopting technology and foreign funds. Further, some heinous innovations too have been made. For example, the extremist communal forces have forged one more weapon, viz. desecration of the places of worship. This process which began in Moradabad a few years ago was adopted in Amritsar, Nabha, Kurukshetra, Delhi, and Patiala last month.

There has been some debate in the press and some other quarters in India about the nature of this phenomenon, about the factors underlying it and about the way it should be tackled. But, quite understandably, the major emphasis in this debate has been on the immediate causes which include: monetary and other inducement; political motivation; police highhandedness or inaction; ill-treatment of Harijans; perpetuation of the caste system and failure to end social inequality. The allegation that foreign money has played a role has, however, been refuted by Muslim converts.

Confusing Picture

As a matter of fact, one is struck by the variety of the response to Meenakshipuram. It covers a wide range of opinions and perspectives: at one end of the spectrum is the nonchalant attitude of individuals like Kuldip Nayar who said "conversions do not bother me," the other end is the impassioned activism of the leaders of RSS and Arya Samaj and heads of religious institutions; and in between these two, we have the lukewarm, opportunistic, pedestrian or simplistic almost Pavlovian reaction of a whole body of commentators and social enthusiasts.

Consequently, we have before us a rather distorted and confusing picture of the conversion phenomenon. It is like a broken-mirror view which does not offer even a faint promise of being considered as a starting point of a coherent and holistic analysis of such a vital problem. We are none the wiser or clearer about the character of the challenge which has been thrown up and the fundamental issues which are involved in our response to that challenge.

This is bad enough. But even in this plethora of arguments and counter-arguments one unfortunate impression has been created that the conversions are primarily and principally a form of protest from Harijans against the various social disabilities and injustices which high caste Hindus continue to inflict on them. This may perhaps be on account of the fact that in almost all personal interviews the converts in Meenakshipuram referred to this aspect.

Consequently, Hindu society and particularly the persistence of inequalities therein, have become not only the basis of all action-programmes in relation to conversions, but has also conditioned the direction of analysis of this phenomenon. Undoubtedly, Hindu society deserves to be censured for the indignities and injustices it continues to inflict on the *dalits*. Every effort must be made to remove this blot on the fair name of this ancient civilization. But it will be unfortunate if this makes us oblivious to other more vital and fundamental aspects of the conversion phenomenon. It is necessary to go beyond this social injustice thesis.

III

Reasons

The exclusively Hindu high caste and social-injustice thesis cannot explain the empirical data relating to the conversions in Meenakshipuram and elsewhere since 1981. Evidence indicates that conversion since 1981 was not a one-way traffic from Hinduism to Islam. In Jessore-Khulna, and Malda districts in W. Bengal there were reports of Christians embracing Islam. In Meenakshipuram itself there were Christian families which covered about seventy five individuals. In other places also many Muslims and Christians changed their faith. And above all, here is conversion with a considerable difference. In Ottapidaram taluk in Tirunelveli district in the month of August 1981, the Harijan atrocities drove the Naicker community to think of embracing Islam. We give below extracts of a report which appeared in the INDIAN EXPRESS dated 30 August 1981.

"In this area Harijans are in a majority. But the Naickers who it is said, settled therein 1500 A.D. are affluent and own ginning factories and have large land holdings. The Harijans make out a living either as agricultural labourers or as workers in the factories. Some miscreants seemed to have succeeded in souring the harmonious relations between the communities in the context of a dispute over land use.

The Naickers were so disgusted and fear-stricken by the domineering attitude of the majority community, i.e. the Harijans that they were driven to the wall and had no other option than to trust in Allah."

A similar instance where caste Hindus live in fear of Harijans was reported on 1 August 1978 in the INDIAN EXPRESS. Five caste Hindus in Amalapuram village in Andhra Pradesh were allegedly burnt to death by Harijans. There were also reports that the Harijans had set up a parallel administration which imposed fines on caste Hindus who dared not defy them for fear of consequences. On the basis of a review of the various reports that appeared after 19, February 1981, we have identified the following reasons for conversion:—

1. As a means of escaping punishment for some criminal activity on the basis of an inducement by communal minded politicians.
2. Personal problems like the Hindu law against bigamy, which doesn't apply to Muslims.
3. As a means of gaining benefits such as promotion in a job, a visit abroad, acquisition of some resources, scholarship, loan funds, comforts, employment.
4. As a means of registering protest against social injustice, police inaction and atrocities including police assault and riots.
5. As a means of achieving economic equality and a sense of dignity and honour in society.
6. As an expression of disgust against a custom or an attitude of a community to which one belongs.
7. a. Reconversion, since the person was forced to change his religion earlier.
   b. Reconversion due to loss of legal and constitutional privileges.
   c. Reconversion due to unanticipated social disabilities in the new religion which the individual embraced.

We quote below references for some of the above-mentioned motives.

Dr. Manoharan, District Medical Officer of Ramanad got converted to Islam because he was in love with a Muslim girl and he could commit bigamy only by going muslim. Dr. Manoharan was already married at the time of falling in love. (HINDUSTAN TIMES–4 June 1981). Many Harijans in Meenakshipuram district were involved in the criminal activity of printing counterfeit currency. This was exposed and the Muslims told the Harijans that if they become Muslims, the police dare not trouble them..." This anxiety for protection coupled with the temptation of financial inducements led to conversion. As per a report submitted by the Parliamentary delegation:

> "Some conversions were a direct result of riots that had taken place in Ramanathapuram in which the Harijans were subjected to atrocities and untold misery unleashed by caste Hindus" (p. 3).

Also there is no evidence to support the view that politically frustrated elements among the Harijans were responsible for giving a fillip to conversion in order to establish their relevance and indispensability to the power apparatus. On the contrary the Harijan community for the areas that reported conversions was strikingly leaderless and its protest over its present plight was articulated by a motley group. The absence of an accredited representative was felt by the Hindu organisations which belatedly bestirring themselves into activity, wanted to dissuade the converts-to-be. Equally important is the fact that, in some cases at least, the lead in the matter of conversions was given by the educationally and economically advanced sections of the Harijans. Resenting social inequalities compounded by police excesses, this section tended to dramatise their chagrin and protest by a demonstrative rejection of the present hierarchical structure.

IV

If we examine the history of mass conversions since the advent of Buddhism up to beginning of the British rule in India, three elemental human motivations can be identified behind the conversions, viz. Conviction or fear or protest or some combination of these three. The Christian missionaries catered to a fourth motivation, viz., the quest for material welfare and social equality on the part of certain individuals in vulnerable groups. As if an elaboration of Christian variety, Dr. Ambedkar in the period 1936-56 conceived of conversions as a means of social transformation and emancipation of a particular cross-section of the down-trodden and the weak. He equated the struggle for emancipation of Harijans from Hinduism with that of India's from the British rule–i. e. both were secular movements. In his speech delivered at Yeola, district Nasik, he said:

> "Those Hindus who ask us as to what can be achieved by conversion alone can be put a similar counter question, that is, what can be achieved by self-Government alone ? If financial and educational progress is the condition precedent for freedom,

what is the good of striving for self-government alone ? After giving careful thought to the problem it becomes clear that conversion is as necessary to untouchability as self-government is to the country. For the untouchables, freedom from Hinduism is as necessary as freedom from the British in India......If freedom is necessary for the life of mankind, conversion of untouchables, which brings them freedom cannot be called worthless..." (speech delivered in the Mahar conference held at Bombay on May 31, 1936).*

In other words Dr. Ambedkar rejected the principle that the people should enmasse change faith solely for reasons 'spiritual'. He made an impassioned and persistent plea for mass conversions for reasons 'secular' also. He assumed indispensability of religion and an organic relationship between religion and social structure, particularly between Hinduism and Hindu society, which in Ambedkar's mind were synonymous. He felt that injustice is inherent in Hinduism. Therefore, he believed that the emancipation of the Harijans from the dominance of the Hindus and heir material progress can only be achieved if they walk out of Hinduism. It may be noted that "Conversion programme was one concrete component of his two-fold secular approach to achieve a very secular objective, viz., promotion of welfare of the Harijans, the other component being to obtain for the Harijans certain preferential, statutory, political and economic concessions."

V

Analysis

The data relating to "Conversions in 1981" is unique, if not unprecedented. It does not entitle these conversions to be categorized under any of the categories mentioned above, particularly the Ambedkar-model. As a matter of fact, since there is considerable superficial similarity between "1981 conversion" and the conversion envisaged by Ambedkar there is a likelihood of a tendency to justify the "1981 conversion" or the basis of Ambedkar's thesis of 1936 and practice of 1956 when his followers turned to Buddhism–enmasse. This must be avoided for various reasons. The "1981 conversions" must be analysed independently and objectively, in respect of all their ramifications. The changes in faith which neither stem from conviction nor fear nor protest nor some laudable and larger secular objective are reversible and are not likely to be durable. When the contingent force or extraneous factors which lead groups to resort to conversion get eliminated, or over-powered by a new contingent force or, extraneous factors there is either restoration of status quo or yet

* Thus Spoke Ambedkar, Vol. IV, Bangalore, 1980, Page 53.

one more change of religion. This is exactly what happened in case of many of the 1981 converts. Although this phenomenon of conversion and re-conversion also took place in the past, its overall national and social consequences were negligible on account of (a) limited means of communication, (b) limited social mobility, (c) other cultural restraints, (d) a particular political structure and (e) a level of social self-awareness and self-consciousness. These did no harm to the moral fibre of the individuals and the society and posed no threat to the stability of this system.

But "1981 conversions" are fraught with very serious national, social and secular implications understood in the best of their respective meanings. For example, with the help of technology and new modes of mobilization of resources and public opinion a cross-section of the Hindu leadership has exploited the 1981 conversion to promote outmoded forms of conservatism, vicious reactionarism and communalism. Reacting unreflectingly to minority fundamentalism, a section of the Hindu leadership has used 1981 conversions for sectarian and even un-national ends and thus unleashed a sort of backlash of majority communalism or fundamentalism, which was not only a denial of Hinduism but wholly un-Hindu. It also reinforced minority communalism. (Please read article in SEMINAR January 1982 by this author for this aspect of conversion). It strikes at the growth of composite nationalism and composite culture and composite national consensus in India; it has also accelerated–the process of de-dharmification of India's psyche.

VI

Dharmic or Secular?

What is *dharma* and what is de-dharmification ?

The concepts *dharmic* and the "secular" postulate two world views, each having its own special aroma which informs their respective derivate or implications and concrete manifestations. Though, fundamentally speaking these two world-views are distinctly different, yet they are not mutually exclusive. However, the acceptance or rejection of the primacy of one over the other does make a qualitative difference all down the scale.

In a fundamental or seminal sense *dharma* is the "spiritual" (innate, essential) nature of everything that "exists".

Thus *dharma* is not a synonym of "religion". But if it is to be related to religion, *dharma* would mean "religion of religious" which the adherents of all credal religions as well as those of Hinduism have incorporated within their respective attitudes towards life.

Dharma is the basis of coexistence of not only religious but also of all the diverse linguistic, ethnic, cultural components of Indian society. *Dharma* created an environment of conciliation and harmony, cooperation and coexistence and thus enabled the diverse ingredients of life even at the micro-level in regard to rituals, occupation, sub-caste etc. To get accommodated, get adjusted and get attuned to each other and thus evolve a social structure as beautiful as a tapestry.

The link between the various ingredients of India's value system and the social system–right down from the smallest to largest unit of formation in human and geographical spread and also in regard to the communication system comprising of signs, symbols, myths, legends, folklore, customs etc. of all religious and cultural groups in India partake of the ineffable aroma of *dharma*.

Consequently, *dharma* imparted a special quality to the enormous sense of accommodation or catholicity of the Indian mind which rejects nothing but takes in and embraces all aspects, sides and dimensions of reality and experience. It recoils from taking a definitive or a final stand on any basic matter. It appears to be a form of pragmatism, but it is something that goes beyond pragmatism, because its roots lie not in a secular world view, but in a *dharmic* world view. That *dharma* oriented humanist values are peculiar to India can be proved in many ways. But, we would like to adduce a semantic evidence. There is no word in any Indian language analogous to the word "secularism" and there is no word in English language at least, which is analogous or synonymous with "*dharma*". The collective mind or experience of people gives rise to language. In other words, the relationship between language and the collective mind is vital.

As Levi-Strauss puts it:

> "The relationship between language and culture is an exceedingly complicated one. In the first place, language can be said to be a result of culture. The language...is a reflection of the total culture... But one can also say that language can be said to be a condition of culture...(p. 68) in two different ways: first, it is a condition of culture in a diachronic way……through the language we learn about our own culture...but also it is a condition of culture because the material out of which language is built is of the same type as the material out of which the whole culture is built: logical relations, oppositions, correlations and the like. Language, from this point of view, may appear to lay a kind of foundation for complex structure which corresponds to the different aspects of culture"...(p. 66).
>
> "If we formulate our problem in purely theoretical terms, then it seems to me that we are entitled to affirm that there should be some kind of relationship between language and culture because, language has taken thousands of years to develop and culture has

taken thousands of years to develop, both processes have been taking place side by side with the same mind", (p. 71)

De-dharmification

De-dharmification means a disposition to give increasing de-emphasis on *dharma* in the social, political, religious and cultural equation or relationships which prevail in India. It means erosion of the will and the material supporting structure so necessary to uphold dharma as the focus of collective and individual existence...It means an attempt to bypass the seminal principle which has been the basis of India's composite culture. Over several centuries, perhaps since the tenth century, there have been set afoot certain processes which brought about a shift in the primacy of the *dharmic* in our view of life, society and cosmos.

But this process got accelerated in the past one century, and instead of *dharmic* word-view we have begun to give increasing emphasis to the "secular" world view. 1981 conversions are a part of this process of de-dharmification of the Indian psyche. The way common people were prompted to change their faiths, the facility with which the changes took place and the petty uses to which the conversion processes were put to, indicates that the hold of *dharmic* world-view as a regulation of life is being relegated to the background.

The fight between leaders for the numerical superiority of their respective religious communities, the fight for establishing the so-called "spiritual" superiority of their respective religions, the fight to out-bid each other in desecrating each other's places of worship are, expressions of death-wish on the part of practitioners of all religions in India. If also means that the sense of awe and reverence, the sense of the sacred and the sublime which is a characteristic of the *dharmic* attitude of mind is vanishing among the common people.

Consequently in the absence of an alternative unifying principle, the various ingredients of our polity are either in a state of cold war or hot war with each other–caste vs. caste, community vs. community, language vs. language–and in Meenakshipuram, it assumed the confrontation of one religion against another religion.

It is an irony of fate that organizations such as the RSS and Vishwa Hindu Parishad should be the most militant agencies of the process of de-dharmification. In their anxiety to create favourable secular conditions for their organised aspect of Hindu religion, they have not fully evaluated the long-term implications of their approach to 1981 conversions. Being guilty of hastening the process of de-dharmification, they have accelerated the process which will lend primacy to the so-called secular world view.

VII

1981 conversions are a symptom of the weaknesses or pathological conditions of our polity in which primacy is being increasingly given to the secular world view of which large scale experiments with liberalism and Marxism, and science and technology during the past 50 years are a few examples. Concretely stated, it means failure of the entire system of reservations in education, political processes, social and economic policies with the help of which we tried to reconcile within the frame work of a nation-state, the conflicting claims of the various interest groups, religious, linguistic and so on.

Indian people, at the behest of its leaders, agreed to adopt a secular world view at short notice without much homework. They did not realize fully that they had to shift the emphasis away from *dharmic* world-view towards a secular world-view as a basis of private and collective existence–what to speak of practical measures to go secular. The leaders could not evolve a comprehensive approach and philosophy of this transformation–the Indian constitution assumes that there is a philosophy, but it does not provide one as such.

Europe went through this kind of process for three centuries since the renaissance in the fifteenth century, prior to which everything there was also a part of the Church. And so everything; economy, society, politics, education, arts and science and attitude towards life, had to undergo a secularistic transformation.

We do not have traditions of what may be called full-blooded "secular world view". We have yet to undergo the grueling and tempestuous experience of leading a dharmically-oriented polity towards a secularly oriented polity. Hence the 1981 conversions. In short, leaderless and inexperienced, Indian people are caught up in the historical process of taking a quantum leap from one type of culture and civilization based on *dharmic* world-view into another type of culture and civilization based on secular world-view. Moreover, a civilization is being transformed into a secular nation-state, as the focus of collective allegiance, stability, unity and security. 1981 conversions are a manifestation of our inability to negotiate the leap and reach our new destination.

1901 Census: The British View

Commenting on the figures of the Census of 1901, giving the respective strength of the three principal religions of India, Sir H. Risley remarked:

"During the ten years preceding the census of 1901, the Mohammadans increased by nine per cent and the Christians by nearly twenty-eight per cent......Hinduism is the dominant religion of India; in all its developments it is intimately associated with caste, and the two sets of factors the social and the religious, can hardly be considered apart. The two rival creeds, Christianity and Islam, for Buddhism may be left out of account, avowedly reject the principle of caste, and have been affected by its influence solely through their contact with Hinduism.

"The statistics of the last census show that during a decade of famine the Mohammadans in India increased by nine per cent. No doubt these proportions were affected by the fact that the famines were most severe in those parts of the country where the Mohammadans are relatively least numerous, but in the fertile and wealthy region of Eastern Bengal, which has never been touched by real famine, though people on small fixed incomes suffer from high prices, their rate of increase was 12.3 per cent or nearly double that of the Hindus. The figures illustrating the proportion of children tell a similar tale, and indicate that in that part of India the Mohammadans are not only more enterprising and therefore better off than their Hindu neighbours, but also more prolific and more careful of their off-spring."

—SIR HERBERT RISLEY
(cf. Writings & Speeches of Lala Lajpatrai, Vol. I, p. 172)

2

Genesis and History of the Politics of Conversion

Sita Ram Goel

Was a Delhi based thinker and writer

While Mao Tse-tung was licking his wounds after the long march to his hideout in Yenan, an American journalist asked him the following question: "A lot of people in the USA have been led to believe by our liberals that you people are not communists, but only agrarian reformers. What do you have to say on that subject ?" Mao Tse-tung smiled mischievously and said: "So long as the belief helps the revolution, we do not care what the sons-of-bitches believe about us."

The Christian missionary and the muslim *mulla* in India can comfortably express the same sentiment about the Hindus who have been led to believe that Christianity and Islam are religions towards which Hindu society should practise the same *samabhava* (sentiment of equal honour) as the various sects of *Sanatana-Dharma* have been practising towards one another throughout Hindu history. Neither the missionary nor the *mulla* will concede for a moment that any Hindu religious sect can claim to be a religion. Neither of them will grant to any Hindu religious sect even the status of an inferior religion. Any missionary who is honest to his calling will confirm that, according to Christianity, the whole of Hinduism is heathenism, which word the dictionaries define as the condition of those who are devoid of any religion whatsoever. Any *mulla* who knows his *kalima* will clarify that, according to Islam, the whole of Hinduism is *kufr* which means "a wilful denial of the one and only perfect revelation."

Nor is the missionary or the *mulla* prepared to practise *samabhava* towards any Hindu religious sect. Each of them pleads his helplessness in this respect because his "scriptures" do not sanction such "sophistry". And each of them appeals to the Hindus to understand his position and help him honour the fundamentals of his faith. The faith of the missionary as also of the *mulla* makes it obligatory on him to convert to his own creed as many Hindus as he can, by all means including force and fraud. The Hindus are expected to understand, indeed appreciate, this obligation also as a proof positive of the missionary's and the *mulla's* profound devotion to his own religion. But both of them deny to the Hindus the same right to convert any of their followers to the latter's ancestral faith. Each of them points out that apostasy is punishable with death according to the fundamentals of his faith. The fact that the missionary or the *mulla* cannot enforce these fundamentals under the present dispensation in India does not mean that the fundamentals have become invalid or should be refashioned. It only means that the Christians or the mu dims should strive to change the dispensation so that they can enforce the fundamentals without let or hindrance.

Meanwhile, both of them hail as very helpful the Hindu slogan of *sarva-dharma-samabhava* (all religions are equal). The slogan proves, if proof was needed, that the Hindus do not mind some of their own flock going over to Christianity or Islam. It does not, should not, make a difference to a Hindu if he becomes a Christian or a muslim. Do not the Hindus proclaim, day and night and from the house-tops, that Christianity and Islam are as good religions as their own *Sanatam-Dharma* ?

Hindu society is thus trapped by a slogan which it has itself coined and made respectable. It cannot turn away from practising *samabhava* towards Christianity and Islam even when these creeds decimate Hindu society by continuous conversions. Nor can it expect *samabhava* from Christianity or Islam when it tries to win back some of its own lost sheep. In such a situation, Christianity as well as Islam can resort to violence which is legitimate according to the fundamental tenets of these faiths.

It is the same sort of trap into which a democracy gets entangled the moment it concedes that communism is also a political ideology as good as the democratic ideology, and that a communist party should be permitted to function as freely as any democratic party. Communism also pleads that its very first premises put it under an obligation to destroy democracy, and that a democracy by its very definition is duty-bound to facilitate the spread of communism. And a communist party can legitimately take to the path of an armed struggle whenever a democracy tries to deny this fundamental democratic right to the party.

Meaning of Meenakshipuram

The mass conversions at Meenakshipuram seem to have shaken Hindu society out of its sloganised slumbers. But the credit for this shock-therapy should go to the spokesmen of Islam, in India and abroad. Hindu society would have taken these conversions also in its stride, as in the past had not the spokesmen of Islam proclaimed publicly that mass conversion of the weaker sections of Hindu society was part of a political plan to win power for Islam, and convert secular India into an Islamic state.

Hindu society has had a full and first-hand taste of an Islamic state in the not too distant past. But it is doubtful if the spectre of such a state would have haunted Hindu society, had not Pakistan and Iran demonstrated the model with such earnest showmanship.

As a cumulative effect of all these events, a new phrase has gained currency in India's prevalent political parlance–the politics of conversion. What was regarded as a religious event till recently has now come to be recognised as a political event. This is a great gain. But it is only the advent of an awakening which would have to go a long way before it achieves an adequate perspective. For, Meenakshipuram has only dramatised a process of subversion which has been preying upon Hindu society for well-nigh thirteen hundred years.

The first current of this process entered India in the persons of muslim merchants and sufis who settled down in several parts of India, particularly Kerala, in the second half of the seventh century A. D. It surged forward when an Arab army under Mohammed bin Qasim succeeded in securing a foothold on the soil of Sindh in the first quarter of the 8th century A.D. It overflowed the ramparts in our North-West when Kabul and Zabul were overrun by the Islamised Turks in the second half of the 10th century A. D. It reached the heartland of India at the close of the 12th century A. D. and spread eastwards and southwards till it touched every nook and corner of this ancient land.

The tide turned at the end of the 17th century A. D. But in the meanwhile large sections of Hindus in the East and the West had been alienated from their ancestral religion and culture. The separation of Afghanistan, Pakistan and Bangladesh from Bharatavarsha was at one time regarded as the culmination of this current. But the consolidation of its aggression has not made it content with what it has already submerged. It is now looking forward to engulfing for good the residue that is Hindustan.

Another current of this process of subversion entered India in the wake of the Portuguese, Dutch, French and British adventurers. A horde of missionaries belonging to different denominations of Christianity and coming from many Western countries including the Americas, swarmed towards our shores. Christianity secured firm footholds in Southern, Central and North-Eastern India while Western imperialism was ruling the roost. By the middle of the twentieth century, Western imperialism was dead and gone. But the missionaries continued to multiply. Their experience over the past five hundred years has emboldened them to envisage a day when India will become yet another Christian country.

The process cannot be understood fully and in its inherent dynamics if we keep our gaze confined to what Christianity and Islam have been doing in India. We would have to travel backwards in time and go to the beginnings when the politics of conversion was first perfected and in the garb of religion and projected into the midst of the pagan societies as unsuspecting as Hindu society. In India itself the politics of conversion is thirteen hundred years old in the case of Islam, and nearly five hundred years old in the case of Christianity. But India is a late-comer in this maelstrom. The world at large has been familiar with the politics of conversion for almost two thousand years. Whole continents had already been conquered by means of these tactics before they arrived in India.

The first principles of the politics of conversion were formulated by the founding fathers of the Christian church in the very first century of what has become known as the Christian era. Its methods were perfected in ancient Alexandria, Antioch, Athens, Rome, Carthage and Constantinople, over a period of 300 years, at the end of which it conquered the Roman empire. In the next 700 years, it conquered the whole of Europe from Ireland to the Urals and from the North Sea to the Mediterranean and the Black Sea. It started surging towards distant shores at the beginning of the 16th century A. D. and, in the course of the next 300 years, it conquered North and South America, the West Indies, the Caribbean, Iceland, Australia, New Zealand, the Philippines and several parts of Africa. Its impact was now being felt in the rest of Africa and over the whole of Asia.

Meanwhile, another politics of conversion was taking shape in Madina in the second quarter of the 7th century A. D. By the end of that quarter it engulfed the whole of Arabia, Palestine, Syria, Iraq, Iran and Egypt. In the next one hundred years it conquered the whole of North Africa, Sicily, Spain, Khorasan and Turkistan, and entered India via Sindh. In the course of the next few hundred years it conquered Asia Minor, Malaya and Indonesia, and invaded the Philippines where it was rebuffed by Christianity which was already getting entrenched in that land.

The same thing happened in Asia Minor and the Balkans. Their fortunes waxed and waned for several hundred years. Christianity came out victorious in the final round at the close of the 15th century A. D. and resumed its conquest of the new world which had just come under its purview. Now the Islamic machinery has revived and is competing with its sister faith on more than equal terms in Africa and India. The petro-dollars have come as a timely shot in the arm of Islam.

It would be interesting to survey the genesis and history of the politics of conversion which now pass as Christianity and Islam. In the process we will discover the fundamental formulas and the mature methods developed and employed by the two for achieving what they have already achieved and what they aim at in future. The discovery may be useful to Hindu society in its encounter with these subversive techniques.

The Church of St. Paul

Christianity generally describes itself as the Church. The designation is derived from the Greek "kuros" which means "mighty". The Greek word is a cognate of the Sanskrit "shoora" which signifies a "warrior". Militancy is thus inbuilt in the psychology which projected this designation.

There is no evidence that Jesus, the son of Joseph and Mary, had any intention to found a religious order or sect. The gospels even when a lot of their language has got garbled in the mouths of their narrators, reveal him primarily as a mystic. He gave to his people, the Jews, a strikingly spiritual message–the Kingdom of Heaven is not to be sought in the world outside, the world of space and time; the Kingdom is within us, in our hearts, as also near at hand for all those who seek it in right earnest.

Moreover, Jesus was too much of a free spiritual seeker to become the founder of any closed community or organisation, far less the founder of a far-flung monolith like the later-day Christian Church. Those passages in the gospels which the Church cites as its source and inspiration are after-thoughts on the very face of it. The passages do not fit in psychically with the rest of what Jesus had to say. The responsibility for converting Jesus into the "only son of god" rests upon his disciples, and also upon Paul, whom the Church hailed as apostles in later history. Christian theology–dogmatics, polemics, apologetics and the rest–is not even remotely related to what Jesus had stated about himself or about God or the world.

It is significant that all disciples ran away or repudiated Jesus when the temple guards of Jerusalem came to arrest him. None of them was present when Jesus was crucified, except John who watched from a safe distance. The body of Jesus was taken down from the cross and entombed by two kindly Jews who had some influence with the Roman governor. Again, none of the disciples accompanied the three women–Mary Magdalene, Mary the mother of James, and Salome–who went to visit the tomb of Jesus two days later.

Yet as soon as the disciples were sure that Jesus was dead and could not contradict them, they started proclaiming that Jesus had appeared to them in a vision, that Jesus had bodily risen into heaven before their eyes, and that the Holy Spirit which was Jesus had entered into them. They flocked back to Jerusalem after the dust of controversy about Jesus had settled down. And they now claimed that they had been endowed by the Holy Spirit with miraculous powers of inspiration, speech and healing !

Saul, who became known as Paul in Christian history, was not even a disciple of Jesus. He had not met Jesus during the latter's life-time. Stephen, a disciple of Jesus had enraged the Jews in Jerusalem by abusing them for their failure to recognise Jesus as the Messiah. He was sentenced to death by stoning. Saul participated in carrying out the sentence. Saul now travelled to Damascus to kill some more followers of Jesus whom he suspected to be hiding in that city. Something happened to him outside Damascus, or so he claimed. Most probably it was the guilt of killing Stephen which had surfaced. In any case, Saul reincarnated himself as Paul and proclaimed that Jesus was the Son of God !

Paul travelled to many cities in Palestine, Syria, Asia Minor and Greece wherever some Jewish communities were to be found. He made some converts to his new-fangled faith. But, by and large, the Jews were not prepared to listen to him. Paul got so angry at this attitude of the Jews as to announce that henceforth men were to be saved not by the Mosaic Law but only by an active faith in Christ as the Son of God. Jesus had by now been transformed into Christ, the anointed one.

There was a great stir amongst the Jews everywhere when they learnt that Paul had repudiated the law of Moses. Paul's life was now in danger, wherever he went, which seems to have had a very sobering effect on him. He rushed back to Jerusalem and offered to repent and undergo the rites of purification at the Temple. The Jews, however, were in no mood to be mollified. He was about to be flogged on orders from a Roman

Magistrate when he revealed that he was the son of a Roman citizen and that, as such, he was entitled to a trial in Rome. That is how he secured a safe conduct to the imperial city.

It is from Rome that Paul fired a number of frenzied letters to Jewish communities elsewhere. The Church eulogised these letters as epistles and incorporated them in the New Testament. It is in these enters that we find the first formulations of what became a full-fledged but completely closed

Christian theology in due course. It is in these letters that, having finally despaired of the Jews, he wrote: "Understand, then, that this message of God's salvation has been sent to the heathen. They will listen to it."

Contours of Christian Theology

According to Paul every man born of woman inherited the guilt of Adam and could be saved from eternal damnation only by the atoning death of the Son of God. Christ was the Wisdom of God as also the first born Son of God. Christ was before all things; in him all things existed; through him all things had been created. Christ was not the Messiah who would deliver the Jews from bondage; he was the Logos who had become flesh and whose death would deliver all men. Paul also promised that "the Lord is coming soon" and that the "appointee time has grown very short." On second thoughts, he amended that, the second coming of Christ would be delayed until after Satan appeared on the scene and "proclaims himself to be God."

John, called Son of Thunder in Christian tradition, took up from where Paul had left. Pointing towards Nero and Rome, he proclaimed that the Satan and his regime of wickedness had already arrived. The Roman Empire, he thundered, was headed towards some great calamities in which all except the Christians would perish. The last judgment would come after a thousand years when the dead would be raised from their graves; all those whose names were not entered in the Book of Life would be "flung into a burning lake of fire and brimstone." The Christians would then "gather for God's great banquet and will eat the bodies of kings, commanders and mighty men... the bodies of all men who have not heeded the call of Christ". Next, a "New Jerusalem would descend on earth" which would be inherited by the Christians who would not know' "death any longer, nor night, nor any grief or pain".

This theology of great promise for the Christians, and great punishment for the rest of mankind, was more or less complete in its essentials by the time John died towards the end of the first century A. D. It had borrowed some of the language of later-day Greek philosophies like Neo-Platonism, as also some symbols from the mysticism of Egypt, Persia and Asia Minor. The language and the symbolism has led some people to give a mystic meaning to this theology. They forget that the founding father had formulated it as literally and historically true. That is why the Church has always laid such great emphasis on the historicity of Jesus who ascended the cross to become the Christ.

Human reason revolves round concrete evidence, emperical or mystical, and has no use for affirmations of mere faith, however, hysterical or high-sounding. But Christian theology had no use for human reason in the realm of its dogma, though it used this reason to the point of casuistry when it came to its own polemics and apologetics. It was based upon a denial of human reason from the first day of its birth in the fevered brains of people like Paul and John. The theologians who followed made this lack of reason the basis of an inverted snobbery. Terteullian, a theologian from Carthage, summed up the case for Christianity when he said: "God's Son died; it is believable because it is absurd. He was buried and rose again; it is certain because it is unbelievable." Who could beat that in a debate based upon evidence of human experience, and human reason ?

Human reason is also the basis of a true universalism. True universalism recognises that although basic human nature is the same, always and everywhere, yet different human beings dwell at different stages of development-mental, moral, psychic and, spiritual–and, therefore, stand in need of a diversity of doctrines, philosophies, aspirations, godheads, and ways of worship. Pagan religions of Europe, Africa and Asia, which Christianity destroyed in due course, recognised this true universalism and, therefore, caused no conflict between different communities or wars between different nations on account of religion. Christianity, on the other hand, prescribed only one historical personality as the *sole* saviour, propounded only *one* theology as the infallible gateway to God, and propped up only *one* church as an exclusive trustee of truth. It was a very gross violation of universalism. It divided humanity into Christians and non- Christians. Christians were now called upon to convert or kill all those who differed from them. At the same time, Christian theologian went about boasting that their creed and church were the harbingers of universalism in human history !

History is a witness that all doctrines, however fantastic or fanciful, have found their fans (or victims) in all societies. Kautilya has elaborated in his *Arthashastra* the psychological principles which alienate some people from their own society, and lead then straight into the lap of those who are out to subvert that society. The first group of people who can be alienated are the *manivarga*, that is, those who are conceited and complain that they have been denied what is their due on account of birth, brains or qualities of character. The second group consists of the *kruddhavarga*, that is, those who are self-righteous, who claim that they alone know how to set things right, and who become angry because the powers that be do not listen to them. The third group comprises the *lubdhavarga*, that is, those who put a price on everything and sell themselves to whosoever can pay the price. The fourth group is the *bheetavarga*, that is, those who have committed crimes, are afraid of being caught and, therefore, collaborate with whoever is out to overthrow the existing order and the laws which threaten them.

A study of the Roman scene in the three centuries, preceding the Christian takeover at Constantinople in 323 A. D., leaves a strong impression that the Church was instinctively employing the psychological principles propounded by Kautilya. The pagan societies in the Roman Empire were encumbered with an elite which had become spiritually bankrupt, morally neutral, and devoid of intellectual discrimination. The common people in these societies loved their gods, flocked to their temples, and rejoiced in their sacrifices and religious processions. But most members of the elite, who had been educated in schools set up by a variety of sophists, could no longer find any satisfaction in the hallowed traditions of their society, nor harbour any aspiration beyond personal ambition for power and pelf.

Myth of Christian Martyrdom

Christian missionaries could find quite a few and easy converts amongst these upper classes precisely because the Church had declared war on their society. Christian theology helped these converts to betrays their Gods, their culture, and their country, with a clean conscience; they could now believe that the betrayal was in the interests of a "higher cause" and a "loftier purpose". Incidentally, it also helped the upper classes to avoid military service to a state, which the Church had placed under a taboo. Like the later-day hippies in the United States of America, the upper classes were now free to "make love instead of war".

Christian historians have made much of the "martyrdom" suffered by the early Christians under several Roman regimes. No pagan records have survived to tell the other side of the story. But the Christian record: themselves provide ample evidence as to who was the sinner and who the sinned against. The Christians abused and poured contempt upon the pagan Gods and Goddesses in the foulest possible language. They denounced pagan culture as degenerate, devilish and immoral. They called upon all Christians not to render military service or pay taxes to a regime run by what they described as the Antichrist and the Devil. John described Rome as the "harlot who sins on the great waters, with whom kings of the earth have committed fornication"; Rome was the "Whore of Babylon", he wrote. Roman society was not yet entirely dead and it was but natural that some Romans reacted strongly against its enemies and in its own defence, every now and then.

Roman records which have survived also show that it was not the ruling classes but the common people who reacted against Christian aggression. Mob action against Christians in many a city street forced the hands of authority quite a few times. But, by and large, the upper classes either remained indifferent, or smiled indulgently on what they regarded as a conflict between tweedledum and tweedledee, or privately advised the Christians not to provoke the "mad" mob. The common people thus found themselves leaderless and felt bewildered in the face of apathy on the part of rulers whom they regarded as their own. On the other hand, the "martyrdom" suffered by the Christians, who were in a minority for quite some time, evoked sympathy for them, particularly amongst the upper class women who could see no "valid' cause for mob violence.

The Christian minority succeeded in the long run because of the two peculiar methods it used–methods with which the pagan societies were unfamiliar, and which these societies did not know how to counter.

First, the concept of a whole-time missionary, who had nothing to do except convert people, was unknown to pagan societies. These societies had their priests who helped them perform certain religious rites, at home as well as at places of public worship and pilgrimage. But the priests themselves were householders who had many other things to do besides helping their patrons. The saints, mystics and philosophers in these societies advised those who visited them about methods of self-improvement or the paths towards spiritual progress. Neither did they know, nor did they have the aptitude to train their devotees in, the art of combat against a rival creed. The Christian missionary thus found the field free for practising his casuistry on simple and straight-forward people who could neither argue with him till the end of time, nor put up a show of piety at which the missionary was a past-master.

The Christian Church: A State within A State

Secondly, the Christian missionaries went on organising into a monolithic and militant Church the community of their converts. The Church was created after the pattern of the Roman Empire–territorially as well as administratively. The entire imperial territory, at the center as well as in the provinces, was divided into parishes, dioceses, districts and other divisions over which priests, deacons, archdeacons, bishops, prelates and archbishops presided with despotic power derived from a "divine revelation". In due course, the Church could raise its own resources, provide for an increasing number of missionaries, build monasteries full of militant monks, and send money to Christian communities in poorer places. The roads, sea-routes and other means of communication which the Roman state had built and devised for its own use also became vehicles of the fast spreading Christian creed. The pagan people, on the other hand, were divided into many communities each of which led its own life in terms of its own cultural traditions. They were hardly in a position to withstand the Christian onslaught which went on gaining might and momentum with the passing of every year.

These methods of the Church were matured and made progressively more powerful in the midst of heresy-hunting and schisms which were inevitable in a community which looked with suspicion on every departure from dogma, and every innovation in ritual. Far from weakening the Church, these recurring quarrels made it ever more ruthless towards those whom it regarded as its enemies. Dogma was doggedly tailored to the needs of church authority, and the authority in turn served the spread of dogma with an uncompromising zeal.

By the end of the 3rd century A.D. the Church had become not only a powerful edifice next only to the imperial government itself, but had also evolved a well-defined dogma deceptively dressed in the language of Greek philosophy and Egyptian mysticism. No wonder that it started finding an increasing number of adherents amongst merchants who had money, amongst politicians who wielded power, amongst military commanders who were superstitions or in need of popular support, and amongst gilded ladies who were out to make the best of both the worlds.

The mother of Emperor Severus (222-235 A.D.) had become a disciple of Origen, a well-known Christian theologian. Emperor Philip the Arabian (240-249 A.D.) had himself become a Christian. The wife of Emperor Galerius implored him, when he fell sick in 311 A.D., to make peace with the "undefeated God of the Christian". He promulgated an edict recognising Christianity as a legitimate religion, immediately before he died the same year. Helena, the mother of Constantine, who converted the Roman Empire into a Christian theocracy, was a Christian convert and exercised considerable influence in the counsels of her son.

Divine Right of Kings

Scholars have debated the question whether the conversion of Constantine was religious or political. It is difficult to give a definite answer at this distance in time, more so because the evidence is conflicting. But one thing which decided Constantine in favour of Christianity was the *divine right of kings* coupled with *dynastic succession*–a dogma which the Church had evolved and was prepared to extend to any contender for power who accepted Christianity as the sole state religion.

The Roman state had continued to pretend to be a republic long after it had become an imperial edifice for all practical purposes. But here was no dynastic succession and no divine right of kings known to Roman political parlance. Every emperor had to wade his way through blood before he could ascend the imperial throne. Constantine saw the future of his family as well as of his own imperial power bound with the Christian dogma of dynastic succession and the divine right of kings. He removed his capital from Rome to Constantinople to avoid resistance which was likely to be stronger in the former city. And he succeeded in the gamble with the help of the Church.

But Constantine was not the last to sanctify his imperial crown with the insignia of the Church. In the years to come, the kings of Celts, Franks, Anglo-Saxons, Germans, Bulgars, Danes and Slavs solicited and obtained the aid of the same Church to proclaim absolute power over their subjects. A king in these pagan societies was only the first amongst equals, and he could be dethroned if he fell foul of the time-honored tradition of allowing autonomy to local units. The Church helped these democratic monarchs to become unbridled despots who, in turn, helped the Church to stamp out all pagan practices–religious, cultural and social.

Destruction of Pagan Religions

The pattern followed by the christianised monarchies vis-a-vis pagan religions was the same in every country of Asia, Africa and Europe.

To start with, the pagan temples were closed, pagan processions were prohibited, pagan sacrifices were declared sacrilegious, pagan priests were deprived of the privileges which they had enjoyed since times immemorial, and state patronage of pagan schools was withdrawn. Simultaneously, finances were made available for building Christian churches, seminaries and monasteries; Christian ceremonies and public festivals were patronised by kings, princes and princesses; Christian sacraments were made obligatory on all citizens; and Christian priests and monks were granted special privileges such as non-payment of state taxes and non-performance of public duties. The Church was permitted to inherit extensive properties from those who wanted to will that way. Soon it became a device to save properties from being sequestered to the state. Those who could not inherit properties legally got them willed to the Church which they themselves joined in some capacity or the other. And the Church was also allowed to hear and decide such legal disputes as were brought before it by the citizens.

In the next round, the pagan temples were demolished or converted into Christian churches; properties attached to pagan shrines were transferred to the Christian shrines; pagan scriptures were burnt; and pagan priests were killed unless they agreed to get converted. The campaigns for destruction of pagan, temples, burring of pagan scriptures, and killing or converting of pagan priests were announced and sanctioned by the hierarchs of the Church and the Christian mobs who carried out the commands, particularly in the countryside, were mostly led by Christian monks living in the fast multiplying monasteries.

It would be a long story if we were to relate, country by country, what the Church did to pagan religions and cultures, prevalent from times immemorial, in Europe, Asia Minor, Syria, Egypt and North Africa. It is a story of how the Church subverted one pagan society after another; how hundreds of thousands of pagan temples and sacred shrines were destroyed; how millions of "heathens" were dispatched to the "Christian hell" by fire and sword; and how the last vestiges of every pagan religion and culture were stamped out.

What is still more painful about this story is how some of the savages and lunatics who instigated, inspired, sanctioned and supported this sanguine saga were sanctified as saints by the Church. Many pious people are impressed as soon as they find the letters "St." added to a name. They would be shocked if they found out what the honorofic hides most of the time.

On top of it all, the Church labelled the pagan people "barbarians" who had "invaded" the then "civilised world" of the Roman Empire. Scholars in several European countries have now delved deeper into the pre-christian past of their societies. The evidence they have pieced together about the quality and character of the pagan people tells an altogether different story. It was not the pagans but the Christians who were perhaps the first barbarians in human history. The doubtful distinction of passing off politics under the cloak religion must go to the Christian church in ancient and medieval Europe.

Christianity in the New World

There was no scope left for expansion after 1000 A.D. or thereabout, because its path towards the East and the South had meanwhile seen blocked by another though similar politics which had taken shape on the sands of Arabia. The new world of the Americas, Australia and New Zealand, and the old world of Africa, India, Southeast Asia and the Far East were not yet accessible to the Church, though its individual missionaries were mapping out the scene in different Asian countries. Meanwhile Christianity had become more and more brutalised as a result of several centuries of heresy-hunting, inquisition and the burning of "witches". Spain and Portugal were in the van of this process of brutalisation.

It was the Spaniards who discovered America towards the close of the 15th century A.D. At about the same time the Portuguese travelled round the western and southern coast of Africa to reach South India, Ceylon, Burma, Malaya, Indonesia, Indo-China, Korea, China and Japan. The Philippines were soon to be invaded by the Spaniards who crossed the Pacific from their base in Mexico. The missionaries found that all these countries and continents were inhabited by pagan societies as unsuspecting as the pagan societies of ancient Europe, Asia Minor, Egypt and North Africa. The politics of conversion called Christianity started playing its game once again, and over a far larger field. The Pope in Rome drew a line on a certain longitude, and handed over the two hemispheres to the two Christian nations–Spain and Portugal.

As soon as the Spaniards saw the vast expanse of North, South and Central America, they were filled with the conviction that it was the very land which their "Lord God" had "promised" to them at the dawn of human history. The "divine promise" was all the more promising because of the plenty of gold it contained, particularly in those parts which later became known as Mexico, Peru and Guatemala. The Red Indians who inhabited these lands appeared to be intruders to the Spaniards. At least that is how the sailors and soldiers of the Church argued amongst themselves. The fact that these Red Indians were welcoming the Christians with open arms, and offering them plenty of gifts including gold, did not change the situation. It only confirmed that the lands for which the Red Indians were not prepared to fight could not really belong to them.

The slaughter and pillage that followed all over America–north, center and south–still remains unparalleled in the annals of human history. It was a slaughter of unarmed people who had given no provocation, and were prepared to share with the Spaniards whatever wealth they had. Their only "crime" was that they were not Christians and the "Lord God" had not "promised" to them the lands on which they had lived for untold ages.

The Red Indians who escaped the sword of the Christian soldiers were enslaved by the plantation pioneers who followed soon after. The missionaries, in their turn, found a rich harvest for conversion in these harassed human beings. The "poor devils" had lost everything in this life. Their bodies were not likely to last for long under the lashes of the Christian slave-drivers. But their souls could be saved for a life everlasting after the second coming of Christ. Meanwhile, the Portuguese were selling to the Spaniards a lot more slaves which the former had captured from all over Africa. The missionaries had their hands full with the work of saving souls.

In course of time, the Christians from Spain were joined by many more from other European countries–particularly the Catholics from France and the Protestants from Great Britain. They frequently came to blows over the division of the land and the loot. But none of them had a thought to spare for the Red Indians who, in due course, almost disappeared from North America and whose remnants were converted to Christianity in Central and South America. It was only when the Dark Age, ushered in by Christianity, came to a close towards the end of the eighteenth century that the Red Indians were recognised as human beings, equal to the Christians who had killed most of them and enslaved the rest. But the Church was not prepared to concede that its mission amongst the Red Indians had been anything except a mission of "Christian mercy". The Church kept on brandishing its belief that the great Mayan culture in Central America was a species of "barbarism", specialising in "human" sacrifices" at the altar of its "blood-thirsty" gods. The Church was to tell similar stories about the Hindus, though in less loud tones, because the Hindus were soon in a position to hit back.

Christian Politics of Conversion in Asia

Due to a number of circumstances, the Portuguese did not do so well in the lands which the Pope had bequeathed to them. But they had an ample opportunity to practise the politics of conversion along the Western coast of India. Francis Xavier who presided over this politics for a few years had the Christian satisfaction of demolishing a number of Hindu temples in South India, and seeing several thousand "heathens" slaughtered in Goa. He invited the king of Spain to use the secular arm for the spread of Christianity in India. The Church sanctified him as the "Patron Saint of the East", and his corpse was enshrined in Goa, to be worshipped in perpetuity by the victims of his politics.

By the time the French, the British and the Dutch appeared on the eastern scene, Christianity had been found out in the West for what it had always been in fact–power-hungry politics masquerading as religion. The later-day European imperialists, therefore, had only a marginal use for the Christian missionary. He could be used to beguile the natives. But he could not be allowed to dictate the parallel politics of imperialism. Moreover, the East had some highly developed pagan cultures, which could discuss on equal terms quite a few fundamentals with the Christian fanatics, and which were also not too weak militarily.

The field for the Christian politics of conversion has become considerably smaller in Asia due to the resurgence of Islam, and the triumph of communism in China, North Korea, Vietnam, Cambodia and Laos. If a missionary converts a single muslim in any Islamic country, he is sure to be murdered immediately by a muslim mob, even before the Islamic state has considered the case for his expulsion. Nor can the missionary find a convert in any communist country. He will be immediately caught as an "imperialist agent" and sent to a labour camp. Buddhist Burma has also seen through his game and barred his entry. It is only in India, Ceylon and Japan that the missionary continues to practise his profession effectively. India is perhaps his most fertile field because India has yet to understand the true character of Christianity in spite of the opportunity provided by the missionaries over the past five hundred years.

Politics of Conversion called Islam

Although Islam entered India some 800 years before Christianity, it appeared on the world scene some 600 years later. By the time Mohammad proclaimed himself a prophet in 610 A. D., the Christian politics of conversion had already conquered all those countries in Europe, Asia and Africa which had formed parts of the Roman Empire at the height of its expansion. The Church was casting covetous eyes towards the North and the East in Europe, as towards the sprawling Persian Empire in the South-East, seeking fresh pastures for its enthusiastic enterprise. The desert of

Arabia did not count for much in the calculations of the Church. Some missionaries had visited the southern parts of the Peninsula and made some converts. But the "chosen ones" had been left to live alone in the company of Arab "heathen" and the "accursed Jews" who had quite a few colonies in the oases spread over the central and northern parts of the desert. Little did the Church suspect that the "heathens" of Arabia were to challenge very soon the Christian monopoly of the politics of conversion.

"Islam" is derived from the Arabic "salam" and has been presented to mean "peace" or "surrender", depending upon the time and place of presentation. In a country and at a time where and when muslims are not in power, it is presented as "peace". But as soon as the Muslims become dominant, it means surrender, and that too at the point of the sword. The surrender is supposed to be made to *allah* the *only* God according to Islam But *allah* is sure to spurn the surrender unless it is preceded by a surrender to the prophet, the sole spokesman for *allah*. In effect, it means a surrender to whichever *mulla* happens to be hailed as the authentic interpreter of the *quran* and the *hadis*, in the eyes of the Sultan who wields the sword, the sole arbiter under Islam in matters moral and spiritual.

While Jesus was not the founder of the Church and had nothing to do with the dogmas of Christianity, the *umm* or *millat*, which became the vehicle of Islam was founded and given a finished form, as well as a fanatic ideology, by Mohammad himself. Again, while the personality, preaching and performance of Jesus can be pitted against the Church and its dogma, there is little in Islam which is not derived directly from the personality, preaching and performance of its prophet.

Allah and His Prophet

What exactly happened to Mohammad in the mountain cave outside Mecca has remained a controversial question. We are told by the theologians of Islam that his "experience" is not verifiable by any other human being, nor his "revelation" subject to human reason. One has to accept Mohammad's word that he was the *last* and the *most perfect* prophet, and that whatever he said or did in a state of *wahi* or otherwise was the pronouncement and prescription from "almighty" *allah*.

Those who took Mohammad at his word and accepted his prophethood were acclaimed by him, as momins, while those who rejected his mission were denounced as kafirs. The momins did not have to be better men than the kafirs in terms of consciousness or character. They had only to recite the *kalima*–there is no god but *allah*, and Mohammad is *the* prophet–and they became qualified to kill as many kafirs as they could, or pleased.

Allah himself had been a part of the Arab pantheon at Mecca for many centuries past. He had shared his divinity with a large number of other Gods and Goddesses worshipped by the Arabs in Mecca, though he enjoyed a certain primacy. The bedouin, who roamed the desert, flocked to Mecca at appointed times for pilgrimage, and worshipped his Gods and Goddesses with whatever offerings he could spare from his meagre possessions. Neither the bedouins nor the nor settled citizens of Arabia had ever suspected that their *allah* was soon going to become the sole cock of the walk, and the cause of a bloody and prolonged strife in many parts of the world.

It is also debatable as to why Mohammad chose *allah* alone, out of a large-sized Arab pantheon. He could have as easily bestowed this singular honour on any other God or Goddess in Mecca, or in the temple of some other town in Arabia. The Gods and Goddesses had obviously no choice in the matter. The only rational explanation is that the sound of the name *allah* was near to the sound of *Elohim*, the God of the Jews. Jesus had also cried out to *Eli* before he died on the cross. There are too many Judaic elements in Islam to rule out this explanation. But whatever the reason for Mohammad's choice, there is no reason to doubt that *allah* would not have assumed the status he did without the help of Mohammad. It is small wonder that *allah* in his turn felt so tender towards Mohammad, and proclaimed the latter to be the last and the most perfect prophet in human history.

Things started happening soon after the covenant between *allah* and his only prophet was struck in the mountain cave outside Mecca, through the good offices of an angel named Gabriel. The Quraish who were the dominant tribe in Mecca would not have minded a member of their clan acclaiming *allah* as the only God. They were used to such prophets appearing in Mecca and other Arabian towns, every now and then. They were a liberal people in matters of religion and did not mind how a man fancied himself or his god. But they were painfully surprised by the proclivities of this new prophet. He had started frequenting the forum outside the *kaaba* to denounce, in a rather strong language, all that they had cherished so far–their Gods and Goddesses, their cultural traditions, their social system, and what not–day in and day out.

Muslim mullas have made a martyr out of Mohammad during his 12 years of prophet-hood at Mecca, the same way as the Church had made martyrs out of the early missionaries at Rome. They have also explained away or justified the vindictiveness of Mohammad towards his own people of the Quraish by citing the "many injustices including violence" which Mohammad had "suffered" at Mecca. No contemporary records of the Quraish have survived to tell the other side of the story. But there is enough in the contemporary Islamic record to clinch the issue as to who was the aggressor and who the aggressed-against. Here was a man sending all ancestors of the Arabs, including his own mother and father, to an eternal hell, and promising the same hell to the present and future generations of the Arabs, unless they accepted him as the *only* prophet of the only *allah*. The Quraish would have been a dead people indeed if they had not reacted, and told Mohammad to leave their city for wherever he could find a more attentive audience.

It is for this "crime" of the Quraish that Muslim mullas have blackened the religion and culture of pre-Islamic Arabia as *jahiliya* (ignorance). The mullas forget that the Arabic language which is their proud possession in the *quran* and the *hadis* was not invented by their prophet at the moment, nor "revealed" by *allah* out of the blue. This rich language had a long ancestry, and reflected the genius of a culture which was deep as well as endowed with diverse dimensions. The pre-Islamic Arabs were a pagan people who allowed a God or Goddess to each according to his or her need and who respected worship from each according to his or her capacity. They had many other qualities of head and heart which the post-Islamic Arab society and culture came to lose progressively.

Islam professes to have brought peace to the warring tribes of Arabia. But its own chronicles tell of nothing except wars, more fierce than ever before, which the Arabs fought, first amongst themselves, and later on with their near and distant neighbours on all sides, soon after they were forced to surrender to Islam.

Islam and Christianity Compared

The Christian Church had taken 300 years to conquer the Roman empire. The Islamic *millat* triumphed much faster over Arabia–in a matter of 10 years after Mohammad arrived in Yathrib which became known as Medina after a massacre of its Jewish population. But in spite of this difference in time-scale, the methods used by the *millat* were more or less the same as were used earlier by the Church. The difference arose because of the different situations in which the two politics of conversion took shape.

The Roman empire was a powerful political edifice. The Church had to build a state within the state before it could subvert Roman society. Arabia, on the other hand, was divided into a number of independent tribal republics, with nothing to share amongst them except a fierce love for local freedom. The *millat* had only to build the apparatus of a centralised state–a reliable revenue system and a standing army—in order to be able to reduce the tribal republics, one by one.

The religious mask worn by the politics of conversion called Islam was also more transparent than the thick veil of verbiage in which Christianity had had to decorate itself. Christianity had its beginnings in an environment suffused with sophistry. It had to acquire a similar language and idiom to percolate itself. Islam, on the other hand, was invented in an environment which was much more simple and straightforward. It could therefore, advocate the politics of conversion with less hypocrisy and shoot straight from the shoulder.

The Momins and Kafirs

If we leave aside the myths and legends which Islam borrowed from Judaism–lock, stock and barrel–the message of Islam was very simple, almost simplistic.

To start with, it divided Arabian society into two tight compartments the momins and kafirs. The momins were asked to muster together into a militant *millat*–armed to the teeth, and ready to use force and/or fraud according as occasion demanded. The *millat* surprised the settlements and caravans of the kafirs in a series of armed raids. The kafirs who were always caught unawares had no choice but to surrender, many a time without a single skirmish. The swordsmen of the *millat* selected and slaughtered, in cold blood, all kafirs who were capable of bearing arms. The movable and immovable property of the kafirs was appropriated by the *millat*. The women and children of the kafirs were captured, and sold as slaves or freed for ransom, after members of the *millat* had their pick of the maidens.

Once in a while, the *millat* discovered that the kafirs were in no mood to surrender in spite of the surprise, and that the armed conflict might turn out to its disadvantage. Then the *millat* made overtures of peace on the condition that the kafirs got converted to Islam. The lives and families of the converts were spared but not their properties which were taken away as booty.

The mullahs take pride that Islam did away with tribal ties and united all Arabs in one solid brotherhood. It must be admitted that the *millat's* method of doing away with tribal ties was very effective indeed. Quite often one or more members of a family or tribe happened to be momins, while their other kinsmen were ranged against them as kafirs. The *millat* encouraged a brother to engage his brother in armed combat, so that one of them was sure to get killed. In case of kafirs who had to be slaughtered after the war, the *millat* searched its own ranks for the nearest kinsmen to perform the "pious" deed. A momin was supposed to retain or recognise no relationship except that of a common creed. All other humanities were now rendered irrelevant.

The momins were, of course, not risking their lives for nothing. Four-fifths of the booty and prisoners captured in a war was their sharp according to a "law" laid down by the prophet himself. The prisoners included quite a number of young and fair maidens who could set any momins mouth-watering. No wonder that the infant state of Islam at Medina was able to assembly very soon quite a number of "dedicated" swordsmen without spending a penny from its own coffers. The principle of lice enterprise applied to plunder and pillage was functioning with full force.

In case a momin got killed in the "holy war", he was promised a permanent place in heaven. "The blessed", said the *quran*, "will be dressed in silk brocades and adorned with gems. They will recline on couches and be served by handsome youths, and eat from trees bowing down to fill their hands. There will be virgins never yet touched by men or jinn...in beauty like the jacinth and coral stone...with swelling bosoms but modest gaze, with eyes as fair and pure as sheltered eggs, and bodies made of musk, and free from the imperfections and indignities of mortal flesh." According to one tradition, quoted by Will Durant, each *momin* was promised 72 of these houries, who would never age or stop being solicitous. According to other traditions, the number could be many times more. It was surely an added attraction.

The balance one-fifth of the booty and prisoners of war were assigned to the Islamic state which the prophet had set up at Medina to start with, and which moved to other cities in due course, under the caliphs or *amir-ul-mominin*. This one-fifth had to be the pick of the bunch before members of a military expedition could claim their share. No wonder that the Islamic state at Medina was very soon rolling in riches. The wealth which flowed to the Islamic state in later times grew progressively in volume and variety, and the stage was set for the flowering of that Islamic "culture" in which the *millat* takes such mighty pride. The prophet and the earlier caliphs, who controlled and commanded these riches, were inclined to lead a life of "poverty". This "piety" impressed the *momins* who had to be satisfied with much less, and served to create many myths about Islamic "ideal of equality." The "equality" never made any difference to the despotic power which the prophet and later on, the caliphs had at their disposal.

Sweep of the Islamic Sword

The prophet of Islam had proclaimed that *allah* had assigned the whole earth to the *millat*. Not a patch was to be left for the kafirs to dwell. And no comer of the world was to be bereft of mosques from which the *muezzin* could call the "faithful" to prayer. But it seems that *allah's* knowledge of geography was not so good. His prophet had not heard of many lands beyond Syria, Iraq, Iran, Ethiopia and Egypt. He knew nothing about India and the Hindus which want of knowledge was to lead to an interesting theological controversy later on.

Notwithstanding this lack of geographical knowledge, the prophet divided the world into two contending spheres–*darul-Islam* (the zone of peace) and *darul-harb* (zone of war). The inhabitants of *darul-islam,* that is, the Muslims were commanded to wage unceasing war upon *darul-harb* till the latter was converted into *darul-Islam*. The frontiers of the Islamic empire were to be pushed progressively in all directions. The theory of Islamic imperialism was thus perfected by the prophet himself, like the later-day theory of communist imperialism which Lenin elaborated as "international proletarian revolution."

The whole of Arabia had been terrorised into surrendering to the sword of Islam by the time the prophet passed away in 632 A. D. The militarised *millat* which had "elected" an *amir-ul-mominin* in the same year, now started seeking fresh fields for the mission of Islam. Iran had exhausted herself in an unceasing war with the Roman Empire. The provinces of the Roman Empire in Asia and North Africa were seething with rebellion against persecution of "heresies" by the Church at Rome which had by now reduced every other ecclesiastical dispensation to a subordinate status. Iran and the Roman provinces fell in quick succession after the armies of Islam had first found out the feebleness of their defences, and then delivered decisive blows.

Thus, within a hundred years after the death of the prophet, the *amir-ul-mominin* at Damascus became the master of a mighty empire, spread over Spain, Sicily, North Africa, Egypt, Palestine, Syria, Iraq, Iran, Khorasan and Sindh. It was a military triumph unprecedented in the annals of human history so far. The triumph could be easily explained in terms of political and military causes and consequences. But the *mullas* chose to attribute it to the might of *allah* which had been "fully and finally thrown on the side of Islam". Henceforward, there was no justification for anyone to dwell in the "darkness of *kufr*". The "light" of Islam was now accessible to all.

The newly conquered countries were inhabited not by thinly spread-out tribal settlements but by populous societies, urban and rural. It was no more possible for the *momins* to kill all *kafirs* who rejected Islam or capture and carry away all their women and children. Besides, the properties which the *kafirs* possessed, and the lands on which they lived were so voluminous and vast. The *mullas,* therefore, developed a more elaborate theory of an Islamic state, out of the embryo of principles which the prophet had already propounded.

The *millat* led by the *amir-ul-mominin* was, of course, the master class under the Islamic state. But this state had a mission larger than providing power and privilege to the *millat*. The state had to see to it that the *kafirs* who had been conquered were brought into the fold or Islam as fast as possible. The *kafirs* were, therefore, given a new status–that of *zimmis* to start with. The *zimmis* were allowed to live under the aegis of an Islamic state, provided they agreed to pay *jiziya* (poll-tax) and other discriminatory taxes, and accepted a status of second class citizens placed under draconian disabilities. It was expected that the burden of taxes and the disgrace of disabilities would force the *kafirs* to get converted to Islam before long. The expectation was more than fulfilled in most countries except India and Spain. The *kafirs* in other countries were not only converted to Islam but were also brainwashed to fulminate against their ancient past, and forget that they had been conquered by a foreign race and creed.

The mullas applaud the concept of a *zimmi* and describe it as a privileged position because, "unlike the *momins*, the *zimmis* are exempted from military service". It is difficult to know how the *mullas* arrived at this self-congratulatory conclusion. They certainly did not consult any *kafir* to find out if he wanted to become a *zimmi* and be "exempted" from military service. The whole thing looks like a deliberate device adopted in order to disarm and emasculate a subject population. People who could not bear arms were in no position to defend themselves against Islamic barbarism which became more pronounced with the passing of every day, in direct proportion to the establishment of "peace" under the Islamic state.

The Islamic state allowed some time to the *kafirs* to "mend' their ways and receive the "true revelation". But it had no patience for the religious and cultural institutions of the *kafirs*. It systematically destroyed and desecrated the temples and shrines of the *kafirs*, killed their priests, burnt their scriptures as well as secular literature, closed their schools and monasteries and heaped insult and injury on every precept and practice that they had cherished so far. It completed the job of "cleaning up" the scene as throughly if not more, as the Christian church had done earlier. The conquered lands were at the same time "adorned" with mosques, *mazars* and *khanqahs* in which the *mullas* mugged up the *quran* and the *hadis*, the sufis sermonised on the *maqams* they had "attained".

Islam: An alibi for Imperialism

For several centuries after its advent, Islam was an alibi for Arab imperialism. And it was an imperialism of a type which the world had not known so far. The Arabs not only imposed their ruthless rule and totalitarian creed on the countries they conquered; they also populated these countries with a prolific progeny which they procreated on native women. Every Arab worth his race "married" scores, sometimes hundreds of these helpless women. Divorce of a wedded wife had been made very easy by the "law" of Islam. A man could go on marrying and divorcing at the rate of several women during the span of a single day and night. What was still more convenient, there was no restriction on the number of concubines a man could keep. The Arab conquerors used these male privileges in full measure. And in a matter of a hundred years,

Iraq, Palestine, Syria, Egypt and North Africa, which had been non-Arab countries for countless ages became Arab countries in race, language and culture. Conversion was not confined to creed alone; it covered one's ancestry as well.

The Arab power declined in due course. The mission of Islam was next taken over by the Turks whom the Arabs had converted earlier. It was the Turks who succeeded where the Arabs had failed–conquering Asia Minor, invading Central Asia, India and Eastern Europe. Asia Minor was wrested from Christianity, converted en masse, and populated by a prolific Turkish progeny. It is known as Turkey to-day. Central Asia, which was already Turkish, became Islamic as well. It was only in India and Eastern Europe that the Turks failed in the final round. But in both places, they crystallised colonies of native muslims to carry forward the politics of conversion under changed circumstances. The success achieved by this Islamic politics of conversion has been quite significant in India so far. How far that politics will progress in future depends upon whether Hindu society understands it or not, at present.

The Situation of Hindu Society Today

The state of Hindu society today presents a close parallel to the state of pagan societies in ancient Europe, Asia and Northern Africa, on the eve of their subversion by politics of conversion called Christianity and Islam.

The pagan societies of the ancient world were also pluralistic societies like the Hindu society, accommodating several streams of social, cultural and spiritual traditions and allowing a large measure of autonomy to their constituent units. And like the Hindu society, these pagan societies also reacted instinctively against totalitarian ideologies like Christianity and Islam.

But these pagan societies were betrayed by their elite which had become spiritually bankrupt, morally neutral and intellectually devoid of discrimination–in short, self-forgetful and self-alienated. Hindu society today is being betrayed in a similar manner by its own elite.

The Hindu masses suspect the slogan of *sarva-dharma-samabhava* in the context of Islam and Christianity, and resist it instinctively. The instinct is very sound because it is supported by the historical experience of what the Hindus have suffered at the hands of these two political ideologies which came from outside, and as accomplices of imperialist invaders.

It is the Hindu elite who must take full "credit" for circulating as genuine the counterfeit creeds Islam and Christianity.

The elite was expected to know better, and in a more systematic manner, the true character of Christianity and Islam. The Hindu scholar was expected to study first-hand the "scriptures" and theologies of these two "religions", and compare them with his own scriptures and philosophies. The Hindu historian was expected to survey and evaluate the record of these "religions" in countries and continents they have conquered.

But the Hindu elite has failed to do its duty towards his society, culture and country.

Most of the time, the Hindu elite is either too pious to believe that "real" religion can be a cause for social or political discord; or too trusting to question the exclusive claims of any creed; or too devoid of discrimination to discern the fundamental difference between *Sanatana Dharma* on the one land, and Islam and Christianity on the other; or too indifferent towards religion to count it as a subject of serious study; or too "compassionate" to remember wrongs suffered by his society in the past; or too preoccupied with his "leadership of all sections of the Indian people" to notice any sentiments or susceptibilities which may divide them. In most members of the Hindu elite the psychological motive is mixed. But in every case the end result is the same–to be impervious to the continuing aggression from Islam and Christianity.

Some sections of the Hindu elite have become too self-alienated to really care for the welfare of the society which gave them birth and brought them up. Most of the times they harbour a deep-seated animus against everything Hindu, and let no opportunity pass to harangue against their own heritage. These are the most privileged sections under the present dispensation, with whom it is difficult to have a dialogue on matters of life and death for Hindu society. They dismiss every Hindu cause with a shrug of the shoulders, if not with utter contempt. They are beyond any appeal of reason or evidence. They need psychiatric treatment.

What is worse, the Hindu elite in general is mortally afraid of being called 'communalist' by the missionary and the *mulla* or the Muslim and Christian elite which functions from all political platforms pledged to what passes as secularism in India at present. One is sure to invite this swear-word as soon as one takes cognizance of any Hindu cause, however legitimate, or questions any claim or "grievance" which the "minorities" may cook up.

And most members of the Hindu elite get frightened out of their wits when the leftists in general and the communists in particular pounce upon them as "reactionary" and "revivalist," working in league with "capitalism" and "imperialism",

This atmosphere of self-forgetfulness, self-alienation, self-righteousness and swearology aimed exclusively at Hindu society, has given birth to a brand of scholarship and journalism which always draws wrong, even perverse conclusions from a right array of facts and premises which it itself marshals, many a time quite perceptively. We have witnessed a lot of such "scholarship" and "journalism" in the aftermath of Meenakshipuram. At the back of it all, there is a mind which can be summed up in one sentence–whatever the facts, its conclusions are the same.

This mind starts by reporting that the spate of conversions too Islam is part of a plan to convert India into a Muslim majority country. It quotes verbatim the statements of the spokesmen of Islam, in India and abroad, to the effect that huge financial resources are being mobilised in all Muslim countries to help the conversion of Harijans. But it ends by citing the actual figures of Harijans converted in this or that town or village, and dismisses the whole affair as too small to justify the "hue and cry which the Hindus have raised." In the final round, this mind concludes that immediate statistics are more meaningful than the long-term strategy.

This mind starts by warning Hindu society that this society is in for serious trouble unless it secures social justice for its underprivileged sections. But as soon as it finds that the RSS, the Vishva Hindu Parishad, the *Mathadhipatis* and the Arya Samaj–the only organisations which work for the welfare of Hindu society–have entered the field for ensuring social justice to the Harijans, it starts shrieking about a "Hindu backlash" which endangers "communal harmony".

This mind ridicules the Vishva Hindu Parishad for expressing satisfaction that the tide of mass conversions has been contained. It also quotes the spokesman of *Ishathul Islam Sabha* of Tamil Nadu to prove that many more thousands are waiting to get converted in the next round which may not be far off. But it sees a danger to secularism if the Vishva Hindu Parishad takes its warning seriously and starts putting in more effort.

This mind cites some significant instances of Harijans having committed atrocities on caste Hindus. It reports that quite often the caste Hindus who came in conflict with the Harijans were only slightly higher than the Harijans in the Hindu caste hierarchy. Its own analysis proves conclusively that the Harijans who clamour the loudest in favour of conversion belong, not to the lower strata of Harijan communities but to prosperous and privileged Harijan elite which has emerged through the prevalent political process. Yet it concludes that there seems to be no other way of securing social justice from the "upper caste Hindus" except, through conversion, and cites several authorities including Dr. Ambedkar in support of this conclusion.

This mind discovers through its own field-survey that most stories of police atrocities on Harijans are pure concoctions, and that quite often the police saved the Harijans from the wrath of another community which the Harijans had wronged. It probes into the motives for conversion and finds that in most cases they are quite low such as the lust for a second "wife" or the lure of gifts and employment in Gulf countries or fear of conviction for crimes committed. It quotes reliable sources that the Muslims can always give a communal turn to any attempt by the police to arrest a criminal who has got converted to Islam in the meanwhile. Yet, when the same facts are cited by some Hindu leader or organisation, this mind starts smelling "Hindu communalism trying to distort some significant sociological phenomenon."

This mind is on record for pressing the point that Kanyakumari district was a paradise of communal peace before the RSS and "other Hindu communal organisations" became active in that area. But it refuses to read the history of Christian proselytisation spread over several centuries as a result of which this district has become a Christian majority district, so much so that the Christians are emboldened to demand a change of its name from Kanyakumari to Kania Maria. An aggression which was not challenged was no aggression, according to the "moral" perceptions of this mind. On the contrary, the aggressor is he, who challenge the aggression and tries to undo the wrongs perpetrated in the past.

To sum up, this mind sees India as a conglomeration of communities–Muslims, Christians, Sikhs, Jains, Buddhists, Jats, Yadavs, Lingayats, Ezhvas, Harijans, Caste Hindus–and address them all from its olympian heights of secularism, national solidarity, non-violence, *dharma*, and so on. It can never find anything to choose in the "unseemly" quarrels of these communities, whatever be the nature of conflict or whoever may be the aggressor. If it is pointed out to this mind that the Hindus should not be thus divided into diverse communities, and that however divided the Hindus may be, they still constitute the nation in the only Hindu home and, it gets alarmed by what it describes as "Hindu chauvinism," and calls upon all secular forces to come together and save "our composite culture" from an imminent danger.

And in the midst of all its contradictions this mind has a constant–for it, the Hindus must always be in the wrong, and the "minorities" must always have justice on their side.

The dominant Hindu elite and its confused, many a time cowardly, scholarship have become irrelevant, if not sinister, in the present situation when the politics of conversion has come out in the open, and is becoming progressively more powerful. A new and ideologically equipped Hindu elite has to emerge and restore the perspective if Hindu society has to be saved from the machinations of this politics.

How the Inquisition came to Goa

The first demand for the establishment of the Inquisition in Goa was made by St. Francis Xavier. In a letter addressed from Amboina (Moluccas to D. Joao III, king of Portugal, on May 16, 1545 he wrote:

"The second necessity for the Christians is that your majesty establish the Holy Inquisition, because there are many who are live according .to the Jewish law, and according to the Mahommedan sect, without my fear of God or shame of the world. And since there are many who are spread all over the fortresses, there is the need of the Holy Inquisition and of many preachers. Your majesty should provide such necessary things for your loyal and faithful subjects in India."

c.f, Silva Regi, Documentacao para a Historia das Missoes do Padroado Portugues do oriente, Vol. III, Lisboa 1950, p. 351.

(Quoted from – The Goa Inquisition by Anant Kakba Priolkar. p. 22)

3

Church as a Tool of Imperialism in the Modern World

MAJ. T.R. VEDNATHAM

Spent many years in North-East India. Now retired and stationed in Madras

Christianity, throughout the ages, has been a politically oriented religion. The unholy church-state alliance which began at the beginning of the 3rd century A.D. acquired a set pattern at the end of the 4th century A.D. under Emperor Constantine. In the centuries that followed, the church-state relationship played an important part in the fortunes of the Empire of Byzantium and was further strengthened under Charlemagne.

The wars that the European countries waged against each other then and in the period that followed, were all instigated by the Popes, who claimed both temporal and spiritual power.

After this came the Protestant Reformation, when Europe was convulsed by a series of wars, called the "wars of Religion", caused by the hostility between the Protestant and Catholic blocks.

The French revolution towards the end of the 18th century and the upsurge of rationalism in the 19th century did weaken the power and influence of the church on the Government.

Medieval Europe was feudal. So was the Church and as a rule they worked hand in glove and shared power. The European invaders brought this tradition to East-Asia & Africa–with them and have always been trying to seize political power.

Christianity proper came to India with the Nestorians also known as Syrian Christians by about the end of the 4th century from Antioch and Damascus. Persecuted in their own country they sought asylum in Kerala and were received and looked after. Having no proselytising zeal, they had a peaceful co-existence with the Hindus for centuries.

Christianity as the "aggressive, ecclesiastical colonialism of the European invaders starts with the advent of the Portuguese, under Vasco da Gama. The Portuguese combined trade with proselytism and colonial expansion. The ships of Vasco da Gama had the Cross painted on their sails, but at the same time carried canons on the deck with which to frighten the Zamorin. His seamen were mostly pirates while at sea, but they took holy orders in the Church when they came ashore for long periods. Force was freely used for conversion. After they got a tiny bit of a territorial footing here, they introduced a branch of the notorious Spanish Inquisition also at Goa.[1]

Vasco da Gama's initial efforts to gain converts were not very successful. He however made it clear to the king of Portugal that territories in this country could not be permanently and successfully held unless the people are made to adopt the Catholic Religion and made loyal to the Church. The king of Portugal then asked Ignatius Loyola to send a battalion of Jesuits to India. Ignatius Loyola could not grant this request. But in 1541 St. Francis Xavier was sent. He was in India for about four years. During this period he is said to have converted at least fifty thousand fishermen along the coast. The fishermen on the southwest and the southeastern coastal regions were being constantly harassed by pirates. One Christian fisherman living at that time in Goa persuaded the fishermen of the Kerala coast to apply to the Portuguese Viceroy for help. The Portuguese were themselves pirates and were only too willing, to do away with their rivals on the Arabian coast. So the Viceroy agreed, subject to the condition that the whole community become Christian and subjects of the king of Portugal. As an initial move, the members of the delegation were baptized. A fleet was sent, and the pirates roaming about the west coast were dispersed, as also on the Coromandal coast. A few weeks later, the rest of the group of fishermen were also baptized. St. Francis Xavier about this time, wrote to the King of Portugal that the only hope of mass conversion in the West coast lay in the use of temporal power of the State. The king responded by issuing orders that in Goa and other Portuguese settlements "all idols shall be sought out and destroyed and severe penalties shall be laid upon all such as shall dare to make an idol or shall shelter or hide a *brahmin*."[2]

He also ordered, that special privileges should be given to Christians so that it acts as an incentive for conversion. This work was followed by Robert de Nobili, the Italian Jesuit who established himself at Madurai in 1605. He was in the long run a failure.[3] This was due among other things to the fact that Christianity was highly exclusive and ridden with untenable dogmas and doctrines. Hence a compromise formula of coexistence before a final transition could not work. He is said to have baptized 87 *Brahmins*, and about a lakh of non-*Brahmins*. But they all melted away after his death. One other important reason that contributed to is failure was that his approach to conversion was somewhat non-political and so he did not get adequate support from the government of Portugal as well as from the Church.[4]

The Protestant missions came to India in the beginning of the 13th century with the landing of the German lutherans in Tranquebar in 1706. Right from the beginning the educational institutions of the missions identified themselves with the political interests of the government. Even as early as two years after the Mutiny (1859), Lord Palmerston the Prime Minister of England announced that it was in the interests of Britain to provide for the diffusion of Christianity throughout the length and breadth of India. The Secretary of State, Lord Halifax appended another statement to it "Every additional Christian is an additional bond of union with this country and an additional source of strength to the Empire."[5]

After the Indian mutiny of 1857 the British were genuinely afraid of interfering with the religious setup of the country. Soon they realised that there was not that much of a risk. They first permitted Christian missionary activities to a limited extent. It paid good dividends. Then they went all out in support of the missions.[6] This policy they have continued with America collaboration after Independence. The attitude of the Govt. of India was one of supreme indifference. The crux of the problem is that the people at the helm of affairs did not understand the seriousness of the threat.

Seventy years of mission work made it clear to the missionaries that the depressed, the untouchables and others at the lower strata were alone amenable and willing to come into the Christian fold. In 1920, the Jesuit missions sent a report to the Pope that there was no hope of the educated elite, the upper castes and the intelligentsia ever becoming Christian. But the harijan communities were excellent targets for their proselytising activities. It was also clear, that with these communities, conversion by faith was out of question. Economic aid and welfare measures as incentives were alone applicable. The object was to build up numbers and they were to be constituted as a separate community isolated from the rest of the people. Disruption of Indian society would thereby follow. The position was the same with regard to the tribals.

Different methods were adopted to keep the churchgoer loyal to the British Empire. One of the common practices in most of the churches was to read out ch. 2 of I Timothy which runs as follows: "First of all them, I urge that petitions, prayers and intercessions and thanksgivings be made for all people, for kings and all who hold high positions that with all reverence and dignity we may lead a quite and undisturbed life......etc."

This Biblical exhortation was interpreted to mean that Christians should be loyal to the British Government and should not have any truck with the agitators of the national movement.

The political ideology of the Christian Missionary has followed the same pattern in different countries during the last one century and more. The missionaries go for the oppressed and the rejects of the society, give them inducements, economic aid, etc. and then prop them up as a force in support of the colonial rule of the ruling class invariably and in most cases the British Govt. of the country.

The same thing happened in China in the 19th century. The missionaries built up a Chinese Christian community loyal to the foreign rulers and hostile to their own country. The part that they played in the "Arrow War" and the "Opium War" is a sordid tale. About a hundred years ago the Dowager Empress of China complained: "First the missionary, then the trader, then the gun-boat, and then the land grabbing. This is the order of events in the Chinese minds." It ultimately resulted in the Boxer rebellion, and the Taiping Rebellion, in which twenty million people died. Majority were Christians.[7]

Towards the end of the 19th century, Christianity was introduced into Burma as well. The tribes known as the karens were the oppressed and the suppressed communities in that country at the time. They corresponded to the harijans of India. The response to Christianity from the Buddhist Burmese was very poor. The Christian missionaries however converted more than 80% of the Karens (aborigines of Burma) to Christianity. They were given schools, hospitals, new houses, economic aids and other welfare measures in support. Even though they became Christians in a way, the majority remained only as animists with their usual beliefs, in ghosts, spirits, and the need for offering sacrifices to propitiate them. There was no religious conversion through faith. By 1920, the more literate among the Karens were put through the seminary at Insein (a township north of Rangoon) and later sent out to reform the tribes. It was a partial success. By 1930, a small band of educated Karens had come up. They groomed the entire lot to accept and adopt western culture, religion and ways of life. They built up a local militia known as the "Karen Irregulars". These were given military training and used to serve as additional flank support to the British forces of occupation in the country. The Karen irregulars were more or less on the same footing as "The Auxiliary Force of India" which consisted of Anglo-Indians and Anglo-Burmese. During the turbulent years between 1920 and 1940 in Burma, when the nationalist upsurge took place the Karen irregulars faithfully discharged their duties and obligations as subjects of the white man, by supporting the British and betraying their own country. When Burma became independent, the Karens were expelled and driven out of the lower Burma regions. They took refuge in the northern triangle and are now collaborating with the Kachins and the Chinese to help the Naga rebels to go to China for training and for their safe return through the Burma border, before reentering India.[8]

There was some talk of the British giving Dominion Status to Burma and installing the Karens in power. It did not however turn out that way. The Karens are today in the wilderness serving as the errand boys of the Chinese, the Kachins and the Nagas. This is a typical example of the way Christianity and the Church had been used to bolster up the colonial empires of the westerner in Asian countries. The standard method has always been to exploit the social inequality and injustice in Asian countries, and then spilt them into hostile groups and support the one against the other in the name of the Church.

The Czarist regime in Russia was a tyranny fully supported by the Greek Orthodox Church. In March 1956 Bishop Raja Manickam met the then Chinese premier Chou-en-Lai in Peking and wanted religious freedom for the Christians to be restored and ties to be renewed with the World Council of Churches. He was told in clear terms "Surely it cannot be on the basis of Ecclesiastical Colonialism". They further made it clear that China had to expel all foreign missionaries who were at heart colonialists and agents of foreign powers and did great harm to China. Chou en Lai also pointed out that in China there was complete religious freedom to every citizen, only subject to the condition that he realises that his religion is his personal and private affair and he cannot and should not try to make an impact of it on his neighbour. No one in the country he said is allowed to bring religion into politics. When Bishop Raja Manickam further questioned him about the Christian leaders imprisoned in China, he was told that "It is simple, because they have tried to overthrow our Govt., under the instigation of our enemies, and no Government worth its name can allow that." Later Bishop Raja Manickam wrote to the editor of the China Bulletin, New York, saying "In my opinion nothing is harming our relationship with our Chinese brethren as much as the circular letters about China written by Americans, particularly ex-chinese missionaries, now at Hong Kong.The same story is now being re-enacted in the Northeastern tribal territories of Nagaland, Mizoram and Arunachal. It is a war declared by the soldiers of the American Baptist Mission on the Hindu Govt. of India. The Americans and the British are reported to have told the tribals that they were not Indians because they were Christians.[9]

The Havoc which the foreign missionaries of the American Baptist Mission Church played in the Northeastern tribal territories, Nagaland and Mizoram, deserves special mention. During the years 1840 to 1920 the then British Govt. took a lot of trouble to subdue the tribals in these areas. There were many expeditions and many casualties on both sides. It may be said that by 1900 the British were fairly successful in bringing those territories under their control for all practical purposes. Once in power, their first act was to ban head-hunting. The Christian missions then started their conversion work. It paid them rich dividends. The then British Govt. gave the missionaries its full support. English education was introduced and with that the western mode of life. When the second World War started in the year 1939 in some areas there were 90% Christians and in others about 50 to 60%. Right from the beginning they were indoctrinated with the theory that they were not Indians because they were Christians and also that being a mongoloid race, and the Indians being non-mongoloid, they certainly couldn't be Indians.

In 1963 one Rev. Scott offered to negotiate with the rebel Nagas and bring about an understanding and then settle the disputes amicably. The Govt. of India accepted the offer. It was then found that right from the start he was actively engaged in instigating them to further intensify the fight. The first advice he gave the rebels was to stand firm on the principle "that the Nagas were not Indians because they were Christians." Result– within 48 hours he was pulled out and thrown out of the country. The short-sighted politicians in Delhi were slowly beginning to see the enormous danger involved in tolerating foreign Christian missionary activity in the country.[10]

During the last six months and more, some strange things are happening in the coastal regions of Tamil Nadu. The Christian evangelists are carrying on a vigorous propaganda among the Christians particularly the fishermen communities along the sea coast and the slum areas in the cities telling them in plain language that a landing of the American Marine Commandos on the Indian coast is imminent. The gist of their thesis is "you are the rejects of Indian society. You are slaves. The American are our friends, they are not only willing but also anxious to liberate you. That will make you enjoy all the fundamental human rights enshrined in the U.N. Charter. So the church has formulated what is known as 'Liberation Theology' and hence this preaching. All of you should now try to concentrate in camps and areas not far from the coast and within reasonable distance of seaports wherever possible. An American landing of troops here is possible any time. The will liberate you and thereafter it will be the kingdom of God for you." A lot more of pro-American propaganda is going on in the name of Christianity. It is all very cleverly worded. In substance it is a direct incitement to rebellion. American help is taken for granted. Communal riots are flaring up. All this has given rise to the opinion in the minds of the public that the Christians are getting organised as the fifth column for USA and the Muslims are getting organised as the fifth column for Pakistan. How far police intelligence is aware of all these happenings and if so what action they would take, remains to be seen.[11]

The stage is now set for a military solution in Mizoram, where all negotiations have failed. During the last world war there was a sarcastic remark against Winston Churchill saying that he was absolutely determined to fight the Germans to the last Frenchman and last Russian. A parallel situation exists in Mizoram today. The tribals are made the scapegoats for fighting the indirect war of the Anglo-American group.

In 1924 an American missionary by name Dr. Stanley Jones toured this country extensively preaching Christianity. To the question "We Hindus are wedded to religious tolerance. We approach the Christians with goodwill and sympathy. We have in our country, Hindus, Parsis, Buddists, Arya Samajists, Brahmos, Theosophists, Vaishnavaites, Saivaites, Sikhs, etc. We get along amicably and take part in each other's celebrations, festivals and congregational worship. As Indians we have a common base. Why is it that Christians alone adopt an attitude of exclusiveness and hostility and refuse to have a common base with us?" Dr. Stanley Jones said "I understand your question very well. You are trying to sell me your idea of the syncretical method. With this syncretical method you destroyed Buddhism in the land of its birth. With this same method you blunted the sword of Islam, If I should accept your proposition then it is only a question of time before the Indian Christian community will become Christianised members of the Hindu-Society. This is a catastrophe that we are determined to prevent."[12] The emphasis is on the negative aspect. There is a saying in the Bible "He who is not with me scattereth abroad." (Mathew Ch. 12.V. 30)

The motivation for Christian evangelism is simple. Disrupt & destroy. The missions make no secret of it. It is a mistake to think that Christian missionary enterprise is a religious movement. The Christians themselves never claimed it to be a religious movement. It was a declaration of war and an attack on the religions and cultural set up of the people of Asia & Africa, and it was always politically motivated.

Traditional religion has collapsed in Christendom, which is no more Christian. This is a post-war phenomenon. The divorce of the Church & State relationship, the old pattern, is now complete. But it has now emerged in a different form. The old theology based on untenable doctrines and dogmas has been totally discarded by the industrialised west with its new religion of scientific technology. The Church therefore is undergoing a process known to social scientists as politicization. The term does not mean merely political activity. By politicization of religion is meant the internal transformation of the faith itself so that it comes to be defined in terms of political values. This has resulted in the entry of the State into areas which were formerly the traditional preserve of the Churches. That means the Church-State relationship has been reinstated in a new form. The Church is today a tool for organising political action as decided and directed by the State. There is a clear distinction between the involvement of religion with politics and the reinterpretation of religious values as political values. This is the politicization that is happening in the modern Church. If the Church does not agree then the justification for its existence just disappears. Christians as a religious body do not exist today in the western world in a meaningful way. But Christian evangelism is still reaping a harvest in the Third World. Thus the political consciousness of the developing world's Christianity actually originated within the politicized churches of the old world. The Christian religion has lost the power and the confidence, to define its areas of influence and jurisdiction even on questions of social morality. In their death agonies, the Churches are distributing the causes of their own sickness–the politicization of religion to the churches in the developing world in Asia & Africa. This can be a fatal inheritance in the eastern countries where religion is not yet so dead.[13]

Liberation Theology – This is the post-war model of the Christian religion. The Christian missions now claim that it has become their duty to liberate the oppressed and the suppressed all over the world. This movement works through the World Council of Churches (WCC) and the International Christian Council etc. These organisations work under the direction and control of the governments of the European superpowers. USA, Canada, Britain, and Australia are in the forefront. USSR and China also seem to have a finger in the pie on their own terms. The Anglo-american groups are keen to liberate, India, Afghanistan, Laos, Kampuchea, Vietnam, Thailand, Cuba, Iran, etc. According to them, Tibet, South Korea, S. Africa, Rhodesia, El Salvador, Nicaragua, Diego Garcia etc. do not come into this scheme. Countries in the Soviet zone of influence feel that these countries like Tibet, Salvador, South Korea etc. have to be urgently liberated from the tyranny of the Imperialists and the Reactionaries. Leftist groups have also been making a lot of noise about the need for drastic action to be taken to eliminate Racism from Africa.[14]

It is interesting to note that many of the high ranking dignitaries of the Church, occupying key positions in these World Councils and the international missionary organisation, happen to be all war veteran of World War II vintage. These Patriarchs installed as the head of the Church hierarchy are talking in the language of exporting revolution to other countries. These Christian organisations when making serious inroads into politics, use some special type of technical phraseology to make everything euphemistic. In the concept of Liberation Theology are also included the concepts of internal disruption, use of violence, civil disobedience, organising resistance movements etc. [15]

While the programme continues and even expands, it is worth noting that most of the money disbursed through these special funds has come not from traditional donors, but from new ones, mostly governments. This governmental element too, worries some critics within the organisation who see in it some dangerous portents. It is a breach of the Church & State relationship brought about not necessarily by philosophical arguments, but by pragmatic ones involving a political approach. An ether serious implication is that some governments will be consciously aiding subversion in some other country. In 1925, in a conference at Stockholm sponsored by the 'life & Work and the Faith & Order Movements' they postulated the slogan "Doctrine divides-Service Unites''. These critics or the dissenters now feel that this slogan has now been reversed to read "Doctrine unites, Service divides." The ethical philosophy of Jesus is dead, and a political philosophy of violence has now taken its place. The developed countries are now making a serious effort to subvert and overthrow the Governments established by Law in the developing countries, using the Churches as their tools.[16]

John Foster Dulles has published a book captioned "*War or Peace*"[18] in 1957 (Macmillan, N. York). In the chapter 'policies in Asia' he writes "In the past the United States policy in the east rested on the foundations of friendly relations with China. Our people, through Govt., missionaries, doctors, and educators, have shared and built Chinese friendship for more than a century. Out of it have come such political doctrines as the 'Hay doctrine, of the open door' in China, the 'Hughes doctrine of territorial integrity'...Out of it have also come the Boxer Fund scholarships, Christian Colleges in China, and Christian medical centres, including a Rockfeller Foundation development at Peking." Here Mr. Dulles is making a clear cut statement that USA has been using the Church and the mission organisations and institutions to build up its close relations with China.

The Church in China is no more under the tutelage of USA. Similar changes are coming up in other areas also.

Sixty years ago Christianity was at loggerheads with Communism. But today Liberation Theology is working in the grooves of Marxism. This has produced a most anamalous situation for the World Council of Churches, which is very much dependent on the Anglo-Americans for its finances. They have to apply this ideology to support the political ambitions of the capitalist west which has and still continues to use the Church as a tool and the Church is only too willing to co-operate.

References

1. *Malabar and the Portuguese* by Sardar K.M. Pannikar.
2. Niyogi Commission Report, Part 11, Chapter 11, p. 13 (Abridged edition).
3. Niyogi Commission Report, Part 11, Chapter 11, p. 13 (Abridged edition).
4. *A Pearl to India* by V. Cronin, Rupert Hart-Davis, Soho Square, London.
5. Niyogi Commission Report, Part 11, Chapter 11, p. 14-15.
6. *The British Baptist Missionaries in India,* by E. Daniel Potts, Cambridge University Press, 1967, Chapter 8.
7. *Christianity in China* by Walter Mann, Rationalists Press Association.
8. *The Loyal Karens of Burma* by San C. Po. The American Baptist Mission Press Rangoon.
9. (a) *Rajah Bhushanam Manikkam, A Biography* by Karl Gustav and Theodox Beemann C.L.S.

   (b) *The Christian Manifesto,* by Y.T. Wu, . YMCA, chapter-The Task in General.

   (c) *Christiaity in Asia* ; Christian Conference of Asia magazine, p. 26.

   (d) *Christianity and Asian Revolution* by Rajah Manickam.
10. The author was serving in the Army in Nagaland in 1963, when Rev. Scott burst upon the scene.
11. The author has passed on a confidential note to the I.G. Police, Tamilnadu regarding this matter.
12. *Christ of the Indian Road,* by Dr. Stanley Jones.
13. *Christianity and the World Order* by Edward Norman, Oxford University Press, 1979.
14. Bulletins of the National Christian Council and World Council of Churches.
15. The Rejuvenation of the Russian Orthodox Clergy—a paper read before the instititute for Study of the USSR, by Nadezhada Theodonovich.
16. To set at Liberty the Oppresscd-W.C.C., Geneva, 1975.
17. Summary of the Niyogi Committee report.

Christian Post-war World Policy

In 1941 during the World War II the 'Commission of the Churches on International Friendship and Social Responsibility' was set up in Britain. In 1942 the commission issued a document on Christian Church and world order viewed from Christian point of view such as common moral purpose, international political framework, economic justice disarmament and the rights of the minority and colonial people. Similarly in U.S.A., the Federal Council of Churches (which had been created in 1908) appointed in 1941, a special Commission on a Just and durable peace under the chairmanship of Mr. John Foster Dulles. In July 1943 the Commission convened a Round Table Conference which issued a Christian message on "World-Order" in which the political propositions previously formulated by the United States Commission as the six pillars of peace were unanimously welcomed and in the section addressed to the Church, the Round Table stressed the opportunity for evangelism on a world-wide basis.

The U.S. Commission on a Just and Durable peace convened in Cleveland, Ohio, in January 1945, set up a National Study Conference which made nine recommendations for improvement of Dumbarton Oak's proposals. These recommendations received wide support among the American Churches and were given careful consideration in Government circles. Similarly, British Council of Churches, formulated in 1945 its recommendations for submission to the British Government. These representations were among the creative influences brought to bear on the San Francisco Conference of the United Nations held in April-June 1945. The religious spokesman at the above conference has been credited with the decision to include, within the Charter, provision for a commission on Human Rights.

At another meeting of the Commission on a Just and Durable peace held in November 1945, it laid stress on the development of Christian unity amongst various Churches on a world-wide basis with a view to bring more effective influence to bear on international affairs. The Commission announced:

"Now, with war ended, world-wide organisation of the Christian Church can be developed so as to co-ordinate, as to substance and timing, the Christian effort (for world-order) in many lands......The Christian forces of the world, though still a minority, must on that very account quickly become a well-organised and militant minority."

(c.f Report of the Christian Missionary Activities Enquiry Committee, Madhya Pradesh-1956. Volume I, Part 1 Chapter, III.)

4

Political Roots of Christianity in India

Bhahm Datt Bharti

Social worker and keen student of Christian missionary activities

In their heydays the Romans had tried to Romanize politics but they achieved very little success. Later the English who had learnt their political lessons from the Romans who held England as a slave colony (from 55 E. C. to about the 5th Cent. A. D.) succeeded a great deal in politicizing Christianity. They used their religion (Christianity) to further their political ends and it is in this context that the politics of Christian conversions with particular reference to India has to be viewed here.

Though the politics of religious conversions, can be traced right back to the scriptures of the two Semitic religions–Christianity and Islam–Christianity aided by circumstances seems to have stolen a march over Islam in this respect. This happened when in 1493 A. D. Pope Alexander VI arbitrarily divided the then known world into two distinctive spheres of political influence between two of his supporters–the king of Spain and the king of Portugal. The history of this division is interesting and has a direct bearing on the politics of Christian conversions.

At this time of history, Spain and Portugal happened to be two main and powerful Christian political states, whose rulers with more than Christian zeal supported and defended the papal claim that the Pope was the undisputed religious as well as the temporal (secular) head of the entire universe! In return the Popes were eager in their own self-interest to wheedle and humour the rulers of Spain and of West Indies. When in 1493 (March) Christopher Columbus was forced to land in Portugal a claim was put forward by King John II of Portugal to the effect that by virtue of the Papal bull, *Romanus Pontifex* (1455) of Pope Nicholas V which granted African territory to Portugal the land (America) discovered by Columbus automatically belonged to him.

Ferdinand and Isabella who then jointly ruled over Spain and were known ardent supporters of the Roman Pontiff, strongly protested to the Pope against this claim. Since Alexander VI found it difficult to displease Ferdinand and Isabella, he hit upon a novel device to pacify both Spain and Portugal. He issued three separate bulls, the second of which (*Inter Caetera Divinae*) arbitrarily drew an imaginary "line from one pole to the other, one hundred leagues west of Azores and Cape Verde islands. Everything west of this line was granted to Spain. The sphere east was to belong to Portugal, It was the 'Line of Demarcation' so established that it put what is now Brazil in Portugal's hands."[1] This line is now known as "Pope Line."

The Second Bull

The second bull (*Inter Caetera Divinae*) had several passages but the two which directly concerned the conversion of non-Christians (heathens) to Christianity laid down inter alia: "We have been informed, indeed, that you intended to seek and discover some remote and unknown islands and main-lands which have not been found by anyone so far, and bring their inhabitants and natives to the worship of our Redeemer and to the confession of the Catholic faith.....But we ordain that by this our donation, concession and grant, no claimed right, belonging to any Christian prince who had actually possessed the said lands and main-lands until the above mentioned day from the nativity of our Lord Jesus Christ, can be understood as suppressed or taken away from him. Moreover, we enjoin you in virtue of holy obedience that you should dispatch–as you have already promised and as we do not doubt that you will, with your very great devotion and royal magnanimity, fulfill this promise–to the said main-lands and islands, honest and God-fearing men, learned, skilled and experienced, to instruct the natives and inhabitants in Christian faith and to imbue them with good morals, and that you should apply all due diligence to this.*[2]

At it always happens with religious fanatics, Alexander VI's bull gave a sort of licence to Portugal and to Spain to use whatever ecclesiastical and civil (secular) means that lay in their power to convert the people of ands which they happened politically to subdue. To know and find out whether the means they employed were Christian and justified and whether these had the sanction behind them of their religion which they claimed to be the only true religion in the world. Portuguese rulers and their Christian missionaries went for guidance either to the Pope or to the Bible. The Pope had already told them "to subdue the said main-lands and islands and their natives and inhabitants with God's grace and to bring them to the Catholic faith."[3] The Pope had further enjoined on them that they were not to suppress or subdue any Christian prince but only non-Christians. And once the non-Christians had been subdued it had been made incumbent upon Portugal and Spain to "dispatch as you have already promised....."[4] (Christian faith till then meant only Roman Catholic religion–Br. D. Bh.).

It was thus about 500 hundred years ago (March, 1493) that a Pope (Alexander VI) parcelled out this world of ours between two of his political stooges without himself in any sense owning a bit of this land. In faithfully carrying out die promise which king John II of Portugal had given to the Holy Father, Pope Alexander VI, the king deputed in 1542 a man–honest, God fearing, learned, skilled and experienced to his Portuguese colonies in India (Goa). This man was Francis Xavier who later was canonized (1522) in recognition of his services to the Christian Church. In 1534 Ignatius Loyola in company with Xavier had formed an association for converting unbelievers. "This was the precursor of that notorious Company of Jesus which has been suppressed and revived, and under the mask of religion has done untold injury to the spiritual and civil liberties of mankind."[5] It was as a member of this Company now known as the Society of Jesus and as a Christian missionary especially commissioned by King John III (D. Joao) of Portugal that Xavier landed in Goa in the year 1542 (May) to use all his diligence and experience to convert the heathens of India (the Hindus) to the Catholic faith.

Birth of the Inquisition

Whenever religion gets organized and regimented it leads to tyranny. Xavier applied his mind and diligence to the problem of how to convert to Christianity the Hindus of Goa who, by and large, had no love or reverence for the Christian religion. Xavier hit upon the idea to get John III interested in the project and told him that unless the Hindus of Goa were converted to Christianity, his political power would never get firmly established in that part of the world. 'Catch them by their weaknesses' is the famous dictum of the Society of Jesus and Xavier knew too well where the weakness of an avaricious king lay hidden. Xavier, in fact, exhorted John III to politicize Christianity in Goa and Christianize his politics so far as it concerned his Indian possessions. In his letter written to John III

Xavier advised the king on how Indians (the Hindus) could be converted to Christianity:

> "I have been able to think of only one remedy for the evil and if this remedy were applied, then, unless I am mistaken, many in these parts would become Christian... Therefore, Sire, whenever a Governor or Commandant writes to your Highness, let him state how the Christian religion goes on; how many, who, what sort of persons, have become believers from among the heathens, what hope or what means there may be of bringing others to the fold... And if, in the province or place where anyone has governed, our holy Church shall have been increased during the time of his command by but a small number of neophytes, while at the same time it is certain that great increase may be made at all times and everywhere, if only the Commandant desire it, then let your Highness seriously, and your royal honour, declare in the diploma in which you institute such persons and confer authority upon them, that you will exact punishment from them for such neglect.
>
> "And I very much wish your Highness to confirm this by oath, and openly pledge yourself, calling in solemn form upon the Holy Name of God, that any officer of yours through whose means may have come to pass that the faith has not been propagated, shall, when he returns to Portugal, be fined of all his possessions, all his money and property be spent on works of mercy, and he himself be detained for many years in chains and severe imprisonment."

As a result of repeated persuasions made by Xavier and the influence he wielded with the Portuguese king, the Inquisition was ultimately established in Goa in 1560 (it was established in Portugal by a Papal bull dated December 17, 1531). Under the protection of the Inquisition the learned, experienced and skilled (they had gained lot of experience in Portugal where Inquisition had been in existence as much as it had been in Spain). Christian priests became the sole arbiters of the destinies of all those Hindus who refused to accept Christ as their personal saviour. The Franciscan friars and the Jesuits used all means, fair and foul, to force innocent men, women and children to renounce their ancestral faith and become Christian but this by itself is another story which need not be told here.

The purpose of the Inquisition was to weaken the Hindu population spiritually, economically and in the end break down their political will to resist the alien intruders. Despite naked coercion in which the Christian civil (secular) power openly supported the Church; inducements offered to people to become Christians ("In some cases he (Xavier) bought his converts with money."[7]) and torture to which innocent people were indiscriminately subjected, the Church succeeded but only little in her endeavor to spread Christianity in Goa. And the political foundations and future of Portuguese Christian colonial empire continued to rest as before on shaky foundations.

The Portuguese did not go to India for the purpose of expanding the kingdom of Christ as is so often claimed in Christian missionary literature. They were there to plunder the colony and its people to enrich themselves. Since religion holds a people together they tried as a first step to destroy the religion of the Hindus whom they had enslaved in order to weaken them politically. Religion was only a facade from behind which they pursued policies of Christian colonial expansion. To break their political will Albuquerque, the Portuguese Governor of Goa, adopted yet another policy. He disclosed in one of his reports to his king "his political plans which aimed at turning the native inhabitants of Goa out of their lands to make place for his own men. He proposed to marry his soldier to 'fair and good looking Turkish women." He suggested to the king: if the people marry in this manner, l think it will be necessary for your Highness to order the natives of the islands (Ilhas de Goa), to be turned cut of the lands and fields so that they may be given to the married; for the lands of Goa belong to none but the King the lord of the land."[8]

The Portuguese continued in their Christian endeavors to convert the Hindus of Goa to Christianity till the year 1738 (January 23), when the Marathas attacked Margao and some other villages around Salsette. Fearing that the Marathas would soon overrun Goa, the Inquisitor ordered most of the record of the Inquisition to be either burnt or transported to Portugal. On some other fronts in India, another Christian political power had been gaining political strength. These people came from England and unlike the Portuguese were the followers of another brand of Christianity which had broken away from Roman Catholicism. In 1757 (Aug. 12), the English lead by Clive; won a decisive victory at Plassey, and his appetite whetted, the Englishman started dreaming of founding an empire in the Indian sub-continent.

The Englishman who came from a nation of shopkeepers, truly concerned himself in India, at least for many more years after 1757, only with making easy money. Neither did he have any well-defined political ambitions nor much of a desire to extend the kingdom of Lord Jesus Christ to this part of the world. All this notwithstanding he soon found the conditions then obtaining in India to be favourable for founding an empire. How to lay the foundations of an English empire that would sustain itself forever and make him the greatest colonizer and the imperialist money lender of the east became his main concern.

Charles Grant

Some years before the close of the 18th Century an Englishman who was born in India applied his mind to this problem more seriously than any other of his countryman had done before him. He was Charles Grant. Grant had been a civilian in India in Malda and was very favourably inclined towards Christian missionaries and their work. Chambers, David Brown and George Udny all of whom thought on similar lines wanted to do something concrete for Christianity. The Christian missions joined hands with Grant to produce a sort of a tract which they called 'A Proposal for Establishing a Protestant Mission in Bengal and Bihar.[9]' A copy of this was sent "from India to William Wilberforce and to Charles Simeon."[10] Grant had forwarded a copy of this pamphlet to the Archbishop of Canterbury and also to the Secretary of the Society for the Promotion of Christian Knowledge (S.P.C.K.) In his covering letter to Wilberforce he had strongly pleaded with him to try to do his best to enlist" support of the Government to the scheme."[11]

Grant went even further. He took this pamphlet to Cornwallis who then was the Governor General but keeping in mind the official policy then being followed, Cornwallis turned down Grant's suggestions. Grant was not however, a man to be easily deterred or restrained. He surreptitiously encouraged many a Christian missionary from England to settle down in Bengal whom he afforded his overt political protection. In 1792 Grant wrote yet another tract which consisted of 116 folios and 5 chapters and which he called 'Observation on the State of Society among the Asiatic subjects of Great Britain particularly with respect to morals, and the means of improving it.' In this he strongly pleaded with the English people that if they wished and wanted to retain India as a colony for all times to come, it was absolutely necessary for them that that they should endeavor to convert the Hindus of India to Christianity.

Initially Grant's Observation made only little impact on the minds of those Englishmen who then mattered in London. There was nevertheless a group of Englishmen led in the House of Commons by Wilberforce and collectively known as the Clapham Sect or the Evangelical Party who fully agreed with Grant's findings and suggestions. Grant had advocated that "the true cure of darkness is the introduction of light. The Hindus err, because they are ignorant; and their errors have never fairly beer, laid before them. The communication of our light (the light of Christian religion–Br. D. Bh.) and knowledge to them would prove the best remedy for their disorders; and this remedy is proposed, from a full conviction that if judicially and patiently applied, it would have great and happy effects upon them, effects honourable and advantageous for us."[12]

What were these effects which were to prove "Honourable and advantageous" to the English people? We can now understand it very well. As a pious and devout Christian, Grant thought and perhaps so believed that converting the Hindus to Christianity was an honourable Christian pursuit no matter what some people in the present secular age might think of the ethics of religious conversions brought to achieve political ends and especially thought it was going to prove advantageous more to the one who converted and not to those who were to be, or had been, converted. As the conversion of the Hindus to Christianity was going to prove politically advantageous to the English people, it happened to be the main motivation behind all English efforts to convert the Hindus to Christianity.

The Ball is Set Rolling

In the year 1813 when the Charter of the East India Company came up before the British Parliament, William Wilberforce (1759-1833 who was the leader of the Clapham Sect repeatedly and copiously quoted from Grant's observations to drive home the point that if the British rule in India had to be perpetuated it was absolutely necessary to convert the Hindus of India to Christianity. In this effort he was actively aided by Henry Thornton (1760-1838) who was the first treasurer of the C.M.S. (Christian Mission Society); Sir John Shore (1751-1834) later Lord Teignmouth and Governor General in India from 1793 to 1798 and by Charles Grant himself who having returned to England had been five times the Chairman and Deputy Chairman of the East India Company.

It was Charles Grant who in fact had first set the ball of Christian conversions rolling in India to achieve English political ends. This policy has since been followed overtly and covertly, in one or the other form and even today there are evangelical action teams working in India to convert the Hindus of India to Christianity. Though the policy and motivation behind religious conversions has been given different shapes and slants to suit the requirements and exigencies of time and particular situation, the main thrust behind these Christian conversions in which the regular and secular clergy have always worked hand in hand continues to be political.

There is no doubt that when Grant put up his plan for converting the Hindus of India to Christianity he had at the back of his mind the political advantages which these religious conversions would bring in their wake. It can be safely surmised that when he sent his tract 'Observations' to Wilberforce he had taken due care to point to him, though only perhaps in passing, the political advantages that would accrue to the English people if they were able to convert the Hindus to Christianity. Grant would have forseen that if majority of the Hindus could be converted (no matter to which brand of Christianity) it would not at all be difficult to create, later and in course of time, a Christian satellite state tied more or less permanently to the English apron strings.

By 1813 Grant's 'Observations' had become almost a *Vade mecum* for William Wilberforce who had freely quoted from it on more than one occasion while participating in parliamentary debates on Indian Affairs. He had renewed his demand for a clause to be incorporated in the new Charter to the effect that Englishmen should be free to go to India and settle down there. He was able to appeal successfully to other like-minded individuals and Christian associations as a result of which they jointly presented as many as "837 petitions"[13] during February to June 1813 asking for this universal permission to be granted. At this time, Grant was the Chairman of the East India Company and lent his full support to whatever Wilberforce said or did to achieve this objective.

In his 'Observations' Grant had emphasised that the evil at the root in India lay in two things; one that the Hindu was ignorant and secondly that he did not have a proper and true religion. He had gone a step further and suggested the remedy which in his opinion was to introduce the English language in Indian schools. In his words: "We proceed, then, to observe, that it is perfectly in the power of this country, by degrees, to impart to the Hindus our language and afterwards, through the medium to make them acquainted with our easy literary compositions upon a variety of subjects; and, let not the idea hastily excite derision, progressively with the simple elements of our arts, our philosophy, and religion. These acquisitions would silently undermine, and at length subvert the fabric of error..."[14]

Thomas Macaulay

The members of the Clapham Sect had been fervently advocating the introduction of English language as had been advised by Grant. Zachary Macaulay the father of Thomas Babington Macaulay (later Lord Macaulay) was an active member of the Clapham sect and a friend of Wilberforce who often visited Zachary Macaulay's home where young Macaulay growing up in this atmosphere often heard these topics being discussed and debated by his father with other members of the sect. When Macaulay was chosen to become the Law Member of India he decided to impose English language on the Indian people. This meant in fact the fulfillment of Grant's dream since he had wanted English language to be used as a vehicle for converting the Hindus of India to Christianity. It has to be admitted that since after then, when by his Minute (Feb 2, 1835) Macaulay arbitrarily made English the compulsory medium of instruction in Indian schools, education has all along been the handmaid of Christian conversion programme in India.

In pre-1813 period there were two distinct schools of thought in England. One was led by Grant and Wilberforce and they favoured conversion of the Hindus to Christianity because in their opinion this would be of great political advantage and would lend strength to English political rule over India. The other group opposed conversions because, they argued that if attempts were made to convert the natives (the Hindus) to Christianity, it was likely to create emotional mass convulsions which, in turn, might jeopardize and destabilize English rule. In either case it was only for political reasons and consequences flowing from them that while one group wanted to convert the Hindus, the other group opposed religious conversions. In 1807, E. Parry belonging to the latter group had made a clear assessment of the situation when he expressed his fears saying: "There appears to be but two principle objections to the scheme of converting the natives to the faith of the Gospel, first the attempt might produce convulsions, and secondly, that if successful the natives would be less easily governed and more ready to shake off our authority than before"[15] But Grant, had offered a different explanation. He had argued in his 'Observations' that the Indians "would become more loyal to the British rule, if they were Christianised, and so put forward his view with emphasis that "in success would lie our safety, not our danger"[16] adding that the introduction of Christianity will "serve the original design with which we visited India...the extension of our commerce."[17]

The renewed Charters of the East India Company (1813 and 1833) virtually opened the flood gates of English immigrants to India. Though nearly all of them went to India to make easy money, more often they were disguised as priests, missionaries and teachers. This influx of Englishmen greatly strengthened the hands of Christian preachers like Carey who were already in India. They became more bold and outspoken. They no longer considered it necessary to hide their innermost feelings vis-a-vis Hinduism as they assiduously did in the past, behind carefully chosen words or pious platitudes. They began to give free vent to their feelings which revealed to the hilt the fact that the real purpose of these conversions was only political.

Grant had made the hidden purpose of Christian conversions more clear when he argued that "religion, and religion only will supply a common principle or bond of union between the Governors and the Governed...If...they embrace our religion, they would have a new cause of attachment to us...which would give us better assurance of their fidelity."[18] This line of thought continued to hold the mind of nearly all Christian missionaries who then worked in India. In 1857 Indians fought their 'first war of independence' (the English historians call it 'mutiny'–Br. D. Bh). and when the English had succeeded in suppressing the national uprising, the Christian missionaries threw all previous caution to the wind. They openly started talking of converting the people of India to Christianity as a means of making them their political bondsmen.

How some Christian missionaries thought of this politically motivated programme of converting the Hindus of India to Christianity is well demonstrated by what Claudius Buchanan said. He was of the opinion that "a Christian policy ever looks to the Christian religion for the perpetuity of the empire."[19] In Buchanan's considered opinion "there can never be confidence, freedom, and affection between the people and their sovereign when there exist difference in religion."[20]

In the course of debates in the Parliament on Indian affairs William Wilberforce had argued more than once on similar lines. Once he had said: "the endeavour to communicate to our fellow subjects in India the benefits of Christian light and moral improvement may not only be made without danger, (to English political interests–Br. D Bh.) but what is more, there is no way whatever by which we should be so likely to promote our political interests in India because there is no other way by which we should greatly strengthen the foundations of our government in that country." [21] On another occasion he remarked: "That remedy Sir, is Christianity."[22]

The Friend of India

Joshua Marshman, a colleague of William Carey then edited 'The Friend of India' (precursor of The 'Statesman' now published from Calcutta and New Delhi). He was more vocal in expressing his views. In a memorandum that was submitted to the Governor of Serampore. Marshman had admitted that the Baptists of Serampore were "happy in the idea that in every real convert they were securing to their country a friend attached to the British nation by new and inviolable ties."[23] Marshman expressed similar views when he wrote to Ryland saying: "We have baptized nearly a hundred natives, and if the English government have a hundred firm and cordial friends among the natives it is among these persons."[24]

Though the Christian missionaries have always tried to give an impression in India, particularly to the Hindus, that they were guided by spiritual motives, they did not hesitate to reveal the real purpose behind their masquerades in the letters which they wrote in confidence to their friends or in their private diaries which they maintained to satisfy their Christian ego. For instance Marshman, who was the real spokesman of the Serampore Baptists, owned in a tract which they distributed in Calcutta; "Every converted Hindoo or Mussalman is necessarily the cordial friend of the British, on the ground of his own interest and security, for on the continuation of their empire in India his very existence depends."[25] In advancing this argument a little further, Marshman completely laid bare the motives that lay hidden behind the so-called Christian love for the India people. He boastfully argued: "...by embracing Christianity he has not only dissolved all the ties which held him firmly to his caste...but he has incensed his friends and countrymen against him and has everything to dread from their ascendancy in India."[26] Marshman so gave himself away that the people now know too well what lay concealed behind the Baptists' love for the people and their Christian desire to serve them.

The political game continued to be played persistently by the missionaries from behind the cross and the pulpit telling Indians all the time that their salvation–social, religious, cultural and political-lay in their accepting Christ as their personal saviour. Great efforts were continuously made, both overtly and covertly, to keep away from the minds of the converts she possibility of conversion ending up as economic-political slavery. As time passed the British government began openly to side with the Church to support the political cause which the missionaries had constantly been nursing from behind the facade of religion. Sir Charles Elliot, the Governor of Bengal, in a speech he made at a Himalayan sanatoriun in Darjeeling, accepted the responsibility for Government's connivance at the Christian missionary's endeavors. He recognized the Christian missionary forming "an unrecognized and unofficial branch of the great movement which alone justifies British rule in Southern Asia."[27]

Strengthening the Empire

The events in India of 1857 had fully unnerved John Bull and the Government in London had been, as a result, very much ruffled. Important English minds were busy in trying to find and suggest ways and means of holding India as a colony. And surprisingly most of them seemed to agree at least tacitly that the only way it could be done was by converting Indians to Christianity. When a deputation headed by the Archbishop of Canterbury called upon Lord Palmerston in London in 1859 the Lord made a confession of great significance. He said: "We seem to be all agreed as to the end. It is not only our duty, but it is in our interest to promote the diffusion of Christianity as far as possible throughout the length and breadth of India."[28] Lord Halifax who was the Secretary of State supported Lord Palmerston saying "Every additional Christian is an additional bond of union with this country and an additional source of strength to the empire."[29]

Though it had been openly accepted only in 1859 that diffusion of Christianity was in the interest of the British colonizers, attempts had since long been made from behind the scenes to promote and propagate this political policy The Christian missionary had for quite some time been trying to sell the idea that if India was to be won over to Christ it was necessary to have more "native teacher-catechists". The real purpose behind this move was to set one Indian against the other. This policy has consistently been carried out under several pretexts and camouflages with some very baneful results for the Indian nation.

In 1857 when Indians revolted against their alien rulers attempts were officially made to enlist the support of Indian converts to fight nationalist forces. Though efforts to keep this information secret have often been made, some missionaries in their overzeal have left the details for posterity. One of these missionaries had recorded; "When the mutiny broke out, the members of this extensive and flourishing mission could have rendered most important service to the Government, through whom they had been permitted to do so. The missionaries had a large number of people including converts inquirers, and others under instruction, through whom they had accurately ascertained the state of public feeling in regard to the Government, and also the condition of the native army in their neighbourhood. They deemed it right, therefore, to warn the authorities of the great probability of outbreak. This was done repeatedly and emphatically. They had also expressed their ability to raise a large force for the service of the Government, consisting of fifteen thousand men, partly native Christians and partly heathens, on whom perfect reliance could be placed."[30]

Some Christian writers have intentionally tried to brush all this aside as unhistorical. Nevertheless, the fact that such an offer had been made by Christian missionaries of Chotanagpur was confirmed by Dr. Alexander Duff according to whom: "As to lovers of us or our rule, in any true sense of the term, probably there are none among any class except the comparatively small body of professing native Christians......

The native Christians of Chotanagpur–a hilly district, offered personal services as police-guards, or in any other capacity."[31] The fact that such an offer had been made was later confirmed by the Government of Bengal which appreciating the action taken by Dalton had observed: "that the Lieut. Governor is highly satisfied with the satisfactory progress that has been made in the enlistment of Kols and Santals in the Chota Nagpur Division and with advance state of discipline and management."[32] This was in connection with a letter Capt. E. T. Dalton had written to the Bengal Government stating that "twenty five Christian Koles had been recruited."[33]

The thinking of an average Christian missionary in matters political can be traced back directly to the teachings of the Bible though these teaching would hardly hold any ground in this age of secularism. He believed that "the dominions of India was consigned by Providence (by Lord Jesus Christ-Br. D. Bh.) to the British nation."[34] This view continued to be held till about the beginning of the Second World War (1939) the conclusion of which in 1945, in the manner it did, shattered many a beautiful dream of Christian colonizing nations.

Let 'Asians fight Asians'

The Christian mission policy to make Indians fight among themselves continued to gain ground even after 1945 under the impact of subtle and circumspect propaganda doled out from the pulpits of churches and in the Christian press. In effect it was the localized version of the American policy to make "Asians fight Asians" (Dr. Eddy Asirvatham admitted that this was the outcome of the aggressive American foreign policy put forth in "slogans like 'let Asians fight Asians"[35] A clever twist however was given to it by telling Indian converts that a Christian owed his allegiance only to Christ which the gullible Indian converts in their innocence believed to be hypothetically true ("No nation–to say nothing of its divine beings–has the right to claim the supreme devotion of Christians."[36] Without realizing that the Christian missionaries, most of whom first propounded this theory, were aliens who were never interested in the political well-being of Indians as a nation. One Indian convert, Samuel Azariah (1874-1945) who had been raised to the position of a Bishop in Dornakal (Andhra Pradesh) in his Christian zeal and a display of complete loyally to those to whom he owed his position in the Church, triumphantly made this position unmistakably clear. In the Report of Church and State which Bishop Azariah had drawn up (1937) in association with some non-Indian Church leaders in Oxford he declared: "Speaking for ourselves, our loyalty to our master (Christ–Br. D. Bh.) comes first, our loyalty to our motherland second. We are first Christians, then Indians. We cannot, yea, we dare not, acquiesce in any act of Government that interferes with our inmost sacred convictions'"[37]

This is what the Christian Church in India, controlled, directed and financed from outside has constantly been trying to tell the Indian converts: They owed their loyally to Christ and not to India–their motherland, and the only purpose has been to subvert his loyalty to the nation. This pernicious idea planted in a very subtle manner in the innocent minds of village folk appears to have caused great mischief. Gandhi was fully conscious of the harm this type of (religious) preaching had been doing. He had once remarked that it was not unusual "to find Christianity synonymous with denationalization and Europeanization."[38]

The English have great qualities as professional diplomats. After the close of the First World War (1918) they clearly read the writing on the wall. They knew only too well that they would no longer be able to hold India as a part of their empire. Therefore they started wooing the United States of America to take over in India the theo-political reigns when time came for them to withdraw. "We have conciliated the United States", Hon. George Peel admitted, "hoping to arouse the interest of the New World in the common good of Christendom, coincident ultimately with its own. We have laboured also abundantly to bring home to our distant dominions of the Newest World that, even if affection or regard for our welfare do not prompt them to dip their feet in the cortex of militarism, it is yet vital for them to know that, on our slaughter, seige will be laid to them, and that our collapse will postulate their catastrophe."[39] The subsequent events amply proved that the astute Englishman had beer, able to convince the American of the urgent need of joining hands with him in the theo-political game at which he had been for more than 200 years.

The American who had long been itching to get into the worn-out English political shoes readily agreed to play the role of the big brother in erstwhile colonies which had gained their political freedom after 1945- the year in which the Second World War had ended. It was in 1813 that the U.S.A. had sent its first Christian missionary to India. Since then the American missionaries have stayed and worked in different parts of India in different fields under different pretexts. In either case, the main purpose behind their work in India has mostly been of the nature of a recce. They have collected information; collaborated with English missionaries whom they helped financially and prepared the ground to ensure a smooth take-over when the English left.

Only very few Indians would believe unless they belonged to a small knowledgeable group that "the foreign politics of the United States of America are foreign missions."[40] That is not all. "The Americas, headed by the U.S.A. give the largest sum of money"[41] to Christian missions working abroad and especially in those countries which till about twenty to thirty years ago were colonies of Christian imperial powers.

When India again became a free land (1947) it dawned on other Christian colonial powers that they could no longer hold their colonies in political bondage. While India justifiably earned the gratitude of countries which later became free, the fact that India had been directly or indirectly responsible for the downfall of Christian colonialism throughout the world rankled in the hearts of all those nations who as a result of this changeover had suffered grievous economo-political losses.

The year 1955 gave a new but an unexpected twist to international politics. Twenty nine countries gathered at a conference in Bandung declared themselves in favour of political neutrality which in course of time came to be crystalized into the creed of political non-alignment as now practised and advocated by India.. As India had already declined (1954) to join SEATO (South East Asia Treaty Organization) which had been sponsored by the U. S. A. to fight Chinese Communism in this region, this new move of leading countries of South East Asia charting out for themselves an independent course of political action nearly angered the American policy makers. They believed that no one could and had the moral right to remain neutral in the fight against communism. This thinking gradually culminated in the formulation of America's foreign relations policy by John Foster Dulles who openly declared that neutralism was "dangerous and immoral."[4]"

As no other country than India had advocated and perhaps practised with greater sincerity the tenets of non-alignment (known now as *Panchshil)* India became a special target of attack by those who wanted India to join SEATO. As India steadfastly refused to relent, the anti-communist powers led by the U.S.A. made up their mind to teach India a lesson. They decided to destabilize India politically. To achieve this political end they enlisted the support and co-operation of the Christian Church who for its own reasons readily agreed to collaborate in this theo-political mission.

While England controlled the enormous Indian revenues, Christian mission agencies working in India used regularly to receive generous monetary help under different pretences. When the Englishman lost this source of easy income he gradually became choosy in giving practical expression to his Christian philanthropic instincts. World-wide inflation and bad economic conditions coupled with mounting unemployment at home added more worries to the Englishman's already existing problems. In consequence, Christian missions working in India "lost a great part of the financial assistance they used to get in the past."[43] The Englishman had no alternative but to seek help of the U.S.A. who finding an opportunity to make use of the large army of Christian clergy spread throughout India, readily agreed to foot the bill.

The task of destabilizing a country of India's magnitude was not easy. It required a large contingent of workers to operate at different levels and a recurring expenditure of large sums of money to be regularly spent on their food, clothing and travel. With the withdrawal of the British from India, the Christian Church had already started finding it very hard to meet its financial obligations to keep the large army of regular and secular clergy from disintegrating. The U.S.A. was in a position to make large funds available but it did not have at its beck and call the services of a large number of men who necessarily had to be engaged in works of subversion throughout India if India had to be successfully destabilized politically. This peculiar situation brought the Christian Church and the U.S.A. together in a bid to achieve what each of them wanted for its own reasons. The Church which wanted more converts in India and the U.S.A. wanted either to force the Indian Government to its knees or in the alternative to destabilize India politically and thus make her pay for her refusal to go over to the American side. So in the bargain thus struck, the Church agreed to place at the disposal of the U.S.A. her large army of workers in India and in return the American government reciprocated by offering to provide necessary funds and wherewithal to keep this religious army intact, working as a cohesive well-knit force.

Communism is to the American as is the proverbial red rag o the Spanish bull in the ring. An average American might at time start getting jitters at the very mention of its name. He wants therefore communism to be fought to the finish but surprisingly he does not want to fight it himself. He usually looks around in the hope of being able to hire some mercenaries to do the lighting for him with the American weapons which he, in his generosity, is willingly ready either to lend free or sell at very liberally extended credit terms. And since the American feels communism to be the arch enemy of the American way of life, the U.S.A. has made it an article of faith and creed to annihilate communism from the surface of this earth. In the process, therefore, to achieve this goal it is but only natural that anyone who even remotely holds the promise to bring about the end of communism would be treated by U.S.A as its bosom friend and an ally. The position of the Christian Church vis-a-vis the U.S.A. is almost identically similar.

Christian imperialism represented in the past by Christian colonial powers and now in the main by the U.S.A. and the Christian Church was able to discover more than one ground of common interest. From the very beginning the Church has been wanting to convert the Hindus of India to Christianity in order that the Christian colonial hold over India could be perpetuated. If India had to be destabilized politically and rendered innocuous, the U.S.A. needed more and more of those Indians who would owe their loyalty first to Christ and only second to their Motherland. Such groups were a necessary ingredient to form a lobby for or against any move–political, economic or intellectual–to be launched by the political block led by the U.S.A. Both these ends seemed possible of achievement only if the members of the majority religious community, the Hindus and the Sikhs, continued to be converted to Christianity. As both agreed on the ends to be achieved, there inevitably grew a regular axis between the Christian Church and the U.S.A.

In the process of trying to convert the Hindus and the Sikhs of India to Christianity, the Church and the U S.A. both discovered to their great dismay that the nationalism of the Hindu and of the Sikh was a great stumbling block in the way of his accepting Christ as his personal saviour. Both tried, therefore, to destroy, by employing subtle and circumspect measures, their nationalism. The U.S.A. as the leading political power in the post–1945 era and opposed vehemently to communism had discovered that "though colonialism was on the way out, whenever we appear to be on its side, we strengthen communism by throwing it and nationalism into alliance."[44] The American policy makers therefore decided that if communism had to be defeated in South East Asia it was necessary first to destroy the nationalism of the people in this region. In this American endeavour the Christian Church again came handy.

The Christian Church had long ago discovered that nationalism of the Hindu and of the Sikh was an article of faith with him. He worshipped his motherland above anything else. The Church knew too well that as long as the Hindu and the Sikh continued to abhor Christianity because he believed it to be an alien faith, he would not be willing to switch over his allegiance to Christ. The Hindu and the Sikh steadfastly refused to accept the Christian postulate that an Indian should owe his loyalty to Christ, or anyone else for that matter, first and in consequence he developed a sort of aversion for Christ and Christianity.

The Christian Church believed that "the surrender of the Christian Church to the rising powers of nationalism is the major betrayal of Christ.[45]"

The Church abundantly recognized this state of affairs and wished somehow to bring about a change in the situation. The schools run and managed by Christian mission agencies where a large number of Hindu and Sikh boys and girls received their education (it is only a misnomer to call it education. At best it is subtle indoctrination or guided habituation–Br. D. Bh.) began to be used to brainwash the students in their more impressionable years. They were told again and again by experienced proselytizers that nationalism was a sort of disease which created so many problems with which the world was beset today. They were advised that if the world had to become one great family, people, especially in India and Japan, must shed their narrow nationalism!

The fight against nationalism was carried to all sections of Indian society. Articles appeared in the press and sermons used to be regularly doled out from the pulpits to Sunday congregations telling them that nationalism was a minor vice and a sin. This theo-political tirade against nationalism received official recognition of the Christian Church when at Lambeth Conference held in the year 1930, where 307 Archbishops and Bishops participated, it was officially resolved: "the Christian Church can make no terms with the idea expressed in the phrase, "My country right or wrong." Great is the debt of service that a man owes to his Fatherland, the claim of Christ remains supreme",[46] Religion holds a people together. If a people have to be enfeebled the easiest way to do it is to destroy the common bonds of religion which hold them together.

Since neither the Christian Church nor the capitalist political powers wanted India to grow strong, both decided in their own way and to serve their own purpose to destroy the religion of the majority community and its nationalism.

The Jesuits, the members of the Society of Jesus, have always formed a very important wing of the ecclesiastical and secular missionary establishment of the Church in India. It was thus natural that when the U.S.A. decided to make use of Christian missionaries–regular as veil as secular for the purpose of destabilizing India politically, the U.S.A. would depend more heavily on the Jesuits in India than on members of any other Christian religious orders. This, however, was not the only reason. The vows of absolute obedience and secrecy under which the Jesuits lived and operated made them an ideal choice for the work of theo-political subversion that was intended to be carried out.

"Unfortunately for the world, the Jesuits have never been able to keep clear of politics."[47] and we also know that when Aurangzeb sat on the throne in Delhi the Jesuits ran their parallel intelligence service.[48] Since "their work had to be propaganda; teaching and insinuation by every possible means of the authority and policy of the Church'[49] the Jesuits found it as a God-sent opportunity to free themselves from the onerous financial burdens which had been nearly crippling the organization in those times of high inflation and also to engage themselves in the type of work which was dear to their heart. They readily agreed to join hands with the U.S.A. in the attempt to destabilize India politically as a step towards giving a blow to Communism and to the Hindu and his nationalism in this part of the world.

The U.S.A., which stood in need of men who would devotedly agree to carry out the new American foreign policy throughout South East Asia in general and in India in particular, willingly enlisted the cooperation of Christian ecclesiastics and the clergy belonging to different religious orders predominant among whom happened to be Jesuits. The fact that the CIA had been making use of Christian clergy for the purpose had been admitted by a high official of American Intelligence. The Rev. James Vizzard, a Jesuit, admitted that the CIA had spent millions in Chile via the Jesuits.[50]

That a Christian owes his allegiance first to Christ and only second to his or her motherland is a piece of missionary sophism for the consumption of the gullible converts in erstwhile colonies. When it comes to himself he conveniently forgets the advice which he so freely gives to the Indian converts. An outstanding example of this dual working of the missionary mind was provided during the First World War when all German and Austrian Jesuits in India had been interned because their loyalty had been highly suspect and it was widely feared that they will work for the enemy. This fact though not very widely known was the subject matter of a book[51] which an English Jesuit wrote to plead the case of his fellow Jesuits.

In all fairness, however, the Jesuits cannot be singled out. Jehovah's Witnesses, another militant sect of Christianity, earned for itself signal notoriety during the Second World War in the British Empire. In the words of an eminent missionary whose opinions cannot be ignored: "This modern heresy has of late achieved unenviable notoriety in the British Empire through being banned on account of its fifth column activities. It masquerades under many aliases: Millenial Dawn, International Bible Students Association; Metropolitan Pulpit, Watchtower Bible and Tract Society, Brooklyn Tabernacle Pulpit, and of late years, Jehovah's Witnesses."[52] Jawaharlal Nehru was of the opinion that "the British often had a powerful fifth column both in the administration and the armies of the Indian rulers,"[53] and more often the Christian clergy formed an integral part of this establishment.

In 1964 an event of great importance, the 38th Eucharistic Congress, was held in Bombay to give a big boost to Christian proselytization in India. In anticipation Church emissaries went to different Christian countries to collect funds needed for 'operation Christianization' of India. One of them, Father Tempra, an Italian residing in Bombay and a member of the Society of St. Paul, went to the U.S.A. for enlisting American support and collect much badly needed dollars for the conversion programme to be especially launched after December 1964. In an interview which Father Tempra gave to Catholic Home Messenger (May, 1963) he advised the Americans: "If the people of India do not find God now, the free world will have lost a formidable ally, and 400 million more souls may foil under the domination of Communism."[54]

Tempra had in fact been trying to kill two birds with one stone. He was asking the American to loosen his purse strings and give him the money he wanted to convert the Hindus to Christianity and also telling them that when these Hindus became Christians they would not go over to Communism which was the enemy of the Americans. How far he succeeded in his mission is difficult to say but he abundantly and fully demonstrated the fact that the Christian Church and the Americans were closely working together for achieving one political goal from behind the smoke screen of religion.

That the Christian Church in India has been interfering in internal politics of the country and actively siding with imperialism in its fight against Communism was more than borne out by the Pastoral letter which the 16 Bishops and Archbishops of Kerala issued in 1961 asking their followers not to vote for communists ("It is our sacred duty to oppose communist.. "[55]) While commenting on this Pastoral letter the Indian Prime Minister, Mr. Nehru had remarked that "The recent pastoral letter on elections was dangerously near interference in politics.[56]

In the past, more than once, great, organized and subtle efforts had been made as they are no doubt being made today to present the Christian conversion programme as a religious endeavor. But in spite of very clever subterfuges having been employed to camouflage its political nature the Indians, especially a more wide awake section among the Hindus, has refused to be taken in by this propaganda. They know it too well that behind all that great facade of religious efforts was hidden the instinct and the ambition of the imperialist and the colonizer to make other people his political slaves.

That Christianity views Hinduism, as, as much a hurdle in the field of religion as imperialism regards Hindu nationalism the greatest stumbling block in the path of colonialism, was made more than clear at a conference of Christian leaders that was held within less than a decade of India becoming a politically free nation. The Christian leaders assembled there were unanimous in their verdict: "Our consideration of the prevailing political ideologies in India leads us to the outright condemnation and rejection of both Hindu Nationalism and Communism since they are opposed to the basic tenets of the Christian religion,"[57] forgetting, however, in their Christian overzeal that India never was a Christian preserve.

There is no doubting the fact that the Christian Church regards Hinduism as a religion which is not true, and since the Church claims Christianity to be the sole reservoir and fountainhead of all truth it foresees nothing but a constant conflict between Hinduism and Christianity. But in their heart of hearts, they are genuinely afraid of Hinduism's revival: "He would be a rash man indeed who dares to predict what lies in the future for a world religion such as Hinduism. Its rennaisant influence is already spreading far and wide over the non-Hindu world."[58] The answer to this was provided by another Christian leader who predicted: "If we kill their (of the Hindustan Br. D. Bh.) faith, they may try to kill our faith too."[59]

This Christian who had the capacity to see beyond his nose had made yet one more startling prophesies: "She (Hindu India–Br. D. Bh) is dead or sleeping. But the sleeper will wake. The corpse of the Indian body politic (Hindu nationalism–Br. D. Bh.) will spring to its feet."[60] Those who are blessed with eyes to be able to see under the surface already know that the body politics of Hinduism has already begun to shake itself out of stupor into which it had been lulled by its enemies masquerading as its friends. More than one political attempt was made in the past to destroy Hinduism but every time these efforts failed. Now that the Hindu has come to know and fully understand the subtleties of Christian politics, any fresh attempt is bound to fail and that too with a bang.

References

1. *The Papal Encyclicals* ed. Anne Fremantle, p. 77.

2. *Ibid.* p. 79.

3. *Ibid.* p. 78.
4. *Ibid.* p. 79.
5. *The Conversion of India* by George Smith, p. 54.
6. *The Life and Letters of Francis Xavier* by Henry James Coleridge, Vol II, pp. 6-15, letter dated Cochin Jan. 20, 1548.
7. *The Conversion of India* p. 58.
8. *Letters of Alfonso de Albuquerque*, Vol. I, p. 63, Pub. Lisbon Royal Academy of Sciences, 1884.
9. *The Centenary Volume of the Church Missionary Society*, p. 2.
10. *Ibid.*
11. *The Life of Charles Grant* by H. Morris, p. 112-3.
12. Observations by Charles Grant. *History of English Education in India* by Syed Mahmood, p. 11.
13. *The East India Company* by C.H. Peilips, p. 165.
14. Observations by Charles Grant. *History of English Education in India* by Syed Mahmood, p. 12-3.
15. Quoted in *the Christian Missions in Bengal 1793-1833* by Kanti Prasanna Sen Gupta, p. 57.
16. Observations Parliamentary Papers. Vol. X, p. 100.
17. *Ibid.* p. 111, *The Christian Missions in Bengal* , p. 58.
18. Bodi. MSS. *Correspondence on Missions in India. Parry and Grant to Dundas,* June 8, 1807. *The Christian Mission in Bengal*, p. 58.
19. *Memoirs of the Expediency of our Ecclesiastical Establishment for British India* by C. Buchanan, p. 29.
20. Ibid.
21. *Parliamentary Debates*, Vol. XXVI, June 21, 1813.
22. *Parliamentary Debates*, Vol. XXVI, June 22, 1813.
23. *Parliamentary Papers*, Vol. X, p. 58.
24. Quoted in *The Christian Missions in Bengal*, p. 60.
25. *Advantage of Christianity in promoting the Establishment of British Government in India* by J. Marshman quoted in *The Christian Missions in Bengal*, p. 60.
26. Ibid.
27. *The Conversion of India*, p. 159.
28. Ibid. p. 233.
29. *Missionary Principles and Practice* by R.E. Speer, p. 29. *Christianity and Government of India* by Arthur Mayhew, p. 194.
30. *Hundred Years of Christian Missions in Chotanagpur since 1845* by Dr. S. Mahto,

p. 54.

31. Ibid. p. 55.
32. Ibid. p. 56.
33. Ibid. p. 56.
34. *Periodical Accounts of Baptist Missionary Society*, Vol. VI, p. 7.
35. *Christianity in the Indian Crucible* by Eddy Asirvatham, p.
36. *The Philosophy of the Christian World Mission* by Edmund Davison Soper, p. 251.
37. *Azariah of Dornakal* by Carol Graham, p. 95.
38. *Young India,* August 11, 1927. *Christian Missions–Their Place in India* by M.K. Gandhi, p. 101.
39. *Future of England* by Hon. George Peel, p. 169.
40. *The Conversion of India*, p. 145.
41. *The Catholic Church Against the Twentieth Century* by Avro Manhattan, p. 51.
42. *My War with the CIA*. Memoirs of Prince Norodom Sihanouk, p. 252.
43. *Catholic Home Messenger*, May, 1963.
44. *The United States and India and Pakistan* by W. Norman Brown, p. 278.
45. *The Betrayal of Christ by the Churches* by J. Middleton Murray, p. 92. This book is full of invectives against nationalism.
46. *Report of the Lambeth Conferene 1930*, p. 99.
47. *Crux Ansata* by H.G. Wells, p. 73.
48. *The Men who Ruled India* by Philip Woodruff, Vol. I., p. 28.
49. *Crux Ansata* by H.G. Wells, p. 72.
50. *Hindustan Times*, New Delhi, July 25, 1975.
51. *The German Jesuit Fathers of Bombay* by Ernest Hull, editor of the *Examiner* Bombay. See *Azariah of Dornakal* (p. 116) for details of internment of missionaries during the Second World War for similar reasons.
52. *Heresies–Ancient and Modern* by J. Oswald Sanders, p. 73.
53. *The Discovery of India* by Jawaharlal Nehru, p. 229.
54. *India for Christ* by Father Tempra.
55. *Times of India* New Delhi, February 5, 1962.
56. *Times of India*. New Delhi. February 8, 1962.
57. *Christianity and the Asian Revolution* by Raja M. Manikam, p. 96.
58. Ibid, p. 137.
59. *The Future of England* by Hon. George Peel, p. 198.

State-wise number of foreign missionaries registered up to 1.1.1973

S.No.	Name of the State	Numbers of Foreign Missionaries
1.	Andhra Pradesh	371
2.	Assam	72
3.	Bihar	379
4.	Gujarat	157
5.	Haryana	10
6.	Himachal Pradesh	33
7.	Jammu & Kashmir	40
8.	Kerala	149
9.	Madhya Pradesh	213
10.	Maharashtra	666
11.	Mysore (Karnataka)	463
12.	Meghalaya	81
13.	Nagaland	3
14.	Orissa	102
15.	Punjab	85
16.	Rajasthan	15
17.	Tamil Nadu	816
18.	Uttar Pradesh	403
19.	West Bengal	415
20.	Manipur	6
21.	Delhi	145
22.	Goa-Daman-Diu	2
23.	Pondicherry	20

Source: Bharat Kalyan Manch

c.f. The Freedom of Religion Bill–Why?
Committee for the Protection of Freedom of Religion, New Delhi

5

British Policy towards Religion in India

DR. S. SARASWATI

Deputy Director, Indian Council of Social Science Research, New Delhi

The success of the English in establishing their hegemony over India was partly due to their calculated religious policy. Unlike the Portuguese who adopted an aggressive pro-Christian posture, the English played a clever game of subordinating their religion to politics. While dealing with the diverse religious groups, the exigencies of politics determined the attitude of the British.

Empire versus Religion

The religious policy of the English started in a clause in the Charter of the East India Company which expressly prohibited religious missions being sent to India, thus severing connection between commercial ambitions and evangelist enterprise. The Company broadly adopted a policy of non-interference in religious matters which was a setback to missionary enterprise. The company's government, as a political tactics, not only permitted native religions to flourish but positively assumed the role of the native rulers in extending patronage to indigenous religious institutions and practices. Thus, the government took over the management and administration of religious endowments and institutions; collected a Pilgrim Tax in return for protection of pilgrims to sacred shrines; incurred expenditure for celebrating temple festivals; and government officials were often seen propitiating Hindu gods and participating in local religious festivals. At the same time, the Company's government refused official support for Christian missionary activities, strongly advocated by Charles Grant and William Wilberforce.

When the Charter Act came for renewal in 1793, Grant came out openly with a proposal to supersede existing religions in India by Christianity as a means of moral and cultural improvement of Indians. He also pleaded for introduction of English education. The House of Commons passed the motion moved by Wilberforce urging to adopt measures for advancement of the inhabitants of British dominion in India in useful knowledge, and religious and moral improvement.

A clause was added empowering the Company to send schoolmasters and other approved persons for the purpose. When the new clauses were redrafted in the form of a Bill stating the ultimate object of sending missionaries and schoolmasters to India for the conversion of Indians to Christianity, the Court of Directors protested that any attempt to convert the natives of India would "result in political unrest". To the proprietors, the idea of converting Indians to Christianity sounded "absurd md impossible". Both Houses of Parliament rejected the Bill.

The East India Company struck to its policy of refusing admission to missionaries in India and "toleration of all religious systems and protection of followers of each in the undisturbed enjoyment of their respective opinions and usages". The Vellore Mutiny of 1806 among the Company's sepoys reinforced the Company's stand. Explaining its religious policy, the government stated its obligations "to protect the inhabitants in the free and undisturbed profession of their religious opinions, and to take care that they are neither harassed nor irritated by any premature or over-zealous attempts to convert them to Christianity". The government based its views on political considerations and regarded missionary propaganda as politically inexpedient.

Missionary Allowed to Enter India

In 1813, the pro-missionary forces succeeded in passing a Bill providing in the Charter Act that "such measures ought to be adopted as may tend to the introduction among them (Indians) of useful knowledge, and of religious and moral improvement, and in furtherance of the above object, sufficient facilities ought to be afforded by law to persons desirous of going to and remaining in India". This clause was intended to cover the missionaries and the Act also provided for the establishment of a Bishopric at Calcutta.

The Charter Act of 1833 created three more Bishoprics in India, at Calcutta, Bombay and Madras and removed the prescription of licence to enter India. The Charter did not refer to the government's role in local religious activities particularly protection of pilgrims and maintenance of order during festivals. A prolonged debate was carried on over these matters leading to an order by the Court of Directors in 1837 that "no customary salutes or marks of respect to native festivals be discontinued at any of the Presidencies; that no protection hitherto given be withdrawn, and that no change whatsoever be made in any matter relating to the native religion, except under the authority of the Supreme Government". Government proceeded with caution in the matter of dissociating themselves from religious matters. The Court of Directors entirely approving the government's policy of sympathy to tradition and practice recalled that the declared intentions of both Parliament and the Directors was to ensure complete freedom of worship to Indians and to protect them from all official interference in matters of religion.

The period between 1833 and 1853 was marked by continuous struggle between the Company's government in India and the pro-Christian religious pressure groups in England to sever the government's connection with Indian religious practices. The clash was again between an authority interested in maintaining its hold over and providing an orderly government in an alien land and the pressure groups interested in Christianizing the non- Christian at any cost. The struggle resulted in gradual withdrawal of the government from religious activities like abolition of Pilgrim Tax, non-participation in Indian religious festivals, and transfer of management of religious endowments to local authorities. A perusal of the records pertaining to this controversy shows awareness among the English administrators in India about the futility of any attempt to convert the Indian people professing an ancient religion.

Partisan Neutrality

The War of Independence of 1857, which was partly a religious revolt of the Indians against the subtle but definite intrusion of Christianity into India with official support, was evidence of the tenacity of the Indian religions to resist and survive. It ended in the Queen's Proclamation which declared, ".......we disclaim alike the right and desire to impose our conviction on any of our subjects. We declare it to be our royal will and pleasure that none be in any ways favoured, or molested or disquieted by reason of their faith or observance but that all shall alike enjoy the equal and impartial protection of the law, and we strictly charge and enjoin all those who may be in authority under us that they abstain from all interference with religious belief or worship of any of our subjects on pain of our highest displeasure."

The declaration was followed speedily with steps to dissociate government from religion. The Act of 1863 relieved officers of government from all duties relating to the appointment to religious offices, the superintending of lands assigned for pious uses, the appropriation of religious incomes, the preservations of sacred buildings, or the management in any form of establishments belonging to the Hindu or the Muhammadan religion. In 1864, by another law the government proclaimed that it would no longer appoint the semi-ecclesiastical Muhammadan Kazis.

Thus ended the system of state patronage in the sphere of religion. What started was a politics of neutrality, applied by an alien ruler in a plural society and in the context of a representative government based on representation of classes, races, interests and territories. Neutrality produced differential impact on various groups and directly intruded into indigenous systems and institutions.

Ecclesiastical Department

British Government, under the cover of religious neutrality was withdrawing every kind of state support and protection to indigenous religious practices and establishments, but at the same time was maintaining an Ecclesiastical Department whose sole purpose was to extend financial and other kind of support to the Christian religious establishments. 'The Government of India on the 3rd Nov, 1876, decided to contribute to the establishment of any church at a civil or railway station where at least 25 British-born European Christian subjects lived. The rate of contribution was to be in proportion to the number of beneficiaries. Indians led by the eminent scholar Dr. Rajendra Lal raised a voice of protest against this partisan policy. People in England also got interested in the problem of the ecclesiastical establishment of the Government of India and William Waxter moved in the House of Commons on the 5th July, 1877 to know the expenditure of Ecclesiastical Department of the Government of India. The Government of India was, in a letter dared the 26th July, 1877 by the Secretary of State to furnish him with the required information. The Government of India after making all the necessary enquiries from the local Governments informed the Secretary of State in a letter, dated the 6th November 1879 that the sanctioned budgets for the department were estimated as follows:

Year	Rs.
1876-77	19,73,000
1877-78	19,66,000
1878-79	19,44,000

In spite of widespread public demand, the Ecclesiastical Department of the Government was not abolished and it continued to give financial aid to the Christian church (Chowdhary, p. 360)*

Christian chaplains accompanied the army to administer the spiritual needs of the Christian in the army, but no such faculty was extended to the persons in the army belonging to other faiths, (p. 360)

Religious Conversions

The official policy of non-involvement in missionary activities, strict neutrality in religious affairs, and imparting of secular education was no boon to the religion of the majority in India. On the contrary, the proportion of Hindus declined between 1881 and 1931 in the official statistics as shown below.

No. of Hindus per 10,000 Population

Province/State	Year 1881	Year 1931	Decline in numbers Loss per 10,000
India	7,432	6,824	608
Provinces	7,197	6,548	649
Ajmer-Merwara	8,162	7,755	407
Bihar and Orissa	4,855	4,304	551
Coorg	9,113	8,939	174
North-West Frontier Provinces	708	590	108
States/Agencies			
Assam	5,921	4,362	1,559
Central Provinces	8,621	7,202	1,419
Cochin	7,152	6,477	675
Hyderabad	9,033	8,435	598
Madras State/Agency	7,467	6,400	1,067
Mysore	9,308	9,174	134
Rajputana	8,750	8,533	217
Travancore	7,312	6,152	160

This significant reduction in the proportion of Hindus was partly due to a rapid rise in Christian population recorded in the census.

* V.C.P. Chowdhary: *Imperial Policy of British in India (1876-1880)* Calcutta, 1968.

Percentage Increase in Christian Population

	1881-1931
India	+ 238.1
Provinces	+ 247.9
Ajmer-Merwara	+ 212.2
Assam	+ 3,412.0
Bengal	+ 153.2
Bihar and Orissa	+ 644.9
Bombay	+ 129.4
Central Provinces and Berar	+ 676.4
Coorg	+ 8.7
Delhi & Punjab	+ 1,455.4
Madras	+ 152.2
North-West Frontier Provinces	+ 192.3
United Provinces	+336.1
States/Agencies	
Baroda	+ 341.9
Central India (Gwalior)	+ 65.2
Cochin	+ 145.6
Hyderabad	+ 1,012.0
Mysore	+ 199.3
Rajputana	+346.3
Travancore	+221.8

This trend needs investigation on the extent of conversions and the type of overt and covert support available from the British Government for religious conversions.

The Report of the Christian Missionary Activities Enquiry Committee in Madhya Pradesh (1956) stated:

"Growth of Protestant church during the period of British Raj in India was due mainly to the great patronage and support the church was getting from the Government of India. Instances of land grants and financial aid to build churches, missionary centers, hospitals, educational institutions etc., are numerous. All cathedrals entrusted to the Bishoprics under the ecclesiastical establishments were built from slate funds. Not only in cities and towns and in military stations in British India, but in almost every state, we can find big churches and missionary buildings erected almost entirely with government aid. To protect the Christian converts and their inheritance in British India, Act XXI of 1850 was passed, as the then prevailing customary law stood as an impediment to conversion of Hindus to other religions".

In the later half of the nineteenth century many parts of India faced severe and prolonged famines due to exploitative British policy and these famines provided a rich harvest of conversions to Christian missionaries. They indulged in mass conversions of Indians into Christianity for the help which they used to give to natives during famine. The *Nusrat-ul-Akhbar*, dated the 21st May, 1878 quoted the Catholic Examiner to support the fact that one hundred thousand natives were converted to Christianity during the late famine between October 1877 and March 1878. The *Khair Khawah Alam,* dated the 3rd January, 1878 complained that children were the special victims of conversion to Christianity, by missionaries for the help that they gave them during the famine and nearly fourteen thousand children were converted to Christianity in Madras during the last famine. (Chowdhary, p. 354).

During the twenty years between 1882 and 1901, Christian population had almost doubled. Several means like education, economic, industrial and philanthropic programmes were undertaken by the missionaries to attract Hindus to Christianity. Conversions were effected in many places *en masse* of entire villages, castes or tribes. Such conversions were motivated by material and not spiritual motives. The census of 1911, quoting from a Roman Catholic Missionary, reports, "As a general rule religious motives are out of the question. They want protection against zamindari and police extortions and assistance in the litigations and came over in whole villages or in groups of villages." Mass conversions were reported, particularly during the great famine of 1878-79 and the converts were actually called "rice Christians" in southern India.

Census Enumeration of Hindus

In pursuance of the policy of neutrality, a policy of recording all denomination of Hindus, castes, sub-castes and sub-sects was followed which resulted in downgrading the religion of the majority–the Hindus–and in many instances making a confusion of religious sects, occupational castes and social stratifications.

The 1931 census of India discloses the controversy in its report: "There was an energetic propaganda by Hindu *Mahasabha* which practically amounted to an advocacy of returning as Hindu, every person whose religion could not be found to have been originated outside India, that is, practically everyone but Muslims, Christians, Parsis and Jews, regardless of whether the followers of other Indian religions wished to be returned as Hindu or not, and equally regardless of the facts of the case. They also proposed to include as Hindus all persons of doubtful position halfway between Hinduism and Islam, without insisting on the *Shuddi* ceremony. In the fear apparently that the depressed classes would not be returned as Hindus, attempts were made to minimise their numbers. Non-Hindu hill tribes such as the Khasi of Assam were claimed as Hindus, though one Assam paper naively distinguished between *kutcha* and *pucca* Hindus while a proposal was actually mooted by certain members of the central legislature that wherever the majority of the members of a hill tribe has been Hinduised, the complete tribe should be shown as Hindu."

The report is critical of what it called the "propaganda of the Hindu missions" and role of the "Hindu enumerators" in recording the religion of the people.

It was in 1931, that the strength of the various religious groups became significant in view of the impending constitutional reform and in view of the depressed class movement for recognition as a political entity. The term 'Hindu' said to be the name of a complex congeries of races, castes and tribes, always presented a problem to the census authorities. In 1911 the problem was tackled by instructing the Provincial Superintendents to enumerate the castes and tribes returned or classed as Hindus who did not conform to certain standards, or were subject to certain disabilities, and to prepare a list of all but the minor castes which:

1. deny the supremacy of the *Brahman;*
2. do not receive the *mantra* from a *Brahman* or other recognised Hindu *Guru;*
3. deny the authority of the *Vedas;*
4. do not worship the Great Hindu Gods;
5. are not served by good *Brahmans* as family priests;
6. have no *Brahman* priests at all;
7. are denied access to the interior of ordinary Hindu temples;
8. cause pollution (a) by touch; (b) within a certain distance;
9. bury their dead; and
10. eat beef and do not revere the cow.

While the classes deemed untouchable in the old order were separated as 'depressed classes' in the census, tribals were always shown as a category separate from the Hindus. Till 1921, aboriginal tribes were classified and tabulated under the heading "Animist" in the census tables and animism was described as "the attitude of those who worship or propitiate the forces and objects of nature and the spirits which they conceive to reside in natural phenomena".

This census policy of categorising tribals from Hindus as a separate religious group was continued in 1931. Special injunctions were given that all primitive tribes were to be tabulated whatever their numbers and slot irrespective of the percentage province-wise for the index of individual tabulation of castes. This policy sharply contradicted the Hindu view of their religion.

The following table revealing the fluctuations in the strength of some important religious groups in the decennial census is significant.

Percentage Variation in Population

Religion	1921-1931	1911-1921	1901-1911	1891-1901	1881-1891	1881-1931
Hindu	+ 10.4	–0.4	+ 5.0	–0.3	+ 10.1	+26.8
Muslim	+ 13.0	+5.1	+6.7	+8.9	+ 14.3	+55.0
Christian	+32.5	+22.6	+32.6	+28.0	+22.6	+238.1
Minor Religions & Religions not stated	+3072.6	–51.5	–71.4	+203.7	–28.7	+ 179.3
Buddhist	+ 10.5	7.9	+ 13.1	+32.9	+ 108.6	+274.1
Sikh	+33.9	+7.4	+ 37.3	+ 15.1	+2.9	+ 133.9
Tribal	-15.3	-5.1	+ 19.9	-7.5	+31.2	+28.8

The official policy of treating the tribals as a distinct group was followed not only for enumeration in the census but for certain socio-political programmes. The Government of India Act 1870 of 1870 conferred upon the Governor-General in Council the power to approve and sanction laws and regulations made by the local Government for the administration of certain special areas to which previously the Secretary of State in Council had applied the Act. In 1874, the Indian Legislature passed the Scheduled Districts Act XIV of 1874 whereby the Local Government was empowered to declare in respect of the tracts specified in the Act the enactments that were not in force therein. Under the Government of India Act 1919 of 1919, the Governor-General in Council was empowered to declare the territories occupied by the aborigines to be a backward tract. That Simon Commission grouped the backward tracts into two large categories–one as wholly excluded areas and the other as partially excluded areas. The Government of India Act 1935, 1935, made a reference to the "Backward Tribes" and the Thirteenth Schedule to the Government of India (Provincial and Legislative Assemblies) Order 1936, 1936, specified certain tribes as backward in the then provinces of Assam, Bihar, Orissa, Central Provinces and Berar, Madras and Bombay. And has, the list of primitive tribes made in the census of 1931 became useful.

A group of the tribes was designated as "criminal tribes" by the Criminal Tribes Act of 1924 and treated as a group prone to criminal tendencies. This Act was abolished by the independent government and the tribes were re-designated as Denotified Tribes and later as Denotified Communities.

The statutory exclusion of the hill and aboriginal tribes had many political implications. Apart from creating an impression of a homogeneous religious group consisting of these tribes with interests distinct from that of the Hindus, such segregation encouraged foreign intrusion into the life and religion of these people. Tribal areas became fertile ground for Christian missionary enterprise. The Education Commission of 1882 recommended literal grants-in-aid to those who were willing to set up and maintain schools in these areas and in doing so, the Commission was well aware of the support it was extending to Christian mission. It said, "We are so convinced it is from missionary agency that most may be expected in education the aboriginal races, that we have emphatically affirmed as the principle on which aid should be given to bodies willing to undertake the work, that of entire abstention from interference with any religious instruction which such bodies may choose to give". This posture encouraged missionary activities. Many tribes like the Kols of Chotanagpur, Paharies of Darjeeling, Khasis in Assam, Santhals of Bengal, Nagas in Borderland were Christianised through education. Over the years, the result, especially in certain areas was, remarkably significant in changing the religion-wise composition of the tribal population as shown below.

Scheduled Tribes by Religion (1961)

State/Union Territory	ST % of Population	Hindu	Tribal Religion (% of SC Population)	Buddhist	Muslim	Christian	Others
India	6.80	89.39	4.19	0.34	0.21	5.53	0.34
Assam	19.35	47.91	14.54	0.93	–	24.01	0.21
Bihar	9.05	72.07	17.34	–	0.03	10.56	–
Nagaland	93.09	4.47	39.87	–	–	55.67	0.01
Punjab	0.07	41.12	–	57.88	–	–	–

State/Union Territory	ST % of Population	Hindu	Tribal Religion (% of SC Population)	Buddhist	Muslim	Christian	Others
Laccadive, Minicoy, Amindivi	97.03	–	–	–	100.00	–	–
Manipur	31.93	0.21	–	–	–	60.97	38.82
Andaman and Nicobar	22.22	–	24.12	0.01	1.56	74.31	–

The developments described in this paper show that at the end of the British rule, the map of religions in India contained a large number of strong pockets of Christian communities throughout the country, and particularly in tribal areas, a large network of Christian institutions and well-established missionary organizations. The independent government that inherited this picture also began to pursue the policies of neutrality and secularism.

"When the missionaries arrived, the Africans had the land and the missionaries had the Bible. They taught us to pray with our eyes closed. When we opened them–they had the land we had the Bible."

-JOMO KENYATTA

Distribution of Christian Population in India–1978

	Christians	Total Population
India	14,233,382	547,949,809
Andhra Pradesh	1,823,436	43,502,708
Assam	667,151	14,957,542
Bihar	658,717	56,353,369
Gujarat	109,341	26,697,475
Haryana	9,802	10,036,808
Himachal Pradesh	3,556	3,469,434

	Christians	Total Population
Jammu & Kashmir	7,182	4,616,632
Karnataka	613,026	29,299,014
Kerala	4,494,089	21,347,375
Madhya Pradesh	286,072	41,654,119
Maharashtra	717,174	50,412,235
Manipur	279,243	1,072,753
Meghalaya	475,267	1,011,699
Nagaland	344,798	516,449
Orissa	378,888	21,944,615
Punjab	162,202	13,551,064
Rajasthan	30,202	25,765,806
Tamil Nadu	2,367,759	41,199,168
Tripura	15,713	1,556,342
Uttar Pradesh	131,810	88,341,144
West Bengal	251,752	44,312,011
Andaman & Nicobar Islands	30,342	115,133
Arunachal Pradesh	3,684	467,511
Chandigarh	2,504	257,251
Dadra & Nagar Haveli	1,198	74,170
Delhi	42,720	4,065,698
Goa, Daman & Diu	272,509	857,771
Lakshadweep	239	31,810
Pondicherry	41,269	471,707

Source – SUNDAY

c.f The Freedom of Religion Bill–Why?
Committee for the Protection of Freedom of Religion, New Delhi

6
'Liberal' Christianity

Ram Swarup

Eminent Thinker, Writer and Philosopher

The practice of Christianity may make a man better in some respects but it does little to widen his sympathies and to open up his heart to the larger spiritual wealth of different peoples and cultures. This is also true of Islam, another revealed religion, but in the present discussion we shall restrict ourselves to Christianity alone.

From its early days, Christianity has claimed a monopoly of things divine. It has held that there is no salvation outside of the church. But the world has considerably changed during the last two hundred years. A wave of rationalism and humanism has reached the shores of Europe. This has made Christian theology with its exclusive claims look pretentious. This has also fostered a new spirit of liberalism and universalism and also a new awareness of a wider human family, including within itself members who are neither European nor Christian and yet are rich in the things of the spirit.

This new intellectual ferment has not left the Christian theologians entirely untouched. In the past, they saw in religions other than their own nothing but the hand of the

Devil and it cost them little pang of conscience to send even the best and wisest of the man of these religions to Hell. But in the new intellectual and humanist climate, this will not do. The Christian Devil and Hell have lost their terror; their old monopolistic claims have also become laughable. In the new context, if they are to be heard at all, they must appear somewhat more modest, and must not appear to reject altogether or too summarily religions other than their own.

So under the changed conditions there is a new theology under construction. This does not regard other religions as the handiwork of the Devil. On the contrary, it says that there is a *natural* religious impulse which has been at work throughout history and throughout the world giving birth to *natural* religions having their own validity. But, it is further added, that this impulse so necessary at a particular stage finds its culmination and fulfillment in the *revealed* religion of Christianity. Other religions are *preparatory* to Christianity.

There is also another problem that the new theologians face, the problem of finding a place in their scheme for non-Christian saints and good men. True, they cannot yet be sent to Heaven–Christian theology precludes that; but they cannot also be so unceremoniously sent to Hell as in good old days–the new intellectual climate does not countenance it.

So some theologians, liberal and ingenious, have been at work trying to find a suitable solution. One of them was the late Cardinal Jean Danielou. In his *Holy Pagans of the Old Testament,* he observes that even the Bible mentions saints who are not biblical. Abel, Seth, Henoch, Daniel, Noe, Job, Melchisedec, Lot, the Queen of Sheba are examples of non-Christian and even non-biblical saints mentioned in the Bible. Abel was anterior to Abraham; and so were Henoch and Noe. Lot was a relative of Abraham but was not a party to the God's Covenant. Daniel was a Phoenician and Job an Idumean; the Queen of Sheba was a non-Jewish princess.

All these examples show that some sort of saintliness or holiness is possible outside the Christian fold though, according to the Cardinal, that holiness by its very nature "must always be inferior to Christian holiness." But "nonetheless, the fact remains that holiness of that sort is possible."

This does not seem to say much or concede much, but considering that it comes from a Christian theologian trained to see Devil in everything connected with non-Christians it is a great deal. Danielou goes on and makes a further concession. He admits that "there are men who did not know Christ either because they lived before Him or because knowledge of Him did not come their way (presumably because a Christian missionary and not reached their locality), and yet were saved; and some of these too were saints." But that is all. For he hastens to add that "they were not saved by the religions to which they belonged; for Buddha does not save, Zoroaster does not save, nor does Mohomed. If they were saved, then it is because they were saved by Christ Who alone saves, Who alone sanctifies. Again, if they were saved, it is because they already belonged to the Church for there is no salvation outside the Church."

II

The new theology will not go as far as to say that the holy men of other religions are damned, though it knows that they are not saved except through the Church.

These holy men are not saved partly because their holiness is not holy enough. There are three levels of holiness, the pagan holiness being the lowest, governed as it is merely by the law of conscience and not by God's own revealed Laws. Danielou tells us that God's will is "expressed on the Christian plane by the law of the Gospel, on the Jewish plane by the Mosaic law, on the cosmic plane by the law of conscience," the last being obviously an inferior agency of holiness corresponding to the inferior religion of the pagan which is merely *natural,* merely *cosmic.* According to Danielou, at the lowest level, which is the pagan level, "holiness within the sphere of the cosmic religion consists in a response to the call of God made known by conscience." At a more advanced stage, God makes His will known through a Revelation to Moses. Finally, God comes down into the world in a human form as Jesus Christ completing His Revelation. Hence the three degrees of holiness and three orders of holy men. "The glory which shines from the face of Jesus Christ overshadows, as St. Paul tells us, that which shone from the face of Moses. In like manner, the glory shining from the face of Moses overshadows that which shone from the face of Noe."

Man's religion, like his holiness, has progressed from the natural or cosmic to the Jewish, to the Christian. "All Christian liturgy–Easter, Pentecost, Christmas–have at the back of their Christian significance, a Jewish significance; and behind the latter there is a cosmic significance."

This three-level development is evident in all spheres and aspects touching on religious life. For example, there is a three-level development in the mode of worship. On the lowest level, the pagan level, there is a cosmic temple. The house of God is the whole Cosmos, heaven His tent, and the earth His footstool. In the Old Testament, this primitive atmosphere still lingers. Abraham has that *parrhesia* with God–that freedom of speech which in ancient Greece was the right of free citizens.

This gave way to the Temple of Moses. The establishment of the Tabernacle, whose ultimate form is the Temple, is the fundamental mission entrusted by God to Moses. The Covenant was Abraham's mission, the Temple that of Moses. Until now, God was everywhere but from the time of Moses till the death of Christ when a still higher stage begins, the Temple is the dwelling in which the glory of Yahweh abides. Up to the times of Moses, sacrifices could be offered to God anywhere. But after that only those sacrifices were pleasing to God that were offered in the Tabernacle. "Ye shall utterly destroy all the places, wherein the nations which ye shall possess served their gods, upon the high mountains, and upon the hills, and under every green tree." (Bible, Deuteronomy 12.2.)

In a divine plan, we are assured by Cardinal Danielou, this was a necessary stage, for the great danger was polytheism; the singleness of the sanctuary was, as it were, the sign of the Oneness of God.

Thus a second great step is taken. The religion of Sinai creates a gulf between God and man. No longer does Yahweh talk on easy terms with the patriarchs. Henceforth He dwells in the secrecy of the Holy of Holies. Separating man from God marks an advance, for it draws attention to two things: first to God's transcendence, His incomprehensibility, that He is wholly Other; no easy-going anthropomorphism any longer; second, to man's sinfulness, his essentially fallen nature. Without this, the next and third step was not possible.

In the next stage, the abode of Yahweh is no longer the Temple, but the Manhood of Jesus. "The glory of the lord dwelt in the Temple until the coming of the incarnation. But from that day it began to dwell in Jesus. The divine presence is no longer to be found in an enclosure of stone, it dwells in Jesus Himself. With Him the Mosaic order comes to an end." There is a qualitative leap, as the Marxists would love to call it or Jesus is not just "a higher kind of Moses. Moses and the Temple ire figures but Jesus is the reality.'

From this to the Temple of the Church was a most natural and easy step. In fact, it was no new step at all. It is a mode of saying the same 'thing. "It is the manhood of Jesus that is the Temple of the New Law, but this Manhood must be taken as a whole, that is to say, it is the Mystical body in its entirety; this is the complete and final Temple. The dwelling of God is this Christian community whose Head is in the Heaven." God now resides in the Church.

There are other variations but the above is the essential theme of the new liberal theologians. For example, there is Henry de Lubac, the author of *Catholicism: A Study of Dogma in Relation to the Corporate Destiny of Mankind* (Publishers: Burns, Oates & Washbourne, London, 1950). In this book he says, "outside Christianity humanity can doubtless be raised in an exceptional manner to certain spiritual heights, but the top most summit is never reached, and there is the risk of being the farther off from it by mistaking for it some other outlying peak. There is some essential factor missing from every religious 'invention' that is not a following of

Christ. There is something lacking, for example, in Buddhist charity; it is not Christian charity. Something is lacking in the spirituality of great Hindu mystics; it is not the spirituality of St. John of the Cross. Outside Christianity nothing attains its end, towards which, unknowingly, all human desires, all human endeavors, are in movement: the embrace of God in Christ."

If this is true, then his conclusion is a fair one: "So long as the Church does not extend and penetrate to the whole humanity, so as to give it the form of Christ, She cannot rest."

F. H. Hilard in his *Man in Eastern Religions* finds that to the question what is man, the Christian answer is the best. According to Christians "man is to be understood as primarily a person and not a mere manifestation". In this view man is "an individual," while the others, "Hinduism, Buddhism and Taoism, agree in thinking of men primarily as an aspect of ultimate Reality.

Nicolas Berdyaev, in his *Spirit and Reality* (Publishers: Geoffery Bles, Centenary Press, London, 1939) says: "Theosis makes man Divine, while at the same time preserving his human nature. Thus instead of human personality being annihilated, it is made in the image of God and the Divine Trinity. The mystery of the personality is intimately related to that of freedom and love. Love and charity can flourish only if there are personal relationships. Monistic identity excludes love as well as freedom. Man is not identical with the cosmos and with God; man is a microcosm and a microtheosis."

Again, he says, "in Hindu and Platonic mysticism everything is diametrically opposed to the dialogical and dramatic relationship between man and God, between one personality and another. Spirituality is interpreted as being opposed to personality and therefore as independent of love, human freedom, and a relation between the plural and the one. The mystical way is that of Gnosis rather than of Eros." According to him, Hindu spirituality "is an austere and unloving mysticism. The absence of love is explained by the fact that this mysticism is unconscious of personality; it is concerned with abdicating rather than preserving the personality."

Evelyn Underhill, the well-known author of the book *Mysticism* (Publishers: Methuen & Co., Ltd., London, Reprint 1952), too seems to share this scheme. She Says: "In Christianity, the natural mysticism which like natural religion is latent in humanity, and at a certain point of development breaks out in every race, came to itself; and attributing for the first time true and distinct personality to its object, brought into focus the confused and unconditioned God which Neoplatonism had constructed from the abstract concepts of philosophy blended with the intuitions of Indian ecstatic, and made the basis of its meditations on the Real."

She repeats similar sentiments at another place. After making the statement that a mystic is "willing to use the map of the community in which he finds himself," which means that mystical experience is compatible with different theologies about it, she continues to add that "we are bound to allow as a historical fact that mysticism, so far, has found its best map in Christianity," and that "the Christian atmosphere is the one in which the individual mystic has most often been able to develop his genius in a sane and fruitful way."

III

In India too, there is a group of Christian theologians working in the direction of liberalism. These theologians have become noticeable after India's independence. While Christian money and missions continue to work by and large in their old style (see the *Report of the Christian Missionary Activities Enquiry Committee,* Madhya Pradesh), there is a group of Christian theologians who want an encounter with Hinduism on a different plane.

Here their greatest difficulty is the rival slogan that is fashionable among Hindu intellectuals that all teachers preach more or less the same things and that different religions are just different paths to the same goal. The problem of these new liberal Christian theologians is how to salvage their religion from this demolishing, equalizing slogan. So they preach that every religion is unique and that we should all meet in our individual richness in a fruitful dialogue. While secretly hoping that this dialogue would prove that they are unique in a superior way, they invite us all to this encounter. And this should be welcome.

Some of them have taken Hindu names, and live in Indian style and have put on Indian dress. Some of them have even donned the habits of Hindu *Sanyasins*. The motives are mixed. Some may be following St. Paul's practice "to become all things to all men, by all means to win over some of them" (1 Cor. 9.22); others because they find this style more informal and under Indian conditions more comfortable; still others, as they argue, in order to understand and enter into the Hindu psyche better. For some it may be no more than a change of tactics and fronts, but there are genuine elements too. They simply don't have the heart to send a whole people to eternal perdition which their orthodox theology demands.

The late Dr. Jacques-Albert Cuttat, the Swiss Ambassador to India in the 1950s, poses the problem and invites us to this dialogue. He says in his *The Spiritual Dialogue of East and West* (Max Muller Bhavan publications): "The West inclines to exclusivism, the East to syncretism. The view that salvation is only possible within the visible Church–a view expressly rejected by the Catholic Church–has been sustained by missionaries and eminent theologians, even today; such blindness for the spiritual riches of the East, for its mystical depth and intuition of the transparence of the cosmos to higher Realities, such blindness always implies a blindness for some basic aspects of Christianity itself. The East is tempted by the opposite extreme, syncretism; it consists in wrongly equating biblical values with Eastern religious categories. Such universalism is undoubtedly more tolerant, less violent than Western Exclusivism, but equally blind to the specific inner visage of Christianity and the other biblical spiritualities". Dr. Cuttat teaches that each religion is unique and different religions should meet and encounter each other in their individual uniqueness. He is a philosopher of *uniqueness, encounter, dialogue,* and *exchange.*

Another eminent name which has to be mentioned in this connect on is that of the late Fr. J. Monchanin. He was attracted to India and settled in Tiruchirapalli. He built for himself a retreat to which he gave the name Sachidananda *Ashram*. He himself assumed the name of *Swami* Param Arubi Anandam and put on the dress of an Indian *Sanyasin*. From these facts one should not assume that he became a Hindu monk. He understood his own mission differently. As the editors of his papers said when he died in the '50s, his "mission here was not so much to become fully an Indian or to realise in himself the final synthesis of West and East as to bring to India in a pure form, yet with a remarkable sympathy and understanding, the riches of a Christian soul." He himself defines his mission in these terms: "I have come to India for no other purpose than to awaken in a few souls the desire (the passion) to raise up a Christian India. I think the problem is of the same magnitude as the Christianization, in former times, of Greece (the Hellenization of Christendom modelled on the forms of Greek sensibility, thought and spiritual experience). It will take centuries, sacrificed lives, and we shall perhaps die before seeing any realizations. A Christian India, completely Indian and completely Christian will be something so wonderful; to prepare it from afar, the sacrifice of our lives is not too much to ask."

Just two years before his death in 1957, he was writing: "I believe more in 'exchange'. India must give the West a keener sense of the eternal, of the primacy of Being over Becoming, and receive, in turn, from the West a more concrete sense of the temporal, of becoming, of the person, of love (of which India alas! knows so little)."

Fr. J. Monchanin found a good deal in Hinduism which he appreciated. But let us see what all this 'appreciation' amounts to. All the merit Hinduism has accumulated is only a pointer to her conversion to Christianity. We give in his own language what he says on the subject:

"India has received from the Almighty an uncommon gift, an unquenchable thirst for whatever is spiritual. From the *Vedic* and *Upanishadic* times, a countless host of her sons have been great seekers of God. Centuries after centuries there arose seers and poets, singing the joys and sorrows of a soul in quest of the One, philosophers reminding every man of the supremacy of contemplation: upward and inward movements through knowledge to the ultimate.

"Communion with Him and liberation from whatever hinders that realization, was for them the unique goal.

"Hundreds and thousands of men and women have consecrated themselves entirely to that end... We may rightly think that such a marvellous seed was not planted in vain by God in the Indian soul. Unfortunately, Indian wisdom is tainted with erroneous tendencies and looks as if it has not yet found its own equilibrium. So was Greek wisdom before Greece humbly received the Paschal message of the Risen Christ. Man, outside the unique revelation and the unique Church, is always and everywhere unable to sift truth from falsehood, good from evil.

"But once Christianized, Greece rejected her ancestral errors; so also, confident in the indefectible guidance of the Church, we hope that India, once baptised to the fullness of her body and soul, will reject her pantheistic tendencies and, discovering in the splendours of the Holy Ghost the true mysticism... etc.

"Is not the message she had to deliver to the world similar to the message of the ancient Greece? Therefore the Christianization of Indian civilization is to all intents and purposes an historical undertaking comparable to the Christianization of Greece."

Hindus may have the necessary underlying spiritual qualities like a sense of the holy in abundance, but the Church has the Truth in its possession. Therefore, "India has to receive humbly from the Church the sound and basic principles of true contemplation. The genuine Christian contemplation is built on the unshakable foundation of revealed truths concerning God and men and their mutual relations." The mystic East should be led by the doctors of theology of the West, the forest-sages by the university men.

On another occasion, he says, "In that mystery, Hinduism (and specially *Advait)* must die to rise up again Christian. Any theory which does not fully take into account this necessity constitutes a lack of loyalty both to Christianity–which we cannot mutilate from its essence–and to Hinduism–from which we cannot hide its fundamental error and its essential divergence from Christianity.

"Meanwhile, our task is to keep all doors open, to wait with patience and theological hope for the hour of the advent of India into the Church in order to realize the fullness of the Church and the fullness of India. In this age-long vigil, let us remember that love can enter where intellect must bide at the door."

He hopes that "India cannot be alien to this process of assimilation by Christianity and transformation into it." But "should India fail in that task, we cannot understand, humanly speaking, how the mystical body of Christ could reach its quantitative and qualitative fullness in His eschatological Advent."

IV

The discussion will gain in fullness if we referred to two colloquia organized by Christian theologians of this approach. These were held at the invitation of Dr. Cuttat who attended them both personally. The first one was held at Almora in April 1961; the second one at Rajpura, Dehradun in the same month next year. A general and sympathetic account of the second one is given by Bede Griffiths in his *Christ in India: Essays Towards a Hindu-Christian Dialogue* (Publishers: Charles Scribiner's Sons, New York). We ourselves shall discuss here only the first colloquy at Almora. It was attended by individuals connected with various Christian institutions, Catholic and Protestent, like Asirvanam Kenkeri, Snehasadan, Poona, Santi Bhavan, Calcutta, Vrindavan Kottagiri, Jyotiniketan, Kareli. One Hindu, Shri Viveka Dutta, was also present at the discussion for the first few sessions. The summary of the papers and discussion was prepared by Fr. J. Britto C.M.I., of Dharmaram College, Bangalore, himself one of the participants. The summary is entitled *Indian Interiority and Christian Theology*.

All the participants in this colloquy advocate a dialogue with Hindu India on a deeper level. But let us see what kind of mind they bring to the proposed dialogue.

As the *Indian Interiority and Christian Theology* tells us, the participants start with the assumption that "Christianity as the one revealed religion for all men, cannot be lacking in any truth necessary for the salvation of man; it has the guarantee of the Divine testimony."

But their procedure is not to be to denounce Hinduism forthright on the other hand, it is to take different categories of Hindu thinking and "after exhausting all the positive points that Hinduism provides as solutions proceed to show that Christianity gives the fuller and ultimate solution to those and all other problems."

The intention is also not to inquire whether "Hinduism has some positive religious values which are wanting in Christianity"; for that is "not logically tenable" believing as they do that Christianity is "the true revealed religion for all humanity." But they are prepared to look at certain particular values more intensely realized by some Hindu sages which may direct "the Christian back to his own religion, in which he finds the same values more naturally embedded." This position is not without its modesty. It seems that Christians, if not Christianity, too can learn a few things even from the heathens though these things are nothing but the neglected truths of their own religion.

But the participants soon forget the learning part and assume the teaching role, probably due to compulsion of habit. They become polemical. According to the procedure they laid down for themselves, they take different Hindu categories of thought and spirit and show that Christianity offers a better answer. One such category is Teacher-Disciple or *Guru-Shishya* relationship, an important spiritual institution in Hinduism. After discussing it, the participants find that "the only person in whom the positive values of the Hindu *Guru* are best verified is Christ."

Similarly, after discussing the Hindu concept of history, the colloquy finds that the positive values found "in the Indian view of history have their full meaning and natural setting in the Christian concept of history."

The participants discuss *Yoga* too, its positive as well as its negative aspects. At the end, they find that while in Christianity the negative aspects are avoided, the positive aspects of Hindu *Yoga* "find their natural setting and full meaning in Christianity. Non-dualism and dualism, *Yoga* absolutism and *Bhakti* personalism, Sankara and Ramanuja are in different ways related to Christianity. The Christian worships the Absolute of Sankara with the devotion of Ramanuja."

The Hindu concept of *Avatarhood* is discussed. It is found inferior to the Christian one. "Christ's incarnation is a unique fact, and not repeated in every age.....He is true Godhead in true humanity."

Hindu symbolism and idol worship have some positive points but the dangers are far greater. "The fundamental defect of Hindu idol-worship is that it is purely a human attempt so to say to trans-substantiate the material things into the divine without a prior incarnation, namely, without a divine guarantee which assumes the human symbol, into the divine economy of self-communication to man. Man cannot by his own powers raise himself to the divine level, which far transcends him. Hence the Hindu conviction that when the priest recites the prayers over the idol it becomes inhabited by the deity is gratuitous assumption and hence superstitious."

But it is different with Christian symbolism. For example, "the Eucharist marks the culmination of human symbolism. In it the food of man is turned into the body and blood of God. There man's attempt to trans-substantiate the material world into the divine is wonderfully realized–the Eucharist may be taken as a summary and completion of all human endeavor to grasp the divine Reality in human symbols. Hence it should form the converging point of all religious cult."

Hindu *Bhakti* too has more demerits than merits. Its chief defects are that (1) "the notion of love itself is not perfect"; that (2) "there is no integration between knowledge and love," - one has to choose between them; that (3) it lacks a "perfect concept of alterity and there is no proper concept of sin."

Nevertheless, the Bhakti of a Hindu could still be a "preparation for the final confrontation with the personal God who manifests Himself in the Christian Revelation."

Discussing *jnanamarga,* the colloquy finds that the Hindu doctrine of Advaita is irreconcilable with the Christian doctrine of Trinity, but even that could become a step to the understanding of the doctrine of the three Persons in One. How ? First by opposing polytheism. Second by its strong metaphysical bias for unity: "Only against the background of the unique and absolute Reality of God can the doctrine of the Trinity and the immortal personality of man be properly understood. God in his providence insisted on the strictest monotheism, and uncompromisingly exterminated all tendency to polytheism, in the chosen people in the Old Testament, before revealing against the background of that monotheism the Trinity of Persons in that one God, in the New Testament. Hence Advaita with its strong metaphysical basis can be a proper *preparatio evangelica* or an understanding of the Christian message."

V

Once it is admitted that Christianity is the uniquely true religion, the summit towards which all religions are advancing, the liberal theologians will not mind conceding certain subordinate spiritual qualities and attributes and values to Hinduism. In this expansive mood, they generously admit that some European Christians "have felt the wealth of India s religious past." The deep interiority which India has inculcated has even "led some of them to deepen their own Christian interiority." Some of them have been "struck by the vision of the spirit of poverty preached by Christ (but) so fully and cheerfully practised by millions in India." The religious outlook in which everything of every event is looked upon as a work of God, a manifestation of the divine, has impressed many. Many have noted with admiration "the so to say natural aptitude for deep prayer and the contemplation of divine things which Indians manifest."

When the Pope came to India in 1964, he "praised" India's deep spirituality. But it is in the light of the above approach that this praise should be understood. It was not anything spontaneous or genuine. It was diplomatic and deceptive. In fact, it amounted to cheating, if cheating includes a double-tongued approach, half-truths spoken and unstated aim. The Pope's "praise" concealed more than it revealed. It meant to say: Hinduism is very good. It is a useful preparation for Christianity. The Pope praised Hinduism for its *secondaries*, hiding a condemnation of its *primaries*.

His deputy in India, Cardinal Gracias, could afford to be more candid in putting forth the unstated aim. He bemoaned: "It is a matter of grave concern for us that hardly three percent of the local population in India could so far be drawn to receive the Grace of Christ over the last several centuries." The strategy may change but the aim remains fixed. It may be a soft-spoken approach now, but the goal is unaltered. Liberal Christianity is like Euro-Communism; the tactics and the slogans have changed but the mind remains the same.

In the past, in the heydays of British imperialism, fanatic Christians like Carey and Wilberforce were telling their people something like this: 'The natives live in the sin and superstition and darkness of paganism. Surely God has not granted us their charge for nothing. He wants us to bring them to the light of the Gospel, to convert them to Christianity.' But it seems the rulers were less convinced about the benefits of Christianity to the natives. But in a Christian country, they could not express this feeling or belief too openly. So they took to a more equivocal course. They pretended to agree with the crusaders but counter-argued thus: You are very correct in your judgment of the natives. But precisely because they are superstitious, we must go slow with them and their religious beliefs; if we touch their religion it would become a law and order problem and we may lose the Empire itself. This attitude of the British rulers saved India from the worst ravages of Christian missionaries.

But now the political equation has changed and also the ideas have changed. What was possible a hundred years ago is no longer possible now. The Church is also less powerful now even in countries nominally Christian. Its pretentious claims jar on the more sophisticated ears and minds of the age. So a new liberal–or at least liberal-sounding–theology is in the offing, which is trying to give up the old method of forthright denunciation and taking the new method of partial praise, a grudging (and sometimes even genuine) appreciation of the values of a religion they aim to supplant.

Behind the praise of the neo-theologians, we can hear, if our ears are attentive, another message expressed sometimes openly sometimes *sotto voce.* They are saying something like this: "You are too good to remain what you are. Your destiny is to become Christians. We see in your country spiritual things deep and uncommon. But God could not have planted these things amongst you in vain. He must have been preparing you for Christianity, for blessing you with the truth he blessed us with; in short, he must have been aiming to make you as good as we are."

The neo-theologians admit that the Hindus have lived a life of dedication and constant quest that they have pondered over things spiritual from times immemorial. But, in spite of that, somehow, the *Truth* eluded them. Why ? Because, as they seem to say, while the Hindus had the seeking, they lacked the key. They did not know Jesus Christ. God has to be found not in God but in Jesus Christ and the Church.

The Bible says: Ask, and it shall be given you; seek, and you shall find; knock, and it shall be opened unto you. But to the Christian theologians seeking and knocking however dedicated and sincere are not enough. For don't we meet the strange phenomenon that while the Hindus asked, as the neo-theologians are ready to grant, God gave it to the Christians; while the Hindus sought, the Christians found; while the Hindus knocked, it was opened unto the Christians? A mystery perhaps a Trinitarian mystery, perplexing to the heathens but easily understood by the Christians.

The Christian theologians call pagan religions *natural,* while their own they call *revealed.* In this they pay to pagans an unintended compliment. The opposite of the natural is not the revealed, but the artificial, and there is something artificial about the Christian theology. A natural religion means that it is about things inherent and intrinsic; it is about a seeking of the heart which is innate; it is about *man* in his deeper search, and not about a particular person or a church; it does not deal with the accidental but with the universal. Its truths are not adventitious, added from *outside* by a *sole* leader or institution; on the contrary, these reside in the "cave of the heart," to put it in the *Upanishadic* phrase. These truths are also not fortuitous, happening by a lucky chance consisting in the appearance of a particular individual, or in the crusading labours of a church burdened with a self-assumed role. On the contrary, these truths happen because man in his innermost being, by *nature,* is a child of divine light. Man grows from *within,* by an inherent law of his being, responding to *That* which he already secretly is. The *purusha* or *person* within responds to the *pususha* without. *Tat tvam asi, tat aham asmi; sah tad asti.* You are That; I am That, he is That.)

Christianity has two pillars: a narrow piety and a word-juggling theology. What is true in it is also found in other religions which it supplanted in the past and which it continues to do in the present as veil; what it claims to be unique to it is merely intellectual blulf.

Christian theology, as it has developed, is not a product of a tranquil and purified heart; rather, it derives from a mind prejudiced, self-centered and self-righteous, a mind contentious and cantankerous, out to prove the other fellow in the wrong. Above all, it is an artificial mental construct; there is little spirituality in it.

7

Conversions: A Christian View

V.V. John

Noted Educationist, former Vice-chancellor, Jodhpur University, former Member, Minorities Commission

In the days when I was a member of the Minorities Commission, some public excitement was generated by Mr. Om Prakash Tyagi's ironically named Freedom of Religion Bill. Its ostensible object was to prevent conversions from one religion to another through force, fraud or undue inducement. This seemingly unexceptionable objective acquired however a sinister dimensions owing to the definitions that were given to force, fraud and inducement. The threat of divine displeasure and the prospect of eternal rewards in the next life, which were the stock-in-trade of a certain type of religious preaching, were sought to be made punishable offences under the proposed law. It also sought to oblige everyone who converted another, or was himself converted, to report the matter to the appropriate civil authority, failure to do so being punishable under the law. If this had become law, religious freedom would have had to be continually reported to civil authority. It would have been as though, under the fundamental right to freedom of expression, a speech-maker were obliged to report to the nearest magistrate every time he made a speech.

A civil liberties organization protested against the proposed law as being fraught with possible threat to individual freedom. A majority of the members of the Minorities Commission took the same view. But two members of the Commission dissented from this view. Their argument was that conversion from one religion to another was to be generally deplored. What about the fundamental right to profess, preach and propagate one's religion? Their stance was not against anyone's right to preach his religion; but this did not include the right to convert anyone. In other words, you may preach so long as your preaching is not effective.

I remember how this matter came up for discussion at the time at a friend's house. Mr. A.D. Gorwala, who was present, rather casually dismissed the matter by observing that we are born into one religion or another, and any effort to convert one from the faith into which one was born, amounted to suggesting that God did not know what was good for us. Did we know better than God ? I was somewhat intrigued that this view should come from a stalwart of the press who had always been trying to convert us to his political views. Why not accept every curmudgeon as having been ordained to be such by God Almighty? But perhaps I should have recognized that changing political views was a matter that could be more calmly discussed than changing one's religion.

And yet, it dawned on me as I reflected on the matter, that if there were not a political dimension to religious conversions, they would not have generated so much heat. We live in a land which was partitioned, and its historic identity ripped asunder, on the basis of differing religious faiths. The integrity of the country has been facing threats of secession from tribes living in border areas, who profess religions other than that of the majority in the country. And there is the ubiquitous phenomenon of party allegiance in the political arena depending on one's caste or community. (The cartoonist Abu pictured a polling booth which, instead of the normal direction: 'Cast your vote here,' said: 'Vote your caste here!') All political parties, not excluding those professing liberal and leftist ideologies, have learnt to count on the support of particular castes and communities. They signify the transfer of votes from one political party to another. The awful result is that religious conversions have come to be discussed in the same terms as defections from one political party to another. Everyone knows that political defections do not ordinarily come because of any change in political convictions. The motivations are different and usually sordid. We have not yet been able to devise an adequate law for discouraging defections among political parties. We have found it so much easier to deal with changes of religion, though one should have thought that a secular state would be less obsessed with its religions than with its political parties.

The political dimensions of conversion underlie the distinction sought to be made between individual conversions and mass conversions. It is disingenuous dialectics to dismiss this by arguing that in matters of freedom, there ought not to be one law for the individual and another for the group. Maybe, the law cannot discriminate, but society may not be inhibited from taking due note of the motivations that prompt mass conversions as distinguished from those that prompt individual conversions.

The most notable instance of mass conversions in recent history was what happened under the leadership of Dr. Ambedkar, who led several thousand members of the depressed classes into Buddhism. The initial impulsions and the occasion were clearly political, but it could be claimed that for most of them, the new faith did not replace anything old but only filled a vacuum. The same could perhaps be said of the large-scale conversions made by St. Francis Xavier in the sixteenth century. The following of the ancient religious traditions of India should be reassured by Paul Johnson's reference, in his recently published *History of Christianity*, to "the almost unrelieved failure of the missions to penetrate the heartlands of the great imperial cults: Islam, the Hindu family, Confucianism, Buddhism or for that matter, Judaism. But among the primitives and the pagans, the hill tribes and the mountains, in swamps and islands–everywhere where cultural standards were low or imperial religions had not yet penetrated–Christianity made spectacular conquests."

Any notion that Christianity thrived in India owing to the patronage and support of Christian colonial powers would be historically untenable. There was a thriving Christian community in India long before the arrival of the colonial powers. St. Francis Xavier's missionary labours were as fruitful outside Goa, where the Portuguese held sway, as inside. It could even be said that the Portuguese, with their persecutions and their destruction of temples, generated such racial resentment that it permanently impeded the spread of Christianity on the subcontinent, and in a land where Christianity had been at home for centuries, it even came to be looked upon as an alien religion. As for the British, the Ecclesiastical Establishment had no missionary aspirations, and the rulers were busier setting Muslim against Hindu, so as to entrench their own position, than in spreading the gospel of Christ.

The colonial experience and our current style of politics have combined to destroy in some measure a major ingredient of our cultural heritage, which consisted of a robust tradition of tolerance and pride in the many-splendoured texture of our religious life. Today one is haunted by the fear that we have lapsed into the condition that Jonathan Swift once described: "We have just religion enough to make us hate, but not enough to make us love one another."

There is reason to suspect that we are not proud enough of the fact that almost alone among the countries on the mainland of Asia, both the letter of our law and the spirit guarantee complete religious freedom in our country. When the enlightened leaders of the Republic wrote into the Constitution, the right of the citizen to practise, preach and propagate his religion, they accepted the possibility of religious conversions and were not dismayed at the prospect. They could not have been unaware that conversions could be used as a political weapon, but they were confident that our democracy would be virile and clear-headed enough to deal suitably with such folly. The cure for the political misuse of religion and for irrational conflicts over forms of observance, such as music and procession before places of worship, is not to ban conversions and to freeze religious allegiances at the point that we have reached as of now. Ignorance and irrational hatred are at the root of these conflicts. The cure for ignorance is knowledge. The cure for hatred is love.

Out of such knowledge and such love could be generated an atmosphere of regard and reverence for faiths other than one's own. It is not necessary for the creation of this atmosphere to accept the proposition that one religion is as good as another. Such a proposition might only help to promote indifferentism, which is not a particularly stable for building a tolerant, secular society. At the same time, those who adhere to the notion that theirs alone is the true faith, should develop the wisdom to recognize that whatever the true believer may claim, God seems to be out looking for the hapless ones that are looking for him!

The true believer may bear in mind St. Paul's warning that though he spoke with the tongues of men and of angels and did not have charity, he would be 'sounding brass or a tinkling cymbal.' He could also take note of one of the possible meanings of Jesus Christ's words: "In my father's house are many mansions."

It is perhaps unrealistic to wish that religious strife were replaced everywhere by religious controversy. For the protagonists of the two are not the same. The effort must nevertheless be made to ensure that wherever conflict exists, it is raised to the intellectual plane, and turned into intellectual encounters. This happy result cannot be achieved unless there is a continuing disposition to study and understand what the different faiths stand for. From the prison-house of ignorance and prejudice, truth will set men free.

There are those who interpret secularism in what may be called fundamentalist terms and would want to insist that religion is a private and personal affair and that the state and society should have no truck with it. Far from being applicable to all religion, it cannot be applied even to the most intensely personal religious experience, namely, the mystical.

Religion is the highest form of sharing, open to the human being. And as G.K. Chesterton once put it: "A man can no more possess a private religion than he can possess a private sun and moon."

The idea of sharing, as the practical expression of love, is he only legitimate basis for conversions. But where conversions are suspect on political or other non-spiritual grounds, the way of wisdom would be to promote the experience of sharing without any search for proselytes. The yearning for higher census figures and the lament or char gin over any fall in those figures have no spiritual dimensions. Since those who get bothered about the census figures currently occupy the center of the stage, the truly religious should not seek any entry there. God's work awaits them on other planes.

Book Review

The Christian Missionaries in Bengal (1793-1833)
Dr. K.P. Sengupta. Firma K.L. Mukhopadhyaya, Calcutta,
1971; 245pp. Rs. 251

This book is an in-depth analysis of the first forty years (1793-1833) of the Protestant missionary activities in Bengal and an attempt to assess their role in the social, educational and religious reforms that took place at that time. An objective analysis of the primary materials has enabled Dr. Sen Gupta not only to correlate between missionary aims and achievements but also to explode some of the myths which have gathered round these achievements. Based on actual missionary records and other primary sources, this work opens up a new horizon in our knowledge of the missionaries and forms a significant contribution to the nineteenth century social history of India.

Questions relating to this important subject which has attracted the attention of scholars in recent years, but which have never been answered before like'- 'What was the object of the missionaries in India? Did they succeed in attaining their objectives? How far were they responsible for social reforms in Bengal?' have for the first time been clearly worked out.

The author Dr. Sen Gupta who hails from Faridpur, now in Bangladesh, took his M.A. in History from Calcutta University and in 1963, went to England where he was awarded a doctorate (London) in 1966. He is Head of the Department of History Tamralipta Mahavidyalaya, Midnapur and is engaged in further researches into missionary activities in Bengal.

That years of painstakingly systematic research into the private correspondence of the missionaries and the Christian journals has gone into the making of this treatise is amply evident.

The author begins with the arrival of the earliest missionaries in Bengal.

'The first missionaries to arrive in Bengal were from the Baptist Missionary Society (B.M.S.), Society for Promotion of Christian Knowledge (SPCK) and London Missionary Society (L.M.S.) during the last decade of the eighteenth century. After passing of the Charter Act of 1813, the missionaries of other societies—Church Missionary Society (C.M.S.) Society or the Propogation of the Gospel, (S.P.G.) Netherlands Missionary Society, Established Church of Scotland, and Wesleyan Methodist Missionary Society—also started coming to Bengal. The period under survey is however distinguished by the pioneering work of Carey, Marshman and Ward. The history of the Missionaries in Bengal between 1793 and 1833 is predominantly the history of the Serampore Mission'.

Although other Missionaries carried on their work with zeal and energy, they were not so prominent as to leave behind any permanent impression.

Objects

'The missionaries of all denominations had one common object the conversion of the Indians to Christianity. The methods they adopted to achieve this end were mainly three—Preaching, Translation and Education' and were motivated to a large extent by a curious mixture of religion and Imperialistic designs. The author quotes among others the arguments of Charles Grant who stated in his *observations* that the demand for a "Popular form of government and assertion of independence ', like the Americans, was "hypothetical" for "political liberty is the last thing likely to flourish" in India. He was of the opinion that the Indians would become more loyal to the British rule, if they were Christianised, and so put forward his view with emphasis that "In success would lie our safety, not our danger". The introduction of Christianity, he argued, will "serve the original design with which we visited India....the extension of our commerce". A similar, almost identical view was expressed by Parry and Grant in 1807. They in their letter to Dundas rejected the objection that the Indians would demand independence as "rests upon mere hypothesis, is destitute of proof and unsupported by probability or experience". As to the safety of the Empire, they declared that "Religion, and religion only will supply a common principle or bond of union between the Governors and the governed... If... they embrace our religion, they would have a new cause of attachment to us...which would give us better assurance cf their fidelity".

In a separate chapter titled "Missionary Object", he says:

The missionaries believed that the religions of the Indians were responsible for their degradation. The remedy therefore was very simple. The Indians must change their religions for Christianity, which to the missionaries was the only true religion of the world. The B.'vl.S. in their first circular to "Christians at large" in 1792, stated that "The object of this society is to evangelize the poor, dark, idolatrous Heathen, by sending missionaries".

How far the missionary methods of preaching, translation and education were successful in gaining converts, what was the social background of the Indian, converts, and their behaviour after conversion are comprehensively discussed. However, contrary to expectations, proselytization understandably progressed at, snail's pace.

Numbers of Converts

'In a joint letter to the committee in 1805, the Serampore missionaries claimed that "The number of native members... is 75'.

'Rev. J. Bough calculated in 1845 the total number of B.M.S. converts up to the end of 1814 as 756.

'An article entitled "Results of the Missionary Labour in India", appeared in *The Calcutta Review* in 1851. The writer states that "a statistical paper, laid before the Missionary Conference in Calcutta, a few years ago, showed that in Lower Bengal, exclusive of Krishnaghur (Krishnagar) the accessions of native converts to the Christian church had been thus:

From 1793 to 1802	27
From 1803 to 1812	161
From 1813 to 1822	403
From 1823 to 1832	675
From 1833 to 1842	1045

The missionaries themselves acknowledged that the number was very insignificant when compared to the vast mass of the Indian population.'

Social Background

The social background of the converts makes interesting reading.

'The first convert, named Krishna Pal, made by the Serampore missionaries in 1800, was a carpenter. Another person who rejected his caste with him was a distiller, another low caste. An analysis of the B.M.S. list would give a fairer idea of the social background of the Indian converts. As this is the only document which gives a somewhat detailed description only up to 188, the analysis would necessarily seem to be sketchy.

The list contained 9 Brahmans. The missionaries mentioned the surname of only one of them. From the surname he appears to be Kulin Brahman, baptised in 1807. There is nothing in the missionary writings which can indicate that he was from a respectable family stated that he was an old man and "very poorly". Of the remaining 8, one was reported to be "excluded", another of a "doubtful character", the other as "gone back" and two employed as Bengali compositors at the Serampore Press. The missionaries claimed none of them to be coming from any respectable family. They mentioned about 12 of their converts as "Kaist" and two as "writer cast (sic)". It is not known that was the distinction if any between these two, as the missionaries never stated the method of their classifications. The Kayastha class contained many sections, both high and low, so without any other descriptions, it is not possible to find out the social status of these converts. In many cases missionaries simply mentioned the converts as a "Hindoo", "A Hindoo widow", "A Hindoo woman" which indicates nothing as to their caste. Where the missionaries mentioned the caste, the majority of them belonged to the lowest class, such as "Carpenter", "Soore", "Dhobe", "Kaibarta", "Jogge", "Till", and others. By profession these people were respectively, distillers, washermen, fishermen, weavers and oilmen. A large number were mentioned as "Byraggees" who lived on begging. Of seven Muslims mentioned in the list, one was employed "as Persian compositor" in the Serampore Press. Of the remaining six, one was "suspended", two "not heard of lately" another one described as "A Musselman having lost cast (sic) by marriage with a *Fering*. The remaining three were s ated simply as "Musselman". The descriptions tend to confirm that most of the Muslim converts also did not belong to any respectable family. Tt appears that one of the Muslim converts was a personal servant of Ward. Incidentally, there is no other description of the Muslim converts in the missionary writings of the whole period under review. The analysis thus confirms the view expressed by Lord Minto that the converts were mostly "those outcastes, who have taken refuge in the Society of Christians, from the scorn of their countrymen."

Ram Mohun Roy expressed his opinion in 1824, that the Indian converts were "generally of the most ignorant class". In 1824 Pearson, the L.M.S. missionary, confessed that the Indian converts mostly belonged to "the lower and poorer class." In 1832 the C.M.S. Record quoted a journal of one of their missionaries from Bengal, stating that the;/ had baptized same adults whose occupation was fish-catching. Pascoe in his history, mentioned that the majorty of the S.P.G. converts at Howrah in 1832 were "of the peasant class", and of Tollygungc in 1833, were "entirely of the Pode and Teore castes."

Motives for Conversion

What prompted the converts to embrace Christianity is best il ustrated in the section: The motives for Conversion.

'The missionaries in Bengal always considered the question of providing shelter and employment to their Indian converts, as an essential part of their duty. As already noticed, Carey was glad to be appointed as Superintendent of the indigo factory at Madnabati, for it gave him enough opportunity to offer "employment" to anyone who "lost cast (sic) for the Gospel." "Ward wrote in his journal that they had purchased land on which they were building a hut for two of their converts. Enough concern was shown for. the employment of the first convert Krishna. When the number of converts grew it became difficult to find employment for all. Ward commented "We are exceedingly puzzled about the employment of the new converts", who mostly lived on begging. In 1105 the Serampore missionaries decided to employ more Indian converts as preachers of the Gospel. The gradual expansion of the missionary work and the Serampore Press, created opportunities for the employment of the Indian converts.

'Those who were poor and in debt seem to have been tempted by the material gains of conversion. Ward recorded in his journal that an Indian came to Serampore mission for conversion but went away soon after when he found that his hope of paying off his debts by becoming Christian might not be fulfilled. Ward feared that the Indian converts might have been primarily influenced by worldly expectations. That such material rewards were sometimes offered by the missionaries is shown by a letter of Forsyth to Carey in which the writer charges the Serampore missionaries with having used "underhand means" to convert people. Ward acknowledged that "Having lent some money to three of our friends... Several others of the newly baptised have been asking to have money lent them."

Behaviour after Conversion

Did conversion to Christianity help them to get rid of their degradation and moral depravity as the missionaries claimed? Did they become any better in their social behaviour after conversion? The author presents very interesting insights into this aspect.

'The desire of the missionaries to remedy all the "miseries" of the Indian people through Christianity, was only possible if conversion could (as the missionaries firmly believed) bring a revolutionary change in the character, attitude and behaviour of their converts.

'Krishna Pal, the first convert and his family, occupy a large part in the early writings of the Serampore missionaries. Ward recorded in his journal that "we have been unhappy this week" because of a quarrel between Krishna's family and Unna, a converted widow "who lived with them (Krishna's family) as servant". After conversion, Unna "got it into her head that as she was a holy sister, it was not right to be Creshnoo's (Krishna's) servant". After the quarrel she left Krishna's house and started living in the house of Gokul—another convert. One evening Gokul came to Ward and asked him "whether it was right that he should always have his mind on Xt's (Christ's) death. He said by always keeping his thoughts on that, his mind got dried (and) exhausted". In connection with Unna, there was a continuous quarrel between the families of Krishna and Gokul. The quarrel reached a climax when "Gokul ... behaved in the most irregular (and) imprudent manner. His conduct is like that of a person insane. He and his wife (and) Unna are full of passion against us (and) Creshnoo's (Krishna's) family. We are very uneasy". They were excluded from the church, but did not leave the two huts, which the missionaries had built for them. Another day Gokul came with a stick and "stamped upon the testament". The same evening he abused some converts. Ward commented: "We fear he makes hemp which has an intoxicating effect. You will conceive how much these circumstances affect us".

'Marshman wrote that the missionaries had a serious conversion with Krishna "relative to some work he had done for us, in which we apprehend he had charged us 15 or 20 per cent above the Calcutta price". He also described in the same letter, a serious quarrel between Krishna and Petumber, another convert. Petumber had lived at Krishna's house for about three months. Krishna sent his servant to demand money for lodging from Petumber. Petumber was offended because Krishna had not told him about the charges before, and the result was a quarrel. During this quarrel Krishna used against Petumber "reproachful language in presence of many people...I leave you to guess the state of our minds. The aggressor our first converst." The missionaries specially advised their women convert "to cultivate love and harmony and avoid particularly all back-biting, tale-bearing and enlarging on other's faults." Women converts manifested more often "a looseness of speaking and coldness in attending upon divine things."

'The relationship between the converts was tinged with jealousy. When Petumber appointed as a preacher, Krishna became disgusted with the missionaries and started preaching separately in his house. Most of the Indian converts joined him. Marshman commented: "The schism of Krishna has filled us with a sensation of grief and fear, which I can hardly describe." Ward's comment on Krishna's action was "we lave this day had a more dreadful schism amongst us than at any former time." After about three months Ward wrote again "Creshno (Krishna) has been dissatisfied with our allowance to him and seems to thinl we have used him hardly. He has said some hardish words to Bro. (Bro iler) M. (Marshman) on this subject." The missionaries decided then to appoint Krishna as an itinerant preacher with a hxed salary.

Even some missionaries themselves lamented that 'the values and morals of the Indians hardly changed after conversion. Haladnar who after his conversion had been forcibly taken away by his father was one day brought back to the Serampore mission by some Indians who demanded money for their service. It was later found that these men were acting on the instructions of Krishna's wife. Krishna's family was found guilty of encouraging an illicit relationship between Haladhar and Goloke, Krishna's married daughter. Apart from be. ng a heavy gambler, Bhyrub, a Brahman convert who married Krishna's third daughter, turned out to be a professional forger. Ward wrote: "This day I caught Bhyrub in a fraud. He had been trying to get money from the Sirkar (Sarkar) by presenting a forged bill in our name. This led to a discovery of more than a dozen other forgeries whereby he fur 1 got from the Sirkar at different times more than sixty rupees." He was excluded from the church. After restoration he was again found "forging a receipt to get money from us. He lately stole from our k use a silver spoon". The missionaries carried the matter to the magistrate who gave Bhyrub "a thorough floggging." On hearing this "Krishnoo (Krishna) has been in a dreadful passion with us...He declared that he would sell his all and wander about the country to warn people against becoming Xns. (Christians)". Another convert Mohan (husband of Krishna's first daughter Goloke) was suspended for indulging in gambling and prostitution. Ward brought to the notice of the missionaries "a practice too much followed by Creshnoo (Krishna) aad a few more of our native brethern viz., the smoking of an intoxicating herb called Ganja".

'Chamberlain in 1804 wrote to Ryland: "Kreeshnoo (Krishna) and his family have behaved in a most unlovely manner...acted in opposition,... have quarrelled and disgraced themselves and others in the open world." He wrote elaborately about Krishna that "his self-conce it and indolence are his misery and ruin. From the former proceeds uncommon anger and stubbornness and the latter produces extravagance and poverty...He was so idle...so little attentive to truth in his engagements, so unjust in his charges, that nobody give him work, and Bret hern find that a heathen does better by far than he did".

'Likewise Carey commented "The state of things among us in some respect painful...I fear that there is a (very) great decline in the vital power of religion among some of our Hindoo friends".

Be that as it may, the missionaries by and large acknowledged their failure. Under the heading: *The Failure and Frustrations of the Missinories* the author says:

'The number of Indian converts, as already noticed, was very insignificant compared to the vast population. The majority of them were from the lowest strata of the Indian society, outcastes, half-castes and even beggars. Their behaviour after conversion scarcely reflected any change in their character or way of life. Thus the missionaries failed to achieve their main object. The missionaries of different societies working in Bengal, were very conscious of this, and frequently acknowledged their failure.

'Charles Lushington, who was for a long time government Chief Secretary, while giving evidence before the Parliamentary Committee in 1832, was questioned whether there was any progress made in Bengal in the conversion to Christianity ? He replied: "I am afraid very little."

'Writers of later periods also pronounced similar judgements. G. Smith, a B.M.S. missionary during the last part of the nineteenth century commented that "The first fact forced on Dull' was that as against the Brahmanized Hindoos, the prevailing missionary methods had failed." K.S. Latourette wrote: "when Duff landed in India, Christian missions, particularly Protestant missions, were still being sharply questioned. In the years immediately preceding and succeeding his arrival, severe criticisms were circulated in Europe by those having first-hand knowledge of the country. Protestant missions were declared a failure."

K. P. Sengupta concludes: 'All these writings pronounce without any reserve, the failure of the missionaries in Bengal, in their main task of converting the people lo Christianity, during the period under present survey.'

–Mumtaz Ali Khan

DOCUMENT

Lord Minto (Governor General in India from 1806 to 1813) on missionary activities

Quoted from Lord Minto's letter to the Chairman of the East India Company

Lord Minto, while declaring the Company's policy with regard to Christian missions emphatically made it clear that the Company's policy was to protect the followers of all religions and to show respect to the traditional and indigenous religious system of the country. While criticising the Bengal Missionaries he said in 1807 that the company should not denounce the religion of the people taught by the fathers and mothers to their sons and daughters. He opposed the way in which the missionaries were functioning. The following passage will afford a sufficient illustration of the truth stated above.

"In the whole course of our administration of the Indian territoriesi t has been our known and declared principle to maintain a perfect toleration of the various religious systems which prevailed in them; to protect the followers of each in the undisturbed enjoyment of their respective opinions and usages neither to interfere with them ourselves nor to suffer them to be molested by others. When we afforded our countenance and sanction to missionaries who have from time to time proceeded to India for the purpose of propagating the Christian religion, it was far from being in our contemplation to add the influence of our authority to any attempts they night make for, on the contrary, we were perfectly aware that the progress of such conversion will be slow and gradual, arising more from a conviction of the principles of our religion itself and from the pious example of its teachers than from any undue influence or from the exertions of authority which are never to be resorted to in such cases..... The principal publications which have been issued by the Serampore Press (the Mission Press worked by the group of Missionaries of whom William Carey was the most famous) in the native language, the sole effect of which was not to convert but to alienate the professors of both religions prevalent amongst the natives of this country. The miserable stuff addressed to the Hindus in which without proof or argument of any kind the pages are filled with hell-fire, denounced a whole race of man for believing in the religion which they were taught by their fathers and mothers....Is this the doctrine of our faith ?.....I am no enemy of the progress of Christianity in India. It is the way, I observe, of some who are personally engaged in the work of conversion.....I do not think we should be justified in refusing the dispensation of the Christian revelation to this great country for our interest or security, but I am not equally ready to sacrifice the great interests which are confided to me to a blind principle of complaisance towards every indiscretion which zeal or negligence may commit."

The court of Directors to the Governor of Fort St. George.

DOCUMENTATION

Christian Reality in India

An Inside View

—Compiled

[Here is a compilation of a few excerpts from the writings of some very devout and responsible Christian scholars, who throw valuable light on the Christian Reality as it exists in India today. They indicate a very welcome and hopeful trend of self-introspection which is beginning to take place in the minds of enlightened and conscientious Christian Indians.

The excerpts compiled here are chosen from the writings of:

a. **Rt. Rev. Sundar Clarke**: Son of a distinguished Pastor and himself a Bishop since 1954; closely associated with several evangelical and social service organisations.

b. **Mr. E.D. Devadasan**: Bar-at-law (London); practising lawyer both in Madras and Delhi; legal adviser to a large number of churches and other voluntary agencies in India. Author of many books on law.

c. **Mrs. D.L. Gopal Ratnam**: President, National Christian Council of India; formerly Gen. Secretary of the Church of South India.

d. **Mr. Frank S. Dewars**: Retired as a high ranking officer in Indian Police; devout Christian patriot.

—Ed.]

Casteism among Christians

Perhaps no one has came out in as bad a colour as the Christians have by the recent development of conversion in southern India. There is a large number of Christian communities in the place where the conversion has taken place, especially in the Tirunelveli district. Those who wanted relief from social oppression, judged Islam and Christianity and found something wanting in Christianity as practised by the Christians in southern India and deliberately chose Islam. It was a discerning judgement on their part that Christians, notwithstanding their conversion, continue to follow caste divisions among themselves. Even after becoming members of the Church, the Christians continue to be divided on basis of caste. Of course, if the members are divided on caste basis, there can be no binding fellowship among the members. Not only in Tamil Nadu, but throughout south India, especially, in Kerala, Karnataka, Andhra Pradesh and Tamil Nadu, the problem of caste and language has bedeviled the development of the Church. Not merely the difference in caste, but also difference in the language have baffled the Church in India. A Roman Catholic Church in Bangalore is openly divided into two sections, one representing the people of Karnataka and the other representing the affluent Christians who have migrated from outside Karnataka into Bangalore.[1]

...Unfortunately this casteism is not confined to any particular denomination. It is prevalent in all denominations in southern India, be it the Roman Catholic Church or the Protestant Church; the Evangelical Church or non-Evangelical Church, a rich Church or a poor Church, an urban Church or a rural Church, a Born-again Christian or some other. This problem of casteism within the Church in Tamil Nadu is not new. It has been there since the beginning of this century. In fact it can be even traced to the early part of the 17th century.[2]

...For instance, on one of the earliest occasions, a section of the Roman Catholic Christians, considering themselves high caste, filed a suit against the Bishop and Presbyter and the so-called low caste Christians. The relief claimed was to erect a wall in the Church so that one portion can be exclusively kept for these high caste Christians and to restrain the so-called low caste Christians from entering into that portion. The right was sought to be established on the basis of a concession granted by an earlier Bishop–*Michael Pillai* vs. *Rt. Rev. Watley.*[3] (1916 m.w.n. 307)

...This caste system has continued to plague the Church and the Christian community in southern India. With the people getting more educated and affluent, the caste difference has become more rigorous and oppressive because added to the caste difference is the added affluence of the stronger section of Christian community. Unfortunately, even those who have been ordained as Pastors and Bishops of the Church have not risen above caste difference. They only reflect the existing prejudices, drawbacks and shortcomings of the flock they lead. In that sense they are not giving leadership, but only following others like sheep. Even where Christians migrate to another area and settle down, strangely, they stick on to their caste groups.[4]

...In most cases the Church in India and the Christians could easily shift the balance on the overseas missionaries but in the present case that cannot be done because even the orthodox churches which trace their origin to the first century and the visit to India of St. Thomas are no better (and in fact worse) than the other churches. The orthodox Christians in India appear to be more an ethnic group than a religious group. They look upon those Indians who have become Christians in recent years with contempt, and keep them out of their Church. Most of them proudly claim that they were converted originally 2,000 years ago from the Nambudripad community and they display condescension in dealing with other Christians in India. It is no wonder that some of the Harijan Christians have also embraced Islam.[5]

...Caste also plays a forceful part in deciding victories or losses in political elections and Church elections. This politicisation of caste in our times has assumed large proportions and has actively helped to keep and continue the differentiations and discriminations. Sometimes it seems as if caste can never be overcome. In the Indian Christian Churches, the tendency exists to cleave to caste in times of marriages, elections to Church committees, elections to schools, colleges, hospitals etc. This is a matter for shame and as a Church we are struggling hard to overcome this...[6]

Position of Women

...The Constitution of India gives equal status to women along with men. Even an ordinance was passed in 1978 to give equal pay for equal work. Even with all these improvements in education, legislation etc., women still remain the oppressed class in the Church...

...they are not given adequate representation at the decision-making bodies in the Pastorate, Diocesan and Synod levels. The CSI Synod stipulated that 25 per cent of representation be given to women at all levels. The representation at the Synod in January 1978 was 8.9 per cent and in January 1980 was less than that...

...These attitudes directly affected the ordination of women in the CSI. The 1976 Synod voted for ordination with a thumping majority, but it fell through because of the failure to secure approval by 2/3rd of the 20 dioceses....[7]

Dowry

...The evil of dowry is raging rampant in many of our Christian societies and we ourselves need to go on an anti-dowry campaign...[8]

Foreign Leadership

...We need to critically examine our leadership. Have we been too dependent on leadership from outside ? Sometimes, a lack of unity drives us to seek leadership from outside...[9]

...Somehow, though we accept this, we also recognize that there still persists in many an Indian Christian a 'complex', a 'dependency complex' or may be even an 'inferiority complex'. Perhaps this has arisen due to a very natural and psychological feeling of being obligated to the Western churches...[10]

...Another occasion for our dependency on non-national personnel seems to be in the choice of our leaders. Our lack of unity has resulted in choosing non-nationals to be leaders in the Indian Church.[11]

...Due to our communal feeling a non-national is forced into accepting a Bishopric. To cite yet another example, our rather narrow linguistic feelings also result in such choices...[12]

...The era when the Indian Church was managed by foreign boards, missionary societies and missionaries is over. To be ourselves, the church must be truly Indian and the leadership of the church in India today must also be truly Indian...[13]

Craze for Everything Foreign

......Even today the Mecca for Christian young men and women involved in evangelistic tasks is the U.S.A. or Australia. They make no secret of this. Are our seminaries useless? Can they not provide the necessary training and motivation? That some of our younger priests have so much to teach and contribute so richly to the deliberations of their Western counterparts is such a refreshing knowledge. One Church group was frantically groping for assistance in Delhi, to get a visa for a young foreign missionary to come and teach English. Another did even better. It wanted a foreign missionary to come and help translate the New Testament into Hindi. Yet another organisation which promoted a Handicraft Export unit to generate employment amongst the poor, as a purely Indian manned unit, very soon found all posts that mattered, taken over by missionary foreigners.

......Very many proudly declare that we have more foreign Christian Missionaries in India today than we had at the time of our Independence. It makes no sense in the context of Indianisation of our religion and it is not known for whose benefit this unwanted propaganda is put across. Foreign evangelists come from abroad for Crusades, Conventions or revival meetings in state capitals. There are colourful banners and posters fluttering all over the town. Eye-catching advertisements adorn English language newspapers and colourful handbills are distributed in thousands. A lot of money is spent. There is nothing wrong in this. But when the same organisation sponsors an equally sincere and effective Indian evangelist, all this paraphernalia is disturbingly absent. What is the nature of the image we are trying to build?

Westernisation

......It is also sometimes noticed that a person changing his faith immediately adheres to the western style of life. Quite often a Hindu after baptising into the church becomes a beef-eating Christian. An urban person who normally wears the Indian *jibba* and *dhoti* after becoming a Christian must conform to the dress habits of his fellow urban church members and must therefore go to church with a suit and neck-tie. These are perhaps rather isolated instances, but nonetheless, they go to prove to non-Christians that the God of the Christians is a God of the West. One has to necessarily conform to the western style of life in becoming a Christian.[16]

......The influence of Western culture in the life of the Indian Church must be seriously questioned and even avoided.[17]......

......We certainly are building more churches in India today, but almost every church that is being built is still striving to preserve the Gothic Spires, the Grecian splendour, the Roman grandeur, the Corinthian columns or perhaps the modern western architectural beauty. What a misfit our church buildings are in the environment of Indian culture. Do we think of an Indian *gopuram* or of Pallava architecture or the Chola beauty, perhaps not! There are very few of our churches that have been built typically on Indian style but one has to make an effort and search for such architecture in the Indian Church. It could be that our church buildings are not Indian enough to attract the non-Christians.[18]

......Our postures at worship also need serious re-thinking. We are becoming very much the comfortable Christians sitting in comfortable pews. Kneeling is going out of fashion. Of course consideration should be given to the *sari* getting crushed or the crease of the suit being lost![19]

......Even in our pulpits and reading desks there is hardly anything Indian. Every pulpit and lectern made today is a true replica of 17th century western Europe or U.K. They appear as finely polished and newly made antique! The candle and the candlestick are still the ever green remnants of past rituals. Why not we replace all candles and candlesticks with the Indian lamp (kuthuvilakku). The Indian kuthuvilakku serves the full significance of the candle and is also in right context with our culture.[20]

......The large receipt of foreign money by the churches is another factor much resented by the followers of the major religions in the country. There is a strong feeling that Christians are losing their culture and becoming Westernised and this is taken by some political parties as a disintegrating force at the national level. From the early days of the mission, colonialism and the British Raj were held synonymous with Christianity. But some politicians had taken maximum advantage of this factor to malign the church.[21]

......It is true our leaders are trained in the West, saturated with Western ideas, theology totally lacking the imaginative adaptation needed to our situation and culture. Very serious action was taken during the past two decades to develop local resources to make the Church free from foreign aid and to maintain our Church, its personnel and evangelistic work. To maintain the institutions we do still need foreign aid. Further, the foreign help is used for social welfare projects irrespective of religion and caste. But there is too much money in the Church and too many people with an easy or no conscience. This leads to corruption at many levels. Qualified young Christians are discouraged to join the church. This is a serious situation...[22]

Elitist Institutions

......These differences and divisions seem to have been reinforced by the institutions the Church has been running during the last 150 years in southern India. Institutions that were started over 100 years ago in order to help the poor and needy have been gradually developed and converted into elitist institutions. Many of the institutions which were started in trust to help the poor have betrayed the trust. They no longer serve the poor and weaker sections of the community. They serve the affluent and richer people and strengthen their exploitative position. Take the case of Christian colleges, convents and other schools that have been started in the last 100 years in all the major cities in India. At present they cater exclusively to the richer classes of the city where they are situated. Eve n the hospitals that were started to help the poor who did not have access to medical service, are more and more devoted to the service of the richer class which alone can pay for their service.[23]

......These institutions have served well to develop an elitist class within the community who have the least interest to serve the poor people. These institutions have served merely as stepping stones for their own advancement and not as a source of service to the poor. It should be possible for us to examine each one of our Christian institutions in India and find that they are wanting in their commitment to the service of the poor for whose benefit alone the Christian institutions should exist and by which measure alone their existence can be justified. Take, for example, the Christian Medical College at Vellore. It is said 40% of the students who came out of its portals are now outside India serving elsewhere, notwithstanding their written undertaking to serve in India. I will be interesting to find out what percentage of these students are from the families of the Church leaders in India.[24]

Royal Splendour of Bishops

......Around the 5th century the Bishop became the sole administrator of the church with all its possessions, property, land and revenues. He came to be looked upon as the spiritual head with temporal powers. In the dark ages the episcopal head came to be regarded as a 'landed magnate'. A.T.M. Parker in his article 'Feudal Episcopacy' contributed to the book *The Apostolic Ministry* edited by K. E. Kirk puts it: 'The Church meant the Bishop. The Bishop was landed proprietor.'

......Towards the end of the 11th century and during the early part of the 12th century we see the struggle between the church and the state. Bishops began to be acutely conscious of the temporal power vested with them, and they often thought themselves to be equals with kings and nobles.[25]

......But a question that naturally arises is–'have we outgrown our dependence on the Western Churches ?' Perhaps 'yes' and perhaps 'no'......[26]

......Several centuries ago the golden ring, the expensive silver staff, the throne, purple robes were symbols attached to and even tied up with temporal power. The Bishop was a friend, guide and a close companion of the emperor or king and as such needed these symbols–the purple robes and the amethyst ring did have significance at a particular period. What do they signify to the Indian church today?[27]

......The very appearance sometimes conveys the impression of a Bishop being a power structure rather than a 'people's man'. Episcopacy in India must be stripped of all pomp, power and prestige.[28]

......We tend to make the church a top-heavy structure, giving more prominence to Bishops, Ecclesiastical leaders, and the clergy. We need to realise that the laity are the real core of the church[29]......

......But now the organizational structure has become such that the leadership of the church has fallen into the hands of a select few–largely comprising of Bishops, Presidents and the Clergy[30]......

......Sometimes our pastors are unable to preach about integrity because it is not practised in their own life[31]......

Scandals

......There is no denying that the church at the local level is the unit of evangelism. But are churches ready? George Verner, a distinguished theologian states: 'The popular notion is that the first duty of the church is to spread the gospel. This is wrong. The first obligation of the church is to be spirituously worthy enough to spread the gospel'. In short the image of the church has to be clean and bereft of blemish if it is to succeed in its evangelistic task.

......Local churches present a disappointing picture today. There is undisguised groupism, casteism, and opportunism. If the Pastor is strong and straightforward, vested interests combine to break him and make his mission and ministry untenable. If he is meek and mild, he is made a nonentity and others thrive at his cost. Either way, he is the loser. If the Pastor is young, energetic and progressive, there is a concerted move by the traditionalists to discredit him and make his ministry ineffective.

......In many churches there is a never ending tussle between the Priest and the Pastorate Committee. In quite a few there is a permanent confrontation between the Pastorate Committee and the Bishops. In a major Christian denomination in India, there are court cases in 21 of the 22 Dioceses making the judiciary wonder as to what are the basic Christian values.[32]

Corruption

......Scandals of major magnitude rock the very foundations of many churches. Mismanagement, maladministration, misuse of funds, neglect of church property and embezzlement are not uncommon. Communal and caste consideration, nepotism and patronage are disgustingly common features in Church administration. In one particular instance, the Church servants were so badly treated, that one of them went to the local Arya Samaj for support and succour. In yet another, one of them went to the local Jana Sangh leader. In one of the major Churches in the nation's capital, election rules were consciously violated to ensure that they got elderly 'yes' men into the Pastorate Committee. In another, the Vicar is so busy finding avenues to spend and account for foreign money received, that he has hardly any time for parish work. In yet another, a deeply entrenched group within the Church has made things so ho for the newly posted young pastor, that he has fled to another parish as a God given relief. There are other instances and innumerable too.

......All this makes disgusting reading, but unfortunately they are true. To make things worse, hostile elements interested in maligning us add on spicy details to these sordid facts and give them the widest publicity. These are matters of serious concern to all of us, particularly, when we plan the onward thrust of the Church.[33]

Groupism and Infighting

......The 20 dioceses in the CSI act as 20 different states under the hegemony of the Synod. There is a scramble for development projects big and small, and for scholarships to go abroad. In every committee, the four distinct regions–Tamil Nadu, Andhra Pradesh, Kerala and Karnataka–fight for representation. At the Synod Working Committee, which is the highest body that runs the affairs of 20 dioceses, the members forget often that they represent the total CSI and no their parochial diocesans and language areas. Fostering trust and confidence among all the dioceses is a herculean task. Dissensions and ill will start over many issues, and dissatisfaction leads to misrepresentation and then to litigation. Large dioceses have been bifurcated not for administrative convenience, but for narrow considerations of prestige, language, grouping, of greed for power and representation. The Synod has a tough time dealing with such problems in spite of the many constitutional safeguards. Sometimes commissions are appointed to go into these matters and rapprochement made. The officers of the Synod call the dissidents and listen to their arduous arguments patiently. In most of the cases, good sense prevails. But, in certain cases, it ends in a cold war that may take the form of non-cooperation, of vicious propaganda or pamphleteering.[34]

Litigation for Property

......For many the Church is the most important secular institution in their lives. In the structures, they seek to affirm their status and prestige in society. Power, foreign experience, allocation of jobs and privileges, handling large sums of money etc., are status-giving privileges. Litigation against the Church is as natural and legitimate as litigation against any secular institution, which has not fulfilled one member's rights, privileges and ambitions. Litigation against the 'sacred' Roman Catholic Church either by the clergy or laity, hardly exists in India. Litigation in the 'secular' Protestant CSI is a plague which threatens to destroy the whole body......[35]

Each diocese is a mini-state, owning vast properties and employing a large number of people. Conflicts over the uses of this temporal power lead to litigation......

In my opinion, the only way to avoid litigation in property matters is to divest the Church of its properties and institutions, and make it devote itself wholly to spiritual matters. This is easier said than done......

The plague of litigation is a sign of deep spiritual malaise. The spirit of gratitude towards the Church as a spiritual mother and the spirit of self-sacrifice for the sake of the Gospel witness appear to be fast dissipating. Nothing less than a spiritual revival is called for. Spiritual character should be the criteria in the selection and training of clergy.[36]

Role of Foreign Money

It is time the Indian Church gave more serious thought to financial independence. There is no doubt that we are what we are financially through the goodness of God, and largely through foreign aid.

Until recently this money was freely flowing in; but all that we had to do was to send an appeal and receive in immediate response. From our standpoint it was 'easy money' and we received it effortlessly and with folded arms, or may be with our arms outstretched. This 'easy money' has not enabled us to realise our responsibility sufficiently...[37]

This sense to absolute dependence on overseas funds has resulted in, what I would like to strongly term, apathy and irresponsibility.

There are still churches in India that expect to pay their pastors from overseas grants......[38]

It is the greatest wrong to pay our pastors from overseas funds......

We have been heavily dependent on overseas support for running, maintenance and building up of many of our institutions......

I often fear that the Christian Church in India is suffering from what may be called a 'poverty complex'[39]......

We are today very dependent on a number of foreign agencies for support towards our poor children and orphans in the rural areas. Many of our boarding schools and orphanages are fully financed and supported by overseas agencies.

We seem to be caught between the horns of a dilemma. We need financial help for the education of the thousands and thousands of our children. At the same time, like power, money can corrupt the Indian Church. Quite often these foreign agencies pour in money and their administrators become demigods. The evils that we see in this unceasing stream of dollars, Dutch marks, pounds etc., need Indian control, absolute honesty and the right and fair distribution of this money. More often than not, there is an improper distribution of resources. People, (clergy and laity) who have not been used to and trained in handling large sums of money fall into the snares of bad accounting, manipulation of funds and swindling of large sums of money[40]......

I am also very unhappy about our children being completely dependent on these foreign grants. Most of our children may not be able to afford their hostel expenses but they must learn to have a share in their hostel and educational expenses[41]......

To me, personally speaking, talking about a moratorium on foreign aid in terms of money is well within our rights and we should perhaps go to the extent of demanding a moratorium on financial aid. I find it difficult to go along with the African Church in asking for a moratorium on missionary personnel. This seem to be un-theological. The very nature of the church is mission, and we will be destroying the mission of the church if there is to be a moratorium on missionary personnel[42]......

To prove our independent and mature existence we should go a step further and have a moratorium on foreign aid for evangelism, for our pastoral and other smaller ministries of the church[43]......

Foreign Money for Social Service

Far from living up to the established traditions, far from highlighting in their methods of work the Christian qualities of compassion, love and selfless service, these Social Action Agencies, fattened by unlimited funds from rich Christian groups from the West, have become cesspools of corruption, maladministration, patronage and incompetence. They seem to look forward to and go in with a flesh whenever there is a national calamity, be it flood, famine or cyclone. On such occasions money comes pouring in. Our agencies do a lot of work, receive and spend a lot of money, and then withdraw from the scene and wait for the next calamity. But it is the backlash that hurts. There are charges of corruption, ineffective and improper implementation of programmes and waste of money and materials. Unfortunately, this is true in many cases. Instead of getting the goodwill of the people and the appreciation of the Government, we at best succeed in arousing their suspicion against us.....

Major Christian Social Action Agencies were involved in relief work in a cyclone devastated area. Lakhs of rupees were spent. The R.S.S. sent a small operation group, spent a fraction of the amount but took many photographs and recorded many statements, most of which condemn all workers of the Christian relief agencies as corrupt, greedy and lacking in tolerance and compassion. In circles that matter, the impression was that the R.S.S., which only used money collected from Indians, did most of the relief work that benefited the people, while Christian agencies, which received huge amounts from foreign Church organisations, swallowed most of it or diverted it for anti-national purposes. There were similar charges in Gujarat, Maharashtra, Andhra, West Bengal and Bihar.

What is more disturbing that no serious effort was made to enquire into these charges and punish the culprits. This hesitancy is something that cannot be satisfactorily explained. Even more intriguing is the fact that we did not even have the courage to refute the allegations. Probably all the charges were true......

On appointments, promotions and project allocations, the methods adopted are scandalous. Since so many and several levels are beneficiaries, all concerned make hay, while the foreign money shines. Nobody, either the secular or the religious officials, are interested in getting things right because it would be like cooking the hen that lays the golden egg. What a sad situation......

Almost all Christian Social Action Agencies get large sums of money from generous Christian donor agencies abroad. The latter do so with the best of intentions. But incompetent management, corrupt practices and lack of Christian motivation have robbed the Christian community of the goodwill that it should have generated from these opportunities. On the contrary, their activities serve as live ammunition to be flung back at us to destroy our credentials as an agency of compassion and honest, selfless service and deep-seated concern for the poor......

There are also scores of petty organisations, often managed by an individual and his family, on a 'dedicated mission' of evangelisation through 'service to the poor'. Gullible Christian agencies abroad pour in a lot of money to such people. To the latter it is a case of rags to riches. But to the community at large, they are additional cases that can be cited against us for unchristian and anti-national activities. The main casualty in these operations is our image. They produce a negative impact and throw us open to justifiable criticism and condemnation. We can hardly defend such groups......

What can we do to set right matters and try and retrieve lost ground and to build up goodwill and acceptance? Let us, at least from now on, try and put a stop to these scandals, be it in C.A.S.A. or C.A.R.E. or the CARITAS or EFICOR or anything else sporting a Christian name. Social Action Agencies should take on themselves the responsibility of refurbishing the Christian image to their former standards of credibility and acceptance[44]......

References

1. E.D. Devadasan: **A Study of Conversion and its Aftermath** (Christian Literature Society, Madras, 1982) P. 53.
2. Ibid, page 54.
3. Ibid, page 55.
4. Ibid, page 55.
5. Ibid, page 58.
6. Mrs. D.L. Gopal Ratnam: "Conflict and Reconciliation In the Church of South India" in *National Christian Council Review:* Vol. CI. No. 9, Sep. 1981 p. 468.
7. Ibid, page 472.
8. Rev. Sundar Clarke: *Let the Indian Church be Indian.* (The Christian Literature Society, Madras 1980) p. 11.
9. Ibid, page 12-13.
10. Ibid, page 13.
11. Ibid, page 14.
12. Ibid, page 14.
13. Ibid, page 15.
14. Frank S. Dewars: *Pilgrimage 2000: Concepts, Contradictions and Concerns* in *National Christian Council Review* Vol. CII. No. 2, February 1982, p. 78.
15. Ibid, page 79.
16. Rev. Sundar Clarke: page 11.
17. Ibid, page 12.
18. Ibid, page 10.
19. Ibid, page 21.
20. Ibid, page 23.
21. Gopal Ratnam: op. cit. p. 473.
22. Ibid, page 473.
23. Devadasan: op. cit. p. 55.
24. Ibid, p. 56.

25. Rev. Sundar Clarke: op. cit. 25.
26. Ibid, p. 26.
27. Ibid, p. 26-27.
28. Ibid, p. 27.
29. Ibid, p. 38-39.
30. Ibid, p. 38.
31. Ibid, p. 32.
32. Frank S. Dewars: op. cit. 78.
33. Ibid, p. 81-82.
34. Gopal Ratnam: op. cit. 469.
35. Ibid, p. 470.
36. Ibid, p. 471.
37. Sundar Clarke: op. cit. 44.
38. Ibid, p. 45.
39. Ibid, p. 46-47.
40. Ibid, p. 48-49.
41. Ibid, p. 50.
42. Ibid, p. 54.
43. Ibid, p. 58.
44. Frank S. Dewars: op. cit. 78-84

Foreign Missionaries and Funds in India

Official statistics presented by the Ministry of Home Affairs (Govt. of India) and cited by late Sh. PRAKASH V1R SHASTRI in Lok Sabha on 19 Feb., 1960.

Number of Foreign Missionaries

1947 (before Independence)	2,200 missionaries
1951	4,377 missionaries
1955	4,877 missionaries
1956	5,391 missionaries
1957	5,521 missionaries

After the Home Ministry put some conditions to regulate their entry, the number fell down in

Jan. 1960 to 4,844 missionaries

Foreign Funds openly received for missionary activities

January 1950 to June 1954	Rs 59.27 Crores
January 1956 to June 1958	Rs 23.92 Crores
July 1958 to December 1958	Rs 4.84 Crores
January 1959 to April 1959	Rs 3.70 Crores
Total (excluding the year 1955)	Rs 61.47 Crores

8

Making of the Muslim Psyche

A. GHOSH

Erudite Scholar and Social Worker

A Sample survey conducted over the past decade to find out how many Hindu intellectuals, irrespective of the regions from where they hail, have a nodding acquaintance with the Koran, the fount of Islam, showed that almost all who were questioned admitted that they had never had an opportunity to peruse it. Even those who are ardent champions of 'All Faiths Unity', of "*Sarva-Dharma-Samabhava*"are found to be delightfully ignorant of the contents of the *Koran*, let alone those of *Hadis* or other components of the *Shariat* complex like *Izma* and *Qiyas*, although they glibly talk about the 'merits' and 'excellence' of Islam. The interest that lala lajpat rai, a foremost leader of the Freedom Movement, evinced in acquainting himself with the contents of the *Koran* and *Hadis* speaks volumes of his spirit of enquiry. The conclusions he arrived at may be gleaned from the famous epistle he wrote to Deshbandhu C.R. Das in 1924 towards the close of the Khilafat Movement:

> "I have devoted most of my time during the last six months to the study of Muslim history and Muslim law and I am inclined to think that Hindu-Muslim

> unity is neither possible nor practicable...... Assuming and admitting the sincerity of the Mohammedan leaders in the Non-Cooperation Movement, I think their religion provides an effective bar to anything of the kind... There is no finer Mohammedan in Hindustan than *Hakim* (Ajmal Khan) *Sahab*, but can any other Muslim leader over-ride the *Koran* ? I can only hope that my reading of Islamic Law is incorrect, and nothing would relieve me more than to be convinced that it is so...... I do honestly and sincerely believe in the necessity or desirability of Hindu-Muslim unity.

"I am also fully prepared to trust the Muslim leaders, but what about the injunctions of the *Koran* and *Hadis* ? The leaders cannot override them......"[1]

Lajpat Rai elaborated this theme in a series of thirteen articles which were published in the *Tribune* in November-December, 1924. He had a hunch that one cannot fathom the depths of Muslim mind unless one has thoroughly studied the *Koran* and *Hadis*.

A famous contemporary of Lalaji belonging to the literary world, sarat chandra chatterjee, also had an occasion to make observations on the problem of Hindu-Muslim unity. He came out with a highly critical and incisive article on the Hindu-Muslim problem in October, 1926. The immediate provocation for this exercise was the widespread riots in the Pabna district of East Bengal where Hindus suffered grievously at the hands of Muslims. In that long article, Chatterjee gave forthright expression to his views on Islam and made a few salient points:

> "If we go by the lessons of history, we have to accept that the goal of Hindu-Muslim unity is a mirage. When Muslims first entered India, they looted the country, destroyed the temples, broke the idols, raped the women and heaped innumerable indignities on the people of this country. Today it appears that such noxious behaviour has entered the bone-marrow of Muslims. Unity can be achieved among equals. In view of the big gap between the cultural levels of Hindus and Muslims which can hardly be bridged, I am of the view that Hindu-Muslim unity which could not be achieved during the last thousand years, will not materialize during the ensuing thousand years. If we are to drive away the English people depending on this elusive capital of Hindu-Muslim unity, I would rather advise its postponement."[2]

Elsewhere in his revealing article, the great litterateur posed the question as to why Muslim leaders never uttered a single word of condemnation when incidents of abduction of Hindu women by Muslim miscreants in various parts of the country came to light. He answered the question himself by saying that Muslim leaders deliberately kept mum because they would have perpetrated the same crime if they had got an opportunity of doing so!

Almost at the same time, the famous poet and thinker Rabindranath tagore came out with his views on the Hindu-Muslim question. His views were translated in an article, 'Through Indian Eyes', in the *Times of India* of April 18, 1924:

> "......another very important factor which, according to the poet, was making it almost impossible for Hindu-Mohammedan unity to become an accomplished fact was that the Mohammedans could not confine their patriotism to any one country...... The poet said that he had very frankly asked many Mohammedans whether, in the event of any Mohammedan power invading India, they would stand side by side with their Hindu neighbours to defend their common land. He could not be satisfied with the reply he got from them. He said that he could definitely state that even such men as Mr. Mohammed Ali had declared that under no circumstances was it permissible for any Mohammedan, whatever his country might be to stand against any other Mohammedan."[4]

In the present article we will follow the cue given by Lala Lajpat Rai and try to throw light on why Muslims all over the world behave the way they do, unraveling in the process the mysteries that underline the making of the Muslim psyche.

The Prophet and the Koran

Professor Joseph Hell in his monograph *Die Kultur der Araber* made a laudable attempt at summing up the revaluation of Arab civilization. While discussing about Mohammad he observed that it was hopeless to expect to understand the development of the Arab people who, through Islam, became the carriers and interpreters of its civilization, without knowing the "teachings" which swayed that civilization, and again, equally hopeless was it to sever those "teachings" from the man who taught them. Mohammad's personality and his message, his message and politics, his politics and the cultural development of his people, are so closely intertwined in the Islamic edifice that they must be considered together in their alternating interplay. Prof. Hell further observed that the life of the prophet, sketched and handed down to us in minute details, seems to be trustworthy only in its main outlines–the rest is the outcome of imaginative piety and pious fiction.

In the present article we shall not concern ourselves with such controversial issues as the nature of Mohammad's prophet-hood **or** the sources of his theology. We shall also steer clear of the assessments of the prophet of Islam as made by h.g. wells in his *Outlines of World History* and by Washington Irving in his *Life of Mahomet.* We are only concerned with those teachings and institutions of the prophet which have a direct or indirect bearing on the making of the Muslim psyche.

In order to have a closer acquaintance with the psyche of a people which has diverse aspects, one has to delve deep into the numerous ramifications of a complex phenomenon. As it is not feasible to undertake such a study within the compass of the present article, we will concentrate mainly on two aspects of the Muslim psyche, viz. (a) attitude of Muslims towards non-Muslims which has a bearing on the current problems confronting our country, and (b) the status of women in the Islamic set-up which will help in throwing light on the social norms that have been evolved by Islam.

The *Koran* is regarded by the Muslims as the infallible word of God, a transcript of a tablet preserved in heaven, revealed to prophet Mohammad by Gabriel. According to Muslim tradition, one night in the month of *Ramzan* in the year 610 A.D., as Mohammad was asleep or in a trance, Gabriel came to him and said: "Recite". He asked "What shall I recite?" The order was repeated three times, until the angel himself said: "Recite in the name of your Lord who created man from a clot of blood. Recite, your Lord is the Most Bountiful one, who by the pen taught man what he did not know." When Mohammad awoke, these words, we are told, seemed to be inscribed upon his heart. The Arabic word *al Quran* means 'the recital". The *Koranic* revelations followed each other at brief intervals and were at first committed to memory by professional rememberancers. During Mohammad's lifetime verses were written on palm-leaves, stones and other materials. Their collection was completed daring the Caliphate of Umar, the Second Caliph, and an authorized version was established during the Caliphate of Usman, his successor (644-656 A.D.). The *Koran* consists of one hundred and fourteen chapters which are called *Surahs* and each chapter is made up of verses called *Ayats*. The *Surahs* are of varying lenghts: *Surah* No. 2 entitled *'Al Baqarah'* (The Cow) consists of as many as two hundred and eighty-six *Ayats* whereas *Surah* No 110 entitled *'Al-Nasr'* is made up of only three *Ayats*. While referring to a particular *Ayat* of a particular *Surah* we shall first indicate the number of the *Surah* and then the *Ayat* number.

Attitude Towards Non-Muslims

We should, however, approach the *Koran* without any preconceived notions and try to find out the extent to which *Koranic* exhortations have been reflected in the behaviour pattern of Muslims in general. A study of the *Koran,* if taken up with this end in view, will turn out to be a fascinating one. The beauty of the *Koran* lies in its clear-cut messages which are concrete in character and refreshingly free from any vagueness which we come across so often in spiritual doctrines of a speculative and abstract nature.

The following *Koranic* observations regarding the fate of unbelievers or non-Muslims are clear and assertive:*

a. "The unbelievers among the People of the Book (Jews and Christians) and the pagans shall burn forever in the fire of Hell. They are the vilest of all creatures" (S. 98:6).

b. "But those that disbelieve our revelations and deny them are the heirs of Hell" (S. 57:19).

c. "When you meet the unbelievers in the battlefield, strike of: their heads and, when you have laid them low, bind your captives firmly. Then grant them their freedom or take ransom from them, until they shall lay down their armour" (S.48:4).

d. "Do not yield to the unbelievers but fight them strenuously with this *Koran*" (S. 25:52).

e. "Mohammad is Allah's apostle. Those who follow him are ruthless to the unbelievers but merciful to one another" (S. 48:29).

f. "When the sacred months are over, slay the idolaters wherever you find them. Arrest them, besiege them and lie in ambush everywhere for them" (S. 9:5).

g. "Make war on them. Allah will chastise them through you and humble them. He will grant you victory over them and heal the spirit of the faithful" (S. 9:14).

h. "Believers, do not befriend your fathers and your brothers if they choose unbelief in preference to faith. Wrong-doers are those that befriend them" (S. 9:23).

i. "Allah has promised the hypocrites, both men and women, and the unbelievers, the fire of Hell. They shall abide in it forever, a sufficient recompense. The curse of Allah is upon them, theirs shall be a lasting torment" (S. 9:68).

j. "Prophet, make war on the unbelievers and the hypocrites and deal rigorously with them. Hell shall be their home-an evil fate" (S. 9:73).

k. "Fight for the sake of Allah those that fight against you.....kill them wherever you find them. Drive them out of the places from which they drove you. Idolatry is worse than carnage" (S. 2:191).

---

* Citation from the Koran have been taken from *Meaning of the Glorious Koran* by Abdullah Yusuf Ali, 2 Volumes, Lahore, 1934.

l. "Believers, do not choose the infidels rather than the faithful for your friends" (S. 4:144).

m. "Believers, take neither Jews nor Christians for your friends. They are friends with one another. Whoever of you seeks their friendship shall become one of their number. Allah does not guide the wrong-doers" (S. 5:51).

n. "Believers, if you yield to the infidels, they will drag you back to unbelief and you will return headlong to perdition... We will put terror into the hearts of the unbelievers. They serve other gods for whom no sanction has been revealed. Hell shall be their home. Dismal indeed is the dwelling-place of the evil-doers"

Punishments for Non-Believers

Let us now switch over to the subject of various modes of punishment to be inflicted on the non-Muslims as per *Koranic* prescriptions.

a. "For the unbelievers We have prepared fetters and chains, and a blazing fire" (S. 76:4).

b. "The wrong-doers shall be known by their looks, they shall be seized by their fore-locks and their feet...They shall wander between fire and water fiercely seething" (S. 65: 41-44).

c. "Flames of fire shall be lashed at you and molten brass. There shall be none to help you" (S. 55: 35).

d. "We have in store for them heavy fetters and a blazing fire, choking food and a harrowing torment" (S. 73: 13-14).

e. "As for the unbelievers, they shall drink boiling water and be sternly punished for their unbelief" (S. 10: 5).

f. "For the wrong-doers, we have prepared a fire which will encompass them like the walls of a pavilion. When they cry out for drink they shall be showered with water as hot as molten brass, which will scald their faces. Evil shall be their drink, dismal their resting-place" (S. 18: 30-32).

g. "Hell lies before them. They shall drink stinking water; they will sip, but scarcely swallow. Death will assail them from every side, yet they shall not die. A dreadful tormet awaits them" (S. 14: 16-17).

h. "Those who have denied the scriptures and the message with which we have sent our apostles shall know the truth hereafter; when with chains and shackles round their necks they shall be dragged through boiling water and burnt in the fire of Hell" (S. 40: 69-74).

i. "But doleful shall be the return of the transgressors. They shall burn in the fire of Hell, a dismal resting-place. There let them taste their drink–scalding water, festering blood and other putrid things" (S. 38: 56-62).

j. "Allah revealed His will to the angels, saying: 'I shall be with you. Give courage to the believers. I shall cast terror into the hearts of the infidels. Strike off their heads, maim them in every limb' " (S. 8:12).

k. "Garments of fire have been prepared for the unbelievers. Scalding water shall be poured upon their heads, melting their skins and that which is in their bellies. They shall be lashed with rods of iron. Whenever, in their anguish, they try to escape from Hell, the angels will drag them back, saying: 'Taste the torment of Hell-fire' " (S. 22: 19-22).

Wine and Women for Believers

As against the eternal hell-fire and the associated torments prescribed for the non-Muslims, the paradise that is promised to the believers i.e. the Muslims is portrayed on the pages of the *Koran* in glowing colours:

a. "But for those that fear the majesty of their Lord there are two gardens planted with shady trees. Each is watered by a flowing spring. Each bears every kind of fruit in pairs. They shall recline on couches lined with thick brocade, and within their reach will hang the fruits of both gardens. They shall dwell with bashful virgins whom neither man nor jinni will have touched before–virgins as fair as corals and rubies. And beside these there shall be two other gardens of darkest green. A gushing fountain shall flow in each. Each planted with fruit trees, the palm and the pomegranate. In each there shall be virgins–chaste and fair, dark-eyed virgins sheltered in their tents whom neither man nor jinni will have touched before. They shall recline on green cushions and rich carpets" (S. 55: 47-77).

b. "As for the righteous, they shall surely triumph. Theirs shall be gardens and vineyards, and high-bosomed maidens for companions–a truly overflowing cup" (S. 78: 31-34)

c. "They shall recline on jewelled couches face to face, and there shall wait on them immortal youths with bowls and ewers and a cup of purest wine (that will neither pain their heads nor take away their reason); with fruits of their own choice and flesh of fowls that they relish. And theirs shall be the dark-eyed houris, chaste as hidden pearls–a guerdon for their deeds" (S. 55: 12-36).

d. "But in fair gardens, the righteous shall dwell in bliss, rejoicing in what their Lord will give them. He will shield them from the scourge of Hell. He will say: 'Eat and drink in joy. This is the reward of your labours.' They shall recline in couches ranged in rows. To dark-eyed houris We shall wed them. Fruits We shall give them and such meats as they desire. They will pass from hand to hand a cup inspiring no idle talk, no sinful urge; and there shall wait on them young boys of their own as fair as virgin pearls" (S. 52: 17-24).

e. "He will reward them for their steadfastness with robes of silk and the delights of Paradise. Reclining there upon soft couches, they shall feel neither the scorching heat nor the biting cold. Trees will spread their shade around them, and fruits will hang in clusters over them. They shall be served with silver dishes, and beakers as large as goblets; silver goblets which they themselves shall measure; cups brimful with ginger-flavoured water from the Fount of Selsabil. They shall be attended by boys, graced with eternal youth, who to the beholder's eyes will seem like sprinkled pearls. When you gaze upon that scene you will behold a kingdom blissful and glorious. They shall be arrayed in garments of fine green silk and rich brocade, and adorned with bracelets of silver. Their Lord shall give them pure beverage to drink" (S. 75: 15-19).

Here is a dream of the other world full of only material comforts such as women, wine and rich food. No trace of spiritual elevation is visible in this salvation.

War Booty

The above extracts from the *Koran* are only illustrative. The *Koran* is replete with almost identically worded descriptions of the Paradise that awaits the Muslims on the Day of Judgment. But what about the enjoyments permitted to the Muslims here on this earth? *Surah* 8 contains instructions regarding division of the spoils of war. After setting apart only one-fifth of the spoils for Allah and his Prophet, the Muslims are free to enjoy the remaining spoils of war which include captive women of conquered territories.

"Enjoy, therefore, the good and lawful things which you have gained in war, and fear Allah" (S. 8: 67).

Position of Women

As regards the position of women vis-a-vis men, the *Koran* is forthright in its declarations on the subject:

a. "Women shall with justice have rights similar to those exercised against them, although men have a status above women" (S. 2: 228).

b. "Women are your fields: go, then, into your fields as you please" (S. 2: 223).

c. "Men have authority over women because Allah has made the one superior to the other, and because they spend their wealth to maintain them. Good women are obedient. They guard their unseen parts because Allah has guarded them. As for those from whom you fear disobedience, admonish them and send them to beds apart and beat them" (S. 4: 34).

d. "If any of your women commit fornication, call in four witnesses from among yourselves against them; if they testify to their guilt confine them to their houses till death overtakes them" (S. 4: 15).

While the *Koran* permits a Muslim male to divorce his wife by simply pronouncing the word *'Talaq'* thrice, no such right has been granted to a Muslim woman. As against the beating and killing (under certain circumstances) of wives permitted by the *Koran*, male offenders are let off rather leniently.

As compared to Muslim women, the fate of non-Muslim women belonging to conquered territories is much worse. Irrespective of whether they are married or unmarried, non-Muslim women who are invariably treated as slave girls are permitted by the *Koran* to be sexually enjoyed by the Muslims in an indiscriminate manner. This licence has been granted to all Muslims right from the prophet downwards. While listing out the categories of women whom a Muslim cannot marry, the *Koran* adds:

> "And all married women are forbidden unto you except those captives whom your right hands possess (i.e. whom you own as slaves)" (S. 4: 24).

Brainwashing and Regimentation

A careful perusal of the tenets of the *Koran* will reveal that a systematic attempt has been made to brainwash the Muslims by making repeated exhortations to obey Allah as portrayed by his Prophet and illustrating the horrors of Hell and the sensual pleasures of Paradise. The official prayer or common prayer is as old as Islam itself. It acquired a special force and significance among Muslims. The wish to correctly carry out the prescribed prostration and bending of the body led by itself to the joint prayer being performed according to a model and under a leader–Mohammad himself mostly leading the prayer. The importance of this form of prayer in awakening and maintaining a spirit of discipline cannot be over-emphasised. The prayer-ground has very justly been described as the first drill-ground of Islam. While accounting for the success of the armed bands fighting under the leadership of Mohammad, Prof. Joseph Hell has observed:

> "The new religion had equipped the quondam Mekkans with qualities unknown to the Arabs: discipline and contempt for death. Mohammad had inculcated discipline by repeated references to it in the revelations of the time. 'Obey God and His Prophet.' This was the refrain of many a Surah. The call for discipline

was further reinforced, improved and perfected by the practice of public prayers. Contempt for death, on the other hand, was born out of the enticing prospects of Paradise which temptingly dangled before those who fell fighting for the faith."

Islamic State: Theory and Practice

How the concept of an Islamic State was moulded by the ideology embodied in the *Koran* was explained by the eminent historian, sir jadunath sarkar, as a result of his lifelong study of the nature and origins of the Islamic State in India:

"By the theory of its origin the Muslim State is a theocracy. Its true king is Allah, and earthly rulers are merely his agents, bound to enforce his law on all. Civil Law is completely subordinated to Religious Law and, indeed, merges its existence in the latter. The civil authorities exist solely to spread and enforce the true faith. In such a State, infidelity is logically equivalent to treason, because the infidel repudiates the authority of the true king and pays homage to his rivals, the false gods and goddesses. All the resources of the State, all the forces under the political authorities are, in strict legality, at the disposal of the missionary propaganda of the true faith... Islamic theology tells the true believer that his highest duty is to make 'exertion *(Jehad)* in the path of God' by waging war against infidel lands (*Dar-ul-harb*) till they become a part of the realm of Islam *(Dar-ul-Islam)* and their populations are converted into true believers. After conquest the entire infidel population becomes theoretically reduced to the status of slaves of the conquering army. The men taken with arras are to be slain or sold into slavery and their wives and children reduced to servitude. As for the non-combatants among the vanquished, if they are not massacred outright–as the Canon lawyer Shaft declares to be the *Koranic* injunction–it is only to give them a respite till they are so wisely guided as to accept the true faith.

"The conversion of the entire population to Islam and the extinction of every form of dissent is the ideal of the Muslim State...A non-Muslim, therefore, cannot be a citizen of the State ; he is a member of a depressed class; his status is a modified form of slavery. He lives under a contract (*zimma)* with the State: for the life and property that are grudgingly spared to him by the Commander of the Faithful he must undergo political and social disabilities, and pay commutation money *(jazia)*... No non-Muslim *(zimmi)* can wear fine dresses, ride on horseback or carry arms; he must behave respectfully and submissively to every member of the dominant sect......"[3]

To illustrate how this theory was put into actual practice, Sir J.N. Sarkar says:

"The history of the world under Muslim rule illustrates how theology has repeatedly prevailed over political wisdom...The demolition of the chief temple in the captured city and the erection of a mosque on its site was an invariable incident of Muslim conquest. But there was at first no wanton or systematic iconoclasm. With the growth of the Muslim population, the long enjoyment of unchallenged power bred in them a spirit of intolerance and a love of persecution. Every device short of massacre in cold blood was resorted to in order to convert heathen subjects.....Rewards in the form of money and public employment were offered to apostates from Hinduism. The leaders of Hindu religion and society were systematically repressed, to deprive the sect of spiritual instruction, and their religious gatherings and processions were forbidden in order to prevent the growth of solidarity and a sense of communal strength among them. No new temple was allowed to be built no any old one to be repaired, so that the total disappearance of all places of Hindu worship was to be merely a question of time...The destruction of temples and the slaughter of Hindus sanctified every war of aggression. Thus a frame of mind was produced in the Muslim community which habitually regarded plunder and homicide as the purest of human acts, as 'exertion in the path of God'. The murder of infidels *(Kafir-Kushi)* is counted a merit in a Muslim. **It is not necessary that he should tame his own passions or mortify his flesh; it is not necessary for him to strive for a rich growth of spirituality. He has only to slay a certain class of his fellow-beings or plunder their lands and wealth, and this act in itself would raise his soul to heaven. A religion whose followers are taught to regard robbery and murder as a religious duty, is incompatible with the progress of mankind or with the peace of the world.**

"Nor has it been conducive to the true interests of its followers. Muslim polity formed 'the faithful' into a body with no other profession than war. As long as there were any fresh lands to conquer and any rich *kafirs* to plunder, all went well with the State. The dominant body prospered and multiplied rapidly: even arts and industries, literature and painting of a certain type were fostered. But when the tide of Muslim expansion reached its farthest limit and broke in vain on the hills of Assam and Chatgaon, or the arid rocks or Maharashtra, there was nothing to avert a downfall. The state had no economic basis, and was not able to stand a time of peace. Repose was fatal not only to its growth but to its very life."[4]

Sir Jadunath Sarkar gave his assessment of the Muslim psyche in die light of events in medieval history. His characterisation of an Islamic State was borne out by an incident which took place in Egypt in 1910. When Butros Pasha was murdered in 1910 by an Egyptian Mohammedan for no personal provocation but for the political reason that he had presided over the court that sentenced the Denshawai villagers, and the guilt of the murder was conclusively proved by evidence, the Chief Qazi of Egypt pronounced his judgment that according to Islam it is no crime for a Muslim to slay an unbeliever. Such is the opinion held by the highest exponent of Islamic law in a modern civilized country!

H. KYSERLING, a widely travelled and profound modern philosopher writes in his *Indian Travel Diary of A Philosopher*: "Islam is a religion of absolute surrender and submissiveness to God–but to a God of a certain character–a Warlord who is entitled to do with us as he wills and who bids us to stand ever in line of battle against the foe. The ritual of this belief embodies the idea of discipline. When the true believers every day at fixed hours performs their prayers in serried rank in the mosque, all going through the same gestures at the same moment, this is not, as in Hinduism, done as a method of self-realization, but in the spirit in which the Prussian soldier defiled before his Kaiser. This military basis of Islam explains all the essential virtues of the Musalman. It also explains his fundamental defects, his unprogressiveness, his incapacity to adapt himself, his lack of invention. The soldier has simply to obey orders. All the rest is the affair of Allah."[5]

Intolerance

As to intolerance towards other religions, Islam is the only religion in the world which teaches that converts can be won at the point of a sword (S 47:4). In his article entitled *The Dead Hand of Islam,* which was published in an American journal, Collin Maine of Australia has observed:

"The intolerance of Islam towards polytheism (the worship of more than one god) has drowned the world in blood.[6] This was particularly the case in India. When Moslems got to India they attacked the Hindus, killed them, and destroyed their temples and images. In Kanauj alone 10,000 temples were destroyed and 50,000 Hindus were killed.[7] The Hindus got on with each other quite well. There has been very little conflict between the various sects of that religion. As far as they are concerned a man can worship anything he wants, or nothing at all. Hinduism is every tolerant in the matter of religion.[8]

"Reports are coming in from all over the world–India, Indonesia, Iran, Lebanon, Cyprus, the Philippines, North Africa–of Moslems fighting each other, as well as with the members of other religions. One does not read of Buddhists, Jains, Parsees fighting with members of other religions. It is always the Moslems who are involved in religious conflicts everywhere except in Northern Ireland where the Protestants and Catholics are fighting each other. One can only conclude that there is *something* about this religion that causes this to happen. It is perhaps the 'Holy' book of Islam, the *Koran*, that incites its followers to attack and kill those who belong to other faiths."[9]

While speaking on the subject of "Practical Vedanta" in London on 18th November, 1896, Swami Vivekananda had said:

> "The more selfish a man, the more immoral he is. And so also with the race. The race which is bound down to itself, has been the most cruel and the most wicked in the whole world. There has not been a religion that has clung to this dualism more than that founded by the Prophet of Arabia, and there has not been a religion which has shed so much blood and been so cruel to other men. In the *Koran* there is the doctrine that a man who does not believe these teachings should be killed; it is a mercy to kill him. And the surest way to go to heaven where there are beautiful houries, and all sorts of sense enjoyments, is by killing these unbelievers. Think of the bloodshed there has been in consequence of such beliefs!"[10]

Apostasy in Islam

So far we have tried to study the psyche which conditions the Muslim attitude towards non-Muslims. But it will be equally interesting to know the Muslim attitude towards a Muslim who, for whatever reason, desires to get out of the fold of Islam and follow some other path of worship, in other words, a Muslim apostate. How is it that we find so few converts from Islam in the world? S.M. Zwemer, who made an intensive study of this problem, writes from Cairo in the preface of this book that "Among the laws that regulate the relation between the Muslim community and those who wish to leave it and join some other faith, is the law of apostasy."[11] According to the *Hedaya,* the *Hanafi* law, "An apostate is to be imprisoned for three days within which time, if he returns to the faith, it is well; but if not, he must be slain......"[12]

There are, in fact, different versions on whether or not some time (three days) be given to an apostate for consideration. An apostate is termed as an 'infidel enemy', who is neither 'protected' nor a *Zimmi*'. If an apostate dies or is slain, his property acquired during his profession of the faith (Islam) goes to his heirs who are Musalmans and that acquired during apostasy goes to the Muslim community, that is, the public treasury. In strict law, a convert from Islam cannot be allowed to exist at all. He is put to death and his property looted.

In India we know the case of the great educationist and nationalist leader, Swami Shraddhananda, who was one of the leaders of the Non- Cooperation Movement launched by Mahatma Gandhi in 1920 in support of Khilafat and "who had won the confidence and esteem of the Musalmans by his bold and courageous action to such an extent that they invited him to deliver an address at the Jama Masjid of Delhi." While in jail he was very much shocked and pained to know the brutalities perpetrated during Mopla riots in Malabar and forcible conversion of helpless Hindus by the Muslims. After his release, he started the Shuddhi movement for reconversions to Hindu fold. But the Muslims would not tolerate it. Swamiji started receiving letters of threat to his life. Finally on 23 rd December, 1926, at 4 p.m., while the ailing old *Sanyasi* was convalescing on his bed at his residence in Delhi, a Muslim young man, Abdul Rasheed, under the pretext of a religious discussion on Islam, sought an interview with Swamiji, who, much against the advice of his loyal servant, granted it. But under pretense of wanting water to quench his thirst, the guest had Swamiji's faithful servant sent out. Then he pulled out his six-chambered revolver, fired four shots and assassinated the great *Swami* in the name of religion.[13] This cowardly and coldblooded assassination sent waves of shock throughout the country. Top leaders including Mahatma Gandhi were stunned. A great Gandhian, Dr. Rajendra Prashad, is on record:

> "...it is difficult to understand how Christians and Musalmans can object to it (Shuddhi Movement) on merits. They are constantly engaged in their proselytizing mission and in converting Hindus to their own faiths. If the Hindus on their side also start converting non-Hindus to their faith, it is no business of non-Hindus to object–especially if they are themselves engaged in the work of conversion. The Hindus have the same right of propagating their faith as others have. But men are not always guided by logic or by a sense of justice and fairness. And there was much bitterness among Musalmans against the Shuddhi Movement and against Swami Shraddhanand personally, as a result of which he fell a victim to a Muslim assassin some time later. Musalmans on their own side started the Tabligh and Tanzim movements."[14]

In the later fifties, a revealing conversation took place between an erudite Muslim headmaster of a school in East Pakistan and his Hindu friend, a reputed author of popular books. While speaking on the subject of Islam, the Muslim headmaster expressed his anguish and pain that he was compelled to bear the stigma of Islam which is nothing but a convenient code of conduct for a group of freebooters given to indulging in their vilest passions. "Islam is hardly a religion. But once a person has entered the fold of Islam it is extremely difficult for him to get away from its clutches. For one thing, Islam gives an enormous sexual advantage to the Muslim males vis-a-vis Muslim females and, secondly, the fear of the sword is always there as Islam secures most of its converts at the point of the sword. The attraction of sex-enjoyment and the deterrent of the sword jointly operate to block the exit from the camp of Islam. It requires exemplary courage to surmount these two obstacles and this is lacking in most of the Muslims." The learned headmaster speculated that he might have made an attempt to get away from Islam, the obvious risks notwithstanding, had he come to know about the real character of Islam at a young age. But by the time he did learn the truth about Islam, he had already become middle-aged and acquired a family with the result that the Taking of a risk was ruled out completely at this stage of his life and he would have to suffer silently the indignity of staying Muslim for the rest of his life. The Hindu friend, who was completely taken aback at this disclosure, asked him how many Muslims shared tins view of Islam. The headmaster replied that the number of such Muslims might not be very large for many of them had developed a vested interest in Islam because of the material advantages it offered, but the number of such dissenting Muslims was not small either.[15]

John Laffin, the famous author of *Arab Mind,* recounting a recent experience, writes:

> "Even Egypt, with the most cosmopolitan capital in the Muslim world, has recently re-introduced the Shari'a laws, including the death penalty for any Muslim-Egyptian guilty of apostasy–renouncing his religion. When I was in Egypt in 1973, upper-class Cairenes were talking of the recent murders of a Christian priest and two Muslims he had converted. No action was taken to find the killers."[16]

So here is a psyche for which logic and conscience have no meaning, which converts others by force and which prevents apostasy by force.

References

1. Ram Gopal, *Indian Muslims: A Political History,* Bombay, 1964.
2. Ibid., p. 164.
3. Jadunath Sarkar, *History of Aurangzib, Vol.* **III,** New Delhi, 1972, p. 163.
4. Ibid., p. 166.
5. *Indian Travel Diary of* a *Philospher,* Bombay, 1959, pp. 102-103.
6. *The Rise of Islam,* A. Bullock, London, 1965.
7. *A Short History of India,* S. Wolpert.
8. *The Truth Seeker,* San Diego, California, U.S.A., March and April, 1982.
9. Ibid, April, 1982.
10. *The Complete Works of Swami Vivekanand,* 1924, Vol. II, pp. 350-51.
11. S.M. Zwemer, *The Law of Apostasy in Islam,* New Delhi, 1975, p. 8.
12. Charles Hamilton, *Hadaya (or Guide): A Commentary on the Musalmans laws,* Vol. II, p. 225.
13. M. R. Jambunathan, *Swami Shraddhananda,* Bombay, 1961, pp. 163-64.
14. Rajendra Prashad, *India Divided,* Bombay, 1946, p. 117.

15. Paribrajak Asliok, ***Marush,may be this word is not correct*** *Musalman O Marxbadi* (Bengali), Brahmachari Shankar Krishna, Shakti Ashram, Calcutta.

16. *The Dagger of Islam,* Sphere, London, 1981, p. 50.

9

Separatism Rooted in Muslim Psyche

LALA LAJPAT RAI

[Lala Lajpat Rai, was extremely shocked and pained by the reports about Moplah riots in Malabar and bloody carnage in many cities of north India from Kohat to Kanpur as an aftermath of the Khilafat agitation of 1920, to which Hindus had given their whole-hearted cooperation under the leadership of Mahatma Gandhi. He decided to delve deeply into the making of Muslim mind in India and devoted many months to an in-depth study of the sources of Islam as well as to the history of Islam since its birth. He presented this study to the world through a series of thirteen articles published in the **Tribune** and other papers in the months of November-December, 1924. The following excerpts have been culled from these articles, which have been included in the *Writings* **and Speeches of** *Lala Lajpat Rai* Vol II, (1920-1928) edited by V.C. Joshi and published by University Publishers New Delhi (1966) —**Ed]**.

Unlike Hinduism, Islam is a faith of dogmas and doctrines. Every Muhammadan must believe not only in the existence of God without a second (La Allah Il Allah) but also that Muhammad was His prophet and that the *Quran* is his final word. He must also believe, according to the orthodox school, that Muhammad was the last of the prophets and whatever he said and did is binding on all his faithful followers. There have been expounders of Islam who have tried to raise it to a kind of high occultism, but their efforts have not met with any considerable success, and Islam remains, to all intents and purposes, with the majority of its followers, what it has been all through centuries past. My Muslim friends will pardon me if I venture to say that too great an insistence on dogma has been the bane of Islam, the cause of its political downfall, and that unless it is given up, it will stand in the way of Islam ever regaining its lost position as a world-wide political factor. Islam is as much divided and subdivided into sections and factions as Christianity once was and perhaps to this day is.

The division and subdivision of Hindu society into sects have one redeeming feature. The general tolerance of Hinduism prevents them from destroying each other. History shows that this cannot be said of Islam.

Intolerance

Religious intolerance of the severest kind has been a handmaid of chivalry, bravery, zeal, learning and piety among the Muslims throughout Muslim history. Three out of the four first *Khalifas* were murdered by their fellow Muslims. The pages of Muslim history are full of similar acts done by religious zealots or political adventurers. One would have thought that recent events in Turkey and Egypt would have chastened Islam at least in this respect. But the stoning to death of an Ahmadia by the orders of the Government of Kabul and the approval of that barbarous act by some of the most prominent and educated leaders of Muslim India have shown that the canker is still there and has not lost an iota of its original violence...

It is a sign of the times that while Mussalman's piety finds such eloquent expression in its fights with Hinduism, it is dumb and powerless in the presence of leaders who openly defy, by acts of omission and commission, the most sacred canons of Islamic Law.[1]

Who is a Kafir?

There was a time when in the eyes of the Muslims all Hindus were *Kafirs* and it was implicitly believed that the property and the women of a *Kafir* were legal prizes of war for a Muslim. The times are changed and with it the conception of a *Kafir* must be changed. No Hindu who believes in and worships one God, can by any stretch of language be called a *Kafir* unless the definition of a *Kafir* be that every non-Muslim is a *Kafir*. In the eyes of a large number of Muslims the latter is the right definition of a *Kafir* and according to *Ulemas* even those Muslims are *Kafirs* who, although believing in Allah and His prophet, do not follow other tenets of Islam as understood and interpreted by them. For example, they pronounced Sir Syed Ahmad to be a *Kafir* and they denounce the followers of Mirza of Qadian also as *Kafirs*. If they are right, then H. H. the Aga Khan is the biggest *Kafir* and so are Ghazi Mustafa Kamal Pasha and Zaghlul Pasha also. If, then, their definition of a *Kafir* is right, there can be no peace between them and the rest of the world. In that case all this talk of Hindu-Muslim unity is superficial, absurd and hypocritical. In the course of the non-cooperation campaign, some of the Ulemas cited particular "*ayats*" (sections) of the *Quran* to prove that Muslims could enter into lawful agreement with such non-Muslims as were friendly towards them, against those who were inimically disposed towards them, brought fire and sword into the homes of the latter and otherwise injured them. Now to be frank, this kind of special pleading does not appeal to my intellect. It is not a mechanical union of this kind that will make a nation of us. What is needed is a chemical union. Are the Hindus *Kafirs* ? If they are, all talk of unity between Hindus and Mussalmans is absurd.[2]

An esteemed Muslim leader has propounded the theory that the fact that the Hindus are rich and Muslims are poor, explains these riots. Assuming the explanation to be correct, how does he explain the irrefutable fact that poor Mussalmans do not loot their rich fellow religionists? The real explanation is that the latter are Muslims and the Hindus are *Kafirs*. This notion has been rubbed into the mind of the Muslim masses and Muslim middle classes, by clever propagandists and influential leaders. It is the duty of the Muslim nationalist leaders to impress on the minds of their co-religionists the truth that Hindus are not *Kafirs* and that even on the occasion of fights and quarrels, their temples, their women and their property are inviolable and unassailable.[8]

Darul-Harab & Pan-Islamism

Add to this the *Fatwa* of the Ulemas that India being a "*Darul-Harab*" (a place of war) every good Muslim ought to leave it and migrate to a Muslim country. We know by this time how the Hijrat movement ended; how much money was wasted over it and how much misery was wrought thereby. The best commentary on it was witnessed by me at Constantinople. On the third or fourth day of my stay there, I met two young Indian Muslims walking in the street. They accosted me first. When I asked them how they fared in Constantinople, one of them burst out almost in tears and said that if he ever returned to India, he would give out a bit of his mind to tell his Muslim countrymen how mischievous was the teaching that India was "*Darul-Harab*" and how false the idea that the whole world was the home of the Muslims. The boy was one of the *Mahajarins* of 1921. He had travelled all over Muslim Asia from Afghanistan through Turkistan to Russia and then back to Angora and Constantinople. His experience was so bitter and his condition was so pitiable that he denounced Pan-Islamism in rather strong terms.[4]

I am afraid Indian Muslims are more Pan-Islamic and exclusive than the Muslims of any other country on the face of the globe, and that fact alone makes the creation of a united India more difficult than would otherwise be the case. I am inclined to think that in this respect, at least, Sir Syed's policy was sounder than that of the Khilafatists. He did not believe in a religious khilafat. He did not accept the Sultan of Turkey as a *Khalifa* and he was opposed to the Muslims of India devoting much attention to the affairs of Turkey or other Muslim countries.[5]

The Muslim movement is also intended to keep the Pan-Islamic movement going. One cannot help noticing, and noticing with regret, that while the Muslims do not open their purses for the relief of Indian sufferers from famine, floods, earthquakes etc., and that while very little Muslim money is spent to improve the educational and economic condition of Indian Muslims, thousands and lakhs are sent abroad under one name or other. The phenomenon is confined to India. One finds no evidence of it in other Muslim nations like Egypt, Turkey, Morocco, Sudan, Syria etc.[6]

Hindus cannot be anything but Indians. They have no other country and no other nation to look to. They cannot, therefore, be accused of any kind of Pan-Hinduism, in the sense in which the term is used in relation to Islam. Hinduism and Indianism are, in their case, synonymous terms.[7]

Origin of Separate Electorates

Sir Syed's attitude towards the Indian National Congress was influenced by the following considerations:

a. That in India the Hindus were in a majority, and if a form of democratic Government was accepted as the political goal of India, the Muslims were bound to be in a minority.

b. That the Hindus were both economically and educationally more advanced than the Muslims, and would monopolise much of Government influence for a long time to come.

c. That a Hindu Raj might possibly mean the death of Islam in India, or at least a position of subservience for it.

I am inclined to think that he did not believe in the possibility of another Mussalman domination in India either with or without the help of foreign Muslim states and he, therefore, favoured the idea of perpetual British rule in this country.[8]

Communal representation by itself is a sufficiently bad principle destructive of, and antagonistic to, the idea of a common nationhood, but separate electorates make this vicious principle immeasurably worse. It our Muslim countrymen are really earnest in their belief in nationalism and in their demand for Swaraj, the least they can do is not to insist on separate electorates.[9]

A Prophecy Indeed!

Maulana Hasrat Mohani has recently said that the Muslims will never agree to India's having Dominion status under the British. What they aim at are separate Muslim States in India, united with Hindu States under a National Federal Government. He is also in favour of mailer States containing compact Hindu and Muslim populations. If communal representation with separate electorates is to be the rule, then Maulana Hasrat's scheme as to smaller provinces seems to be the only workable proposition. Under my scheme the Muslims will have four Muslim States: (1) The Pathan Province or the North-West Frontier, (2) Western Punjab, (3) Sindh, and (4) Eastern Bengal. If there are compact Muslim communities in any other part of India, sufficiently large to form a province, they should be similarly constituted. But it should be distinctly understood that this is not a united India. *It means a clear partition of India into a Muslim India and a non-Muslim India.*[10]

There are men who assure us that this is a passing phase, that Hindus and Mussalmans can be made to and will eventually forget what has happened at Multan, Saharanpur, Delhi, Allahabad, Lucknow, Shahjahanpur, Lahore, Amritsar, Amethi, Sambhal, Gulbarga and Kohat, that they will not only shake hands but embrace each other in love and fraternity, as soon as Englishmen will have left us, and that therefore, all that is wanted at present is a union which will result in the expulsion of foreigner. They do not tell us, however, how, in face of the prevailing distrust, this union is to be brought about, how the foreigner is to be expelled and lastly how the expulsion of the foreigner, even if it was practicable, would, by itself, solve the problem of Hindu-Muslim differences. Is it the foreigner that loots and desecrates temples and mosques? Is it he that kills people and burns property? Is it his hand that strikes children and women or dishonours the latter? No, they say, the hands are those of the Indians, but the brains are of foreigners.[11]

References

1. Page 220
2. Pages 226-27
3. Page 228
4. Page 238
5. Page 238
6. Page 248
7. Page 241-42
8. Page 242-43
9. Page 250
10. Page 252
11. Page 259-60

Achievements of Islam in the Twentieth Century

'Within Islam, the 'dagger'–in the form of machine gun, bomb and hangman's rope–is well bloodied. Men–and sometimes women–are struck down with a frequency and ferocity which is only dimly perceived in the Western world. Assassination is an accepted means of political expression. Between 1948 and 1979, 25 heads of state and prime ministers were murdered and another 20 ex-prime ministers or senior ex-ministers. One was killed in London. Numerous unsuccessful murder attempts were made on the lives of other leaders–including fourteen known attempts to kill King Hussein of Jordan. In the same 30-year period there were 22 inter-Muslim wars and civil wars and on 32 occasions between 1958 and 1979 Muslim states broke off relations with other Muslim states–apart from the mass Arab repudiation of Egypt in 1979. During the years 1968-79, twenty six foreign, mostly Western, diplomats were assassinated Muslim in countries. That Islam's dagger will be used and used again is not just a matter of speculation, the Lebanese War of 1975-76 alone proves that. Some other massacres are horrifying in their immensity. For instance, in March 1970 about 30,000 members of the El Ansar religious sect were killed in Aba Island in the Nile by the Sudanese army.'

Report by Radio Amman, January 12, 1971. Egyptian estimates put the figure at 'several thousand',

John Laffin

The Dagger of Islam, Sphere Books Limited, London, 1981. (p. 158-159)

Christianity versus Islam in Africa

ALASTAIR MATHESON

NAIROBI, Jan 13,1983 – Despite huge sums of money spent by oil rich Arabs on trying to convert Africans to Islam, Christianity still holds the lead.

The Rev. David Barrett, an Anglican missionary based in Kenya who has devoted more than 10 years to compiling comparative statistics of religions throughout the world for his World Christian Encyclopedia, puts the number of Christians throughout Africa in 1980 at 203 million compared with 189 million Muslims.

At the turn of the century fewer than 10 million African Christians existed (compared to 34 million Muslims), but in 1970 the two religions had about 140 million followers each.

However, the Christians' lead is likely to be challenged soon by Islam's new aggressive tactics. Chief among Islamic organisations dedicated to spreading the *Koran* further afield is the International Congress on Propagating Islam (I.C.P.I.)

At a recent meeting in Khartoum, the I.C.P.I. laid down guidelines aimed at an Islamic revival and recommended ways to resist the "cultural invasion" from the West. After dismissing radical calls for Christian missionary work to be sabotaged, the Congress voted to set up new Islamic style missionaries. Cairo's prestigious Al Azhar University was chosen to be the centre for the I.C.P.I.'s Islamic revival.

Islam's most likely recruiting ground is believed to be the semi-arid strip south of the Sahara Desert, stretching all the way across Africa from Senegal to the southern Sudan where most of the population are pagans. Ironically it is the very same part of Africa where the Christian missionaries see most of their potential converts.

Father Barrett describes the situation of Christian missionaries in the southern Sudan today as "balanced on a knife-edge." Because of pressure from fundamentalist Muslims, the Khartoum Government is making life harder for Christian missionary workers ; many complain of long delays in getting visas to work in the south, and some organisations deliberately play down their Christian affiliations to be able to remain and work among tribes such as the Dinka, Shilluk and Nuer. In Somalia, an openly Islamic State, Christian missionaries can only work where tie re are expatriate groups they can minister to. In religiously tolerant Nigeria, riots and even massacres are frequent, usually on the grounds that Christians are making too much headway, or that the Islamic leaders are straying too far from the *Koran*.

– By arrangement with *The Observer*, London.

Published in the *Tribune*, Chandigarh (January 14, 1983).

10

Social Reality in Islam

DR. B.R. AMBEDKAR

[The following excerpts are culled from Dr. Baba Saheb (B.R.) Ambedkar's monumental work **Pakistan or the Partition of India** (Bombay, 1945). They give us a glimpse of the insights which Baba Sahab, a great intellectual and social reformer of our country, had into the character of Islam, as he saw it–**Ed].**

One may well ask if there is any social evil which is found among the Hindus and is not found among the Muslims?

Take child marriage. The secretary of the Anti-Child Marriage Committee, constituted by the All-India Women's Conference, published a bulletin which gives the extent of evil of child marriage in the different communities in the country. The figures which were taken from the Census Report of 1931 are as follows:

TABLE: Married Females aged 0–15 per 1000 Females of that age

	Hindus	Muslims	Jains	Sikhs	Christians
1881	208	153	189	170	33
1891	193	141	172	143	37

	Hindus	Muslims	Jains	Sikhs	Christians
1901	186	131	164	101	38
1911	184	123	130	88	39
1921	170	111	117	72	32
1931	199	186	125	80	43

Can the position among the Musalmans so far as child marriage goes, be considered better than the position among the Hindus? (p. 215)

Caste System

Take the caste system. Islam speaks of brotherhood. Everybody infers that Islam must be free from slavery and caste. Regarding slavery nothing needs to be said. It stands abolished now by law. But while it existed, much of its support was derived from Islam and Islamic countries. While the prescriptions by the prophet regarding the just and humane treatment of slaves contained in the *Koran* are praiseworthy, there is nothing, whatsoever, in Islam that lends to the abolition of this curse. As Sir W. Muir has well said*:

"...rather, while lightening, he rivetted the fetter... There is no obligation on a Moslem to release his slaves..."

But if slavery has gone, caste among Musalmans has remained. As an illustration one may take the conditions prevalent among the Bengal Muslims. The Superintendent of the Census for 1901 for the Province of Bengal records the following interesting facts regarding the Muslims of Bengal:

"The conventional division of the Mahomedans into four tribes–Sheikh, Saiyad, Moghul and Pathan–has very little application to this province (Bengal). The Mahomedans themselves recognize two main social divisions, (1) Ashraf or Sharaf and (2) Ajlaf. Ashraf means 'noble' and includes all undoubted descendants of foreigners and converts from high caste Hindus. All other Mahomedans including the occupational groups and all converts of lower ranks, are known by the contemptuous terms, 'Ajlaf', "wretches" or "mean people": they are also called Kamina or Itar, 'base' or Rasil, a corruption of Rizal, 'worthless'. In some places a third class, called Arzal or 'lowest of all, is added. With them no other Mahomedan would associate, and they are forbidden to enter the mosque or to use the public burial ground.

"Within these groups there are castes with social precede ice of exactly the same nature as one finds among the Hindus.

* *The Coran, Its Composition and Teaching*, p. 58

I. *Ashraf*–or better class Mahomedans.

1. Saiyads
2. Sheikhs
3. Pathans
4. Moghul
5. Mallik
6. Mirza

II. *Ajlaf* or lower class Mohamedans.

1. Cultivating Sheikhs and others who were originally Hindus but who do not belong to any functional group, and have not gained admittance to the Ashraf community e.g. Pirali and Thakrai.
2. Darzi, Jolaha, Fakir, and Rangrez.
3. Barhi, Bhathiara, Chik, Churihar, Dai, Dhawa, Dhunia, Gaddi, Kalal, Kasai, Kula Kunjara, Laheri, Mahifarosh, Mallah, Naliya, Nikari.
4. Abdal, Bako, Bediya, Bhat, Chamba, Dafali, Dhobi, Hajjam, Mucho, Nagarchi, Nat, Panwaria, Madaria, Tuntia.

III. *Arzal* or degraded class.

Bhanar, Halalkhor, Hijra, Kasbi, Lalbegi, Maugta, Mehtar."

The Census Superintendent mentions another feature of the Muslim social system, namely, the prevalence of the "panchayat system." He states:

> "The authority of the panchayat extends to social as well as trade matters and...marriage with people of other communities is one of the offences of which the governing body takes cognizance. The result is that these groups are often as strictly endogamous as the Hindu castes. The prohibition on inter-marriage extends to higher as well as to lower castes, and a Dhuma, for example, may marry no one but a Dhuma. If this rule is transgressed, the offender is at once hauled up before the panchayat and ejected ignominiously from his community. A member of one such group cannot ordinarily gain admission to another, and he retains the designation of the community in which he was born even if he abandons its distinctive occupation and takes to other means of livelihood...thousands of Jolahas are butchers, yet they are still known as Jolahas."

Similar facts from other provinces of India could be gathered from their respective Census Reports and those who are curious may refer to them. But the facts for Bengal are enough to show that the Mahomedans observe not only caste *but also untouchability. (p. 218-220)*

Position of Women

There can thus be no manner of doubt that the Muslim society in India is afflicted by the same social evils as afflict the Hindu society. Indeed, the Muslims have all the social evils of the Hindus and something more. That something more is the compulsory system of *Purdah* for Muslim women. As a consequence of the *Purdah* system a segregation of the Muslim women is brought about, *(p. 220)*

Take the position of women....the Muslim woman is the most helpless person in the world. To quote an Egyptian Moslem leader:

"Islam has set its seal of inferiority upon her, and given the sanction of religion to social customs which have deprived her of the full opportunity for self-expression and development of personality."

No Muslim girl has the courage to repudiate her marriage, although it may be open to her on the ground that she was a child and that it was brought about by persons other than her parents. No Muslim wife will think it proper to have a clause entered into her marriage contract reserving her the right to divorce. In that event, her fate is 'once married, always married.' She cannot escape the marriage tie, however irksome it may be. While she cannot repudiate the marriage, the husband can always do it without having to show any cause. Utter the word *'Tallaq'* and observe continence for three weeks and the woman is cast away. The only restraint on his caprice is the obligation to pay dower. If the dower has already been remitted, his right to divorce is a matter of his sweet will..(p. *216-217)*

Anti-Science, Anti-Progress

The question may be asked why arc the Muslims opposed to social reform?

The usual answer given is that the Muslims all over the world are an unprogressive people. This view no doubt accords with the facts of history. After the first spurts of their activity–the scale of which was undoubtedly stupendous leading to the foundations of vast empires–the Muslims suddenly fell into a strange condition of torpor, from which they never seem to have become awake. The cause assigned for this torpor by those, who have made a study of their condition, is said to be the fundamental assumption made by all Muslims that Islam is a world religion suitable for all peoples, for all times and for all conditions. It has been contended that:

> "The Musalman, remaining faithful to his religion, has no progressed; he has remained stationary in a world of swiftly moving modern forces. It is, indeed, one of the salient features of Islam that it immobilizes in their native barbarism, the races whom it enslaves. It is fixed in a crystallization, inert and impenetrable. It is unchangeable ; and political, social or economic changes have no repercussion upon it.

> "Having been taught that outside Islam there can be no safety, outside its law no truth and outside its spiritual message there is no happiness, the Muslim has become incapable of conceiving any other condition than his own, any other mode of thought than the Islamic thought. He firmly believes that he has arrived at an unequalled pitch of perfection; that he is the sole possessor of true faith, of the true doctrine, the true wisdom; that he alone is in possession of the truth–no relative truth subject to revision, but absolute truth.
>
> "The religious law of the Muslims had the effect of imparting to the very diverse individuals of whom the world is composed, a unity of thought, of feeling, of ideas of judgment."

It is urged that this uniformity is deadening and is not merely imparted to the Muslims, but is imposed upon them by a spirit of intolerance which is unknown anywhere outside the Muslim world for its severity and its violence and which is directed towards the suppress on of all rational thinking which is in conflict with the teachings of Islam. As Renan observes:

> "Islam is a close union of the spiritual and the temporal; it is the reign of a dogma, it is the heaviest chain that humanity has ever borne...Islam has its beauties as a religion.. But to the human reason Islamism has only been injurious. The minds that it has shut from the light were, no doubt, already closed in their own internal limits; but it has persecuted free thoughts. I shall no say more violently than other religions, but more effectually. It has made of the countries that it has conquered a close field to the rational culture of the mind. What is, in fact essentially distinctive of the Musalman is his hatred of science, his persuasion that research is useless, frivolous, almost impious–the natural sciences, because they are attempts at rivalry with God; the historical sciences, because they apply to times anterior to Islam, they may revive heresies..."*

* Nationality and Other Essays

11
Position of Converts During Muslim Rule

Dr. K.S. Lal

Professor of History, University of Hyderabad

It would be a truism to say that Islam is a proselytizing religion. It would again be a truism to assert that every Muslim is a missionary of his faith. Sufis, Ulema, merchants, invaders, rulers–all participated in proselytizing activity. However, since documentary evidence in the form of medieval chronicles pertains mostly to the activities of invaders and rulers, our knowledge of the spread of Islam at the hands of these people is available in some detail, and is also more or less authentic. As M. Mujeeb rightly points out:

> "There was never any doubt in the minds of the Muslims of their right to spread over the earth...As this could not, in the opinion of kings and warriors, be achieved without the subjugation of non-Muslims and occupation of their territory, the propagation of Islam became identical with war and conquest. The *Hidayah* is quite explicit about the legality of *Jihad* (holy war) against infidels even when they have not taken the offensive."[1]

The concept of *Jihad* is multi-dimensional; one of its aims is the conversion of non-Muslims to Islam. All invaders like Muhammad bin Qasim, Mahmud Ghaznavi and Muhammad Ghori proved to be great missionaries of Faith and achieved great success in their mission. When armies march to spread a religion, the process of conversion is quick.[2] In India armies never ceased to march, at least in its early years and invaders like Mahmud of Ghazni openly swore to convert Hindus to Islam. While Subsequent invaders, conquerors and rulers followed the same policy, Muslim merchants introduced and spread Islam on the Malabar Coast and Gujarat. Belief in the proselytizing achievements of the *sufi Mashaikh* too is not entirely without foundation.[3]

The concern of the present article, however, is not with the way in which Muslim population grew in India, but with the equation obtaining between the foreign immigrant Muslims and indigenous converts to Islam, in other words, the treatment meted out to Indian Muslim converts by foreign Muslims of the ruling classes. Muslim political power in northern India was firmly established with the founding of the Delhi Sultanate at the beginning of the 13th century, and it is from this point of time that the situation may be studied.

Class Character of Converts and Rulers

The Hindu converts to Islam fall into two general categories. Firstly, there were the poor, low caste and vulnerable sections of people, who could neither resist the force of the conquerors and rulers, nor the temptation of the prospect of release from the Hindu social bondage of low caste, which the Sufi missionary endeavour dangled before them. Within this section were also vocational and professional groups like *Julahas, Qassab, Mahauts* (elephant drivers), tailors and *Hajjam* who found it profitable not only to serve Muslim clientele but also to convert to a faith in which they could find advantages of service in their vocation.[4] The second category was of those Hindus who were ambitious but finding that employment under Muslim government was confined to Muslims primarily (before Akbar's time at least), chose to convert to Islam to claim a share in administration and polity. We will study about these sections in the reverse order.

The administrators or the governing class may be termed as *nobility*. The foundation of Muslim rule in India was laid by its exertions and achievements. The founders of Muslim rule were foreigners. These foreign nobles belonged to Turkish, Persian, Arab, Afghan, Mongol, Abyssinian and Egyptian stock but were known by the generic name *"Turk"*, and constituted the ruling oligarchy. They were army commanders-cum-civil administrators, officers in-charge of provinces and districts and holders of other similar appointments of various grades and ranks. Most of them had risen from humble beginnings; many of them were just slaves. But conquest of Indian kingdoms had proved to be very lucrative. So greatly had they benefited during campaigns and wars, and so great was their gain in holding and administering the newly acquired territories, that they all became men of power and influence.

The material change which the conquest had brought to the individual Turks can be best assessed from the statement of FAKHR-I-MUDABBIR, a contemporary historian. "Even a poor householder", he writes, "who did not possess a single slave, became the owner of numerous slaves, horses and camels; a man who originally owned only one horse became a *sipahsalar* and possessed a kettledrum, standard, naubat, all of his own."[5] This resulted in two things. *One:* the Turks gave up the idea of going back to their homeland and stayed on in Hindustan to enjoy the fruits of victory. *Two*: Once they were here they naturally tried to monopolise all important positions in the state and maintain their racial and exotic identity. This attitude was also shared by their children and children's children who, though born in India, psychologically felt that they were Turks of foreign stock. They treated the Indian Muslim converts with contempt.

They were so class conscious and suffered from such superiority complex that ZIYAUDDIN BARANI, writing in the 14th century both in his *Tarikh-i-Firoz Shahi* as well as *Fatawa-i-Jahandari* credits the Turks with all possible virtues and the Indian Muslims with all kinds of vices. He says:

> "They (the Turks) alone are capable of virtue, kindness, generosity, valour, good deeds, good works, truthfulness, keeping of promises... loyalty, clarity of vision, justice, equity, recognition of rights, gratitude for favours and fear of God. They are, consequently, said to be noble, free born, virtuous, religious, of high pedigree and pure birth. These groups, alone are worthy of offices and posts in the government...Owing to their actions the government of the king is strengthened and adorned."[6] On the other hand the "low born" Indian Muslims are "capable only of vices–immodesty, falsehood, miseriness, misappropriation, wrongfulness, lies, evil speaking ingratitude... shamlessness, impundence..... So they are called low-born, bazaar people, base, mean, worthless, plebian, shameless and of dirty birth."[7]

Now neither the one could be that good nor the other that bad but Ziyauddin Barani rightly depicts the prevailing attitude. What worried him most was that the Indian Muslims were appointed to

> "high offices and are successful in their work...they will make people of their own kind their helpers, supporters, colleagues. They will not allow (Turkish) nobles and free-born men and men of merits to come anywhere near the affairs of the government."[8]

In his support Minhaj Siraj bluntly declared that **"Turks of pure lineage and Tajiks of noble birth could not tolerate the tribes of Hind to rule over them."**[9] The way in which some of the highest Indian Muslim noblemen like Imaduddin Raihan, Nasiruddin Khusrau, Khan-i-Jahan Maqbul and Ainulmulk Multani were referred to or treated by the Turks shows the contempt in which the Indian Muslims were held by their foreign co-religionists.

No Jobs for Converts

In short, during the period of Muslim rule, a bitter struggle of wit and influence for power was going on between the "foreign Turks" and Indian Muslims.[9] The former felt that they were founders of Muslim rule in India they belonged to blue blood and deserved special consideration. It was their right to keep to themselves all high offices, for they possessed merit and were superior to the "Julahas". The latter knew that the Turks were good fighters, but for administrative work the indigenous Muslims were better suited if not indispensible. Muhammad bin Qasim and Mahmud Ghaznavi used to employ Hindus in administration and army. But the policy of the early Turkish rulers in India was to keep the Hindus excluded from offices and appoint only Muslims. Consequently, some ambitious Hindus converted to Islam tried to obtain offices. They were originally *Brahmans* or *Kshatriyas* or of other high castes and perhaps belonged originally to that of *Raja, Zamindar* or warrior families. To them the Turks were all slaves.[10] At least the Indian Muslim officers did not feel inferior to the Turks. In this struggle the foreign Muslims had an edge. They were closer to the Sultan and had influence with him. With a view to denigrating Indian Muslim officers, the "Turks" were ever doing research on their ancestry, and informing the king about the same with a view to see that no low born people or Indian Muslims joined their cadre, and made attempts at the removal of those who had infiltrated into it.

Ziyauddin Barani derives a genuine pleasure in writing about the exclusion and expulsion of low born Muslims from state employment. He says that Iltutmish dismissed thirty three persons from government service by one stroke of the pen on account of their *low* birth.[11] He also writes that the Vazir, Nizamul Mulk Junaidi had appointed one Jamal Marzuq as the *Mutsarrif* (Superintendent) of Kanauj. The Sultan not only cancelled the appointment of Marzuq, he even went into the antecedents of Nizamul Mulk himself on the representation of Malik Qutbuddin Hasan the Barbak and Malik Izzuddin Salari, the Vakil-i-Dar. It was not difficult for interested persons to prove that the Vazir's grandfather had descended from the Julaha class, and it is said that the latter lost confidence of the Sultan. Barani writes that no Indian Muslim could be retained on an *iqta* or appointed to the post of *Khwajgi, Mutsarrifi* or *Mir Muharriri.*[12] It is true that Balban also made detailed enquiries about the families of all his officers and removed one Kamal Maiyhar from the *Khwajgi* of Amroha because he was an Indian Muslim.

Struggle for Power

In short, Indian Muslims did not take this discriminatory treatment by the Turks lying down and fought back as is evident from the case of Imaduddin Raihan, but the prejudice of immigrant Muslims against Indian converted Muslims continued in varying degrees throughout the medieval period. Iltutmish invited and welcomed foreign Muslims to settle in India.[13] Balban employed Afghans to garrison his forts against Indian rebels. Mohammed Bin Tughlaq gained notoriety for preferring foreign to Indian nobles. The Afghan rulers lured their Afghan compatriots from abroad, in preference to Indian Muslims, and they a rived in large numbers like "ants and locusts".[14] The Turco-Mongol polity was familial and tribal. Indian Muslims could not be freely accommodated in it, and if they tried to push in, they were treated with derision.

It is not possible to go on giving similar examples for a long period of five to six centuries in a paper of this size. It would suffice to close with one instance given by Niccolao Manucci. He states that three Hindu *Rajas* embraced Islam against promises of temptations offered by Aurangzeb but later on regretted their decision[15] for, writes Manucci in a laconic style that Hindu converts to Islam commanded little respect.[16] Right up to the 19th century the Iranis and Turanis remained prominent in the Mughal Empire and India's politics.

Plight of Toiling Masses

If this was the position of the elite among the converts, the situation with regard to those who manned lower professions could not have been better. They formed the toiling masses of Muslims like shopkeepers, artisans, masons, water-carriers *(saqqa),* barbers, tailors, bullock-cart drivers, fish sellers, *goalas* (milkmen). Some were masters of their craft like blacksmiths who manufactured line flexible swords; the needle workers made thin thorn-like needles, and Muslim weavers, called *Julahas*, turned out fine fabrics. Beef sellers were called *Kassai* and meat ṣellers *Qassab*. There were tailors, *Rangrez* and *Qalandars* or beggars moving from place to place.[17] On a deeper study of the original sources in Persian it would appear that professions of pharmacistry, perfumery, milk-selling, tailoring and carpentry were valued, while socially rejected classes were of weighers, camel and donkey drivers, falconers, leather workers and barbers, while the menial, included scavengers, entertainers, funeral workers, refuge collectors, wrestlers, clowns and singing women, moving about in the streets, irregularly employed, knocking about for a living associated with vice and begging.[18]

However, all these sections, all converted vocational groups of Muslims remained poor. Muslims of foreign extraction looked down upon them and were not prepared to treat them on equal terms. To add insult to injury the chronicler Ziyauddin Barani, a confirmed believer in the racial superiority of the so-called Turks and the baseness of Indian Muslims, recommends:

> "Teachers of every kind are to be sternly ordered not to thrust precious stones down the throats of dogs or to put collars of gold round the necks of pigs and bears–that is, to the mean, the ignoble, the worthless, to shopkeepers and the *low born.* They are to teach nothing more than the rules about prayer, fasting, religious charity and the *Haj* pilgrimage along with some chapters of the *Quran* and some doctrines of the faith without which their religion cannot be correct and valid prayers are not possible. They are to be instructed in nothing more. They are not to be taught reading and writing, for plenty of disorders arise owing to the skill of the *low born* in knowledge.[19]

> "The *low-born,* who have been enrolled for practising the baser arts and the meaner professions, are capable only of vices...So they are called *low born,* bazaar people, base, mean, worthless, plebeian, shameless and of dirty birth."[20]

Conversion by Force

The problem was this: the process of the conversion of indigenous Hindus to Islam was hurried. All of a sudden the invader appeared in a city or region, and in the midst of loot and killings, a dazed, shocked and enslaved people were given a choice between Islam and death. The choice was so limited that it was hardly a choice. Those who got converted had their names changed. They were hastily taught to recite the *Kalima* and to say the prescribed prayers, and then the invading army marched forward for further conquest.

The Arabs in Sind had made some provision for teaching the neo-converts the ways of Muslim worship and prayer. *Tarikh-i-Yamini, Rauzat-us-Safa* and *Tarikh-i-Ferishtah* speak of construction of mosques by Mahmud of Ghazni. Similarly, *Rauzat-us-Safa* mentions construction of mosques and schools by Masud, while Muhammad Ghori and his successors constructed mosques from the debris of or at the site of old Hindu shrines.[21]

But there was no programme for the social or economic uplift of the neo-converts in the scheme of proselytization and they remained poor and downtrodden. For instance, Fakhr-I-Mudabbir in his *Adab-ul-Harb* says that if any one paying *Kharaj* (land tax collected from non-Muslims became Musalman, he was liable to pay the same amount which he paid before conversion. Also if any Musalman purchased *Kharaj* land from a *zimmi,* he had to remit the same old amount in revenue.[22] Similarly, *Jaziyah* appears to have continued to be paid by early converts, else there was no reason for Firoz Tughlaq to emphasise that those who became Musalmans would be exempted from the poll tax.[23]

No Uplift of the Converts

If Ziyauddin Barani's recommendation constituted the actuality prevalent, then there were no facilities available for educational and moral development of the newly converted Muslims. No wonder, the converts could not get equality in the democratic Muslim social order. The high class Muslims would not mix or even eat with them if modern practices are any indication for the medieval.[24]

The converts, or at least some of them, were aware of their humiliating position. It was a practice to call them by the generic but contemptuous term "*Julaha*". Surely all the converts could not have come from the weaver caste, but the word *Julaha* became synonymous with an Indian Muslim convert, and he was condemned as the low born. It is interesting to note that in the Punjab the *Id-ul-fitr* or *Ramzan ki Id* is called the special festival of the *Julaha* weavers as the *Id-uz-Zuha* is called the festival of the Qassab butchers.[25] Surely the Indian converts could not forever live with such inferior status and such humiliating appellations, ant they have tried by various means to break the chains of bondage and claim equality with 'foreign' Muslims.

Return to Original Faith

In the early years of Muslim conquest, many converts used to try and succeed in returning to their original Hindu faith. Muhammad bin Qasim invaded Sind in 712. A.D After his departure not only the Arab power there declined, but most of the neo-converts too returned to their former faith.[26] Even during the hell days of Mahmud of Ghazni, men like Nawasa Shah and Rai Sal tried to return to Hinduism.[27] In response to large-scale conversions in the wake of Muslim invasions works like the *Deval Smriti*[28] and other treatises of a similar nature[29] appeared laying down liberalised rules for the reconversion of neo-Muslims back into the Hindu fold. During the course of a century and a half that is between the death of Mahmud Ghazni and the invasion of Muhammad Ghori (1191-92), such opportunities of the conversion were many, even on a large-scale.[30] However, such a situation was not sustainable by the traditional rigidity of the Hindu caste system which precluded re-conversions on which Alberuni writes an elaborate note[31] as well as the aggressive attitude of the Muslims in not permitting defection, apostasy in Islam being punishable with death.

Caste Hierarchy Among Muslims

The other course open was to improve one's economic position and status to such a degree as to be counted among the Muslim elite. On conversion the neo-Muslim carried his caste, vocation and economic status with him. He was generally poor and exploited, and was treated with contempt by high class or foreign Muslims. His redemption lay in somehow joining their cadre and for this he could hope only if his economic position registered a rise. But since it was a difficult proposition in the society thriving on exploitation, he could only pray and dream for better days: "Last year I was a *Julaha* (weaver); this year a *Shaykh;* and next year, if the harvest be good, I shall be *Saiyyid*."[32] This prospect was not in the luck of all.

Therefore, the one trump card he could use was to actually join the cadre of the master class by claiming descent from foreign Muslim stock of Shaikh, Saiyyid, Mughal, Pathan. The terms Saiyyid and Shaikh imply Arabian origin; the former being used exclusively for descendants of the Prophet's family through his daughter Fatima, and the latter being used to designate any other of Arab origin. The term Mughal includes Turks and Pathans had their origin in Afghanistan and its neighbourhood. "There is a strong tendency for the converts from among the Hindus to assume a position in one of the recognised groups of *Sharif-lats* just as soon as practicable."[33] "In Bihar a converted Hindu of the *Brahman* or *Kayasth* caste is usually allowed to call himself a *Sheikh* and to associate and intermarry with genuine Sheikhs. A *Babban* or Rajput in the same circumstances becomes a Pathan... In Mymensingh, high caste converts are given title of *Khan* and call themselves Pathan, (even) the lower castes.....after a lapse of some year are gradually recognized as Sheikhs."[34] This is the position with regard to other states of India too and there are people with the title of Nawab and Thakur in one.

The high and low caste Hindu converts during Muslim rule in India are all dead. But their descendants are very much alive. However, hardly any one admits to having descended from Indian stock. Most of them lay claim to foreign ancestry and trace their descent from Turks, Mughals and Arabs. There is nothing surprising in this. In theory all Muslims are equal; in practice some are more equal than the others. It is because of the condescending and humiliating treatment accorded to the Indian converts by the outsiders that Muslims of Indian extraction, to wash off the stigma of Hindu origin, have ever tried to join the ranks of the conquering and ruling foreign Muslims through non-available and unverifiable geneologies.[35]

References

1. M. Mujeeb, **The Indian Muslims,** George Allen and Unwin (London, 1967), pp. 676d citing Hidayah, Kitab al Siyar wa'l-Jihad, Mujtabai Press, Delhi, 1331-32 H. p. 539.
2. K.S. Lal, **Growth of Muslim Population in Medieval India** (Delhi, 1973) pp. 99-108, 113-140.
3. For controversy in this regard, see **ibid.,** pp. 162-64.
4. Ziyauddin Barani, **Tarikh-i-Firoz Shahi** Persian Text (Calcutta, 1862) pp. 273-74; Shams-i-Siraj Afif, **Tarikh-i-Firoz Shahi** Persian Text (Calcutta, 1890), p. 271 also K.S. Lal, **Twilight of the Sultanate,** 2nd edition (Delhi, 1980) p. 271.
5. **Tarikh-i-Fakhruddin Mubarak Shah,** ed. Denison Ross, (London, 1927) p. 2). Trs. and cited in Habibullah, p. 315.
6. Barani, **Fatawa-i-Jahandari** (English) by Afsar Begum and Mohammad Habib, Kitab Mahal (Allahabad, n.d.) pp. 97-98.
7. Ibid., p. 98.
8. Ibid., p. 99.
9. Minhaj Siraj Jurjani, **Tabqat-i-Nasiri,** Persian Text (Calcutta, 1864) and Eng. trs, by Major H.R. Raverty, (London, 1881); Raverty p. 829.
10. Iltutmish ever remained conscious of his humble origin. Barani: **Tarikh,** op. cit. p. 137.
11. Barani, **Tarikh,** p. 38-39.
12. Ibid. p. 38.
13. Ferishtah, **Tarikh-i-Ferishtah,** Persian Text (Lucknow, 1865) pp. 66-67, 75. **Tabqat-i-Nasiri** pp. 157-60.
14. Niamatullah's **Makhzan-i-Afghana,** English trs. by N.B. Roy (Santiniketan, 1958) pp. 67-69.
15. Niccolao Manucci, **Storia do Mogor,** English Translation by W. Irvine, 4 vols. (London, 1906), II, p. 436.
16. Ibid. p.451.
17. Amir Khusrau, **Aijaz-i-Khusravi,** iv, pp. 45-48. also **Subh-ul-Asha** by Otto Spies, An Arab Account of the 14th century (Aligarh n.d.) p. 50.
18. Ira Mervin Lapidus, **Muslim Cities in the Later Middle Ages** (Cambridge, Mass. 1967) p. 83.
19. **Barani,** *Fatawa-i-Jahandari,* **p. 49.**
20. Ibid. p. 98.
21. Utbi, **Tarikh-i-Yamini** English trs. by James Reynolds (London, 1958), pp. 322-25, 462, also Elliot, II, p. 37, Ferishtah, I, p. 44.

22. **Adab-ul-Harb,** fol. 157 (a).

23. **Fatuhat-i-Firoz Shahi,** Elliot & Dowson, III, p. 386.

24. A.K. Nazmul Karim, "Muslim Social Classes in East Pakistan," in **Changing Society in India and Pakistan,** University of Dacca, (Oxford University Press, 1956), pp. 120-130, 138-143. Also E. A. Gait, **Census of India Report,** 1901, Vol. VI, pp. 439-442 and Vol. II, p. 544.

25. Jafar Sharif, **Qanun-i-IsIam,** trs. by G. A. Herklots as **Islam in India,** ed. by William Crooke, Oxford University Press, 1921, p. 211.

26. A1 Biladhuri **Futuh-ul-Buldan,** written in 9th century; Elliot, I, pp. 124-125. Also Denison Ross, **Islam** p. 18 and Idrisi, **Nuzhat-ul-Mushtaq** (written 12th Century) in Elliot, I, p. 89.

27. Utbi, in Elliot II, p. 39. Also Wolseley Haig; **Cambridge History of India,** Vol, III, Delhi, Reprint 1958, p. 47.

28. Published by Anandashrama, Sanskrit series, Poona and Translated into English by M.N. Roy in the Journal of Bihar and Orissa Research Society, 1927.

29. **P.V. Kane,** *History of the the Dharma Shastra Literature,* **4 Vols., II, pp. 390-410.**

30. Ferishtah, I, p. 45.

31. Alberuni, Abu Raihan Muhammad, **Alberuni's India** English trs. by Edward Sachau, 2 Vols. (London, 1910), II, pp. 162-63.

32. Murray M. Titus, **Islam in India and Pakistan** (Calcutta, 1959) p. 177. The saying has a variable like "The first year we were butchers, the next Shaikhs; this year, if prices rise, we shall become Saiyyads".

33. Titus, op. cit. p. 177.

34. **Census of India Report,** 1901, VI, Pt. I, Bengal, pp. 165-181.

35. E.g. Dewan Fazle Rabbi, **Haqiqat-i-Musalaman-i-Bangla** to show that Bengal Muslims are mainly of foreign extraction. Its English translation is entitled the **Origin of the Muhammadans of Bengal,** Thacker & Spinck Co., Calcutta. 1895.

Confessions

a. **Gamal Abdel Nasser,** President of Egypt, in *The Philosophy of the Revolution*, 1955:

'When my mind travels to the eighty million Muslims of Indonesia, the fifty million in China, and the several other millions in Malaya, Siam and Burma, and the hundred millions in Pakistan, the hundred or more in the Middle East and the forty millions in Russia, as well as the other millions in the distant parts of the world, when I visualise these millions united in one faith, I have a great consciousness of the tremendous potentialities that cooperation among them can achieve.'

b. **Dr. Ali Issa Othman,** for some years adviser to UNRWA on education; quoted by Charis Waddy in *The Muslim Mind*, Longmans, 1976.

'The spread of Islam was military. There is a tendency to apologise for this and we should not. It is one of the injunctions of the Koran that you must fight for the spreading of Islam.'

Muslim Attitude towards Scheduled Castes

Another illustration would be the attitude of the Muslims towards the problem of the Untouchables. The Muslims have always been looking at the Depressed Classes with a sense of longing and much of the jealousy between Hindus and Muslims arises out of the fear of the latter that the former might become stronger by assimilating the Depressed Classes. In 1909 the Muslims took the bold step of suggesting that the Depressed Classes should not be enrolled in the Census as Hindus. In 1923 Mr. Mahomed Ali in his address as the President of the Congress went much beyond the position taken by the Muslims in 1909. He said:

"The quarrels about ALAMS and PIPAL trees and musical processions are truly childish; but there is one question which can easily furnish a ground for complaint of unfriendly action if communal activities are not amicably adjusted. It is the question of the conversion of the Suppressed Classes, if Hindu society does not speedily absorb them. The Christian missionary is already busy and no one quarrels with him. But the moment some Muslim Missionary Society is organized for the same purpose there is every likelihood of an outcry in the Hindu Press. It has been suggested to me by m influential and wealthy gentleman who is able to organize a Missionary Society on a large scale for the conversion of the Suppressed Classes, that it should be possible to reach a settlement with leading Hindu gentlemen and divide the country into separate areas where Hindu and Muslim Missionaries could respectively work, each community preparing for each year, or longer unit of time if necessary, an estimate of the numbers it is prepared to absorb or convert. These estimates would, of course, be based on the number of workers and funds each had to spare, and tested by the actual figures of the previous period. In this way each community would be free to do the work of absorption and conversion, or rather, of reform without chances of absorption and conversion, or rather, of reform without chances of collision with one another. I cannot say in what light my Hindu brethren will take it and I place this suggestion tentatively in all frankness and sincerity before them. All that I say for myself is that I have seen the condition of the "Kali Praja" in the Baroda State and of the Gonds in the Central Provinces and I frankly confess it is a reproach to us all. If the Hindus will not absorb them into their own society, others will and must, and then the orthodox Hindu too will cease to treat them as untouchables. Conversion seems to transmute them by a strong alchemy. But does this not place a premium upon conversion?"

Dr. B.R. Ambedkar

Pakistan or Partition of India
Bombay, 1945 (p. 235-36)

12

Muslim Fundamentalism & Pan-Islamism

Dr. M.S. Jain

Head of the Department, History & Indian Culture, University of Rajasthan, Jaipur

Two Islamic movements have become, during the last two decades significant on account of their international bearings. The first is *Pan-Islamism* and the second is *Islamic Fundamentalism.* Both have sought inspiration from certain values enshrined in the *Quran* and have been put forward by traditional and conservative elements.

Fundamentalism v/s Modernism

The advocacy of a return to pristine Islam and to model the life of Muslims on the basis of *Quran* and *Hadith* is Islamic Fundamentalism. This fundamentalism has a long history. Leaving aside the early medieval attempts in this direction, there is a long chain of such movements in the Islamic world from 18th century onwards. The consciousness of the corresponding need to remedy social evils in the Muslim society brought forth reform movements which have sought to rid the Muslim society of causes responsible for its degeneration. The more effective and long-lasting among them have advocated a stricter implementation of the *Quranic* rulings and *Hadith* in the realm of social behaviour precluding any substantial rethinking of the social contents of Islam. The impact of the political domination of the West over Middle East encouraged the growth of Islamic liberalism/modernism for some time. The westerners turned a blind eye to the earlier fundamentalist movements and side-tracked such movements during the period of their domination over the Muslim world. The Islamic modernists advocated the adoption of western education, ways of life and interpreted Islam as if it were advocating western values. Muhammed Abdul and Taha Hussayn in the Arab world, Namik Kemal and Tevfik Fikret in Turkey, Abdul Aziz, and Lutfias Sayyid in Egypt, Sir Sayyid Ahmed and Amir Ali in India, Hajji Aqus Salim in Indonesia have been some of the reputed modernists. However, all of them put forward liberal exposition of Islam but no Islamic exposition of liberalism. Liberalism was not formulated to envisage its dynamic truth within the central structure of Islam.[1] The liberalist forces in Islam were bound to suffer because while analysing causes of decline in the position of the Muslims corporately, they could not agree to a rethinking on the basic social religious norms and values. Western liberalism failed to bring about a revival of their corporate Islamic personality. The Muslim liberalist movements ultimately underwent transformation and split into three streams–one diverting towards fundamentalism, another towards pure Westernism, and the mid-modernist stream degenerating into pure apologetics. The experience of a majority of Muslim countries with the West created a situation where any links with a western trend of thought became a strong argument against its acceptability in the Islamic world. Modernist movements have further declined because of the logic of struggle for liberation from western domination.

Nationalism and Petro-Dollars

The conservative forces were anxious to find a way to be able to face the onslaught of western civilisation and value system. Resistance to the advancing western cultural onslaught could be and was offered only by the traditional elements. In the Islamic world the *ulema* have generally come forward to protest, be it Egypt, Morocco or Iran. Almost everywhere the fundamentalist movements have been in the forefront of national liberation struggles. Nationalism and Islam have fought hand in hand; differences and discussions in this process have been discouraged, this has been a gain to fundamentalism.[2] The indifferent performance of imported western institutions–parliamentary form of government, educational system and the danger from the ideology of 'communism' has led almost everywhere to modern problems. Buttressed by economic affluence and petro-dollars, a new self-assertion is noticeable in Muslim countries which confidently and boldly advocate the relevance of Islamic fundamentalism. The full measure of the failure of effective modernism can be judged by the fact that pure Westernism is only a product of the virulence of resurgent fundamentalism.

The sources of strength of the fundamentalists need to be explored a bit deeply to avoid hasty generalisation. Their greatest source of strength is the Muslim belief that Islam as a true and revealed religion was not meant for a particular time-period only, rather it holds true for all times to come. Therefore, in any situation of crisis, the ultimate inspiration should come from the *Quran* and the *Hadith*.[3] This has not been a feature of Muslim orthodoxy only but all modernists have also appealed to the same source and have tried to justify their liberalism on the basis of the teachings of the *Quran* and the *Hadith*. When both the fundamentalists and the modernist liberals appeal to the same source, it becomes a question of choosing the 'valid' interpretation which would ultimately depend on whether the *ulema* by and large agree to that or not.

Roots of Iranian Revolution

Another source of strength of the fundamentalists lies in the fact that it is they who have invariably raised the banner of revolt against foreign domination and western cultural values.[4] Whether it is the case of organising opposition to the decadent Egyptian monarchy in the 30s and later, or it is the question of leading resistance to foreign rule in Morocco or criticising the pro-American policies of the Shah of Iran, it is the *ulema* (the fundamentalists) who are in the vanguard. Nasser took advantage of the *Ikhwan* in Egypt, though later on he himself had to take measures to curb the violence and fury of the members of the *Ikhwan*. It was the *ulema* in Iran who had led the revolt against the Qajar dynasty, against Moosaddeq and against the Shah of Iran. It would be a total misunderstanding of the movement to try to call it an upsurge only on account of the failure or consequences of the socio-economic policies of the Shah. The prevalence of corruption or the prosperity of a 'class' as a consequence of his economic measures only tended to make the fundamentalist appeal popular and emotional, but its roots of inspiration were fundamentally different from what some modernists would like us to believe.

The ouster of the Shah of Iran by the Islamic fundamentalists has led the western media to talk of Muslim fundamentalism and the dangers it poses. In truth, it is like the proverbial shepherd boy's cry of "wolf, wolf". The western media's portrayal of Islamic fundamentalism has prevented its evaluation in a historical context. Some scholars are trying to present this phenomenon as the outcome of social and economic dissatisfaction generated by the overthrown political authority and thus put forward different models of fundamentalism constructed on the basis of individual countries. Dr. Moin Shakir advocates that Islamic fundamentalism has been used by non-democratic rulers for the legitimisation of their authority; in the same article he also argues that the Muslim countries, even if they have liberal or democratic set up, cannot effectively counter the threat of fundamentalism unless radical changes are made in the economic system.[5] In developing countries it is facile to put forward economic factors as the only determinants of any or every movement. One has only to remember that when a particular movement crosses its geographical boundaries and the state of economic development, it must have some internal self-propelling force of its own. Islamic fundamentalism is one such movement whose internal strength has to be understood clearly.

Rule of Ulema in Iran

It is probably not appreciated by the outsiders that the *ulema* in Iran have enjoyed far more political power than the *ulema* in other Middle Eastern countries, and it is worth noting that they, quite unexpectedly, became willing partners to a large measure in modernising the constitutional revolution in Iran from 1905 to 1911. For historical reasons, they have enjoyed great political power and popularity in Iran. The *ulema* have been acting consistently in the interest of the preservation of their own power; their reaction appeared to be 'progressive' when it was against imperialism and appeared 'reactionary' (fundamentalist) when it went against modernisation and westernization.[6] The Shah of Iran, by centralizing power with the help of army and bureaucracy and by the creation of a modern educational and judicial system, was directly trying to curb *ulema's* power and influence. The religious-nationalist alliance, having a long history, reappeared in the movement against oil nationalisation in the early 1950s and in opposition to the government's policies in the 1960s. The government's autocratic ways and subservience towards the U.S. led the nationalists and the *ulema* to forge unity again.

Opposition to tyranny has been a characteristic of *Ithna ashari Shii Islam* and has influenced the *ulema* in Iran. In their hostility to the hate in recent times, the *ulema* and the urban mercantile classes have tended to complement each other. A strong self-assertive State threatens; the judicial and other prerogatives of the *ulema* and was likely to tax the merchant community heavily. The *ulema* and the merchants gave each other aid and refuge; the protection of the mosque was a refuge from State tyranny and the closure of the markets gave the *ulema* a powerful instrument of building pressure upon the government.[7] The *ulema's* role in recent years is a continuation of their traditional political role of opposition to state absolutism and foreign domination, exhibited a number of times during the 20th century. The attempt to present Khomeini's agitation as directed solely against government plan of land reform and women enfranchisement, though given almost universal credence in the western press, will not stand the test of close scrutiny.[8] The creation of a literary corps and a religious corps by the Shah was a brutal attack on the influence of the *ulema*. Severe opposition in Iran to U.S. during the last 4 years is only an index of the hostility reused against foreign hegemony over Iran. The recent political role of the *ulema* in Iran cannot be regarded as an "anachronistic curiosity". Despite all the inroads of the modern age, the Iranian national consciousness still remains wedded to *Shii Islam.* When the integrity of the nation is held to be threatened by internal autocracy and foreign hegemony, protests in religious terms will continue to be voiced and the appeal of men like Khomeini will be widely heard.

Emergence of Pan-Islamism

There was another aspect of the danger to conservative forces in the Islamic world which consisted not in the growth of western liberalism but in the growth of radicalism and leftist forces. During the sixties the conservative forces in the Muslim world were anxious for a defensive mechanism to check the growth of radical forces, emerging under the leadership of Nasser in Egypt and the Baathists in Iraq and Syria.[9] King Feisal, of Saudi Arabia, the Shah of Iran and the Shah of Morocco held mutual consultations to form a defensive mechanism. The *Quranic* exhortation that the Muslims of the world belong to one *'Ummah'* was utilised to form a joint front to contain radical forces. This sentiment of religious cohesion, called 'Pan-Islamism' by the western writers, had been utilised in different directions during the last hundred years. Jamaluddin Afghani used this sentiment to rouse Muslim countries against European imperialism. Sultan of Turkey used it, during the First World War, to encourage Muslims to revolt against the British; while the Khilafat leaders in India utilised it to politicise the Indian Muslims.

In the sixties, a number of conservative Islamic states felt the need to institutionalise this sentiment of cohesion to check the forces of radicalism. It began initially as 'summit diplomacy' during 1964-65 leading to a temporary cessation of propaganda warfare among the Arabs.[10] But radical Syria broke apart. King Feisal of Saudi Arabia then adopted the strategy of appealing to Islamic solidarity and putting forward Islam as a heavy counter-weight to nationalism-based radicalism. The gain of the conservatives after the defeat of Egypt and Syria in June 1967 was counter-balanced by internal radical revolts in Libya and Sudan. This appeal to Islamic solidarity with a view to containing the leftist forces had the tacit support of U.S.A. which wanted to restrict the growth of radical/Soviet influence in the region.[11] The Islamic solidarity appeal was further sustained by hostility to Israel. The institutionalization of the sentiment of solidarity received a tremendous boost by the *Al-Aqsa Mosque* Fire Incident in 1969. The Rabat Summit of 1969 finally agreed to give concrete shape to the idea of a Pan-Islamic organisation.[12] The radical states, Egypt and Libya, could not ignore the symbolic and historical dimensions of the issue. However, it was only in 1972 that the Charter of the Islamic Conference was adopted and an Islamic Secretariat was created at Jeddah.[13] The radical and secular Muslim states joined it cautiously and in phases. The leadership of the Islamic Conference during the last ten years has passed into the hands of the conservative Arab states.

Proselytisation

Another lever operated by the conservative Arab states to contain the growth of radicalism was to advance Islamic *Da'wah* (propagation and proselytisation) for encouraging solidarity with Muslim minorities. By this method the conservative Arab states have sought to project their anxiety to preserve the cultural and religious identity of Muslim minorities everywhere in the world. This would serve the cause of Pan-Islamic cohesion as well as of Islamic fundamentalism. In 1962 Saudi Arabia utilised the annual Haj congregation of Muslim *ulema* at Mecca and founded a non-official organisation called the *Rabetat-al-Aalam-al Islami* with headquarters at Mecca. During the last 20 years it has been able to acquire control over almost all the leading Muslim associations and organisations in all the continents of the world and has been aiding construction of mosques, Arabic teaching in non-Arab countries, providing scholarships for higher Islamic learning, and for training Muslim preachers for Islamic *Da'wah.* The Muslim minorities are declared to be part of the Islamic *'Ummah'* and the *Rebetat* has organised different forums to implement the Islamic *Da'wah.*

The appeal to Islamic sentiment of cohesion has helped the conservative Arab states to impart to the Muslim countries a significant undreamt of 20 years ago. Islamic *Da'wah* has been able to considerably reduce the impact of western values on Muslim minorities.

Thus Muslim fundamentalism, Pan-Islamism and Islamic *Da'wah* have been complementary aspects of a single urge to preserve the political interests of the conservative sections of the Muslim society. All these movements operate to assert the 'Islamic' personality in political affairs at national and international levels. The basic undercurrents and mainsprings of these movements are political. These forums have been forged for waging a political battle for the preservation of a position of leadership for the conservative interests under the garb of preservation of Islamic corporate personality.

References

1. **W.C. Smith:** *Islam in Modern History,* **p. 66.**
2. *Cambridge History of Islam,* **vol. ii, p. 650.**

3. Ibid. p. 648.
4. Nikki R. Keddie (ed.): **Scholars, Saints and Sufis,** Introduction, p. 6.
5. Anwar Moazzam (ed.): **Islam and Contemporary Muslim World.** Moin Shakir's article: "Politics of Islamic Fundamentalism," pp. 22-23.
6. Nikki R. Keddie's article: "The roots of ulema's power in Modern Iran" in **Scholars, Saints and Sufis,** p. 227.
7. Hamid Algar's article: "The oppositional role of the ulema in 20th century Iran," in **Scholars, Saints and Sufis,** p. 236.
8. Ibid. p. 246.
9. **Philip Windsor (ed.)** *The Middle East: Nations, Super Powers and Wars,* **p. 51.**
10. Williard A. Beling: **Quest for an American Policy,** pp. 64-65.
11. **Impact** (fortnightly magazine), 26 March, 1976, p. 8.
12. Muhammad Heikal: **The Road to Ramadan,** pp. 77-80.
13. Chaudhary Nazir Ahmad Khan: **Commonwealth of Muslim States** (Lahore, 1972), pp. 157-158.

13

The Two Faces of Islam: Expansionism and Revivalism

MUZAFFAR HUSSAIN

A Conscientious and Patriotic Muslim Indian Writer

After a lull of about 25 years, the winds of Islamic expansionism have again started to blow. Following the conquest of Iran in the seventh century, the fierce winds of Islamic expansionism had blown for about one thousand years. Putting on the mantle of Caliphs of Islam, the Muslim monarchs subjugated many countries in Asia, Africa and Europe. But the winds of Islamic expansionism ceased to blow with the emergence of European colonialism in the middle of the seventh century. The people of Britain, France, Portugal, Holland and Spain were at the vanguard of this colonial movement. The waves of European colonialism engulfed most countries of the Muslim world. The conflagration of the two world wars dealt such a severe blow to the doctrine of Islamic expansionism that even the caliphate in Turkey, which was the foundation of this expansionism, was swept away.

In their book entitled *The Islamic Bomb of Pakistan,* Major D.K. Palit and Shri P.K.S. Namboodiri have observed:

> "From the seventh to the seventeenth century Islam spread to new areas in the orient. While militant Islam spread the message up to the banks of the Indus, a more persuasive and gentler Islam won over Malaysia, Indonesia and East Bengal to its faith. However, from the mid seventeenth to the mid twentieth century the power of Islam declined. Barring Saudi Arabia, Iran and Yemen, the entire Islamic world was colonised by European colonial powers..." (p. 4)

The Politics of Oil

But in the meantime, a very significant event took place and it was the discovery of mineral oil. The discovery of immense oil-wealth in the countries of West Asia kindled a ray of hope in the prevailing atmosphere of despondency in these countries and once again they began to wield considerable influence. The use of oil as a political weapon in the seventh decade of the present century whetted the appetite of the Muslim politicians for starting yet another movement for Islamic expansionism. An idea was mooted that all the Islamic countries of the world should be brought on a common platform in the name of Islam and the affluent and developed countries of the West should be brought to their knees by using oil as a weapon.

The former Prime Minister of Pakistan Mr. Zulfikar Ali Bhutto and the Petroleum Minister of Saudi Arabia, Mr. Zaki Yamani, wore the principal architects of this doctrine that mineral oil should be used as an Islamic bomb and all the Muslim countries of the world should unite themselves against Israel under the leadership of Saudi Arabia. The former Shah of Iran had already conducted an experiment to show that the countries of the West could be put under one's thumb by using oil as a weapon. By using this weapon, the Shah of Iran compelled the United States to dance to his tune and it had to concede all his demands whether legitimate or illegitimate. In return, the United States maintained its massive supply of weapons to this part of the world including Pakistan, Turkey and Iran.

Terrorism against Israel

From the sixth decade of the present century, the issue of Israel had assumed such serious proportions that the solution of this issue had become a matter of life-and-death for Arabs. They did not feel any hesitation in taking recourse to violence in order to tackle this issue. A new chapter was added to this terrorism with the hijacking of a plane by Laila Khalid. From then onwards, the *'al-Fateh'* organisation of Yasser Arafat adopted terrorism as its creed.

This terrorism and the unlimited oil wealth of Arab countries acted as a catalyst to the activities of those Muslim fundamentalists who had maintained a low profile so far. There was an organisation in Egypt called *"Akhwan-ul-Musalmin"* which became active in the name of Islam because of the issue of Israel. All this shows that the Islamic revivalists thought that for achieving their objective i.e. Islamic rule it was essential to bring about unity among the Muslim nations. Whatever one may say about Islamic unity, it should be borne in mind that this Islam would be neither a religion which is adapted to modern scientific age, nor an Islam based on the ideologies of our modern age, such as Communism or Socialism. Actually this Islam would be the purest form of Islam which was established 1,400 years ago during the reign of the Caliphs.

Israel which is their enemy is the land of Jews. Western countries supplying arms to Israel are inhabited by Christians and the population of the Third World comprises mainly of Hindus and Buddhists. It was Zulfikar Ali Bhutto who took full advantage of the call given to the Muslims of the world to unite against Israel. He unleashed a virulent propaganda that India, a subcontinent in the East, was also like Israel an enemy of Islam and that the defeat suffered by Pakistan at the hands of a Hindu nation in 1971 war was tantamount to an insult to the whole Muslim world and therefore, it was the moral responsibility of the Arab nations to support Pakistan in her *jehad* (holy war) against India. Thus, as the call for Islamic unity grew louder and louder, the revivalist and expansionist forces also became stronger.

At the time when Pakistan and Saudi Arabia were chasing the will-o'-the-wisp of an Islamic empire, a miracle took place before the eyes of the whole world. The Raza Shah of Iran had to surrender his throne and to flee to a foreign country and Ayatollah Khomeini, living as an exile in Paris, became the all in all in Iran. This successful revolution by *Mullahs* acted as a shot in the arm of the revivalist elements. A fierce propaganda was mounted for bringing about Islamic revolution in other Muslim countries also. Even the Sunni states like Pakistan and Saudi Arabia, forgetting their centuries-old Shia-Sunni differences showered praise on Iran for this achievement and highlighted the fact that it was Iran wherefrom Islam had begun its victorious campaigns which lasted till the end of the seventeenth century. They said that as Iran had once again taken the lead in giving the call for a revolution, an Islamic empire would be again established in the world as had been the case in the past.

Islamic Fundamentalism

The success of the Iranian revolution, the climate of terrorism and the immense oil wealth of Arabs nurtured the roots of this revivalist movement and as a result, these forces have intensified their activities in all those countries where Muslims are either in a majority or minority.

Today the horizons of no country in the world are free from the clouds of Islamic fundamentalism and expansionism.

It is an interesting as well as a revealing fact that, though these fundamentalists and expansionists talk in terms of an Islamic Army, Islamic Bomb, Islamic Bank and an Islamic Stock Exchange, one can see that there is considerable disunity among all those organisations which are operating in the name of Islam. This explains the fact that possibly no other group of countries in the world are riven by so many dissensions as exist between the Arab countries. It is a difficult task to bring about unity in the Arab world because of the existence of tribalism in Arab countries. But Islam has not been able to bring even the 160 million Arabs on a common platform though the fundamentalists want to unify the entire world on the ideological basis of Islam.

Modern historians have referred to the disputes that existed between the Aryans and non-Aryans in the Indian subcontinent. Similar disputes existed between *'Arabs'* and *'Azams'* in Arab territories which were based on regionalism. The word *'Azam'* signifies Iran and its literal meaning is 'dumb' or inarticulate. The word *'Arab'* means a person who is 'articulate' and possesses the power of expression. The Arabs were very proud of their art of speaking and poetic talents. Hence they described themselves as *'Arabs'* and though their neighbours possessed a very fine culture, they described them as *'Azams'*.

Though the Iranians accepted defeat at the hands of the second Caliph, they did not accept him as a caliph rather acknowledged Hazrat Ali as their *Imam*. In other words, the Iranian people became a community of Shias despite suffering defeat at the hands of Sunnis. Thus, regional feelings took a communal character under the very roof of Islam.

An Arab first and Muslim afterwards

It is a curious fact that whenever the expansionist aims of Islam were sought to be achieved, it was said that doctrine of nationalism was contrary to the tenets of Islam. But the same standard was not applied in the case of a conquered territory. A conquered territory was declared an Islamic state and nation forthwith. Thus one would come across contradictions in Islam at every step and these have arisen as a result of the loss of individual liberty in the Islamic world. The application of double standards is a natural corollary to the suppression of individual liberties in any social system.

Whatever one may say about the supremacy of Islam, it is an indisputable fact that even today the Arabs consider themselves as Arabs first and Muslims afterwards. In the eyes of the Arabs, an Arab Jew is more honourable and worthy than a Muslim belonging to a non-Arab country.

During the recent conflict between Israel and Lebanon most of the Christians living in Lebanon fled from their country. When these Christians arrived in the Gulf countries, the Governments of those countries accorded a warm reception to them. Even today one may notice hundreds of Christians with *crosses* dangling from their necks, walking on the streets of Kuwait, Abu Dhabi and Dubai. They say that they were Arabs first and hence they had an unalienable right to live in the land of Arabs. Even in Israel, the Arab Muslims and the Arab Jews have very intimate relations with each other. Both of them are proud to belong to the Arab stock.

Myth of Islamic Brotherhood

The Iran-Iraq war has pricked the bubble of Islamic expansionism. All those walls on which the artificial cement of Islamic brotherhood and *Nizam-e-Mustafa* was sought to be applied, have collapsed in no time. Four salient facts have emerged as a result of this war:

1. It was the expectation of Ayatollah Khomeini that the Shias in Iran, who constituted 55 per cent of the country's population, would raise the banner of revolt against their own Government out of sectarian considerations. But the Shias in Iraq have remained loyal to their country even at the hour of its defeat. Thus this illusion cherished by Khomeini that communal feelings could override the feelings of nationalism has been completely shattered.

2. The fact that the leaders of Islam who cherished the dream of an Islamic bloc failed to stop the Iran-Iraq war proves conclusively that the unity sought to be achieved in the name of Islam was like a palace without a foundation.

3. After the fall of Khorram Shahr, the Arab countries formulated a plan to unite on a common platform in order to teach a lesson to Iran. This proves the fact that Arabs are still swayed by feelings which make a distinction between an *Arab* and an *Azam*.

4. By getting assistance from Israel and the Soviet Union, the rulers of Iran have proved that to them their country and government were dearer than Islam.

On one hand, the Iran-Iraq war has given a blow to Islamic expansionism and on the other, it has posed the danger of Shi'ite expansionism by Khomeini supporters. The weapon of Islamic expansion which was being used by Muslim countries against non-Muslim countries till yesterday is now proposed to be used by one Muslim country against another. Under the banner of Shi'ite expansionism, Khomeini wants to establish his rule over the Sunnis. In other words, the *'Azams'* want to bring the *'Arabs'* under their suzerainty. Two years back, there was a declaration about the arrival of *Mahdi* at the sacred mosque of Mecca. Then there was a conspiracy to overthrow the regimes in Kuwait and Bahrein. Moreover, Iran has refused to agree to a ceasefire despite reoccupation of its territory which was annexed by Iraq in the war. All these incidents are links in the chain of Shi'ite expansionism.

The Weapon Boomeranged

This success of Iran has caused the greatest worry to Saudi Arabia because of the fear that wave of an Iran-type revolution can sweep away the throne of King Khalid any day. Shah Hussain of Jordan is also placed in a more or less similar position. The Sheikh of United Arab Emirates may also be dislodged from power in the event of a revolution in the name of Islam. A Khomeini-led or Khomeini-inspired revolution in Arab states having a centralised power structure is also possible.

The late King of Saudi Arabia, King Khalid, wanted to revive the Caliphate to perpetuate his power. In Pakistan Gen. Zia, realising that Islamic rule was an elixir of life for him, declared that he would establish *Nizam-e-Mustafa* in Pakistan. The first hurdle faced by Gen. Zia in enforcing the Shariat rule was the opposition of Shias in regard to the imposition of *Zakat* and other religious taxes. The Shias constitute 15 per cent of the population of Pakistan. Gen. Zia has been aide to remain in power by using the crutches of economic assistance given by Arab states and his campaign for Islamisation but when the Arabs themselves are beset with their own internal problems, the question arises as to what extent they would be able to support Gen. Zia in his hour of crisis. Revolt against Gen. Zia is inevitable. It may be delayed for some time but there can be no two opinions about its ultimate outcome. What would happen to the dream of an Islamic empire in the event of a revolution in Pakistan?

On the basis of above-mentioned facts, one could imagine as to what would happen to Islamic expansionism and revivalism after the exit of Gen. Zia and King Fahd. Even if the Arabs are able to engineer a counter-revolution against Khomeini, all the schemes of Islamic rule would come to nought forever. In short, the internal feuds and dissensions between the Arabs have reduced the revivalist movement to a mockery. Once this revivalism receives a strong blow, the bubble of expansionism would be automatically pricked.

Bloodstained Power Struggle

A fierce tug-of-war is going on over the question of leadership in this game of power grabbing in the name of Islam. The two leaders of Egypt–Col. Nasser and Anwar Ali Sadat had all along wanted to become supreme leaders of the Muslim world on the issue of Israel. King Fahd wants to become the leader of the Muslim world in the name of Mecca and

Medina. Khomeini has also advanced his claim for being acknowledged the leader of the Muslim world by showing to the world that he alone could bring the United States on its knees.

As long as Mr. Bhutto was alive, he tried to secure the leadership of the Muslim countries by projecting his intellectual image. Now Gen. Zia has also staked his claim for leadership in return for what he has done for the establishment of Islamic rule in Pakistan. Col. Qadhafi of Libya is also asserting his supremacy in this field by establishing Islamic socialism in his country. Moreover, a tug-of-war is going on between the terrorist organisations which have come into being in the name of Islam. In this situation it is difficult to find any Muslim leader whose leadership is acceptable to all the Muslim nations of the world. If there is no unanimity in regard to the leadership question, the question of unanimity in regard to policies and programmes does lot arise at all.

Islam talks about *"Majlis-e-Shura"* and *"Izma"* on the basis of its ideology. But we see wars of succession and monopolisation of power everywhere in Islamic countries and the system of Government in these countries is a form of military dictatorship. The ambition to grab power takes them to the politics of violence. The history of Islam shows that from the time of the third Caliph Hazrat-e-Usman down to the time of the Sultanate of Bani Umayya and Bani Abbas, the bloodstained story of power struggle had remained the same. The Karbala incident is a permanent blot on the face of Islam. This tradition of violence came to India also and according to this tradition, the aspirants for the throne slew their own kith and kin. If on one page of the history we find Alauddin Khilji killing his own uncle on the other page we find a ruler like Aurangzeb usurping the throne of his own father and putting him behind bars. Even today the politics of murder is having its undisputed sway over the Muslim countries of Asia and Africa. Even the Islamic countries of the Indian subcontinent have not been able to refrain from following the bloody trail of the politics of murder despite the fact that many generations of the people of these countries had lived under the umbrella of Indian culture for thousands of years. The murders of Mujibur Rahman, Ziaur Rahman, Liaquat Ali Khan and the execution of Zulfikar Ali Bhutto are recent examples which prove this point.

There is an interesting aspect of Islamic expansionism. The expansion of the Islamic empire resulted in an increase of Muslim population. But side by side a deliberate conspiracy was going on to narrow down the concept of *'Ummat'* or society as far as possible in the name of Islam. All the rules, regulations and customs of Islam have favoured the rulers while the interests of the common man have been totally ignored.

Conversions–a Part of Power Game

The doctrine of *'Darul Harab'* *'Darul Aman'* and *'Darul Islam'* was set forth to create separatist forces in the society. Though the concept of *'Tabligh'* was the basis of this doctrine, it became the most potent instrument of gaining power. A campaign was started to convert *'Darul Harab'* i.e. non-Muslim countries into *'Darul Aman'* and *'Darul Islam'* i.e. Islamic countries. At the same time a campaign for conversions was also started which resulted in a clash between the followers of Islam and the people belonging to other faiths. But according to the injunctions of Islam, Muslims are required to leave those countries where conditions for the establishment of Islamic rule do not exist. This is known as *'Hijrat'*. Despite this injunction no Muslim has ever left such countries. Islam describes Christians and Jews as followers of the religion of *'Ahale Kitab'*. Hence the rules and regulations governing their conversion to Islam are not so hard and they are not subjected to cruelty during the process of conversion. But the attitude towards the followers of those religions which have originated from the Indian subcontinent is characterised by extra ordinary ruthlessness. The following excerpt from the Economist of London, dated 8th August, 1981, gives an indication–howsoever dim–regarding the recent wave of conversions in India which has been secured by with the help of petro-dollars:

> "The conversion controversy has been fuelled by a report in the *Arab Times* of Kuwait, saying that the Islamic Cultural Centre in London is privy to a plan to convert 80 million of India's 120 million untouchables with the help of Gulf money. According to the Kuwaiti newspaper, 50 families of untouchables have agreed to embrace Islam, while benefiting from an agricultural project costing Rs. 50,000.
>
> "Moslem institutions in India have been getting generous help from abroad and consider it their duty to use this money for propagating the faith and improving facilities for their community. One village where mass conversions took place secured a supply of drinking water for the first time. In another village, converts have been given new clothes and offered education and books at Moslem schools."

Islam as Tool of Politics

On account of this fundamentalism, the Islamic countries do not show any tolerance towards the non-Muslim minorities. That is why Bahais in Iran and Kadiyanis and Hindus in Pakistan are victims of his religious bigotry. In the game of power, the minority Muslim Governments in some Islamic countries have victimised even the majority itself. This has happened in the Indian subcontinent. Today, the best example of how these minority Governments have perpetrated atrocities on the majority can be found in Syria. The President of Syria, President Hafiz Asad Alvi belongs to the Shia community. Shias form only 14 per cent of the population of Syria whereas the remaining 86 per cent population consists of Sunni Muslims. The minorities there have the support of a terrorist organisation '*Akhwanul Musalmin,* This organisation wants to bring about a bloody revolution in the name of Islam and therefore the Asad Government does not have any compunction in the massacre of Sunni Muslims. Islam has only a secondary place in his game of power. The ruling clique goes to the farthest extent to keep itself in power. In such a situation it is very difficult to define 'Islamic values.'

The present Government in Uganda which came to power after the fall of Idi Amin has achieved popularity and stability. But the Government of Saudi Arabia is not pleased with this Government. The Muslim population in Uganda is only one-tenth of country's total population out in spite of this, Saudi Arabia's Government is creating a climate of revolt against that country's Government by inciting fanatical Muslim elements. Idi Amin is at present living as an exile in Saudi Arabia. He is a great supporter of the international interests of Saudi Arabia and therefore the Government of Saudi Arabia is also lending its support to a discredited tyrant and despot like Idi Amin. The following excerpts from the Islamic world reviEw, No. 5, January 82, gives an idea about the undesirable activities of Saudi Arabia in Uganda:

> "The type of lawlessness rampant in today's Uganda has led the religious leaders of all denominations to come together as an outspoken critique of Obote's regime. Tired of making declarations of concern in mosques and churches, the clerics demanded and obtained audience with the President. Catholic Archbishop Emmanuel Nsubuga, Anglician Archbishop Sylvanus Wani, Orthodox Bishop Theopheodos Nankyamu and Uganda's Islamic leader, the Chief Khadi Kassim Mulumba together told Obote: 'The Uganda you lead is bleeding to death.'
>
> "The religious leaders further told the government that security in several areas is going from bad to worse. They said in their statement: 'Innocent men, women, children and old people are being murdered mainly by the people who are there to protect the citizens of Uganda. They hold the army responsible for the carnage. Much of the recent killing, rape and looting has taken place in Uganda's West Nile district and Buganda which happen to be the home areas of the majority of Uganda's Muslims'. It was out of concern about the well-being of the Muslim community and about its unity that had led to a considerable activity by Saudi Arabia and the World Muslim League in Makkah. Reconciliation talks chaired by Sheikh Mubarak al-Zayid of the Muslim League

have led to a new unity among Muslims, something that cannot be ignored by Obote."

Kashmir Issue

Though Kashmir is an integral part of India, most of the Muslim countries supports the claim of Pakistan in regard to Kashmir in the name of Islam. Sheikh Abdullah used to say that the people of Azad Kashmir should have the right of passage in Jammu and Kashmir as the people of Azad Kashmir were Kashmiris. Does it not show that Sheikh Abdullah had cherished the dream of an independent state of Kashmir and now his son and successor is also following his footsteps? The Muslim nations are interested in converting the Kashmir problem into a Muslim problem and this attitude is a part of the Islamic expansionism. A fanatical and fundamentalist organisation like the *Jamaat-e-Islami* has given a free role to its Kashmir unit and the *Jamaat* of Kashmir does not come under the *Jamaat* of either India or Pakistan. The members of the *Jamaat* of Kashmir are also entitled to cast votes in elections as the *Jamaat* allows its members to exercise their right of franchise in *'Darul Islam'* countries. In the view of the *Jamaat*, India is a *'Darul Harab'* country and hence this organisation does not allow its members to cast their votes in India.

The aforesaid analysis of Islamic expansionism makes it clear that this expansionism, which was like a boon to Islam till the recent past, has now become a curse due to the activities of Khomeini. The same thing applies to revivalism also. Islam has so far considered revivalism as its shield but now terrorism which is a product of this revivalism has become a challenge to the Islamic rulers themselves. Those who had encouraged the policies of Yasser Arafat had not known that the terrorist organisations supported by them would dislodge them from power.

Islam and Communism

A comparison between Islam and Communism, which are the two expansionist forces in the world today, would lead to the conclusion that they are more or less similar. Outwardly, communism is based on materialism and Islam is based on religion. Though both Marx and Mohammad had evolved the concept of internationalism based on an ideological brother hood, this concept could not transcend regionalism. Both camps are plagued with disputes regarding leadership. Communists called Marshal Tito a revisionist. Similarly in the Islamic world Col. Qadhafi and Khomeini call each other revisionists. Mao had adapted the doctrine of Communism to the geographical and social conditions of his motherland, China. Similarly, not only the Caliphs and Sultans but also the present leaders of Islamic countries have adapted the expansionist doctrine of Islam to their requirements. But now the arms of the clock are going in the reverse direction due to international situation. While on one hand

Islam and Communism are making frantic efforts to dominate the world on the other, both these forces are rapidly disintegrating. Communism had penetrated the countries of Asia and Europe but when it could not strike roots in those countries, it took the form of nationalism. Similarly, those leaders of Islam, who had once cherished the dream of painting the whole world with the green colour of Islam, are finding themselves embroiled in the Iran-Iraq dispute. Islamic expansionism is acceptable to them only so long as it enables them to remain in power. In other words, Islamic expansionism is compelled to seek refuge in nationalism.

Individual freedom has no place either in Islam or Communism. In both systems, one person deprives millions of others of their individual liberties. Both cannot tolerate any dissidence within or difference of approach outside. But the two systems represent entirely different and conflicting approaches to life and its problems. Both are antagonistic to each other. If these differences lead to a clash between the two, it may pave the way for a fresh and healthy change for the whole mankind.

14

Money-Power and Politics of Conversion

Sita Ram Goel

Erudite Scholar and Writer, based at Delhi

Christianity and Islam have tried several strategies to convert Hindu society to their respective creeds. But Hindu society has survived in spite of significant losses in certain areas. The latest weapon wielded by these alien creeds is massive finance they receive from their friends abroad. It is to be seen if this new weapon will win the battle for them.

They tried the sword–Islam for several centuries and all over India, Christianity for several decades along the West Coast. Islam converted a large population in the west and the east. Christianity could convert only a few thousand fishermen. But the resistance and repulsion they provoked in Hindu society was profound.

They tried their patronage during the days of their political domination. The converts to Islam were taken to the courts of the ruling sultans, heaped with presents and praises and quite often conferred with *mansabs* and *jagirs*. The converts to Christianity were granted many concessions by the East India Company and treated preferentially over the other natives. But the overwhelming majority of Hindus spurned such allurements and despised those who fell for them.

They tried their monotheism. The Muslim *mulla* proclaimed that *allah* was the *only* true god and that Mohammad was that god's *last* prophet. The Christian missionary claimed that his god was the *only* true one and that Jesus was the *only* true saviour. Some Hindus here and there might have been impressed by these claims for a monopoly of truth and salvation. But the majority of Hindus laughed at what they regarded as ridiculous.

They tried their heaven and hell to attract and frighten by turn. Sophisticated Hindu spirituality, however, found these promises and threats quite crude.

End of Political Power

But the *mulla* and the missionary refuse to learn any lesson. They refuse to realise that the fault lies not with the "heretic" Hindus but with the falsehoods of their own exclusive and external creeds. They refuse to recognise that Hinduism represents a great spiritual vision which cannot be obscured by their crude theologies. They fail to see that Hindu society harbors a deep culture of the soul which is beyond comparison.

The political power of Islam and Christianity in India is a story of the past. The missionary and the *mulla* can no more rely on the sword or prosper on patronage. Their theologies have become threadbare. Their "only true" gods sound hollow, if not horrible. The only saviour of Christianity now causes scepticism even in those lands which have prized him most. More and more people are coming to know of the life of the "last prophet" and they find it truly unedifying.

Yet, the missionary, as well as the *mulla,* has suddenly revived his hope about his full and final victory. The missionary continues to hope that India will be a land of Christ in a not too distant future. The *mulla* continues to be convinced that this *dar-ul-harb* will become a *dar-ul-Islam* before long.

What is it that makes the missionary and the *mulla* entertain this hope? There has been no change in their dogmas which remain as dismal as ever before. There has been no change in their methods which repeat the same stereotypes. Islam and Christianity will cease to be what they are if they changed their dogmas or modified their methods. What is it, then, that has undergone a change?

Looking at the scene that has been unfolding in this country in recent years, the contours of the change can be identified. The change has taken place along two lines: (1) an unprecedented swelling up of the coffers of Islam and Christianity by a flow of mammoth finances from abroad and (2) a progressive degeneration in the perceptions of Hindu society, particularly the Hindu elite.

II

Post-Independence Scene

When India achieved independence after a hard and prolonged struggle against successive waves of foreign imperialism–Islamic and Western–the missionary and the *mulla* were seized with fear and panic. They no more saw any future for their conspiracies in this country. The missionary had started packing his paraphernalia in order to take it back home. The *mulla* was also beginning to lose heart.

But their fears proved false. The class that rose to power in India assured the missionary and the *mulla* that they had no cause for panic and that they could continue their crusades in the interests and under the patronage of a secular state.

The missionary was assured that he alone was competent to impart quality education to the sons and daughters of the new class, as also to take care of the health of those who mattered under the new dispensation. He was complimented for the "excellent care" he had taken of our orphans and lepers and the otherwise handicapped in the past, and requested to go on rendering his ministrations in future. And his services were requisitioned to multiply, as fast as he could, his schools and colleges, hospitals and 'homes' for the handicapped. As the missionary could not shoulder this onerous responsibility without multiplying his ranks, he was allowed to do so with a liberal grant of visas and citizenship facilities.

The second industrial revolution in Western Europe and Northern America followed soon after. The West was now rolling in riches it had never known before. The missionary in India was also allotted his due share of this vast wealth. Huge funds were made available to him by the Defence and Foreign Policy departments of many Western countries. The missionary had been maintained by these establishments in the past as well. The hats that did the rounds in Christian communities all over the Western world for collecting funds in the service of the *only* saviour were now filled to capacity. The wealthy ones who did not care for Christianity but happened to be large-hearted otherwise, were told that the "poor, starved, sick and illiterate Hindus" were crying for crumbs from his table. The cumulative effect of all this affluence and effort was that, in the words of Mother Teresa, the missions could not always use all the money that was raised for them.

Harvest of Secularism

In like manner, the *mulla* was assured very soon that he had no reason to feel small, that the suspect in India was not Islam but "Hindu communalism which had divided the motherland", and that he could go about his normal work in "the second largest Muslim country in the world". He was also told that India was very proud of the "rich Islamic heritage", that the medieval *sultans* whom the "Hindu communalist" was accusing of imperialism, despotism and religious bigotry were illustrious sons of the soil, and that he himself had much to tell to a caste-ridden and superstitious Hindu society.

The *mulla* lost no time in resuming his age-old role of manufacturing "grievances" against the state which he said was secular only in name. He now came forward as the champion of Muslim "rights" which according to him had been denied although guaranteed by the democratic constitution. For all practical purposes, he became the foremost defender of secularism and democracy in this country.

If a "Hindu communalist" or a "Muslim renegade" appealed to the *mulla* to give up his separatism and join the mainstream of Indian nationalism, he started shouting from the housetops that his religion and culture were being threatened with extinction. At the same time, he reserved his right to be partisan towards the Islamic state of Pakistan, both in war and peace, and to support Islamic causes, right and wrong, all over the world. He also felt free to stage a riot whenever he thought that the Hindus were disregarding the unequal privileges he had enjoyed under the Muslim and the British rule, or that India's foreign policy had strayed away from an all-out support for Islamic causes, or that the Hindus were not showing sufficient concern for calamities in Muslim countries.

Oil Power and Petro-dollars

Meanwhile, a windfall for the *mulla* was preparing to burst out of the womb of human history. The second industrial revolution in the West, while it had made the West wealthy, had at the same time exhausted its reserves of coal and oil. The West was now becoming more and more dependent on oil reserves in the Persian Gulf and North Africa, all of them controlled by Islamic countries. An unceasing and progressively swelling flood of petro-dollars had started flowing towards Iran, Iraq, Kuwait, Libya, Oman, Saudi Arabia and United Arab Emirates. An idea of this vast wealth can be formed by the oil revenues of Saudi Arabia which is now earning 350 million dollars per day.

The Islamic countries were now making money far in excess of what they could use for renovations at home, or for buying military hardware from East and West, or for securing a life of dream-like luxury for their sheikhs in five-star hotels and holiday resorts all over the world. A fat lot of this money started flowing towards *mullas* in the poorer Islamic lands. And a large share of this money was made available to the Indian *mulla* who now ascended the pulpit in new robes with a re-acquired self-confidence. The Islamic divines in India declared that *allah* was not a fool when he put all this wealth under the feet of the faithful.

To start with, the *mulla* used this money for renovating the old and building new mosques on a grand scale. Archaeological sites and other ruins were ransacked in search of *mazars*, Muslim tombs and relics of old and deserted shrines. Many more places were claimed as places of Muslim worship and painted afresh. An army of loafers was recruited to look after these "shrines" with incense and flowers and to manage a regular flow of "pilgrims". And all mosques, even in places where there was no Muslim population, were fitted with public address systems.

Next, the *mulla* invested his wealth in *maktabs* and *madrasas*, periodicals and publishing houses, and real estate on a large scale. The *maktabs* and *madrasas* were to train more *mullas*. The periodicals and publishing houses were to remind Muslim society in India that Islam was the *only* true religion, that Islamic cultural heritage was an incomparable heritage, and that the armies of Islam had at one time conquered and ruled over this vast land. The Muslims were being prepared to resume the role of *ghazis* in the image of their "forefathers". Nobody was supposed to tell them that their forefathers were Hindus who had been converted to Islam by force and fraud, and that very few of them were descendants of the Arab and Turk invaders.

The neo-rich Muslim nations had asked the Indian Muslims to shed their minority complex. The Muslims in India, they were told, were a nation by themselves and should behave as such. There were many pockets all over India where the Muslim population lived in comparative concentration. These pockets were to be cleared of whatever Hindu population had remained near or in the midst of them. Almost all Hindus who lived in the midst of or near Mulims *mohallas* happened to be Harijans. So we had Jamshedpur and Moradabad and Meerut where Harijans were the main victims of Muslim wrath. While they were staging the riots on one hand, on the other they were maligning the police and other security forces. A new chapter was thus being written in the history of Islam in India.

III

Money Factor in Mass Conversions

Hindu society had so far failed to measure the magnitude of this money in the hands of the missionary and the *mulla*. After Moradabad, Kuldip Nayar had coined the thesis that "Hindu communalists" were creating riots wherever they found the Muslims becoming prosperous in industry and trade. The Muslim press and politicians picked up this thesis immediately. They proclaimed that the Muslims had every right to use their prosperity for renovating their places of worship and their private properties. Nobody noticed the contradiction that the same champions of the Muslims were simultaneously presenting the Muslims as a poor and persecuted minority.

It was in the midst of this Hindu carelessness and Muslim casuistry that mass conversions to Islam took place at several villages in the south, particularly Meenakshipuram. The journalists who visited these places in the first flush of excitement were told by the converts themselves that the latter had been given money, new clothes and several types of presents and promises of jobs in the Gulf countries. The spokesmen of Islam denied any use of material inducements whatsoever. They assured their countrymen that Harijans had flocked to the fold of Islam in search of social equality which they had failed to find in Hindu society and which Islam assured to them in ample measure. Reacting to such reports, a Harijan leader from New Delhi protested that caste Hindus were casting aspersions on the integrity and honesty of the Harijans.

Ever since, this new and massive money in the hands of the *mulla* has been the subject of a sharp political controversy. In the heat of this controversy, the money in the hands of the missionary has been almost forgotten. But it has to be remembered that Islam is a novice in the use of money for conversions. Its tried and tested weapon so far has been naked and unashamed violence. It is Christianity which has perfected the art of using money and other material inducements to win over members of other societies.

A country-wide field survey to find out the comparative poverty or prosperity of Muslims as a community after Independence has never been carried out. Some time ago a survey was carried out in Karnataka. It revealed that the Christians were the most prosperous community while *Brahmins* were the poorest. Muslims were placed fairly high in the scale of prosperity. If such field surveys are conducted, the Karnataka scenario is likely to be confirmed in other provinces also so far as the Muslim community is concerned. Such studies will reveal that the myth of Muslim poverty such as is circulated by the spokesmen of Islam and the secularist politicians does not seem to have any foundation in the facts of the case. Muslims seem to be fairly prosperous as artisans, shopkeepers, traders and exporters, not to speak of smugglers amongst whom they form a majority. Those who talk of Muslim poverty look like keeping only big Hindu capitalists in mind, and forgetting that, by and large, Hindus bear the brunt of poverty in equal, if not larger, measure as compared to the non-Hindu communities.

Swami Vivekananda had calculated the amount which Christianity was spending in India on an average in order to win a single convert, it

I remember aright, the figure given by him, while addressing a Christian audience in America, was Rs. 24,000. That was almost a century ago. The average at present must be many times more due to inflation as well as acceleration in the volume of Christian money-power.

Another significant thing to be noticed is the new language of salesmanship adopted by both Christianity and Islam. The missionary has started selling his superstitions in the name of social service and social revolution. The *mulla* is now hawking Islam in the name of human brotherhood. The use of money for conversions is thus sought to be hidden under a mass of high-sounding verbiage. In the process, Hindu society has been put against the wall as a society Jacking in even elementary social ethics and having no conception of the dignity of man

IV

Foreign Conspiracy for Conversions

The first salvo for Islam in India was fired in the middle of 1980 by the Islamic Cultural Centre, London. As reported at that time by the *Arab Times* of Kuwait, the Centre had made plans to convert 80 million Harijans to Islam with the help of money to be made available by oil-rich Islamic countries. Mass conversions in South India followed soon after. But the plot was discovered and received wide publicity. Hindu organisations all over the country sat up and appealed to the government to stop the mischief.

Much water has flown down the Yamuna since those eventful days in the middle of 1980. The subject has been studied in some detail not only by some Hindu organisations but also by others who normally frown at what they describe as Hindu communalism. They have all come to the conclusion that Islam in India has a plenty of petro-dollars at its disposal and that a large part of these funds is being used for promoting conversions amongst poorer sections of Hindu society.

The *Times of India,* New Delhi, was the first amongst our prestigious newspapers to make some significant facts known in its issue of March 21, 1981 under the heading 'International Conspiracy for Mass Conversion of Harijans'. It reported:

> "Plans to convert poor Harijans to Islam and setting up of a host of organisations of journalists, youths, trade unions and *kisan sabhas* with the help of 'friendly' Arab countries and Islamic organisations in London and Europe have come to light. The Union Home Ministry is perturbed at these developments and is investigating reports about the activities of extreme Muslim organisations such as *Jamaat-e-Islami*...
>
> "Plans to convert Hindu Harijans were later published in the *Arab Times* of Kuwait. Quoting London-based Islamic Cultural Centre's

reports, the paper said that plans were afoot to convert 80 million out of 120 million Harijans. These poor Harijans could be lured to Islam with financial largesses from oil-rich Islamic Gulf States and other Arab Nations.

"According to this report 50 Hindu families in India had secretly adopted Islam. They were lured by a grant of about Rs. 4 lakhs for an agricultural project.

"The Centre's director, Mohamed Abdul Kheir Badawi, in his report, told Muslim nations that the time was ripe for converting poor Harijans. Such a move would raise the Muslim population in India from 80 million to 200 million in the next decade. He suggested sending to India Urdu-speaking Arab proselytizers. These preachers will carry out work discreetly so as not to arouse suspicion of Hindus.

"The Home Ministry has evaded direct reference to the involvement of the *Jamaat* or any Arab state in the recent communal riots in U. P. and other parts of the country. But the Home Minister and the Prime Minister have referred to a foreign hand behind these riots. The Saudis were giving money to Haj pilgrims from India, some of whom abetted communal riots.

"Apprehension has been expressed in some quarters at the massive grants given by Saudi Arabia and some other countries to institutions like Darul-ul-Uloom, a Centre for Islamic Studies near Moradabad...

"The *Jamaat* has been receiving funds not only directly from the Islamic countries but also through the Islamic Foundation in London and several other such organisations based in UK and Europe. Dr. Mustafa Tahan, a representative of the Islamic Foundation, attended the *Jamaat's* Hyderabad conference. Representatives of the U.K. Islamic Mission were also present. Among those present were Sheikh Mabrook, a Minister in the Saudi Cabinet, and Abdullah Turki, Chancellor of Riyadh University. Many other representatives, who had come to celebrate the 15th Centenary of the Hijra, also attended the Hyderabad function."

Flow of Foreign Money

The *Hindu* of Madras reported as follows in its issue of September 23, 1981 under the heading 'Foreign Money From Muslim Nations Influenced Conversion':

"Reports reaching here spoke of monetary help of the *Ishathul Islam Sabha* from Saudi Arabia and more than one country, particularly the *Rabita-e-Alam-e-Islami,* Mecca, for the Malabar Education Society (MES).

"While the *Sabha*, according to the information, provided jobs to converts and supplied sewing machines and cattle for self-employment to the poorer among them, the MES arranged the medical aid.

"The programme was administered by the London Centre, which had planned a surveyor the conditions of Indian Muslims and reported that the climate for conversion of Harijans to Islam was favourable.

"The reports spoke of the unusual interest shown by Pan-Islamic elements in Indian Muslims and referred to a Karachi organisation, called the *Motamar-al-Alam al-Islam,* primarily set up to bolster Pakistan's image in Muslim countries and its proclaimed desire to help Muslim groups in India in accelerating the spread of Islam among Harijans, especially in the south.

"The organisation set a target of 50,000 Harijans to be converted to Islam this year, and 200,000 by the end of next year.

"The London Centre's plans were more ambitious–to convert eight crore Harijans. Mention was also made of the receipt in India of huge amounts from rich Muslim countries for such activities as construction and renovation of mosques.

"The *Jamaat* had reportedly chosen 33 mosques in Tamil Nadu, each of which was to be given Rs. 3 lakhs. It was only a channel for the money received from the Mecca organisation through the Indian Council of Mosques, a newly-formed body."

Oil Fuels the Faith

Next, the fortnightly *India Today* published from New Delhi carried an article, Oil Fuels the Faith, in its issue of November, 30 1981. It said:

"The hue and cry in India over conversions to Islam and the heated debate on whether Gulf money was involved are watched with surprise and not a little amusement in the Gulf countries. It is admitted here that a share of the huge bounty from oil is spent for promoting Islam. As one official of the Islamic and Awkaf Affairs Ministry in Kuwait admits candidly:

> 'Of course we spend money on spreading Islam. What's wrong with that? We will spread the word of the prophet with all the resources at our command.'

"The Sheikhdoms of the Gulf–Kuwait, the United Arab Emirates (UAE) and Saudi Arabia–have been spending more and more to propagate the faith ever since the oil price hike in 1974. Even after funding the most grandiose welfare projects, sizeable surpluses of money remain which cannot be spent usefully. A good part of this surplus has been officially allotted to what is termed as 'spreading Islamic culture'.

"There is no element of secrecy about these activities; quite the opposite, in fact. The Ministry of Awkaf, which is in charge of these matters actively encourages conversions. In Kuwait anyone who converts to Islam is entitled to a ministry grant of 1,000 Kuwaiti dinars (Rs. 34,000). Larger sums are also sometimes sanctioned at the discretion of officials if they feel the case merits it. These conversions are given wide publicity and stories of conversions are treated as a matter of pride and satisfaction.

"Muslim politicians and leaders from countries like India, South Korea and China are especially welcome. Gulf governments felt a particular duty to promote Islam in these countries where Muslims are in a minority. It is common knowledge that among Muslim politicians who visit the region, not a few return with pockets bulging with money which is never accounted for. This money is described as personal gifts from the Ministry of Awkaf.

"The Gulf governments keep quiet about these payments only because their recipients request them to do so. 'They would have problems at home, you know. All sorts of motives are attributed to them', explains a ministry official...With regard to India, officials admit that some money could well be going towards converting Harijans. Says one, 'Certainly, we have no way of checking. We don't ask for an audit. *But we would consider that our funds were well spent even if a single person converted himself from idolatry. It is one of the finest services a good Muslim can render to his brother in his life.*'

"At a conservative estimate the officials reckon that Saudi Arabia, Kuwait and the UEA together spend about US $ 200 million (Rs. 180 crore) every month directly or indirectly to promote Islam abroad.

"The Gulf governments defend their attempts at proselytisation. '*It is our sacred duty and our religious obligation to spend our money for such a sublime purpose,*' says an official. The latest step in this drive to spread the word has been the setting up of the Kuwait National Committee for Education, Science and Culture. The Committee, which has been charged with the duty of spreading the faith, is headed by no less a person than the country's Education Minister...

"Besides this, an International Centre for Islamic Teaching was inaugurated in October to 'supervise curricula in the various stages of teaching in the Islamic world'. The Centre has strong connections on the Indian subcontinent and its director, Dr. Mohammad Jamil Khayyat, says openly that the Centre is '*the product of meetings held in Mecca, Islamabad and Dacca*'.

Home Ministry's Findings

In an article published in *Business Standard* of Calcutta dated November 16, 1981, Kuldip Nayar leaked out a confidential report compiled by the

Ministry of Home Affairs, Government of India. According to him this report had blamed the Arab countries for Harijan conversions. Similar news appeared in *The Statesman* a year later, on 16 November, 1982 to be exact. Finally, a New Delhi monthly published the full text of this Government of India report in its issue of January 1983. Referring to the use of money, this report says as follows:

"There is enough indication that the zeal with which the *Jamaat-e-Islami-Hind* and other revivalist groups are working in this area to accelerate the conversion of Harijans, is at least partly attributable to the resources these parties have acquired from the Muslim countries and the Pan-Islamic organisations over the last two or three years. The affluent Muslims of this region who have close commercial links with the Gulf countries as well as the Muslim countries in the South East supplemented the efforts of the Muslim organisations. The Karachi-based *Motamar al-Alam-al-Islam* (World Muslim Congress) has claimed credit for the mass conversions in and around Meenakshipuram. It has stated that the target for conversion of Harijans to Islam for the year 1981 was 50,000 of which some 1,700 had already been converted. This number was expected to swell to 200,000 persons by the end of 1982. The London-based Islamic Cultural Centre is reported to have worked out plans to convert 80 million of the 120 million Harijans in India to Islam with financial largesses from the oil-rich Islamic Gulf states and other Arab nations. The move is stated to be aimed at raising the Muslim population in India from 80 million to 200 million in the next decade."

All these reports, however, have revealed only the tip of the iceberg. The full extent of the use of money-power by Islam has yet to be investigated in depth and detail. The results of such an investigation are sure to surpass the most liberal estimates made so far.

Christianity which started using money-power in India much earlier has at its disposal financial resources which far exceed the funds acquired by Islam in India so far. Even if we leave aside the missionary schools, colleges, hospitals and homes for the handicapped, which are working in the interests of Christianity indirectly, the monasteries and seminaries, which house foreign missionaries and train native crusaders for the direct work of conversion, add up to an impressive number. The foreign finances which flow for maintaining these insidious institutions are colossal. That has also to be surveyed and scrutinised. That will provide the key to a correct understanding of the separatism inspired and instigated by Christianity in several states in our North-East.

V

But money-power of Christianity and Islam would have also failed to make an impact on Hindu society if they had not been helped by another factor which has entered the situation. This new factor is the state of Hindu society at present. This society has not only lowered its guards against its inveterate enemies after the attainment of independence; it has also bred in its own ranks a species of self-alienated skunks. The skunks have sprung up most speedily in those sections of Hindu society which have had a past record of collaboration with Islamic and Western imperialism.

At one time, these sections saw nothing objectionable in Islamic conquerors who were murdering their countrymen *en masse* and trampling under foot everything cherished by Hindu society. On the contrary, they welcomed Islamic culture as a superior culture and collaborated with their Muslim masters in humiliating Hindu society. Some scions of these sections wrote histories of wars waged by the Muslim marauders in which the Hindus that got killed were sent to hell and the Muslims who fell were hailed as martyrs, *a la* their contemporary Muslim historians.

But as soon as the British came out victorious, the same sections started singing praises of the new master and his "incomparable" culture. They were now aping the "master race" in pouring contempt over everything Hindu, particularly Hindu spirituality and the Hindu social system.

The system of education devised by Macaulay during the early days of the British rule has bred many more self-alienated people from other sections of Hindu society. The missionary schools and colleges in particular have multiplied such people much faster, and have invested them with a smug sense of superiority which cannot be shaken easily. They know next to nothing about Hindu history or Hindu society, not to speak of Hindu spirituality and culture. Their contempt for everything "native" is to be seen in order to be believed.

The same system of education has been extended on a large-scale after the attainment of independence. It continues to spread self-alienation in larger and larger sections of Hindu society. What is still more ominous, these self-alienated people have managed to monopolise almost all places of power and prestige under the present dispensation.

Lastly, the language of leftism in general and of communism in particular, which has flooded this country during the last sixty years has imbued these self-alienated people with a sense of self-righteousness also. Now they can swear at Hindu society and heritage in the name of science, socialism, secularism, progress and the march of human history.

Islam and Christianity can safely depend on these people to act as their sappers and miners, to damage all Hindu defences, ideological as well as psychological, and to cry wolf whenever and wherever Hindu society tries to strengthen itself. Hindu society, therefore, has a twofold task before it: (I) expose Christianity and Islam as ideologies of imperialism employing imperialist methods to subvert Hindu society, and (2) to purge itself of the self-alienated people who sabotage it from within.

Manifestations of the money-power of Christianity and Islam do not require much of an effort to be seen. Nor do the skunks fail to spread their smell far and wide. Both of them can be easily located for what they are, where they are.

JIHAD IN TWENTIETH CENTURY!

In October, 1968, at the fourth conference of the Islamic Research Academy *AL-AZHAR* University of Cairo (Egypt) Sheikh Abdaliah Ghoshah, Supreme Judge of the Hashemite Kingdom of Jordan, presented a paper on *JIHAD* in which he made the following significant revelation:

Jihad is legislated in order to be one of the means of propagating Islam. Consequently, non-Muslims ought to embrace Islam either willingly or through wisdom and good advice or unwillingly through fight and Jihad. Scholars lay the foundation of the foreign policy of the Islamic states on the following bases:

1. It is unlawful to give up Jihad and adopt peace and weakness, unless the purpose of giving up is for preparation, whenever, there is something weak among Muslims and their opponents are strong.
2. War is the basis of the relationship between Muslims and their opponents unless there are justifiable reasons for peace such as adopting Islam or making an agreement with them to keep peaceful.
3. The abode of Islam is the homeland which is subject to the rules of Islam.....
4. Muslims are free to break their covenant with enemies if they are uneasy lest the enemies should betray them.

This paper is available in the complete transactions of this conference published in 1970 by the Egyptian Government Printing Office in Arabic (3 Vols.) and in English **(1** *Volume, 935 pages***)**

cf: **John Laffin:** *The Dagger of Islam* (London, 1981) pp. 54-55)

DOCUMENTS

A Conspiracy That Failed

Relevant extracts from the letters written by RAGHIB AHSAN (Member, Working Committee, Bengal Provincial Muslim League and All India Muslim League Council) to M.A. JINNAH are reproduced here from *Quaid-e-Azam Jinnah's Correspondence* Edited by Syed Sharifuddin Pirzada (Publishers: Metropolitan Book Co. Pvt. Ltd., New Delhi- 110002, Indian Edition, 1981, pp. 303-318).

-Ed

I

Calcutta, 13th August, 1944

Copy to Quaid-e-Azam:

My dear Sir Nazimuddin,

1. The question of the outline of East Pakistan has been engaging my mind from the beginning. It was with this very idea that I several time visited Ranchi, met Mr. Jaipal Singh 'Munda' M. A. (Oxon), the President of the Adibasi Mahasabha and the champion of Adibasistan and leader of National War Front in Chota Nagpore. After this evening discussion of the problem of Pakistan in the Working Committee it has become difficult for me to sleep peacefully. It is clear that some members are taking a very narrow and parochial view which will be fatal.

I am enclosing a note on the subject which I have sent to Mr. Jinnah. Kindly go through them and oblige me.

Reduce Muslim Majority But Have Burdwan & Singhbhum

2. It is a matter of greatest joy for me that materially we agree on this subject. I would be ready to reduce Muslim majority to the barest minimum say 52 p.c. and grant caste Hindus the most generous terms and liberal concessions but we must insist on having Burdwan Division and at least Singhbhum (containing Jamshedpore and Iron Mines) and Mayorbhanj State which is politically a Bengal State and in the Census and Government reports is included in the orbit of Bengal plus Balasore and parts of East Purnea bordering on Dinajpore, Mayorbhanj supplies iron ore to Tatanagary.

Confederacy of Pakistan and Adibasistan

3. The Chota Nagpore and Santal Parganas, Surguja and other adjoining territories are really speaking the Homeland of Adibasis-the aboriginal Tribals who are demanding separation from Hindu Bihar. Chota Nagpore or Adibasistan (which cannot stand alone at present)

and Bengsman (East Pakistan) should form a Confederacy. They should have their separate legislatures and Governments but should jointly manage (1) Bengal Nagpore Railways; Communications; (2) Customs; (3) Defence; (4) Foreign Policy; (5) Currency; (6) Post and Telegraph; (7) Common port of Calcutta and such matters. The two will form a joint development board and agree to work for industrialization on lines of democratic socialism for the uplift of the poor masses of Adibasis, Muslims, Scheduled Castes and Hindus. Only State Socialism can checkmate dangers of the Capitalism of Birla-Tata clan.

The Bengal League has adopted the abolition of landlordism as the first item of its programme. Let it now adopt the policy of Socialization of Heavy Industries, Public utility services and Defence industries as its next step. This will win over the Adibasis whose leaders have joined the Radical Democratic Party of M.N. Roy.

The Adibasis, the Muslims and the Scheduled Castes and even general mass of the caste Hindus will equally welcome Socialism and combine to make it a success. This will on the one hand break the backbone of aggressive communalism and on the other free Muslims to spread Islam and Islamic culture by way of peaceful penetration. It will lift and remove fear complex.

Like Peace of Hudaibya

In fact Treaty for such a Confederacy of Adibasistan and Pakistan will be a blessing like the Peace of Hudaibya by which Mecca recognized the independence and integrity of Medina although under very disadvantageous and bad terms for the Muslims of Medina, so much so that Hazrat Omer was not ready to surrender to it. But the Prophet accepted it for it granted the Muslims recognition as an independent power and gave opportunity to make peaceful penetration by Education and Tabligh into Mecca and Arabia with the result that Muslims were able to Islamize whole of Arabia only in two or three years after this peace.

As Muslims let us be optimist and courageous and liberal. Let us give up inferiority complex of fear. Let us free our minds from defeatism.

41 p.c, on Education Board 51 *Versus* p.c. in Every Department of Government

4. If Muslim culture could not be destroyed by the complete Anglo-Hindu domination in education, Government, legislature and everything in the last 150 years when the Muslims of Bengal had not even 1 p.c. representation on the University and the Government, the poor caste- Hindus, after their dream of All India Hindu *Raj* at the Centre has been completely smashed, can never break and destroy

Muslim culture when the Muslims will have at least 50 or 52 p.c. solid and genuine representation on legislature, University education and in every department of Government. The position will be otherwise. Because economically the Muslims, Scheduled Castes and Tribes will pursue a proletarian or Socialist policy and combine, for, their economic and political interests are common.

Then we have agreed to accept only 41 p.c. Muslim representation on the Bengal Secondary Education Board according to Secondary Education Bill of 1944. If we hope to protect and develop our culture by 41 p.c. we can more than protect and develop ourselves by 52 p.c. or 50 p.c.

Progress of Adibasis in Education

5. Sir Nazimuddin's argument that Adibasis are backward is based on wrong information. In fact, Adibasis of Chota Nagpore are more advanced in education and lighting capacity than many parts of Bengal. There are many M.As and M.Scs. Their ladies give masterly oration in fluent and beautiful English on the independence and separation of Chota Nagpore.

Adibasis and Muslims Traditionally Friends

6. Then by race and tradition the Adibasis are most friendly with Muslims. In fact most of the Nagpuria Musalmans are by race tribal and speak their language. The Adibasi flags fly side by side with League flags. They raise slogans of *PAKISTAN ZINDABAD* with their cry of *Adibasistan Zindabad.* Even at times of riots they have invariably sided with Muslims and fought against the Hindus. I personally know that Jaipal Singh, their leader, was the first to come in the field for the defence of the Mosque at Doranda (Ranchi) from the Mahabir Dal Procession. Jaipal Singh led the Muslim Deputation before the Commissioner of Chota Nagpore. Jaipal Singh fought against Birla's tactics to harm Muslim weavers of Chota Nagpore.

From the very beginning "Nagpuria" Muslims and Adibasis have been jointly working for the separation of Chota Nagpore from Bihar. The first Memorandum of the Adibasistan was signed equally by Adibasis and Muslims. In all elections to District Boards, Adibasis and Muslims have worked and voted jointly as friends and allies.

Meet Mr. Jaipal Singh

I suggest, therefore, that you should meet Mr. Jaipal Singh and have free and frank talk. *Adibasistan will alone solve the problem of East Pakistan.* A Confederacy of Adibasistan and East Pakistan will be practical, defensible, solvent and self-sufficient. In fact, it will make it invincible and the richest and most powerful in India.

What Amery & British Think

It will be also in accord with the latest trend of Mr. Amery's policy and British mind as revealed in the recent parliamentary debates, particularly Mr. Elliot's suggestion of having more than two Units and Mr. Amery's support to the suggestion. Mr. Elliot (Conservative) supported Prof. Coupland's Four River Basin Planning, (1) Indus (2) Ganges Valley (3) Brahm Putra and Ganges Delta (Bengal and Assam) and (4) Daccan or Dravedanad and also the Five States Plan of Sir Feroze Khan Noon viz: (1) Pakistan (2) Hindustan (3) Dravedanad or Dravedistan (4) Maharashtra and (5) Bengsman (Bengal and Assam).

This is what Mr. Walter Elliot said in Parliament:

"Pakistan solution suffered from over simplicity and a dual solution was a solution to perpetuate antagonism...This is to produce an impossible situation and some means to escape must be found from it whether a dualist solution or more than a dual solution, *the setting up, it may be, of four or five units.*" Mr. Elliot said he was more attracted by a solution such as the River Basin Scheme (of Coupland) which suggested *four great Units* and there had been other suggestions including the *Five States Scheme* (of Sir Feroze Khan Noon). "But", added Mr. Elliot, "on the principle of two or more than two it seems to me that *two* is more dangerous solution than *many* because two seems to make for antagonism which would be exacerbated more as years go on".

Mr. Amery Favours More Units Plan

Mr. Amery, Secretary of State for India, replying to the Commons' India debate said:

"I do agree with my Right Honourable friend Elliot that a division of anything into two may be more difficult to reconcile with ultimate cooperation than a division into a number of Units. I agree with him and indeed it underlies the present situation in India but any Constitution which may be framed, that economic development to be effective must have the support not merely of passive acquiescence, but involve something in the nature of patriotism". *(Dawn* 30-7-44).

Christians Will Support Adibasistan-Pakistan Union

It should be realized that Pakistan depends on the agreement of the British, the rulers of India, and that they will hotly favour Adibasistan-Pakistan Confederacy because it will give free scope to Christian missions in Chota Nagpore.

As a matter of fact the Christian Adibasis are more zealous supporters of Adibasistan than the Animist Adibasis, because they are educationally more advanced than the latter.

The Christian missionaries of Chota Nagpore have been pressing the demand of Adibasistan because Chota Nagpur and Bengal industries are interdependent.

Another point to be noted is that all the heavy industries of Bengal e.g. Bengal Iron Steel Works of Kulti, Burnpore (Burdwan), Cossipore Gun and Shell Factory (Calcutta) and the Rifle and Ordnance Factory, Ichapore, Bengal Assam Railway Workshop which is being fitted for producing Railway Locomotives and jute mills all depend on Singhbhum and Mayorbhanj for iron ores and on Burdwan and Barakar (Hazaribagh) for coal, mica, shellack, manganese etc.

Even if Chota Nagpore is left out in Hindustan, Pakistan must get free access to those mines and the same rights it is enjoying at present for utilization of the mines. In return Calcutta port will give them the same facilities.

Yours sincerely,
Raghib Ahsan

II

Calcutta District Muslim League
8, Zakaria Street, Calcutta
Dated: 1-9-1944

My dear Quaid-e-Azam,

...I will send you tomorrow my note on my demarcations on the map of India (enclosure No. 1) showing the boundary lines of (1) East Pakistan and (2) Adibasistan according to my idea. East Pakistan Zone proper has been marked *red* and Adibasistan Zone has been marked *blue.* In brief my East Pakistan proper is composed of the whole of Assam and Bengal plus Akayab District and the 'excluded' tribal frontier tracts of Arakan Hills, Chin Hills, Hukawang Valley, then the Eastern one half of Purnea. It will have at least over 21 lakh Muslim majority.

My idea of Adibasistan is that the Chota Nagpur Division and Santal Parganas with an area of 32,592 sq. miles and population of 9,750,866 should be formed into a separate autonomous state as the homeland of the aboriginal Adibasis, in confederal Union with East Pakistan. This Zone alone is more in area and population than Orissa. Orissa has an area of 32,198 sq. miles and a population of 8,728,544; that is less than the area and population of Chota Nagpur and Santal Parganas. The Chota Nagpur state which are all Adibasi and Mayorbhanj which is also Adibasi in majority should be placed under its suzerainty.

The coal and iron reserves tables will show you that the assertion of Prof. Charles Behre of the Columbia University, in the Foreign Affairs

Quarterly as quoted by *A.B. Patrika* on 13-8-44 that "The Pakistan State of Bengal would industrially speaking die" and that "about 90 p.c. of Indian coal and 92 p.c. of iron would belong to Hindustan" is absolutely wrong and based on the baseless supposition and propaganda that Chota Nagpur is a Hindu majority province. But Singhbhum, Bustar, Rajmahel, Jharia and Adibasistan areas are not Hindustan and should never be allowed to be grabbed by Hindustan.

Yours sincerely,
Raghib Ahsan

III

Calcutta,
Dated: *10-10-1944*

My dear Quaid-e-Azam,

...General belief is that failing an agreement the British will make Pakistan dependent and contingent upon the votes of the present provinces-per Cripps Plan. In that case, it is vital that we should win over the (1) Depressed Classes, (2) The Adibasis (one p.c. in Bengal and 25 p.c. in Assam), (3) The Kisans, Ryots, Labourers, Socialists and other peoples. If we have pacts with the two–*the Adibasis* and the *Depressed Classes*–we will triumph.

Yours sincerely,
Raghib Ahsan

IV

Calcutta,
3 November 1944

My dear Quaid-e-Azam,

(1) I am sending you the Puja Annual Number of the *Amrita Bazar Patrika* under registered cover. I specially invite your attention to the article:-"Changing the Map of Bengal: The Politics of Boundaries" on page 34 by a Bengali Hindu. The article broadly represents the Bengali Hindu mind.

Your plea for Greater Bengal consisting of at least the whole of the present Provinces of Bengal and Assam has really pleased the heart of every Bengalee, Hindu or Muslim. It should be noted that in case the Burdwan Division is left out of the Pakistan Scheme, the Hindus will have another weighty reason for their opposition to the Muslim demands out of their perpetual antagonism to the Muslims, namely (1) the division and fragmentation of the Bengalee people and consequent damage to Bengalee language and culture; in addition to the general Hindu objections to

Muslim majority. Your plea for Greater Bengal is really a plea for living space for the whole Bengali race which is rapidly growing and which has the highest density of population in India and Burma.

Mr. M.K. Sen, has made much capital of and built his thesis on the foundation of Linguistic Basis and on that ground he has demanded the reincorporation of the Bhums–the Singhbhum and Manbhum.

But language is neither the chief criterion of nationality or culture nor of administration. Lt.-Col. Jaipal Singh Munda M.A. (Oxon), President of the Adibasi Mahasabha, the leader of the Tribals of Chota Nagpur and the Champion of Adibasistan declared that by race and religion the vast majority of the peoples of Manbhum and Singhbhum are non-Hindu, non-Aryan and Adibasi (Tribal). He says that sociologically and ethnologically language is no criterion of race or nationality. Moreover, it is not correct that the peoples of Manbhum and Singhbhum speak Bengali. Large majority speak Tribal Languages. Col. Jaipal therefore is opposed to the Bengali Hindu demand for annexing Manbhum (Dhanbad-Jharia) and Singhbhum (Tatanagary) to Bengal and demands that the Bhums and Chota Nagpur should be constituted into a separate free Homeland of the Adibasis having treaty alliance with Bengal.

Adibasis Ready for Alliance and Pact with Muslims

Col. Jaipal Singh, however agrees that Chota Nagpur is more akin to Bengal than to Behar, and will therefore forge stronger links with East Pakistan for mutual benefit He has even agreed to enter into a formal Pact with the League for Adibasi Muslim collaboration in the fight for Pakistan and Adibasistan and to effect an Alliance for Economic Reciprocity.

This and this alone–viz. Alliance of Muslims and Adibasis–is the affective way of checkmating the Hindu machinations and at the same time of preserving Muslim majority in Bengal and getting line on the coal, mica and iron mines of Chota Nagpur.

Adibasis Will Support Pakistan in Case of Plebiscite

It is also noteworthy that the vast majority of the people of Burdwan Division is composed of non-Hindu elements viz. Muslims, Adibasis, Depressed Classes. The caste Hindus in Burdwan Division are a minority.

If we have a pact of friendship and alliance with the Adibasis we will be able to defeat the caste Hindus even in a plebiscite on lines of Cripps Plan.

Your sincerely,

Raghib Ahsan

(Member, Working Committee
Bengal Provincial Muslim League

Social Equality in Islam–a Myth?

The core belief in the Unity of God (Tauhid) and the fraternity of Man led to the creation of an egalitarian polity in the early phase of Islam, with a zeal and devotion unparalleled in the annals of the human race. But this brief heroic period of idealism could not last more than 52 years (610-661 A.D.), namely the 22 years of the Prophethood of Muhammad and 30 years of the Four Righteous Caliphs (Abu Bakr=2-1/2, Omar = 10, Osman = 12 and Ali = 5-1/2). With the transfer of the Caliphate by Muawiyya, from the bedouin-mercantile Mecca to the affluent commercial city of Damascus, the entire ethos of Muslim social organisation and political authority changed. It was no longer a society of equals but a nucleus of an empire system, no more based on consultation of the Wise and the Pious *(Shura)*, but on dynastic rule of succession and oligarchic hegemony. It was a far cry from the pristine simplicity and directness of administration, arresting ambiance of equality and brotherhood that exuded a fresh breadth of life and gave a radical distinction to the polity that the Prophet of Islam had built.

......the new Muslims of non-Arab extraction were referred to as *Mawali* (clients), who were recognised as inhabitants of the subject areas outside Arabia. The *Mawalis* were discriminated against in the time of the Ommayyid Caliphs and the Abbasid Caliphs as well.

Even within Arabia, the tribe of Qurayash in its two main streams, *Hashmite* and *Ommayyide* became the new aristocracy. Likewise the progeny of the *Muhajirin* (fellow 'emigrants' from Mecca who accompanied the prophet to Medina) and the *Ansar* (the natives of Medina who were the 'helpers' of the Prophet) staked their claims to special treatment, if not superiority among the fellow believers. The new category of *Ashraf* (nobility) emerged in Arabia and in the newly acquired lands including North Africa, Iran and Central Asia. The *Ashraf* originally included only the descendants of the Prophet's daughter Fathima and her husband Ali, the fourth Caliph, but later it extended to mean all the descendants of the Prophet (referred to as Sayyid). Later, especially in India, *Ashraf* included apart from the *Sayyids,* also the progeny of the ruling ethnic groups like the Moghuls and the Pathans and the priestly class known as the *Shaikhs.* An interesting development in contemporary Arabia linking genealogical status with land-power, is indicated in the fact that *Ashraf,* as descendants of the Prophet, not only form a separate and exalted community, but also own large tracts of lands.

Prof. Rasheeduddin Khan M.P.

Professor and Chairman, Centre for Political Studies, Jawaharlal Nehru University

(Extracts from a paper titled *"Islamic Concept of Human Equality and the Caste System"* presented in an International Seminar on "Islamic Contribution to the Culture and Civilization of the World with special reference to India" which was held on 28-30 January, 1981 at Vigyan Bhavran, New Delhi).

15

Castes among Muslims: A Study of Hindu–Muslim Interaction

Dr. M.M. Sankhdhar

Reader, Department of Political Science, University of Delhi

The early Hindu society did not know the caste system: *Varna* was not a caste. The *Vedic* institution of the fourfold order *chaturvarna* is miscalled the system of four castes. While the caste is an endogamous and hereditary subdivision of an ethnic unit occupying a position of superior or inferior rank of social esteem in comparison with other such subdivisions, the *varna* was a theoretical concept–a fiction in the historical period, though the occupational grouping became a reality. The existence of the caste system in any form does not find reference in the *Rigveda*.

Varna, is not Caste

A confusion has thus been generated by the use of these two words- *varna* and *caste*–as synonyms. Sociological characterization of caste, without reference to *varna* as a concept, has obfuscated clear thinking on this subject. The theory of *varna* seriously jeopardises the racial hypothesis of the origin of caste. The word *caste* comes from the Portuguese *casta* or the Latin *castus,* both meaning the race. This racial origin of the caste system has been widely accepted by Western indologists. Some Hindu scholars tend to ascribe economic origin of the Hindu caste system as it later developed. Perhaps the literal meaning of the Sanskrit word *varna* as complexion or colour has helped the Western racial hypothesis of caste.

In the present paper attention has been focused on the theme of interaction of the Hindu and Muslim caste systems on the basic assumption of the caste systems as historical phenomena in the two societies having conformed to some common characteristics. The conceptualization of the ancient *varna* as an ideal has to confront the reality of degeneration of the old Hindu society into a category of the caste system. It is like the erosion of the Islamic concept of equality into the sociological notion of caste-society.

It is generally believed that the caste phenomenon is a peculiar feature of the Hindu society. It is also commonly held that Christians or Muslims are uncontaminated with this evil. But recent researches have shown to the contrary that although the Hindus have failed to materialize the *varna* system in actual practice and have witnessed distortions in what was designed to be a perfect functional-organization, because of the corruptions introduced by historical forces, other societies have willingly accepted the caste system. It is instructive how the infection of the Hindu caste system caught the Muslim society napping where the spirit of equality could not last more than 50 years (622-672 A.D.). In comparison, however, the Hindu myth of *varna* had a glorious record of age-long survival.

Contemporary sociologists and behavioural scientists have vitally ignored the theological basis of caste i.e. *varna* and have fallen into the methodological error of identifying the caste phenomenon with evil. This is not to suggest that the historical degeneration of *varna* into caste should be lost sight of, but only to emphasise the need for the functional merit of caste as a balancing factor and an important variable in our analyses.

The conceptual framework of *varna-ashrama-dharma* as the trilogy of value-system and a way of life would be of utmost benefit for an accurate comprehension of the Hindu caste system. Social behaviour in early Hindu society was well conceived by the needs of society, status consciousness, sense of duty of a particular station and an eugenic notion of the virtues of heredity–all rolled into one Relationships were not governed by formal agreements or contractual obligation. *Varna* was treated as a social-micro in which a man was born and functioned, his choice of vocation being primarily determined by his birth. There has been a flexibility too in so far as the birth factor could be bypassed if a man was not capable or was incapable of performance of the vocation of his caste. The fourfold division of society could be interpreted as a theory of division of labour based on differentials of aptitude and inherent natural capacity for particular jobs. So while the *varna* was to be preserved for utilitarian and divine ends, it was supplemented by the disposition of duty, i.e., *dharma* and the prescription of four stages in man's life: *brahmacharya, grahastha, vanaprastha* and *sanyasa* whereby man could have a wholesome experience of worldly material life as also of the self-restraint and discipline for high spiritual evolution.

Islam Face to Face With Hinduism

When Islam made inroads into Hinduism, it was up against such a Hindu social order with its strong *varna-ashrama-dharma* foundation. Being a comparatively young religious order, Islam faced a major challenge on the Indian sub-continent from Hinduism with a rich philosophical tradition and key concepts of *Karma* and spiritual spiral of evolution and a wide degree of tolerance for other faiths. The Muslim society encountered the fear of absorption in the powerful cultural Hindu stream. The conviction that Hindu religion was eternal, *sanatana dharma* and was philosophically open, unlike Islam, which defied the narrow definition of religion by taking a universalist view of human life, it had an irresistible appeal to the reflective, contemplative and intellectualized or spiritually oriented Muslims. The Hindu metaphysics, with wide range of interpretations suited to diverse schools of thought, gave secular overtones to Hindus' love for tolerance. Here was a system of caste so deftly integrated with a world-view that unless the caste was construed in isolation from the totality of Hindu experience, it was well-nigh impossible to propagate a contrary view. Caste system, rooted in *varna* theology, was unassailable.

The Islamic concept of equality came handy to the critics of Hindu society, especially its hierarchical and discriminatory caste structure. The ethno-centric view predicated on the concept of ethnic exclusivity sought to undo the age-long love for hierarchy and social status. Perceptions were reversed from 'openness' to 'closeness' in the Hindu fold. A new consciousness of degeneration of the old *varna* system into a caste system vas engineered by the impact of Islam. The Hindus, too, became aware of the ugly super structure having developed over the pristine glorious foundation of the *varna*. The vulnerable points became too obvious and the cracks in the Hindu social order surfaced. The Hindu society was pushed to the defensive by the equalitarian thrust of Islam. The practices of endogamy and hypergamy in marriages, the *gotra,* lack of inter dining and inter marriages, restrictions and social taboos, discriminatory customs and festivals, sanctity of temples, higher caste privileges, denial of employment opportunities on caste basis, the notion of pollution or contamination, social immobility and rigid patterns of outlook and orthodoxy, helped Islam in fostering an appeal of the heterogeneous and fractured character of Hindu society on the one hand and an impression of its own cohesive and fraternal organization having no concept of higher and lower.

Myth of Equality in Muslim Society

How false has been this impression can be seen in the scholarly studies bringing out the facts of a literal caste system prevalent in the Muslim society. On the wrong assumption of equality among Muslims as a propaganda device, the Muslim rulers confronted in Indian society an order which despite its evils of caste system was thoroughly rooted in tradition. Hinduism revealed a model of stability unknown in societies developing from tradition to modernity in so far as preservation of its undying culture is concerned. The process of interaction between the political superiority of the Muslim along with its message of fraternity and the Hindu conservative ethos brought two fold results. A class of Sufi saints who were inspired by the Hindu transcendentalism emerged on the one hand to advocate reforms in Hindu society, large-scale conversions of the lower Hindu castes by force and inducements occurred on the other. The Hindu converts into the Muslim fold acquired a most reactionary character and tended to be demonstratively hostile to the Hindus, they found it difficult to give up the needs or compulsions of a caste system in the Muslim society and by the back-door brought it in.

For different reasons although, Muslim societies in the Islamic world outside India violated the *Koranic* injunction of brotherhood and developed closely bound caste character. New Muslims of non-Arab stock known *Mawalies* were a lower caste since they were belonging to a class subjugated by the Caliphs. In Arabia, Hashmites and Ommayids were superior to *Ansars*. Like Mughals and Pathans in India, the Ashrafs and Sayeds were in a descending order of social status based on land ownership. The *Ailafs* and *Arzals* were the lowest and menial castes which included weavers, washermen, potters, sweepers, butchers, tailors barbers and the like.

The Muslim rule in India produced a landed aristocracy likewise, but somewhat differently to the pattern elsewhere. Higher and lower *zats* like Hindu *jatis* appeared on the scene. *Mansabdars, zamindars, taluqdars* and *jagirdars* were the new castes occupying exalted position. Subsequently at lower levels there were greater caste stratifications with propensity among Muslim groups for sectarian, hierarchical and cultural distinctions. These castes have precluded inter marriages and intercultural communication. The ruling dynasties have perpetrated a closed caste system further augmented by conversions. The converts like *Meos* of *Mewat* who were originally Rajputs belong to the lower strata of Muslim society. *Shias* and *Sunnis* have had a long-draw n conflicting caste relationships giving rise to riots as between Hindus and Muslims. There are trading castes like *Ismaili, Ashanashri, Khojas, Dawoodi Sulemani Bohras, Kutch Memons* and Tamil Labbas. In the lower order, again, there were sub castes like *Qureshis, Ansaris, Momins* and *Khans. Jirgas* and *Biradaris* thus, signify the exclusivity of the Muslim castes vitiating the spirit of the Islamic faith where brotherhood of man has been emphasised as the basic core of Islam.

Sociologists on Muslim Castes

Castes as they exist and operate among the Muslims have not attracted attention. While castes among Hindus have been torn out of the context and genesis and interpreted as an undesirable category of social functioning, the real caste system with all the features of stratification, discrimination and hostility are left out of social intellectual discourse. Since the Muslim caste system escaped notice, the myth that the Hindus were the only people on earth to have an abominable caste system remained unexploded for long.

However, Ghaus Ansari's study *Muslim Castes in Uttar Pradesh* (1960) and E.R. Leach's (edited) *Aspects of Cases in South India* the same year followed by R. Levi's *Social Structure of Islam* (1962) along with articles on the subject in some leading journals by L. Dumont, Ziaur Khan, E. B. Harrier, F.G. Baley and others have brought to light the new phenomena of caste among Indian Muslims both as an independent outgrowth and as an interaction among Muslims and Hindus. These studies covering almost two decades have added a novel dimension to our social stratification.

Imtiaz Ahmed has recently edited a volume: *Caste and Social Stratification among Muslims in India* (1973) which had run into a second revised and enlarged edition in 1978 as investigative literature on this crucial subject. The work is a collection of papers written by sociologists with the help of data. Most contributors define caste on Hindu basis and then examine the extent to which Muslim social stratification conforms to the Hindu model. Hindu caste system is defined in terms of cultural traits in the form of a syndrome. The following are the main features of the caste: endogamy, occupational distinctions, hierarchy ideological-religious basis. There are variations and exceptions to these broad characteristics in different parts of the country. There is a general agreement among scholars that these features are by and large present in the Muslim social structure.

Dumont and M.N. Srinivas are quoted in support of the theme of the Hindu caste. It is maintained that certain theological notions like *karma* and *dharma* support and reinforce caste divisions among Hindus. There is no such philosophical support to castes among Muslims, for Islam stands for equality of status. A philosophy of life with a life experience and a vigorous metaphysic at its back sustains the Hindu *varna* structure. It is a different matter that it is difficult to work it out in modern times, which is the fate of many a Hindu ideal. A long period of Muslim rule followed by British rule, in my view, has snapped our ties with the glorious past with its belief-system that a man is born again and again in accordance with his *sanskaras* and *purushartha* of preceding mortal lives. He plays his part in the drama with steadfast duty in the role he is set out to carry out. A mysterious calculation of reward and punishment operates for him over which he has no control. His *varna* is accordingly determined. The *varna* helps him in the growth of his personality in terms of higher evolution whereby he finally attains the *Brahma*, the absolute state of consciousness and he ceases to be reborn. A sum total of his actions in the long spiral of existence in the previous and present births puts him into a situation from where he has no escape. The only way out for him is to respond to the call of higher duty for his station in the soul's journey accords with his station in life. The soul's journey is an eternal quest for the attainment of the highest goal of attaining the absolute consciousness. E.E. Bergel in his *Social Stratification* (1962) has rightly observed that the "caste system (of the Hindus) cannot be understood unless it is recognized as a religious institution". Theological complexion of *varna* as the fundamental structure gives to the social system its unique and distinctive character. This is not so in the case of the Islamic society and its caste structure.

Pratap Aggarwal and Ranjit Bhattacharya have brought out the differentiation by referring to the *Koranic* tradition which explicitly rejects gradation of groups and individuals on the basis of birth and ideology of pure and impure, and find that the only criterion of social evolution recommended by Islam is religious piety. Formal religious values of Islam are opposed to any rigid system of ethnic and social stratification. M.K.A. Siddiqui asserts that the hierarchical order among Muslims militates against the traditional values of the Muslims.

Ideologies behind Muslim Castes

But it is also held by other contributors that there is an alternative Muslim ideology which sanctions the caste. While the formal Islamic ideology rejects caste, the actual beliefs held by the Muslims not only recognize caste distinctions, it also seeks to rationalize them. This dichotomy of values might have been a product of Hindu Muslim cultural interaction. There is, however, no evidence of any obvious conflict of values among the Muslims with regard to their acceptance or otherwise of the caste patterns.

Imtiaz Ahmad draws clearcut differences between the Hindu and Muslim models of caste. Firstly, the Muslim caste system is weak, for it lacks support from traditional ideology. Second, it has not attained the degree of elaborateness of the Hindu model. Third, it allows a greater interplay of wealth and other secular factors in status determination unlike the Hindu love for a purely theological value-structure. Lastly, there is no concept or practice of a pure caste like *Brahmans* in the Muslim society. That is to say, there is no charisma attached to Muslim caste.

The volume under discussion raises an interesting controversy at the end whether the castes in Muslims stem from Hindu acculturative impact or are inherent in Islamic typology. The general view favours a direct link with Hinduism, especially with reference to the conversion phenomenon. The Hindu psyche of the converts with Hindu blood running through their veins could not bill have been prone to the adoption of a caste system in a powerfully Hindu environment. It doesn't make sense to accept Dumont's argument that the Muslims consciously compromised or "entered a tacit and reciprocal compromise" with the Hindus. The fact that a large majority of the Muslims were converts from the lower rungs of Hindu society deluded by the hope of an equal treatment in the Islamic fold were unconsciously importing the Hindu behaviour traits and habits is enough testimony of the Hindu influence. Conversions by peaceful persuasions was not possible nor would a Hindu easily change his *dharma.* Threats, force and material and political inducements or the false promises of social mobility worked towards the hastening of the process of conversions. This also is the secret of Islamization's reinforcement rather than weakening of the caste structure among Muslims. Muhammad's prophetic statement that "there are no genealogies in Islam", as an evidence of equality of all believers, finds stark contradiction in Islamic Law as practised in India. It is doubtful whether further research would alter the basic contradiction in theory and practice of Islam.

16

Muslim Reaction to Mass Conversion

BRIJ BHUSHAN BHATNAGAR

The news of mass conversion at Meenakshipuram and some other places in South India shocked the Hindu conscience throughout the country. It culminated in the emergence of a powerful mass awakening movement *(Jan-Jagran Abhiyan).* Almost all political leaders, though belonging to different parties, felt that mass conversion of this type went against the spirit of secularism based on *Sarva-Dharma-Sambhava.* But some intellectuals like Khushwant Singh *(Hindustan Times,* Aug. 22, 1981), Kuldip Nayar *(Sunday,* Calcutta, Aug. 23, 1981), B.G. Verghese *(India Today,* New Delhi, Oct. 1, 1982) and Dr. Gopal Singh, Chairman, Congress I–Panel for Minorities *(Nai Duniya* Delhi, November 3, 1982) took objection to this Hindu resurgence on the plea that "Conversions are no concern of a secular nation" and that these conversions do not involve "change of nationality" or "political defection". Looking at their patriotism, one may appreciate this criticism as an expression of their deep commitment to the ideal of secularism, though one may not agree with their understanding of the implications of these mass conversions.

On the other hand, it is difficult to find any influential Muslim voice condemning these conversions. Most of the Muslim politicians or intellectuals either chose to keep mum on this issue, or the chosen few, who spoke out, condemned not the mass conversion to Islam but the Hindu reaction to it. And they also did it in the name of secularism! Syed Shahabuddin, M.P. *(Hindustan Times,* July 27, 1981) and Syed Ahmed Hashmi, M.P. (Jamiat's Daily *Al Jamiat,* Sept., 20, 1981) used the same stick of secularism to beat Hindu anxiety on mass conversions to Islam. Both these M.P.s are members of the Working Committee of *Jamaat-ul-Ulema-i-Hind,* Shri Shahabuddin being its special invitee member (vide *Al Jamiat,* Delhi, Aug. 8, 1981).

Two other Muslim leaders Shri Muhyuddin Shawl, M.P. (Jamaat-e-Islami's Weekly *Radiance,* Delhi, Oct. 18, 1981) and Maulana Mufti Atiqur Rahman Usmani, President, All India Muslim Majlis-e-Mushawarat *(Radiance,* November 15, 1981) also took shelter under secularism to support the conversions and to critise the Hindu resistance to them.

Curiously enough the Working Committee of *Jamiat-ul-Uiema-i-Hind* also passed a resolution condemning the Hindus' *Jan Jagran Abhiyan* (Mass awakening campaign) in the wake of Meenakshipuram conversion, called it a danger to the nation and the country and demanded legal ban on the organisations engaged in it. This resolution was published with reiteration of the theme, editiorially and otherwise in *Al Jamiat* (3-4 May 1982, 4-11 June, 2-8 July and 9-15 July 1982.) Another resolution on almost identical lines was passed by Jamaat-e-Islami-Hind, publisher with editorials on the theme in its periodicals *Radiance,* weekly, Daily *Dawat* and *Sehroza Dawat* of 16 and 19 May 1982, 5,7,10 and 13 June, 4,5,7, and 13 July and 11-17 July 1982).

Jamaat-ul-Ulema-i-Hind and *Jamaat-e-Islami* along with Indian Union Muslim League are considered to be the three most representative Muslim organisations in India with a long history behind them. When these organisations advance secular arguments in support of conversions to Islam and against Hindu *Jan-Jagran,* one may be tempted to welcome their posture as a victory of secularism upon pre-partition separatism. But before we welcome these new converts to the secularist club, it will be desirable to probe their credentials as to whether there is any genuine change in their outlook or line of thinking from pre-to post-independence period or is it just another strategic cover to hide the same old designs.

Jamaat-e-Islami-Hind

As is fairly known, this organisation openly stands for the domination of Islam through *Jehad,* and the establishment of an Islamic State in India. As far back as 1939, its founder Maulana Abul A'la Maudoodi, elucidating the objects of *Jamaat-e-lslami,* in a speech had made it clear:

"Islam is not merely a code of religious beliefs and certain prayers, but a comprehensive system that wants to enforce its reformist plan...For this, it gives *'Dawat'* (a call) to all humanity. Those who accept this *Dawat* become members of Islamic organisation..... or *Ummat-e-Muslimah* (Muslim community). As soon as this party comes into being, it starts *Jehad* to fulfil the aim for which it has been formed. Its very existence demands that it strive to annihilate the rule of un-Islamic forms of State and to establish instead the rule of that moderate and balanced code of culture and community life which is expressed through the comprehensive term of *'Kalimtullah'* in the *Quran*.....This is not a body of preachers or missionaries for the spread of religion, but a party of God's soldiers.....*Ayat* says: "Wage War against them till the rot is finished and there is allegiance to God alone" (that is, belief in God and system of life are established, as ordained by Islam)'. And these same aims and means continued to be propagated by the *Jamaat-e-Islami-Hind* among its co-religionists all along.

For instance, we find the same objective reiterated by Syed Ahmed Urooj Qadri, Member, Advisory Council, *Jamaat-e-Islami Hind*:

"It has been proved that it is the duty (of the Muslim community) to make the true faith (meaning Islam) dominate over false religions and exalt it, for which (duty) the *Quran* uses a comprehensive term, 'the *Iqaamat-e-Deen* (the establishment of the religion of Islam). The object of conferring the position of *Shahad-e-Haq* on the *Ummat-e-Muslimah* and the task for which *Allah* has chosen this *Ummat,* is the establishment of the *Deen* to the full; it is (the execution of) the duty of *Jehad* in the way of God."[2]

Presidential address read before the *Jamaat's* Sixth All India Conference held at Hyderabad on Feb. 20, 1981, exhorted the Muslims not only to follow and preach Islam, but also to strive tirelessly against other systems of life or religions. It said:

"To strive for *A'la-i-Kalimtullah* is not the obligation of one country or one organisation. We are thankful to God that different organisations in different countries are engaged in this task in their own way. Representatives of many of these organisations are present among us today. We have a golden opportunity to benefit by their ideas and experiences....

"To establish *Deen* is the purpose for which *Ummat-e-Muslimah* has been brought into existence. To consider the striving for the establishment of *Deen,* a wordly pursuit, or shirk it for a life of seclusion, even after these clear testimonies (*Quranic* exhortations) is not at all correct. It is as well true that only *Dawat* and preaching of Islam is not enough to fulfill the duty of establishing *Deen*. It is also necessary that not only do we sincerely follow' Islam, but continue striving tirelessly against all wrong and false systems of life till the religion of *Allah* completely dominates (every other system/religion)".

A call for striving for the establishment of *Deen* is essentially a call for *Jihad*, as should be clear from the following observation, made in this conference by Sadaruddin Islahi:

"Another term for *Jehad* in the way of *Allah* is 'striving for the establishment of *Deen*."[3]

Indian Union Muslim League

Muslim League's role in the Partition of India up to 1947 is too well known. After the Partition Muslim League was declared to have been dissolved in Indian Union. But after a lapse of few years an organisation under the name of Indian Union Muslim League came into being. For a few years an impression went round that this new organisation had nothing to do with the pre-Independence Muslim League or its ideology based on two-Nation theory leading to the demand for separate homeland for Muslims. But the spokesmen of the new Muslim League have again and again made it clear that they are the successors of the same old Muslim League organisationally as well as ideologically. This is evident from the following comments published in *Haftroza Jamiat Times*, Delhi, dated 27th July, 1973:

> "The statement of Umar Bafaqeeha Thengal that the Indian Union Muslim League is the same that was founded in 1906 and whose moving spirit was Mr. Mohd. Ali Jinnah, and the statement of Janab Ibrahim Suleiman Sait, President of the Indian Muslim League, that the Indian Union Muslim League would in no way tolerate any contemptuous reference to the Muslim League of the pre-Independence days, have compelled us to ply our pen."[4]

The *Haftroza Mustaqeem*, Delhi, the official organ of the Indian Union Muslim League, not only confirms the above view, but reveals more facts in its support. It says that the present Muslim League is out to solve the problems of the Muslim minority left behind in the partitioned India. *Mustaqeem* writes:

> "Congress leaders, especially the young elements in it, have protested against the statement of Janab Umar Bafaqeeha Thengal that the present Muslim League is a part of the same Muslim League that was founded in 1906. Janab Abou Baker, Joint Secretary, Kerala State Muslim League has claimed that even in 1950, Qaed-e-Millat Alhaaj Janab Mohd. Ismail had made it clear that the present Muslim League is the succession of the Muslim League which

was formed in 1906 for the protection of Muslims. The demand for Pakistan was made in 1940, but its fulfillment does not at all mean that the problems of the Muslim minority are over.'[5]

That the present Muslim League is working hand in glove with *Jamaat-e-Islami-Hind* is clear from the speech made by its President Janab Ibrahim Suleiman Sait at the sixth A.I. Conference of *Jamaat-e- Islami-Hind* at Hyderabad. There, he said: "the fourteenth century *(Hijri)* has passed, and now the fifteenth has commenced. The latter half of the fourteenth century witnessed a number of Islamic movements and Islamic personalities. Personages like Shah Waliullah, Syed Ahmed Shaheed, Allamah Iqbal and above all Maulana Maudoodi appeared on the scene. Their movements awakened a new feeling (among Muslims). These movements have led us to believe that Islam is not a mere ode of certain prayers, but a system of life which encompasses all aspects of (human) life and that with us there is no room for difference between politics and religion.

"The present century (fifteenth century *Hijri*) is the century for the revival of Islam; it is the century for the ascendancy of Islam. Along with this, I have to say that here (in India) while various things are necessary for the advancement of Islam, protection of our *Deen* and *Shariat* is also essential for the sake of our community self *(Milli Wajood)*. Simultaneously with this, we have to discharge the duty of *Iqaamat-e-Deen.*

"I pray that Almighty God may make this Century, the century of the revival of Islam, the ascendancy of Islam and the domination of Islam."[6]

Jamiat-ul-Ulema-i-Hind

Lastly we come to *Jamaat-ul-Ulema-i-Hind*. This organisation has been projected as a nationalist party, which, unlike Muslim League, has been an ally of the Congress Party in its Freedom Struggle before Independence and continues to be its ally even after. Its opposition to the demand of Pakistan has been very much publicised to establish its credentials as a nationalist party. Therefore, it becomes necessary to look into the real considerations which led it to adopt this posture *vis-a-vis* the demand of Pakistan. Reacting to the Lahore Resolution of Muslim League, Maulana Hussain Ahmed Madni in his Presidential address to Jaraiat's Annual Session held at Jaunpur (U.P.) in 1940, said:

> "*Pakistan And Opinion About it:* If it (Pakistan) means establishment in the Muslim-majority provinces of an Islamic State based on the traditions of the Prophet, wherein all commandments of Islam viz. '*Hudood*\ '*Qisas*' etc, are enforced, then Masha' Allah it is indeed a very noble scheme. Not one Muslim can have exception to it. But under the present circumstances such an achievement appears to be beyond imagination".

It is evident from the above remarks that *Jamiat* was not opposed to the basic concept of Pakistan, but kept away from this demand simply because it was not sure of its feasibility. In fact, like its predecessor *Ulemas*, the *Jamiat* had always been working in its own way for achieving *A'la-I-Kalimtullah,* which includes the twin aims of establishing an Islamic state and domination of Islam over all other religions, even through war *(Jehad).* It was made clear in a joint appeal to Muslims for co-operation and funds, made in 1940, under the signatures of Maulana Hussain Ahmed Madni, Maulana Ahmed Sayeed, Allamah Mohd. Sajjad, Mufti Kifayatulah, who were then respectively the President, Vice-President, General Secretary and an important member of the Working Committee of the *Jamiat*. It said.

> "*Iqaamat-e-Deen* (the establishment of the religion of Islam) as detailed and expounded by *Allah* and the Prophet is imperative. It is for this high aim that *Jehad* is provided for in the true religion (meaning Islam). And the very meaning of *'Litkun Kalimtullah-Hial 'ulia'* is that the *Kalima,* that is, the commandments and laws of *Allah,* reign supreme, superseding the commandments and laws made by all human beings and only the laws of *Allah* ought to be enforced and brought into operation. For the realisation of this great aim one form of *Jehad* in the way of *Allah* is lighting in the way of *Allah* which involves the loss of countless lives and property. But as compared with the gains that accrue from the enforcement and execution of the laws of *Allah* (Islam) for human society in this world and the Hereafter–loss of life and property has no value at all. But fighting...is the last method of work when no other method is availing and time and circumstances also favour (the adoption of) this method of work"[7]

If *Jamiat* had in any way helped the freedom movement, by joining hands with the Congress, it was not out of its belief in secularism and democracy rather, it was a sort of compromise with the realities of Indian situation. Keeping its eye fixed on the establishment of Islamic state in India, *Jamiat* leadership had calculated that independence won through common efforts would pave the way for the achievement of its "real aim". Maulana Hussain Ahmed Madni's Presidential address to *Jamiat's* Annual Session, held at Lahore in 1942, clearly lays down this strategy:

"It is extremely essential that this *Nizam-i-Khudawandi* (Islamic State) is strongly established. All along the *Ulemas* of India have made efforts for the achievement of this very aim. But as ill-luck would have it, the real aim could not be achieved. Then it was thought essential that the principle of *'Ahavan-ul-baliyatain'* (the lesser of two evils) be adopted and part taken in common efforts for the independence of India. And though independence won through common efforts would not be called *Nizam-i-Islami* (Islamic

State), yet by removal of a number of difficulties and hard obstacles the way will be opened for the achievement of the real aim".

In a letter written before Independence to one of his Muslim Correspondents Maulana Hussain Ahmed Madni stated the position of the *Jamiat*:

> "Hindustan is *Darul-Harb.* It shall continue to be a *Darul-Harb,* as long as it is dominated by *Kufr* (that is ruled by non-Muslims)"[8]

After the partition of India in 1947 also, Madni reiterated the same view. In a letter dated November 17, 1950 he made it clear:

> "Hindustan has been a *Dar-ul-Harb* ever since Islamic rule ended here. *Juma* is surely proper and imperative in *Darul Harb*"[9]

But, is the *Jamiat* prepared to reconcile itself with this reality of *Darul Harb* in India? Certainly 'not', because all the official pronouncements made by the *Jamiat* till date lead us to one conclusion only that the *Jamiat* is very keen to convert this reality of *Darul Harb* into *Darul Islam* in India.

AL JAMIAT, the official organ of the *Jamiat*, reproducing extracts from Maulana Hussain Ahmed Madni's book *Muttahida Qaumiat Aur Islam,* wrote on January 27, 1972:

> "When possessed of no Sultanat, the only duty of (Muslim) individuals shall be that so far it lies in their capacity, they make efforts solely for the establishment of Islamic State"

Again, Maulana Asad Madni, son of late Maulana Hussain Ahmed Madni and his successor as President of *Jamiat-ul-Ulema-i-Hind* (who is also a Cong. (I) M.P. in Rajya Sabha) in a message to the Muslims of India and the world, reminded them of the mission of *A'la-i-Kalimtullah*:

"Today by the grace of *Allah, Dar-ul-Uloom* is the centre of activity for *Dawat-e-Deen* and *A'la-i-Kalimtullah* not only for our country, India, but the whole world. On the occasion of the Centenary Celebrations of the *Dar-ul-Uloom,* my only appeal to Muslims of India and those of the world, is that they strengthen this center of activity for *Dawat- e-Deen* and *A'la-e-Kalimtullah.*"[10]

> "We, the feeble servants and members of the Working Committee of *Jamaat-ul-Ulema-i-Hind*...are going about courageously for *A'la i-Kalimtullah.*"[11]

These efforts by the *Jamiat* for *A'la-i-Kalimtullah* have now acquired international ramification. On 22nd March, 1980, a world body of the *Fazala* (Old boys) of *Darul Uloom,* Deoband has been founded under the name 'Aalmi Motamar Fazala'-e-Darul Uloom, Deoband, with its headquarters at Deoband (India) and branches not only in various states of India, but also in foreign countries like Pakistan, Bangladesh and England etc. Its President is Maulana Asad Madni himself, but Vice-Presidents are from Pakistan, Bangladesh, England and Africa. Immediately after its birth the Motamar started calling for the establishment of *A'la-i-Kalimtullah* with a quickened pace.[12]

Common Strategy

It is clear from the above discussion that all these Muslim organisations are striving to achieve the common aim of establishing an Islamic state in India, which is an antithesis of the concept of a secular state. Hence, the use of secularist arguments by them is not borne out of any genuine conviction in secularism rather it seems to be a tactical move to confuse and divide the Hindu society in general and its power-hungry political leadership in particular. While in the name of Islam and minority interests, they irrespective of their different political labels, can openly assemble on a common platform, and dictate terms from a position of strength based in their block-votes, the Hindu politician, with an eye on their block-votes becomes a split personality within himself. He does not speak out the truth from public platforms, rather under the pretext of secularism he chooses to submit before their communal dictates.

The Muslim leadership seems to have decided to make full use of this weakness of Indian political leadership. This explains the memorandum presented by 45 Muslim M. P.s, under the leadership of Shahabuddin, and others belonging to different political parties including the ruling Congress-I to Prime Minister Mrs. Indira Gandhi on 5th November, 1982. Quite interestingly, this unabashedly communal memorandum dares to dub some Hindu organisations-mainly *Vishwa Hindu Parishad* and *R.S.S.* as communal organisations and demands a blanket ban on their activities. This demand has been so blatantly partisan that one of the signatories on this memorandum, Rafiq Zakaria had to publicly criticize it. He admits that "while the memorandum listed some Hindu organisations as being communal-the *Vishwa Hindu Parishad* and the *R.S.S.* -it did not refer to Muslim organisations which are not less guilty of practising 'communal hatred. Had we not so defaulted, our bonafides might not have been suspected'. (*Times of India,* Feb. 22, 1983). Zakaria has made an interesting revelation by leveling a charge against S. Shahabuddin that he had violated 'the solemn understanding unanimously arrived at among all signatories that the contents of the memorandum would not be released to the press" *(ibid)*. So, this memorandum was going to be a *behind-the-curtain* blackmail tactics!

Jamiat in its True Colours

This memorandum by 45 Muslim M.Ps. was followed, almost immediately by an ultimatum submitted separately by *Jamaat-ul-Ulema-*

i-Hind, which under plays the recent mass conversions and protests against the "verbal assault launched under the leadership of the *R.S.S.* and *Vishvva Hindu Parishad* against the entire Muslim community, over *a few* conversions in Meenakshipuram". The *Jamiat*, on the point of a threat of a mass agitation, demands **"30 per cent reservations for Muslims in PAC and BMP, purging of government services of persons affiliated to the *RSS* and deletion of the clause from the Indian constitution relating to the uniform civil code".** *(Times of India,* Feb. 20, '83)

While the *Jamiat* has for the time being, stopped at issuing an ultimatum for launching a *Mulk-o-Millat Bachao Tehrik* (have Communists and country Agitation) the Indian Union Muslim League has already started implementing this ultimatum by sending *Mujahidins* to jail in the Capital of the country, perhaps to malign India win the eyes of the heads of state attending the Non-Aligned Conference in Delhi and to in the sympathy and support of the Muslim representatives among them. This united action on the part of various Muslim organisations coupled with a new aggressiveness against forces of law and order reminds us of that phase of Muslim politics which was started in 1940 and had resulted in the partition of our motherland. Shall India allow the history to repeat itself?

References

1. *Jihad-fi-Sabilillah* Speech of Maulana Abul A'la Maudoodi in 1939, Reprinted in Feb., 1968 and Jan., 1978 by Maktaba Jamaat-e-Islami Hind. Delhi-6, pp. 22 to 24.
2. Syed Ahmed Urooj Kadri: *Iqaamat-e-Deen Farz Hai*. Published by Markazi Maktaba, Delhi, Sept., 1970; pp. 59, 60, 63.
3. *Mussalman Aur Dawat-e-lslam*: A paper read by Sadaruddin Islahi at the Jamaat's Hyderabad conference, published by Jamaat's Ishayat Islam Trust in J981, p. 10.
4. *Haftroza Jamiat Times,* Delhi dated July-27, 1973. p. 1.
5. Haftroza Mustaqeem, Delhi, *Indian Union Muslim League Ka Tarjuman*, July-27, 1973. p. 7.
6. *Dawat*, Delhi ; Ijtima Number, April 14, 1982 p. 102.
7. *Tazkira,* 1940. Published by the Jamiat.
8. *Maktubaat-i-Shaikhul Islam* , Vol. II, letter No. 23.
9. Ibid: letter No. 64.
10. *Al-Jamiat,* Darul Uloom (Deoband) Number, March 26, 1980, page 13.
11. *Al-Jamiat,* dated 5-11-1971, 12-10-1973, 28-8-1977, Darul Uloom Number, 26-3-1980, p. 15.
12. Fazala-e-Darul Uloom Resolution–Weekly Aljamiat 8-4-1980 and reports on the Motamar–Aljamiat 27-3-1980, 21-5-1981 and 24 to 26-5-1981.

17

"Liberation Theology" A New Church Strategy

G.N. Singhal

Lecturer, Shivaji College, Delhi University, New Delhi

The Second World War marks the beginning of a new chapter in the history of Christianity throughout the world. At the end of the war, the Church discovered, to its dismay, that although the western Christian powers led by the U.S.A. had emerged victorious in the war, the rising tide of western colonialism and imperialism, which had started in the 16th century, had not only lost its momentum but had started moving in the reverse gear with the following results:

(a) Half of Europe was lost to communist Russia and her puppet governments. The Soviet block emerged as a serious military and ideological rival to western imperialism and capitalism. Addition of China to the communist block in 1949 gave communism a new respectability and aggressivism throughout the world.

(b) Western imperialism, battered from within during the war, had to retreat from India in 1947, which gave a new phillip to national freedom movements in various Asian and

African countries, giving rise to more and more independent nation states in these two continents.

(c) The Church because of its close identity with the foreign colonialists and oppressors, after their departure came under fire everywhere. In China, the communist government ordered expulsion of all the foreign missionaries and by 1950-51 made all of them to leave China under threat of arrest or torture. Scope for proselytisation was getting more and more circumscribed in the newly born independent States.

Challenge of Science and Technology

In the post-war world the Church had to face the worst crisis in its own heartland, i.e. Europe and America. Industrial revolution resulted in the establishment of a very high material civilisation and a comfort-loving consumer society, making all the old social institutions and values irrelevant and leading to a spiritual vacuum in the lives of youngsters. But Christianity could neither provide an alternative set of values and institutions nor an atmosphere for the fulfillment of spiritual quest. As an eminent Indian theologian Dr. M.M. Thomas says, "The technological world has become aggressive towards man, and Christianity has become marginalised in that world."[1] In fact, this process of marginalisation or alienation had started long back because 'on the whole, the world of science and technology itself developed in alienation from the Church and outside the discipline of the Christian faith'. Dr. Thomas admits that "the Christian conceptual frame work about Nature, Humanity and God has not yet been worked out in its challenging relevance to the modern world."[2] Crisis of values and spiritual vacuum in the post- industrial society added more and more to the alienation of the westerners from Christianity, resulting in the 'emptied churches in Europe, only to fill up *Ashrams* in India and the West'.

Internal Conflicts

Besides this ideological crisis, the Church found itself caught in a situation of civil war among Christians in many of the Christian countries. In Latin American countries covering an area of almost eight million square miles and accommodating more than 300 million out of total 700 million Roman Catholics in the world, the conversion task had been completed long back. But after more than four hundred years of uninterrupted Christian rule, their vast masses found themselves drowned in the sea of poverty, illiteracy, cultural discrimination and exploitation. To their shock they found that their own governments had been callously indifferent towards their fate and the U.S.A., which had emerged as the sole leader of the Christian world, was backing these governments militarily. This made them anti-church and anti-U.S.A. In such a situation, communist theory of class-struggle seemed to be the only way open for their liberation. This realization paved the way for successful communist revolution in Cuba in 1959 under the leadership of Fidel Castro.

Efforts for Church Unity

To meet these challenges, the three main churches, Orthodox, Roman Catholic and Protestant, tried to set their own house in order as a first step. Eastern Europe, where Orthodox Church had its following, was mostly controlled by the communist regimes. Roman Catholic Church being centrally organised with Pope at its head, was not so much bothered about unity, although it was also forced to set its tune according to changing times. But for the Protestant Churches, having different denominations and national origins, problem of unity was really complex and difficult. Some of the Protestant Churches joined together in 1948 at Amsterdam to form a loose federation called the *World Council of Churches* (WCC). But it became a really effective organisation in 1961 when, in a World Christian Conference at New Delhi, *International Missionary Council* born in 1921 also declared its merger with WCC. Its membership has been continuously increasing (in 1980 it rose to 293 Churches from 146 Churches in 1948). Although all its efforts of unity with Roman Catholic Church have failed so far, majority of the Orthodox Churches have joined its membership. Byzanatine and Orthodox Oriental Churches including the Orthodox Syrian Church of India officially accepted its membership in 1948; the Orthodox Churches of Eastern Europe joined its membership in 1961.

The first conference of the leaders of East Asian Churches was organised in Bangkok leading to the establishment of the *East Asia Christian Conference* (EACC) which was rechristened in 1973 as the *Christian Conference of Asia* (CCA). Many similar regional councils have come into being since then, such as *All Africa Conference of Churches* (AACC), *Movement for Latin American Evangelical Unity* (UNELAM), *Middle East Council Churches* (MECC), *Pacific Conference of Churches* (PCC) and *Caribbean Conference of Churches* (CCC) etc.

In India, efforts of unity of Protestant Churches turned out to be more difficult and slow. A *National Missionary Council* established in 1913 rechristened itself as the *National Christian Council of India* in 1923, and as *National Council of Churches in India* (NCCI) in 1976, perhaps to fall in line with the *World Council of Churches*. It is one of the 'Associated Councils' of WCC and functions through 14 regional committees.

But this ecumenical movement for church unity has not been able to make much headway beyond a certain point. No church is ready to lose its independent identity which means a complete surrender of its financial resources, hierarchical structure and property to any central organisation.* On the other hand, Roman Catholic Church, because of its vast resources and central organisation, is dreaming of swallowing all other denominations and thus emerging as the only Church.

Origin of Liberation Theology

If a situation of civil war was emerging in the Christian world of Latin America, the Church was facing a serious problem of racial conflicts in U.S.A. and Southern Africa also. Black power was rising in U.S.A. itself. In the Republic of South Africa which with 11 million Christians has the largest concentration of Christian population in any African country, 'many Christians support a government representing a white minority that imposes its will upon a black majority by coercion, threats and frequently by violence,' to fight which 'many black Christians and even some whites find themselves pinning their hopes on taking part in liberation movement.'[3]

All these internal conflicts posed a serious problem of survival before the Church. Inspired by the success of communist revolution in Cuba, communist ideology and techniques of struggle became very popular in various Latin American countries giving rise to guerilla warfare. This upsurge shook the Roman Catholic Church down to its foundations It was not able to decide whether to stand with the tyrant minority governments or to join the struggle of the oppressed majority. While the Church was caught in this dilemma, some foresighted bishops in Latin America jumped into the struggle of the masses and became the prophets of Liberation Theology. To sum up, in the words of Zachariah,

> "Liberation Theology had a dual origin in the political repression common in most of the Latin American countries for many decade, and in the Churches' lack of adequate concern for the poor and for the injustices in society. The theologians, intellectuals, priests etc. who felt solidarity with the poor used the Marxian analysis of society as a framework to organise their thoughts and evolved a sort of shirt-sleeved political theology. Since this was an answer to a felt need it attracted considerable following."[4]

This fusion of Christ and Marx has been very succinctly described by Paulo Freire. who worked for mass awakening in Brazil in 1960, was interned in 1964 and externed from Brazil in 1968; was appointed education and consultant to WCC in 1971, as follows:

> "I went to the slums of Brazil not because of Marx but because of

---

* According to an estimate, the Church in India owns extensive properties. "The Church of South India (CSI) in a moment of confusion declared truthfully that it owned Rs. 2000 crores in property and other assets. The Roman Catholic Church, much larger, must be worth more than that."

Christ. The people in the slums told me, "Go, meet Marx". Their conditions sent me to Marx. Now I meet both Marx and Christ and I have no problems. I continue to do that in peace."[5]

It was with this background in mind that the Third Assembly of WCC in New Delhi in 1961 exhorted the churches to realize that "The revolution is taking place whether we recognise it or not and without Christian leadership it may be tragically perverted."[6] and therefore "where oppression, discrimination and segregation exist, the churches should identify themselves with the oppressed race in this struggle".[7]

Success of this new strategy inspired some Latin American priests to give it a theological garb. Gustav Gutierrez of Peru wrote *A Theology of Liberation*; Paulo Freire wrote his *Pedagogy of the Oppressed*. Latin American Bishop Conference put its seal of approval on the new strategy (*Medellian Documents*) in 1968. Roman Catholic Church took serious note of this new trend in the Second Vatican Council (1965). This line was taken up in an All India Catholic Seminar held at Bangalore in 1969. Pope Paul VI through his encyclical letters encouraged this new trend.

Programme to Combat Racism (PCR)

In 1961, a WCC secretariat on Racial and Ethnic Relations was established.[8] The fourth World Assembly of WCC at Uppsala in 1968 commended a *Programme to Combat Racism* (PCR). It was confirmed by the Central Committee meeting in Canterbury in 1969 and a Special Fund of $ 5,000,000 was established the same year under PCR. In fact this meeting openly exhorted the Churches **to move beyond charity, grants and traditional programming to relevant and sacrificial action and to become agents for the radical reconstruction of society.**[9] The WCC Executive Committee meeting in 1970 at Arnold Shain (FRG) laid down the policy guidelines for allocation of grants from the Special Fund. According to these guidelines, among other things,

> "(1) The proceeds of the Fund shall be used to support organisations that combat racism rather than welfare organisations and (2) while grants are made without control of the manner in which they are spent, they are at the same time a commitment of the PCR to the causes the organisations are themselves fighting for".[10]

Following these guidelines, "From its inception (in 1970) until March 1974, Special Fund Grants totalled $ 1,050,000 distributed to 55 organisations, with $ 688,000 being allocated to liberation movements in Southern Africa".[11] But "Grants to liberation movement aroused the opposition and concern, sometime anger, of some member Churches. Did the World Council endorse violence? Did the Council have a right to disburse any part of its general funds for such controversial programmes?

Who speaks for the churches? Is money to be given to movements without any control or reporting back?"[12]

It was also noted that "Most of the money disbursed through the Special Fund had come, not from traditional donors, but from new ones including governments. That governmental element, too, worried some critics who saw in it a dangerous breach of the separation of the Church and the State."[13]

Development versus Liberation

To mollify this criticism, the WCC Central Committee, in its meeting at Addis Ababa in 1971, asked its sub-unit in Church and Society to conduct a two year study on the problems and potentialities of violence and non-violence in the struggle for social justice. The long statement submitted by the above sub-unit in 1973 built a case in favour of the use of violence in struggle for 'social justice' and the WCC Central Committee with its seal of approval circulated it to its member Churches.[14] Before this exercise had begun, the WCC had established in 1970 the *Commission on the Churches' Participation in Development* (CCPD) 'to co-ordinate various efforts and to take further measures to promote the development concern'.[15] But by then the concept of 'development' had entirely changed. Consequently, in 1974 meeting at West Berlin, the CCPD invited Richard Dickinson to prepare a document for presenting this new strategy, while the PCR received an extended mandate with authorization to continue the Special Fund.[16] Dickinson's work was published by the CCPD under the title *To set at Liberty the Oppressed*. Explaining this shift in strategy, Dickinson says,

> "The programme to Combat Racism (PCR) has highlighted distinctions between 'development' and 'liberation', a shift in terminology which often has subtle but important implications Liberation is a political and theological concept, as well as an economic one.....Liberation suggests discontinuities and possible conflicts, while development implies an orderly and harmonious evolution (reformism and gradualism) without major discontinuities and conflicts."[17]

Commending 'violence' he says, "the programme forces the churches to define more precisely their understanding of the legitimacy of violence as an instrument of social change and justice".[18]

This sudden shift to "Liberation Theology" has raised man; basic issues;

> "What is the right balance between the Church's social, political and spiritual aims? Will the Church endorse the use of violence (many Latin American priests joined guerilla groups) or counter violence? What should be the Church's attitude when

confronted with autocratic regimes? How far can Marxist ideas be incorporated into Christian thinking?"[19]

But without caring to find satisfactory answers to these basic questions, WCC leadership rushed with its decision to export Liberation Theology to the third world countries, because they felt that "Liberation Theology has struck a sympathetic chord in third world countries, where poverty and injustice are the experience of millions".[20]

Liberation Theology Comes to Asia

Under the cover of PCR, it was decided to export the Liberation Theology to Asian countries including India and efforts were made to identify communities in these countries which could be termed as racial and ethnic minorities. One finds in the minutes of a meeting of WCC, held in Kingston in January, 1979: "The Central Committee in 1976 requested PCR to give major attention to racism in Asia. In 1977, the Central Committee recommended that 'regional ecumenical bodies be involved in the development of PCR's agenda'. In pursuance of this recommendation a workshop was held in Auckland on 'Race and Minority Issues in Asia' in 1978."[20a]

Consequently, the discussion on this new strategy gradually percolated in the regional ecumenical bodies also such as CCA, NCCI etc. CCA (formerly EACC) in its 1968 Assembly at Bangkok called Christians and churches "to participate and, where necessary, even to initiate a revolution in thinking as well as action among the inarticulate masses in the rural sector–the peasantry, the artisans and the landless labourers–as well as among the working sections of urban communities."[21] This Assembly recommended Christian participation even '*in the form of riot, rebellion and revolution*'[22] and radically questioned 'nationalism as an ethos'. And to bring this new strategy still closer to the Marxian jargon, the EACC Working Committee meeting of June, 1972 changed the world 'community' to 'peoples'.[23]

The next step was a full-fledged programme Christian Action in Asian Struggle (CAAS) which became the main theme for discussion at the 1973 Bangkok Assembly of CCA. For the implementation of this strategy a new set up called Urban Rural Mission (URM) was created by CCA to initiate and guide the poor and powerless people in different countries of Asia.

In the Fifth Assembly of CCA held at Penang in 1977, besides 'continuation of work among urban poor and industrial workers', three specific areas were named for development: rural mission, race and minority issues, and women workers.[24]

To initiate field action Rural Youth Programme (RYP) was launched in September 1975, and in the period from late 1975 to 1976 the RYP began to take root in the form of projects initiated in live Asian countries: India, Sri Lanka, Thailand, Malaysia and the Philippines.[25]

Methodology

As far as the methodology of Christian action in people's struggle is concerned, the Auckland workshop (1970) provides a very interesting clue to it: "The self-interest of the people leads them to organize and it is this organisational pattern that forms the keynote of the struggle for the people."[26] Bantorn Ondam elucidated it in the Rural Youth Workshop organized by CCA-RYP at Manila in 1980:

"Dissatisfaction with any existing order is a most practical point of departure from which the whole CO (Community Organization) could take off. But it must be brought to the attention of the people. Discontent, conflict, or contradiction must be recognized and understood by the people. Hence, the need to focus the conflict on something specific–specific issues which the people feel most intensely about–must be identified. Mobilization takes place after the problems have been identified, analysed and selected and when the people think that they can do something about them. It must be launched with the end in view of motivating the oppressed to act on an issue."[27]

In short, local discontentment are sought to be exploited through localised action for precipitating violent conflicts under the cover of the Marxian jargon of people's struggle.

But this is only the first step. The next step, Bantorn Ondam says, lies in "moving from simple, immediate, short-term, personal and localised issues to more complex, long term, national and systematic issues."[28] The Christian Institute for the study of Religion and Society (CISRS) Basic Document of December 1977 says, "Another major concern is the relation between the micro-level activities with the macro-level of regional, national and internal forces and movements."[29] Since this was a long and difficult process, hence CISRS, advising caution and patience, suggested that "We must accept for the time being some of our limitations which are not dependent on our own decisions and not indulge in stances which jeopardise our more serious objectives."[30]

Purse Controls Policy

In this way local Christian Action Groups, guided and financed from abroad, came into being in different Asian Countries including India. As to the financial resources and life style of the Christian Action Groups using marxian jargon and working for a 'social revolution' in India, we get very interesting and meaningful hints in the National Christian Council Review (NCCR). Its September, 1975 issue says:

> "One finds that in the third world, these groups are heavily dependent on foreign money. Further, one finds that their style of life and operation are expensive. In this matter they don't seem to be in any way different from the Churches they criticise."[31]

WCC has created separate commissions and other agencies to give financial support to different type of activities going on in the third world such as Special Fund under PCR, CCPD, CICWRS and URM (Urban Rural Mission) etc. Now-a-days Urban Rural Mission serves the purpose of linkage and cover for the financial support and guidance given to various types of Christian Action Groups in third world countries. According to the report presented by George Ninan as General Secretary of CCA-URM to the Eleventh Committee meeting held at Hong Kong in February: 1980. "Major share of our finances comes through WCC-URM and we accord our appreciation with thanks to them. Western funding agencies are ready to support URM related groups."

The Financial Report of the CCA for the period 1977-1980 while admitting that, "for extensive programmes which we run, we are heavily dependent on funding agencies in Europe and America" throws some light as to how this financial dependence has been used to dictate programmes to the churches in the third world. Narrating its own experience the CCA Report says:

> "For some years past, the CCA has been sending staff to Europe and America to discuss with our partners in these countries aspects of common interest. What began in 1970's as a fund raising programme quickly changed into a discussion on basic theological questions about mission."[32]

In fact, the shift from 'developmental programmes' to 'liberation theology' in church strategy was reflected in its funding policy also. Dickinson writes,

> "There seems to be a waning amount of church money available for development programmes in the third world. This is quite marked in the United States, where budgets of mission boards have decreased dramatically over the past six years,"[33] although "between 1968 and 1973 giving through WCC/CICARWS increased impressively. Even contribution from North American sources through WCC increased by 33% despite declines in overall giving to projects and programmes by these churches."[34]

Obviously, all these funds were diverted from '*developmental programmes*' towards '*liberation movements*' because, in words of Dickinson,

> "The Churches have come to appreciate far more the fact that projects should be limited, and to be more deeply aware of the

danger of pre-occupation with projects only. There is now far more attention to structural issues and structural change."[35]

Financially dependent third world churches could hope to get more funds only if they agreed, though unwillingly, to toe this new line. A CCA Report, while claiming 'A special fraternal relationship between the WCC and the CCA' admits that 'there are always strains in this family relationship through misunderstandings on programme emphasis'.[36]

International agencies like CCA-URM and WCC-PCR/CCPD etc. besides financial assistance, have been providing two types of support service to these action groups.

1. **Documentation and Information**: According to CCA Report "Documentation has been a strong aspect of URM work. In Asia it is known as DAGA (Documentation for Action Groups in Asia). As a pan of the world URM movement it is actually responsible to WCC Geneva, but the Asia URM makes full use of its service... As the name suggests, its documentation service revolves around specific items on the agenda of local action groups. Its specialised work has given very significant support to local groups and enabled factual evidence to be provided."[37]

2. **Centralized Training Programme**: Centralised training programmes are organised for leaders of these action groups called 'Community Organisers' or change agents. Many such centralised training programmes for selected activities are held in different countries at different times.[38]

Christianity or Marxism

It is obvious from the above facts that the Church through immense money power at its disposal has been dictating to the third world churches the action programme and methodology, which have nothing to do with spiritualism or religion. In a way it has completely switched over to a political role couched in Marxian jargon and methodology.

Then, why should not the Church openly admit the defeat of the traditional Christian ideology of love, compassion and non-violence; of 'love thy neighbour' and of 'turning the other cheek' before the Marxian ideology of class struggle and violent revolution? Has not the church ceased to inspire its adherents for a higher and purposeful action in a changed situation? If the church leadership is convinced that Marxian analysis and communist techniques are the only way to lead to the liberation of the poor and the oppressed, why should they not boldly admit the inadequacies and failures of Christianity as ideology and an vacate the field gracefully for others to play their historical role? Why this artificial mingling of Marx with Christ? Why this sudden outburst of love for the poor and oppressed? Why this switch over to Marxian jargon? Could one say that the recently born Liberation Theology or the Black Theology are natural stages in the evolution of Christianity and the Church? What has been the role of the Church in history?

Church versus People in History

The WCC symposium of Essays on the relation between the Church and the Poor during the 18th and 19th Centuries of the Industrial Revolution and the Western Colonial Expansion, published recently by the CCPD/WCC (Geneva, 1978) under the title *Separation without Hope*[39] documents the large scale alienation between the Church and the awakened poor in the past. Andre Bieler's study of this relationship in Europe concludes that the Church's rigidity (against the advance of political democracy and working class betterment) 'strongly encouraged, in the middle classes first and then in the working class, a spiritual quest outside the frame work of traditional Christianity since the latter was serving as an ideology of reaction', and that the "religious fanaticism however contributed to strengthen the anti-clerical ardour of the democratic bourgeois and then the militant atheism of the proletariat".[40] Writing on the North American scene, Ronald White Jr. says: "Calvinism which was under sway accepted economic inequality as a result of divine ordination. The corollary of this belief was that the poor continued to exist in their conditions because of sin or sloth or that wealth was a sign of the *elect*."[41] The virtual identification of Christian missions in Asia, Africa and Latin America with western colonialism and white racialism could not generally be avoided and hence also their alienation from the struggles for political independence and racial justice.[42] Regarding churches in the independent nations of the post-war world, C. I. Itty observes that 'the totality of their membership who were drawn from the poorer sections of society continued to remain poor'.[43] M. M. Thomas concludes, "It is clear from this brief survey that there exists a large gulf in all continents between the churches and the revolting poor"[44] and raises the question "can the Church become the Church of the awakened poor, awakening the poor and lighting with the poor for social justice in our time ?"[45] But what is the urgency for this new and reverse role for the Church? To this question, Thomas has only one answer: "Without it the poor would continue to seek the spiritual framework of their struggle outside the stream of Christian faith. This is dangerous both for the Church and for the social revolution "[46]

The Third Assembly of WCC at New Delhi in 1961 asked the churches to join the struggle of the oppressed since "the revolution is taking place whether we recognise it or not, and without Christian leadership it will be tragically perverted."[47] A similar argument advanced in favour of a new role by the All India Catholic Seminar held at Bangalore in March

1969 with the blessings of the Vatican was: "The Church had lived far too long in a ghetto largely of its own making.. She must plunge into the mainstream of change and suffuse it with Christian values. Otherwise, she will be bypassed by the modern world and, like a relic of a bygone age, her relevance will fade, her appeal will diminish, her strength will ebb."[48] The WCC Assembly and the Catholic Seminar do not answer as to who had stopped the Church from giving leadership to revolution in the past and has not the Church itself been responsible for forcing the people on to the path of bloody revolution? An official statement, approved and circulated by the Central Committee of WCC in 1973, has this to say about the role of Church in history: "Churches and Christians are realizing that they have too seldom been on the side of the poor and the oppressed. They have too often supported the powers of an unjust social order. They often have profited from the poverty of others. They have in the worst used force, when they were in power, against those who differed from them in belief or ideology". After having said all this the statement exhorts: "Their first word to this problem must be one of repentance. Repentance however means a change of mind and heart, and new-forms of action for justice."[49] But where is the urgency to repent now? Is it an urgency by external pressures or born out of a new spiritual awakening? Repentance imposed by external circumstances can never be more than skin-deep while a repentance born out of an inner craving results in discarding the old forms and institutions by the repentor.

Survival for What?

Is it not a call of the instinct for survival only? From every responsible Church forum the only argument advanced in favour of this radical change is 'a crisis of survival' and 'fear of loss of leadership'.

The question arises: is it really so simple and easy to transform an instrument of oppression and exploitation into an instrument of liberation and social justice? Where are the historical theological foundations in clerical tradition for such a transformation? One could expect such a change of heart on the part of a few enlightened and nobler souls but could it be applicable to a large world-wide organisation rooted in a long historical process? Merely a call of survival cannot bring about a genuine change of heart in an old institution like the Church, a fact testified by a Christian activist in Maharashtra, Father D'Mello S.J. alias Pradip Deshbhakt Prabhu in his dialogue with Paulo Freire, "The Church is afraid of losing its position. We cannot opt to be on the side of the poor. The inevitable result of this is that the Church is feeling bad as it is being bypassed by history."[50] After all, why should the Church be so keen to save its physical existence and lose its soul and spirit? The basic question is 'Survival for what?'

Baptism and Conversion

This bring us naturally to the question, whether the Church has finally decided not to press its claims about the 'uniqueness of Christ' or that 'Christianity is the only path for human salvation'? Has it really renounced its basic mission of baptism and conversion? Or, does it mean only a shift in strategy for the fulfillment of the same mission?

Here one should admit that many personalities, impelled by the higher human urges, had been able to rise above the forms, institutions, rituals and thought-structures, within which they happened to be born; to see objectively through their inadequacy to meet the challenges of changing times and formulate new ideologies and thought-structures and to carve out new paths for future action. But such visionaries and prophets renounced old forms, rituals, institutions and thought-structures just as a sprouting seed would discard its own shell. How can an instrument which was designed for a definite purpose in a particular environment be effectively used for a different purpose in an entirely changed milieu?

We see no symptoms of such a transformation in the attitude or the organisational set-up of the Church. The failure of the ecumenical movement to bring about church unity is in itself a proof that in spite of all the tall talks of identity with the poor and the oppressed or the smuggle for structural changes, the church leadership still seems to be obsessed with the preservation of its position and power acquired in the name of religion. The Report of the Boston World Conference of scientists, technologists and theologians on Christian Social Ethics held in 1979 laments: "The present brokenness of the churches which weakens and discredits Christian Witness is one reason for the failures and injustices of societies. The ecumenical movement is indispensable for the validation and influence of the ethical convictions supported by Christian faith."[51]

Transformation or Opportunism?

Strong instinct for survival and commitment to its basic mission of evangelisation have been forcing the Church to take contradictory postures and to make the worst type of compromises in different situations.For example, the Church had been always projecting itself as an ardent champion of parliamentary democracy in India but EACC (now CCA) in its First Assembly in 1958 at Kuala Lumpur seriously questioned its usefulness. It asked: "Is Parliamentary Government the best method of all circumstances for preserving those Christian values enshrined in the word 'Democracy'? And is not the development of a more authoritarian system in certain circumstances a more effective means of safeguarding them?" It further asked about the possibility of an indigenous and dynamic form of democracy.[52]

Was it not an apologia in favour of People's Republic of China to flatter its communist rulers just to save Church's existence in China? Similarly, explaining CCA's attitude towards nationalism, M.M. Thomas in his opening address before 1973 Assembly said,

> "In the 1958 Assembly we thought nationalism would provide an adequate ethos for the struggle for social justice and in fact in this sense we have talked about nation building". And "one of the striking things the 1968 Assembly (at Bangkok) did was to radically question nationalism as an ethos for a genuinely human process of modernisation and the realisation of a just society in Asia."[53]

This naturally leads one to surmise that if the Church leadership is taking recourse to liberation theology, it may not be out of genuine love for the poor but may be a calculated move to save its existence and prepare ground for mass evangelisation at some opportune time.

This apprehension gets strengthened when one scans through the debate that has been going on within the Church leadership at different levels–World, Asia and India–about its basic mission of evangelisation. In April 1980 Zachariah, while discussing the deadlock that evangelisation was meeting in India, wrote: "In the secular and religious situation in India the concern for evangelism in the sense of an open and explicit proclamation of Jesus as the Saviour, and the invitation to men to be committed to Him and join the Church may not evoke much interest. In such a situation what do we do, and what do we proclaim?"[54] Pointing to an earlier debate he wrote, "At this point....one cannot ignore the interesting and profound discussion which got started at the close of the sixties on the whole question of baptism and conversion. In fact, one can trace the beginnings of this discussion to the 'Cosmic Christ' debate which began at the New Delhi Assembly of the WCC in I961."[55]

Evangelisation: How and When?

In fact, the Church has not for a moment been able to think of a different role for itself except evangelisation i.e. to baptise and to convert. The focus of discussion has been on how to overcome the obstacles and resistance which Church had been facing in the fulfillment of this mission in different countries. Describing such efforts the NCCR wrote in February 1975: "There is today a visible and renewed interest in evangelism among the churches all over the world. In the WCC related churches a new awareness of the urgency of the evangelistic task has developed, especially since the Bangkok Conference on 'Salvation Today' (1973-Ed). Over two hundred Roman Catholic priests gathered recently at the Vatican in the Fourth Synod to discuss this theme. The Evangelicals met at Lausanne last year (August 1974) for a Conference on World Evangelisation."[56]

But the situation was not found favourable for direct conversion because, as Zachariah admits, "In many countries in the world today the Church faces the context of the rejection of Christianity and there is increasing resistance to the work of the Church at different levels."[57] Pointing to the new Liberation Theology he says, "There are signs of hope visible in the movement towards the liberation of man everywhere."[58] In fact, the main thrust behind the extension of Liberation Theology movement to third world countries seems only to prepare ground for the fulfillment of its evangelic mission. M.M. Thomas in his opening address to the EACC Conference in 1973 on *Christian Action in Asian Struggle* (CAAS) made a categorical statement:

"I agree that the Church's central mission is the mission of presenting Christ as the Saviour of human spirit". He said, "The pastors and the theologians have a large responsibility to sensitivise themselves and the churches to the ethical demands of the Asian struggle and to relate Christian Action in it to *worship, evangelism and faith of the Church*."[59] The Basic Document (December, 1977) of CISRS made it all the more clear when it said: "The question of participation in the struggle of the people for social justice and transformation of society was seriously taken up by CISRS as an integral part of the evangelisation and mission."[60] The dogged resistance offered by the Indian Church in 1978 to the Arunachal Pradesh Freedom of Religion Act and the Freedom of Religion Bill presented in the Lok Sabha in November 1978 which did not mean any harm to the Church in any way except seeking to restrict religious conversion through force, fraud or inducement, showed that Church had never lost sight of its basic mission of conversion through any means. In fact, the Church has been wavering between its new tactical line and its basic mission of conversion. This dichotomy present in the clerical mind comes out very sharply in a day long discussion which prominent Indian Christian intellectuals and liberation theologists had with Paulo Freire during his visit to New Delhi in Feb. 1979. Towards the end of these discussions, S. Santiago, Executive Director, Indo-German Social Service Society asked: "Is it (evangelism) possible at all in the whole process of liberation? Whether you call it conscientisation or not? Where do we place the role of the prophetic Church to bring at least the basic mission of the Church to give good news to the people and in black and white terms to baptise and to convert?"[61] He went on to assert that "Its basic theological evangelical missionary purpose is one of the very purposes of existence of the Church. When it is dealing with social, economic destinies of the people, it does so at a certain level without fulfilling one of the basic missions of trying to see that as many as possible come over and get baptised and so on. I don't want the Church to die like that."[62]

This is exactly how the average Churchman looks at the Liberation Theology of people's struggle. For him Liberation Theology is just another name of the strategy or politics of conversion. If he is getting ready to use the Marxian analysis and techniques, it is with an expectation that it will be able to pave the way for evangelisation in future through subversion and disintegration in the third world countries. Perhaps this is what Paulo Freire had in his mind while replying to Santiago's question, he talked of the 'prophetic Church' in Latin America and hinted that "may be in the next century there may be other aspects in the historical priorities."[63]

This only shows that the compulsions of an adverse or difficult situation have made the Church a split personality and Liberation Theology is still not a part of its convictions. It is an exotic plant, not born from within. If Liberation Theology had its roots in a genuine love for the poor and the oppressed, its genesis and operation would have drawn its sustenance from the meager local resources and not from the same old foreign funds. Liberation Theology seems to be a cover for the same old expansionist role, which had used imperialism as its cover in the past. If the Church intends to be sincere about Liberation Theology it will have to renounce its evangelistic mission of baptism and conversion or of Christianity as the only path for human salvation. Then it will have to prepare itself for its own total transformation into an entirely new identity. As long as the same money power, the same centralized planning mechanism and the same international organisation which had led and controlled the Church in the colonial era operates, people will be led to believe that Liberation Theology is nothing but another name for the global conspiracy, which had formerly exploited imperialism and colonialism for the sustenance and expansion, is now using Marxism as its cover or tool. For Church, it seems, the Liberation Theology is nothing more than a strategy or politics of conversion.

References

1. M.M. Thomas: *Religion and the Revolt of the Oppressed,* I.S.P.C.K., Delhi, 1981, p. 19.

2. *Ibid.* p. 55.

3. *Struggle for Social Justice* (WCC), Delhi, 1973.

4. M. Zachariah: *Christian Presence in India.* C. L. S,, Madras, 1981, p. 78.

5. *A Day with Paulo Freire* (Ed. G. Mathew), ISPCK, Delhi, 1980, p. 3.

6. *WCC Statements & Documents on Racism* (1948-1979), Geneva, p. 13.

7. *Ibid.* p. 13.

8. *Ibid* p. 15.

9. R. D. N. Dickinson r *To set at Liberty the Oppressed,* CCPD/WCC, Geneva, 1975 (2nd Printing 1978), p. 23.

10. WCC Statements, *op. cit.* p. 31.
11. R. D. N. Dickinson, *op. cit,* p. 23.
12. *Ibid.* p. 23.
13. *Ibid.* p. 23.
14. *Struggle for Social Justice,* op. cit.
15. R.D.N. Dickinson, *op. cit.* p. vii.
16. *Ibid.* p. 24.
17. *Ibid.* p. 31
18. *Ibid.* p. 30.
19. M. Zachariah: op. cit. p. 78-79.
20. *Ibid.* p. 79.

20a. Minutes of the 31st Central Committee meeting, WCC, Geneva 1979, p. 60.

21. M.M. Thomas: Christian Action in the Asian Struggle, CCA, Singapore, 1973, p. 6.
22. *Ibid.* p. 6.
23. *Ibid.* p. 9.
24. *From Penang* to *Bangalore,* CCA, Singapore, 1981, p. 60.
25. *Rural Awakening,* CCA, Singapore, 1980, p. 57.
26. *No Place in the Inn.* CCA/URM, Tokyo, 1978, p. 119.
27. Bantorn Ondam: *Rural Awakening, op. cit.* p. 18.
28. *Ibid.* p. 18.
29. Saral K. Chatterji: Foci of C.l.S.R.S. Responsibilities in India Today, CISRS, Bangalore, 1979, p. 70.
30. *Ibid.* p. v.
31. M. Zachariah, *op. cit.* p. 75.
32. Front Penang to Bangalore, op. cit. p. 12.
33. R.D.N. Dickinson, op. cit. **p. 46.**
34. *Ibid.* p. 46.
35. *Ibid.* p. 46.
36. From Penang to Bangalore, op. cit. **p. 11.**
37. *Ibid.* p. 62.
38. *Ibid.* p. 62.
39. Religion & Revolt of the Oppressed, op. cit. p. 39.
40. *Ibid.* p. 39.
41. *Ibid.* p. 41.

42. *Ibid.* p. 41.
43. *Ibid.* p. 42.
44. *Ibid.* p. 42.
45. *Ibid.* p. 42.
46. *Ibid.* p. 42.
47. cf. reference 6.
48. *The Social Mission of the Church* (Ed. V.H. Devadas), I.S.P.C.K., Delhi, 1982, p. xi.
49. Struggle for Social Justice, op. cit. p. 7.
50. A Day with Paulo Freire, op. cit. p. 54.
51. Religion & Revolt of the Oppressed, op. cit. p. 9.
52. Christian Action in Asian Struggle, op. cit. p. 3.
53. *Ibid.* p. 8, and *Ibid,* p. 6.
54. M. Zachariah, op. cit. p. 82.
55. *Ibid.* p. 82.
56. *Ibid.* p. 53.
57. *Ibid.* p. 53.
58. *Ibid.* p. 54.
59. Christian Action in Asian Struggle, op. cit. p. 10.
60. Saral K. Chatterji, *op. cit.* p. 48-49.
61. A Day with Paulo Freire, op. cit. p. 88-89.
62. Ibid. p. 87.
63. Ibid. p. 90.

18

Church Goes Political in India

S.K. Agrawal

Lecturer, Shri Ram College of Commerce, Delhi

The withdrawal of British power on 15th August 1947 left behind in independent India an eight million strong Christian community crestfallen, dazed and demoralised. Suddenly it found itself reduced from the position of rulers to that of a small minority-hopelessly divided against itself. It felt like being orphan or alien in its own land of birth.

Perhaps in some moments of self-introspection, a noted Indian Christian theologist D.D. Pitamber said:

> "When freedom came in 1947, we found ourselves in an awkward situation. Our relation with the West and our identification with the Christian faith–the faith of the Colonialist–created a sense of doubt in our identity as Indians. Our dependence on the West for survival produced doubt in our capacities and abilities, and our failure to live up to the expectation of the society created shame in our personalities. Such a dependence created hesitation to commit ourselves, with a free will, to our autonomous identity."[1]

Consequently, a fear psychosis, born out of a feeling of deprivatism seemed to have gripped the Indian Christians."[2]

In these moments of bewilderment, identity crisis and fear psychosis they found themselves led and controlled by a church organisation, which had no roots in Indian soil and, to quote an eminent Christian theologian T.V. Philip, was "understood in terms of Western missionary expansion. It was seen only as an appendix of the church in the West or a dot on the missionary map."[3] Naturally, such a church could never identify with our national struggle for freedom.[4]

Three Trends

When battered by the Second World War, British Imperialism was left with no option but to withdraw from India, there emerged three distinct trends in Indian Christianity. *One,* the church hierarchy controlled by one or the other foreign missionary society which depended entirely for its leadership and financial sustenance upon the country of its origin, popularly known as its "Home Board." This priestly and missionary class which looked upon India as a recruiting ground only was worried more about its own survival in the changed situation, and was interested in the protection of its property, position and money inflow. *Two,* there arose a microscopically small section of enlightened patriotic Christian intellectuals, eager to atone for the sins of the past and to identify itself with the national euphoria that India was witnessing on the eve of the Independence. The *third* was the majority trend representing the vast Christian masses, who were till then fed upon a false pride of' heir religious identity with foreign rulers, but now, deprived of that found themselves in no way different from or superior to other sections of the Indian masses, submerged equally in the abyss of social and economic inequality, ignorance and poverty. Naturally, they were led to think:

> "Whether conversion to Christianity has really led to a higher spiritual life and to a real and personal experience of Christ, or whether it was simply a change of rites, myths, concepts and social customs..." and to most people "baptism appears to be an act by which a person repudiates his cultural heritage and accepts an alien culture."[5]

The church was now required to meet on equal terms the challenge of Hindu reality, which though poor in economic terms was proving to be much richer in spiritual field not only in India, but in the heartland of Christiandom also. *George Soraes Prabhu S J* Professor in De Nobili College, Poona, explaining the seriousness of this challenge said, "Christian prophets of doom once gleefully predicted the imminent end of traditional Indian religion, brought on by the onslaught of a secularism which, they had persuaded themselves, was in fact some sort of a prodigal son of biblical religion. Alas for such wishful thinking! Secularism, if it has indeed a Christian ancestry, has proved itself a most undutiful child. For the wave of secularism that has swept through the post-war world has emptied churches in Europe, only to fill up *ashrams* in India and the West. God may be dead in post-Christian secular city of the West, he appears alive and well in India today."[6]

The church was faced with some real problems. How to proclaim the uniqueness of Christ before such a society? How to carry on the basic mission of the Church i.e. baptism and conversion in a pluralistic society believing in equality of all religions *(Sarva-Dharma-Sambhav)?* How to uphold in a secular state the biblical claim that "Neither is there salvation in *any other* for there is *none* other name under heaven given among men whereby we must be saved." What was superior in the Indian Christian society to justify church's claim of 'uniqueness and the only path of human salvation"?

Freedom of Religion, but

Against this background the church leadership felt greatly relieved when the Constituent Assembly of India, at the end of a heated debate, voted in favour of an amendment conferring the "right to propagate religion" under article 25 (a). Making full use of this they made intensive and vigorous efforts in North-East India achieving tremendous success in converting a large segment of tribal population to Christianity after Independence. Encouraged by their success in North-East India the Church leadership decided to concentrate all its efforts and resources in tribal belt of Bihar, Orissa and Madhya Pradesh. But the objectionable missionary activities among the tribals of Madhya Pradesh; where 57.4% population comprised of members of Scheduled Castes, Scheduled Tribes and other Backward Classes forced the Madhya Pradesh Government to appoint on 14th April, 1954, "The Christian Missionary Activities Enquiry Committee" popularly known as "Neogy Committee" named after Justice Bhawani Shanker Neogy who headed this Enquiry Committee. The report of this Committee, submitted in three volumes in 1956, made startling disclosures about the designs and techniques pursued by the Christian missionaries, mostly foreigners, for conversion of poor and illiterate sections of Indian population. The publication of this report strengthened much the already prevailing suspicion about the political aims behind the missionary activities. The demand for expulsion of foreign missionaries and stoppage of foreign money to church organisations gained momentum. And without the leadership of foreign missionaries and inflow of foreign money it was not possible for the church in India to maintain the vast infrastructure of its relief and welfare activities in the field of education, medical aid and help to orphanages etc., which were the main tools of its proselytisation activities.[6a]

In 1967 the Swatantra Party Government in Orissa with R.N. Singh Deo as Chief Minister in spite of stiff opposition from the Church passed a 'Freedom of Religion Act' banning conversions through "force, fraud or inducement". This was followed in 1968 by a Freedom of Religion Act passed by SVD Government of Madhya Pradesh. The passing of such Acts by various state governments shook the Church to its foundation.

Besides, the gradual shrinking of the inflow of foreign personnel and financial resources, the Church found that its monopoly over welfare activities in backward areas and backward sections of the Indian society was being challenged by the massive welfare efforts initiated by the Central and State Governments of independent India. When the Tribal Welfare Department of Madhya Pradesh Government started some schools for tribal children, the Roman Catholic missionaries had carried on persistent propaganda against such schools and had represented this to the State Government also. Although Father Vermiere had intimated that he had no objection to Government starting schools in Jashpur side by side with the Mission schools, the Roman Catholic Bishop of Ranchi kept on representing that this should not be done. But this resistance put by the missionaries did not succeed and various Government agencies launched massive welfare projects for the economic, social and educational development of the tribal and backward sections of the Indian society.

The society at large also awoke to its duty towards these long neglected sections of the society and undertook service activities in these areas to supplement the governmental efforts. Now, Church found itself logged in a competition against the whole society backed by state power in the field of service and charity; which made it difficult to use these service institutions for proselytisation purposes.

Rethinking about Service Role

This made the church leadership to rethink about the role of the service activities,

> "The service role of the church is being increasingly diminished in our welfare state and the state is moving into areas-education, medical aid, community service-in which it was the privilege of the Church to serve. Christian institutions have been drawfed by the massive institutions of the state and other agencies."[7]

National Christian Council of India in its 17th Assembly a Kottayam in September 1971 whose basic theme for discussion was "*The Indian Church: Identity and Fulfilment*" took note of this difficult situation in the following words:

> "The church in India through its schools, colleges, hospitals md other service projects had tried to do this with varying degree of

success. But today the church's involvement in society with its service agencies has become an apple of discord. The church's image is today vitiated by the power, money and the institutions which it commands."[8] and therefore, NCCR in its August 1971 editorial lamented:

"It is obvious that in India we live today in the context of the rejection of Christianity and this is due to socio-religious md political reasons. There is a strong resistance to the work of the Church at different levels."[9]

Reservation policy introduced by the Indian Constitution in favour of Scheduled Castes and Scheduled Tribes also proved to be a big hurdle in the ways of Christian proselytisation efforts among these two major target groups. Concessions under reservation policy were not applicable to the converts to other religions and therefore,

"The protective discrimination for Scheduled Castes and Tribes reversed at a blow the possible economic and educational advantages of conversion to Christianity and instead provided new and compelling disincentives to conversion from the under privileged groups. On the one hand this liberated the Church from *large-scale* conversions for primarily economic motives."[10]

To get over this hurdle, Church has been carrying on a concerted campaign demanding the extension of reservation policy benefit; to Christian converts also, but to no effect so far.

Faced by this dilemma, a serious debate started within the Church about its mission and techniques. This debate is partly reflected in a book *The Indian Church: Identity and Fulfilment* published by the Study Department of NCCI on the eve of its 17th Assembly held at Kottayam in 1971. Reviewing this book, NCCR in an editorial note in September 1971 issue, admitted:

"Today the old classical methods of proclaiming Christ are no longer open or relevant. So we are now seeking new methods and new frontiers of witness."[11]

"There is no gainsaying the fact that the poor success met by the Church in preaching the gospel is to a large extent due to the way in which Christianity has been preached and lived in India."[12]

Later in May 1973, NCCR wrote:

"Even the traditional channels of church's compassion through time-honoured methods of service are losing relevance. Our institutions have been dwarfed by the massive institutions of the Government and on the whole we live in a context of the rejection of the Christianity."[13]

Thus, bereft of the exclusive patronage of State power after independence, coupled with increasing vigilance and restrictions against the inflow of foreign money and personnel, the Church in India fell upon the Liberation Theology couched in Marxian jargon and advocating violent means. This theology was born and perfected outside India in the context of the extraordinary situation prevailing in Latin America.

Liberation Theology in India

The early 60s debate that was going on in the higher circles of W.C.C. and Vatican about the utility and application of Liberation Theology in the interest of the survival and expansion of the church base in third world countries, found its echo in Indian church and Christian intellectual circles also though the process was a little slow and tardy.

As to the foreign origins of the 'Liberation Theology debate' in India, there can be no doubt. Admitting this fact a Catholic scholar George Soraes Prabhu S.J. of De Nobili College, Poona, says:

> "Christianity has, of course, been impelled by its own specific clan to put out an immense and exuberant system of education, relief and welfare works of which Mother Teresa has become a much publicized symbol. But it has only now begun to realize (and that too largely at the prodding of secular ideologies like Marxism) that its education is not often education for justice that its development projects are helping to maintain an unjust social order, not change it, and that its works of welfare are rescuing the victims producing oppression itself. As with so much else in Christianity, this awareness has first appeared in the West (still the Christian heartland) and has yet to trickle down to India in a significant way. The extraordinary radical social encyclical; of the recent popes, or the strong pronouncements of W.C.C. on justice and race are little known here. And neither the political theology of Moltmann or Metz, nor the more radical and (to us) more relevant Marxist inspired liberation theology of the Latin Americans (Gutierrez, Segundo, Sobino, Schaull) have made a serious creative impact on the thinking of the Indian churches."[14]

N.C.C.R. (National Christian Council Review,) the monthly organ of the National Christian Council of India (NCCI) also writes,

> "For some time the discussion as to whether the church's work of charity and grace are to be limited to relief and rehabilitation etc. or whether it should risk its resources and move into a biblical ministry of justice to the poor, has been taking place in the churches around the world. This issue brought about a crisis in the Church World Service (the service arm of the NCCC, U.S.A.)

over a year ago and led to discussion on the national level of the whole question of the politics of charity. This discussion has now percolated into the church in India."[15]

In India many intellectual and ecumenical bodies like National Christian Council of India (now, National Council of Churches in India) NCCI, with its headquarters at Nagpur, Christian Institute for Study of Religion and Society (CISRS) Bangalore, Ecumenical Christian Centre (ECC) Whitefield, Bangalore with M.A. Thomas as its founder director, Christian Retreat and Study Centre (CRSC) Rajpur, Dehradun under the leadership of Director R.W. (alias DICK) Taylor, Ecumenical Study and Industrial Institute (ESII), Durgapur with Rev. Kenyon Wright as its Director, William Carey Study and Research Centre (WCSRC), Serampore (West Bengal) took up this debate in the Protestant circles, while the Catholic Bishop Conference of India (CBCI) gave the lead in Roman Catholic circles.

Role of CISRS

Of course, it goes to the credit of CISRS that with about twelve year's patient research studies and painstaking efforts it created the necessary intellectual and information base for the acceptance and application of Liberation Theology on a wider scale in Indian situation. CISRS had come into being in October, 1957 with the blessings and support of WCC,[16] with an avowed object that it "shall specially assist the churches in India in educating their members regarding their total task of witness and service..."[17] Under the intellectual leadership of Dr. P.D. Devanandan, M.M. Thomas and Saral K. Chatterji as its first, second and third Directors "it has contributed much to the thought and leadership of the N.C.C.I., the EACC (now CCA) and the WCC".[18] *The Basic Document on the Foci of CISRS responsibilities in India Today* prepared by its present Director Saral K. Chatterji, discussed and adopted by the Biennial Council of CISRS in December, 1977, gives us a complete conceptual framework and the action strategy to be followed for the implementation of Liberation Theology in the Indian situation. Referring to a definite shift in the "social and political studies of the CISRS from the sixties onwards", it says,

> "During this period also the earlier emphasis, necessary at that time, on nationalism, democracy, development etc., gave place to the ideas of mass struggle, transformation of structure of power and the proximate goals of socialism."[19]

While CISRS was busy in preparing an intellectual rationale for this strategic shift, National Christian Council Review (NCCR), the official organ of NCCI, was trying to sell this idea to the church leadership in India. In May 1969 it wrote:

> "Schools, hospitals, farms etc. once so important in promoting social justice have no longer the cutting edge in relation to key issue and so the churches have to seek new areas of service."[20]

In April 1970, it went a step further and started talking of social revolution.

> "The development process is often regarded by the Christians as the distribution of money or materials or doing some form of social service... Social service will not re-create a nation, only social *revolution* can do."[21]

In June, 1971 it drew attention to a Consultation jointly sponsored by the Church of South India (CSI), CISRS and Community Service Centre (Madras) which was held in early 1971. This Consultation, according to NCCR:

> "has begun a process of thinking which if taken to its logical conclusion will make us evaluate the goals, the methods and performance of our service institutions in order that they may serve at the point of the needs and struggles in India today."[22]

In May, 1973 it gave an open call to organise action for revolution, "The aim of the Church should be to involve itself at the lower levels at which the *social revolution* in India ought to make place.....One area into which we must enter is that of landless peasantry (agricultural workers, share croppers etc.)"[23]

And that "We are today called to participate in action groups that will create the ethos for the much needed social revolution".[23a] In Catholic circles also an all India Catholic seminar was held in Bangalore in March 1969, with the blessing of the Vatican to discuss this new strategy. Of course, these discussions, consultations and exhortation could not sway the church establishments to wind-up their service institutions and jump overnight into the so-called 'revolution'. NCCR laments.

> "Some inconclusive discussion took place in the early 80's, but it did not proceed much, nor was it picked up in the churches. It remained at a highly elitist and theological level. This discussion was interpreted by some as a rationalisation of our failure in the area of evangelism."[24]

Referring to the Church dilemma, CISRS Basic Document (Dec. 1977) also says,

> "The question of the mission of Church in India, in spite of numerous conferences and discussions for the last twenty years is today more distant than ever, for the churches and the congregations. Instead we see evangelistic campaigns

and religious euphoria and illusions taking hold of a stagnant situation."[25]

Action Groups and Funding Agencies

While this debate was still going on, many local action groups sprouted up in different parts of the country in the late sixties and early seventies. These groups led by Christian activists under the cover of rural development started local action in selected areas. New organisations such as Village Reconstruction Organisation of Father Windey got themselves registered in 1969 onwards and embarked upon intensive grass root work in some selected groups of villages in Andhra Pradesh, Tamil Naḍu and Orissa etc. Father Ferrer, who was expelled from India, had started work in some areas of Maharashtra and Andhra. Simultaneously, many foreign funding agencies also came into being, professedly for the purpose of helping the cause of rural development in India. In fact, in the post-war situation when national governments of newly independent countries in Asia and Africa tried to restrict the inflow of foreign money for church missionary activities, it was discovered that the same money could be pumped into these countries under the cover of aid to developmental activities especially rural development which was given top priority in all these countries.

The Directory of Voluntary Action published by AVARD gives a long list of such foreign funding agencies, e.g. Helpage India, Christian Children's Fund, Australian Catholic Relief, Bread for the World (West Germany), CARE, Catholic Relief Service, Christian Aid (London), Canadian International Development Agency (CIDA), Community Aid Abroad Australia (India), Danish International Development Agency (DAN1DA), Division of World Outreach–ICC (Toronto), EZE (Protestant Central Agency for Development and Aid), For Those Who Have Less (Australia), Indo-German Social Service Society, Lutheran World Federation, Lutheran Relief Work, Netherlands Organisation for International Coordination (NOVIB), Swedish International Development Agency (SIDA), Swiss Aid, Swiss Development Corporation, Terre des Hommes India Programme, OXFAM, Food and Agriculture Organisation (FAO) etc.[26]

A study of NCCR and CISRS Basic Document shows that many of these Christian action groups came into being without the approval and support of Church leadership and sometimes even out of disenchantment with the Church functioning. NCCR writes:

> "In the given conditions in India the established churches have found it difficult to make bold moves and the initiative has been left to small community-based groups scattered all over India (perhaps over 150 in all)."[27]

In another issue NCCR writes:

> "Often they are small groups of young people, highly critical of the authoritarian and bureaucratic churches...... They want structural revolution in the church and in society. Members of the churches they often are, but a sort of reluctant members."

And pleads that

> "The Church's responsibility to them is one of understanding pastoral care. Their great concern for the poor should be incorporated in the Church and its programmes."[28]

Similarly, the Basic Document of CISRS, referring to the estranged relationship between the action groups and the Church says,

> "While the churches do not extend themselves to these fellowships, the latter or at least a significant part of them, deliberately act outside the churches."[28a]

and that

> "without proper nurture these groups, individuals or movements are likely to lead to a parallel existence without any significant meeting point with the mainstream of church life."[29]

Therefore, "the developing context is that of two brotherhoods or fellowships without any concrete link to mould them into one body."[29a]

NCCR's anxiety about the inflow of foreign funds to these action groups and the resulting life-style is reflected in its September, 1975 issue,

> "One finds that in the third world, these groups are heavily dependent on foreign money. Is this not an affront against their own integrity? This militates against the very genius of their existence...... Further, one finds that their style of life and operation are expensive. In this matter they don't seem to be in any way different from the churches they criticise."[30]

Again in April 1980 issue, it writes:

> "These groups have two major weaknesses. The style of life and operation of many of them leave much to be desired. Secondly, their heavy dependence on foreign sources for money will eventually lead to the very negation of everything they stand for and work for."[31]

This shows that in the beginning the foreign funding agencies had established direct links with these action groups but gradually the Church stepped in an organised manner. Roman Catholic Church in India created an apex funding body CARITAS–India. Taking cue from the Catholic Church, the Protestants also established their own apex body for funding in 1976, under the name: Church Auxiliary for Social Action (CASA). Its object has been defined as "to channelise aid from Protestant churches (World Council of Churches, Church World Service, Lutheran World Service, CSI, CNI etc. to project-holders within India."[32]

A New Strategy

Given this background, CISRS with the backing of NCCI concerned itself with the following tasks:

1. To identify target groups and areas for the operation and implementation of Liberation Theology in India and to evolve a common strategy and action plan.
2. To coordinate and fuse these scattered action groups into that common strategy and action plan.
3. To bring them within the orbit of church organisational process because in the CISRS view, this "relationship is vital for both, *more* for the churches than, perhaps, for the groups."[33]
4. To divert churches' energies from "development and relief activities" because "these activities are a hindrance to the full participation of the churches in the messianic mission in which they are called as well as they *alienate* them from the people'[34] and to involve the church establishments with all their influence and resources in the implementation of liberation theology, fur "in this way lies its own freedom from alienation from the people."[35]
5. To break the isolation of Church in Indian society and create acceptability for its new strategy by building bridges of contact and dialogue with non-Christian intellectuals, social workers and political activists. The CISRS has realized that in the prevailing atmosphere of secularism and socialism in India, operation of Liberation Theology on socio-economic plane would serve Church interests better than working on the same old lines making a direct religious appeal as it had become suspect in people's eyes.

Preparation of Ground

In pursuance of the open call given by the WCC in its Uppsala Assembly (1968) and Nairobi Assembly (1975) and EACC (CCA) in its Bangkok Assembly (1973) for Christian Action in Asian Struggles, the CISRS had started working seriously in this direction since 1974. Jointly with William Carey Study and Research Centre (WCSRC), Calcutta and with the cooperation of PCR/WCC it organised a national seminar on caste and class in Calcutta. It was attended by about thirty sociologists, economists, political scientists and theologians, none of whom belonged to scheduled castes or tribes. There it was suggested that two separate consultations of scheduled castes and scheduled tribes leaders be organised to discuss the problems relating to their struggle for justice. Of course the PCR offered to support such programmes.[36]

From 24th to 29th October, 1974 the CISRS organised another conference on "Emerging Styles of Struggle for Social Justice in India" in which about forty youngmen directly engaged in some or the other social and political movement and representing a variety, from reformist movement in Chaibasa to a radical movement like Dalit Panther, were brought together. In April, 1975, a consultation of social scientists was organised at Bangalore by the CISRS in which it was proposed to develop an informal fellowship of Christian social scientists from all over the country.[37]

After having prepared this ground, in 1975 the CISRS together with WCSRC launched a Joint Programme of Social Action and Reflection with an apex committee having Dr. M.M. Thomas as its Chairman and Mr. M.J. Joseph as its Secretary, and under it initiated a programme of coordinating and supporting a number of action groups in different parts of the country.[38] The same year the Biennial Council meeting of CISRS suggested national consultations of women drawn from the Church Women's Fellowships and other groups.[39]

Next major task was how to involve church establishments in this process. Towards this end, the CISRS along with others took initiative to form the Fellowship for Justice Concerns including social action-groups, organisations, clergy fellowships and individuals.[40]

In order to establish regular contacts with the churches and their devotees as well as with various action groups the CISRS appointed many full-time regional secretaries in different parts of the country.

After having created this organisational infrastructure, the CISRS came out with a comprehensive and integrated action plan in the shape of Basic Document of December 1977.

Target Groups

As far as the identification of target groups is concerned, the NCCR, following the guidelines laid down by the foreign funding and ecumenical agencies, had already identified the target groups and areas as "*adivasis*, harijans, scheduled castes, landless peasants, urban workers, fishermen, share croppers, rickshaw pullers, etc."[41] Naturally the Basic Document of the CISRS also focuses its attention on the same target groups:

1. Tribals
2. Scheduled Castes under Caste-Class Study Programme
3. Unorganised labour and poor in rural and urban areas
4. Women

The tribals and scheduled castes were to be treated as racial and ethnic minority problems and therefore to be covered under PCR of WCC, while the other two sections were to be organised for struggle against social injustice and deprivation of human rights i.e. as justice concerns. In fact, tribal population, scheduled castes and poorer section of the society had always been the target groups for the church. Formerly it used to approach them through relief services expecting immediate results in the form of conversion, but now it decided to approach them in the name of struggle for human rights without talking of immediate returns in terms of conversion to Christianity, which means in Paulo Freire's language, that the Church has decided to play a 'prophetic role' postponing its priorities to a remote future.[42]

Action-Strategy

The action-strategy suggested by the Basic Document has been summarised in the Director's Report for Jan.-Aug. 1978 in these words:

a. The policy of decentralisation through regional implementation of the CISRS programmes,

b. involvement in the struggle of the weaker sections and the building up of solidarity and network among groups in action,

c. action related studies on different aspects of the struggle for social justice and transformation of society,

d. documentation of and reflections, both theological and social, on the experiences of the people, and

e. theological reflections on the experiences of people in suffering and struggle.[43]

1. *Decentralisation*: As to the long-term perspectives behind the decentralisation approach, the Director's Report (April 29, 1979) has this to say:

   "a long term perspective as well as coordination are necessary for

   (a) strengthening of what is already happening
   (b) promoting leadership in these regions within the Christian community and outside
   (c) maintaining regular contacts with the academic and intellectual groups and movements in the regions and (d) collaborating, sharing more meaningfully with organisations, groups and individuals, with similar objectives and concerns."[44]

2. Area Studies, Research and Documentation: Following the lead of WCC and CCA (formerly EACC), CISRS also gives top priority to area studies, research and documentation in its scheme of things. The Basic

Document says:

> "Studies for social action groups and political activists as well as for political education of the people in general should be a major responsibility of the CISRS."[45]

and "the deeper consideration which ought to motivate social studies are "first, to understand the nature of *social reality* and secondly, to contribute towards *changes* in social order. But the comprehension of social reality does not come from generalisation and abstraction alone. It is the result of a *creative tension* between generalisation and the specific experience and situations. *Action-reflection* is or should be one way of comprehension through involvement in local situation." And therefore "the CISRS must seriously consider the possibility of initiating such studies as on the proximate goals of socialism, the domestic and international forces of exploitation, the nature of power structure and the current social, political and economic problems."[46]

The Document further says that "These studies must involve a deliberate attempt to decentralise the programmes and to concentrate them in areas where groups of persons who share our perspectives have already been formed."[47]

With this object in mind, the CISRS has been sponsoring micro-level area studies into the realities and problems of its target groups. To give a few examples, it claims to have already conducted area studies about scheduled castes in Vidarbha, Karnataka, Gujarat etc., about tribal identity in different parts of the country, about bonded labour problems in Karnataka and on the status of rural women etc. Along with area studies, it gives top priority to the programme of documentation.

3. *Dialogue and Consultation*: In order to build bridges with non-Christian intellectuals and activists the CISRS organises dialogues and consultations with them on specific topics and issues.

4. Linking local struggles with national and international movements and agencies such as PCR/WCC, CCA/URM etc. The Basic Document says, "Solidarity with struggling groups, organisations and individuals not only within India but also in other parts of the world, especially is a programme to which the CISRS will have to pay increasing attention."[48] It further says, "Another major concern is the relation between the micro-level activities with the macro-level of regional, national and international forces and movements."[49]

Strategy Unfolds Itself

Soon after the adoption of the Basic Document in December 1977 a Delhi Forum of Christian Concern for People's Struggles was formed in January 1978 in order to bring the scattered Christian action groups within a common fold. In March 1978 the Delhi Forum organised the First National Convention of various Christian action groups at Delhi. This March convention formed the Coordination for Socialist Studies with groups in Delhi, Calcutta, Madras, Bombay and other cities. The first all-India Convention of this Coordination was held at Bangalore in October 1978 with George Mathew as the National Convenor and Kishan Patnaik, a staunch Lohiaite, as one of the many coordinators.[50]

As a result of these concerted and planned efforts by the CISRS and NCCI in Protestant circles and CBCI in Roman Catholic circles, within a few years a close liaison between the Church and the scattered Christian action groups seems to have been established on national as well as international level.

A newly created forum under the name of Urban Rural Mission (URM) provides the necessary cover and linkage between the local action groups on one hand and the WCC and CCA on the other. In a National Report on India, presented to the eleventh committee meeting of CCA-URM at Hong Kong (Feb. 3-6, 1980), we get authentic information about the number as well as foreign links of these action groups:

> "There are 20-25 groups working all over India related to URM. There are also new groups emerging in several parts of the country. The first concern of the National URM Conference was the National Solidarity of these groups working throughout the country.[51]

Obviously referring to CISRS activities, this Report says:

> "There is a programme called the Joint Programme for Social Action. This relates to about 20 groups. Another programme is more related to the ethnic minorities and also caste-class oppression. We are related to similar programme of 75-100 action groups directly."[52]

The linkage is not confined to the provision of financial aid or programmaticguidelinesonlyratheritextendsuptothetransfers,promotions or deputation of personnel also. For example, we find in a CCA Report that an Indian Christian activist, George Ninan, who after completing his studies in Philips University, Enid, Oklahoma in 1972 had organised a local action group called Bombay Urban Industrial League for Development popularly known as BUILD, to work in the slums of Bombay and had served as its first General Secretary, was appointed a full-time secretary of CCA-URM in March 1979 with its headquarters at Hong Kong, because its earlier secretary Oh Jae Sliik had "changed his desk to International Affairs."[53]

Similarly, this Report mentions that T.K. Thomas, editor at the Christian Literature Society of India (Madras) joined as a permanent staff member of the CCA at short notice and afterwards worked for the WCC in Geneva.[54]

Imported Action Programme

All these action groups carry out programmes which are formulated outside India by the CCA-URM or WCC-PCR. In the Minutes of Rural Local Contacts meeting of CCA-URM which was held in Changmai (Thailand) on May 26-31, 1979 we find a detailed outline of the programmes and strategy to be followed by these action groups. In part III of these minutes, dealing with planning and policy we find the following given under the title *INDIA–Programme of priorities*,[55]

(a) Primary task: – Organization of rural poor for power

Rural Poor:
- Landless agro-labourers
- Marginal and small farmers
- Share croppers
- Fishermen
- Artisans & Workers in organized cottage & village industries
- Plantation workers
- Dalits
- Tribal groups
- Women

(b) Issues in the contexts of:

(i) Minimum wage
(ii) Implementation of land reforms
(iii) Employment
(iv) Participation in decision-making process
(v) Tribal identity and self-hood
(vi) Human dignity
(vii) Equal participation of women/rights of women
(viii) Human rights

(c) Programmes:

(i) Identification of groups involved in organisation of rural poor
(ii) Forging links between these groups
(iii) Forging links between groups of rural poor to promote solidarity in issues affecting each other
(iv) Sharing of material
(v) Collection of relevant information
(vi) Information – secondary data – encouraging groups to share experiences and documenting these

(vii) Dissemination to groups in local or regular languages
(viii) Research to complete data which can be used by peasant organisations
(ix) Research – history of peasant movements in different areas
(x) Training - community organizers and primary level change agents
(xi) Contents - structural analysis, society envisaged and strategies for organization
(xii) Organization – North and South basis and at local level

Time schedule–3 years, 1979-81.[56]

In continuation of the same minutes we find an outline of a training programme for rural organizers and secondary level change-agents and another training programme for Research and Documentation. Detailed break-up of the budget allocation for these training programmes is also given there.[56]

Foreign Funds

In fact, it is an open secret that practically all the Christian organisations and programmes in Asia and Africa depend to a *la*rge extent for their sustenance upon the funds flowing from Europe and America.

Roman Catholic Church with its well-knit international organisation under the leadership of the Pope never had any difficulty in regulating the flow of foreign money into India and this fact has always been a source of envy to the Protestant leadership. Commenting on the first All India Catholic Seminar held at Bangalore in March, 1969 the NCCR writes,

> "While there was a lot of talk about self-support and indigenous leadership, one found it impossible to get any idea of the finances of the Church, particularly as to the money received from abroad. The finances of the Roman Catholic Church seem to be as closely guarded as confessional secrets."[57]

But now Protestant churches after having created their own ecumenical apex bodies like WCC, CCA and NCCI etc., have also established a regular pipeline for the inflow of foreign money from WCC to NCCI level via CCA or directly. As far the finances of NCCI are concerned former General Secretary of NCCI, late John Sadiq, wrote:

> "The total contributions raised in India do not amount to more than a fraction of the annual budget, which is met largely from contributions sent from abroad. The major portion of support from overseas comes from the United States and Great Britain gives an amount equal to half of the American contribution. Some

of the continental missionary societies are also beginning to send small contributions, and Australia and New Zealand are showing interest in helping the Council."[58]

About the foreign funds flowing to CISRS, the Director's Report for the years 1977-79 mentions the names of many foreign agencies such as Netherlands Missionary Council. The Jaffna Fund, Committee for Society Related Services of the Evangelical Church in Germany NAGKED (W. Germany), I.C.C.O. (Netherlands), the Methodist Church Overseas Division (London) etc. which have been liberally contributing to the various programmes and projects launched by CISRS like Joint Women's Programme, Study of Religion and Caste-Class Programme etc.

Precipitating Caste Conflict

At this point, it may be worthwhile to examine the nature and dimensions of the various programmes sponsored by the CISRS with foreign support and guidance. The study of CISRS documents shows that caste-class study programme covering the scheduled castes population of India has been accorded the highest place in its scheme of things. How this programme is being utilised to create a situation of anarchy and destabilisation within the country as well as to malign India in the eyes of the world needs a detailed in-depth study, which is not possible here. But its essential features may be summarised as follows:

(a) To conduct area studies about the scheduled caste population for identifying their local grievances against other caste groups.

(b) Documentation and dissemination of this information to Christian Action Groups.

(c) To create new leadership and organisations among scheduled castes in different regions.

(d) Forging alliances between scheduled caste leaders, Muslims and Christians.

(e) To incite these puppet scheduled caste leaders and organisations for demanding the scrapping of the reservation policy and its originator Poona Pact and for the creation of autonomous Dalitsthan on the lines of Pakistan.

(f) To engineer local caste conflicts and to widely publicise caste atrocities on Harijans.

(g) To build pressure upon the Government for arming the Harijans in the name of their self-defence and to prepare ground for an armed civil war for breaking the center.

(h) Internationalisation of the issue.

Tribal Policy

The tribal issue attracted CISRS attention long back. Its Director M.M. Thomas along with R.W. Taylor published in 1965 a book titled *Tribal Awakening*. Later on Ranjit Chowdhry was deputed to collect data on the separate state movements in the tribal areas of the north and analyse them for a proper understanding of the problems, sufferings and aspirations of the people of these areas.

Among tribal population the Church was already well entrenched. In North East India three Christian dominated states–Nagaland, Meghalaya and Mizoram–had already come into existence and with this dominant position the Church has been dreaming to carve out a compact territorial slice for itself in North-East India. But the existence of non-Christian majority states of Manipur, Tripura and *Arunachal* are proving to be major hurdles in the fulfillment of this dream. Therefore, the new church strategy in North-East India revolves round the following points:

1. To arouse a separate identity consciousness among tribals of Manipur and Tripura.
2. To instigate 'son of the soil' sentiment in them and foment disaffection between local population and other linguistic groups so as to divert it against administrative, economic and political integration of these areas with the rest of the country.
3. To build pressure in the name of secularism and democracy for the abolition of permit system for entry in Arunachal Pradesh.
4. To encourage violence for creating a situation of anarchy.

Any investigative in-depth study will prove that this church strategy is playing a key role behind all the agitations, riots and turmoils going on in our eastern region. In the rest of the tribal areas also the Church has been trying to encourage separate statehood demands such as Jharkhand in Bihar, Kolhan in Orissa, Chattisgarh in Madhya Pradesh and Udayachal in Assam.

Political Role

It is obvious from the study of the above documents that because of circumstantial constraints the Church has now decided upon a strategy of working under the cover of socio-economic issues instead of its earlier religious cover. By following this strategy, it may make use of the prevailing atmosphere of secularism and socialism in this country to break its isolation and get cooperation of non-Christian activists and intellectuals, who are genuinely interested in the socio-economic transformation of the country and therefore out of their infatuation with secularism may join hands with any agency professing similar objectives, without going deeper into its real motivation and linkages.

A deeper study of the church literature and reports would prove that Church has now decided to play a political role. The National Report on India presented to CCA-URM conference held in Feb. 3-6,1980 at Hong Kong says,

> "As you know, Mrs. Indira Gandhi has come back to power with a massive mandate... We can expect a lot of resistance to any kind of organising work that, for instance, URM groups in India and others are engaged in. Apart from political parties, the need for organising people has become more urgent now than before for various reasons...We must try to relate to the non-Christian secular leadership that are at work. We must come to a closer understanding with them."[59]

It is in pursuance of this strategy that the front organisations like CISRS have been trying to build bridges of contact with Gandhian institutions such as Gandhi Peace Foundation, Delhi, and Institute of Gandhian Studies, Varanasi etc. on one hand and through, 'Coordination of Socialist Studies' with socialists and Marxists on the other.

That the Church has a political action in mind is obvious from the statement on the deliberations of a meeting of 45 activists which was held in Delhi in July 1981 'to discuss the political process in the country and the role of Action Groups.' This statement says,

> "Many such groups are functioning all over India who represents a significant force. Collective strength of all these is a potential for political action."[60]

It emphasised,

> "The only hope lies in masses getting organized and capturing power under the leadership of an existing left political party or by giving birth to a new political party".[61]

After discussing various options before Action Groups in political field, the meeting came to the following conclusion:

> "The best option for Action Groups in the existing situation of growing crisis is to offer critical collaboration to one or the other left political parties".[62]

Another report says that 95 Catholic scholars and grass-root workers assembled at the National Biblical Catechetical and Liturgical Centre (NBCLC), Bangalore from October 19 to 24, 1981 to discuss the theme "The Indian Church in the Struggle for a New Society". The seminar took place after a laborious preparation for the past nine months during which more than 40 research papers were written. According to this report:

> "Provoked by grass root level workers who are actively involved in the struggles of women workers in industry and rural areas the group reflected areas of involvement and collaboration with non-Christians and even Marxists who are committed to sharing in a new society".[63]

In order to play this political role more effectively in collaboration with the non-Christian leftist intellectuals and activists, these action groups have decided to adopt Marxian jargon as a cover for their activities and programmes. The statement on Delhi meeting of July 1981 clearly says,

> "Some of them (Action Groups) *motivated by their religious convictions* are making use of Marxism as a tool of analysis to understand the reality and plan their strategy".[64]

An example of a crude application of Marxist jargon to naked communal situation may be found in a statement, originally published in the Catholic paper *The Examiner* (Bombay) and reproduced in NCCR (Nagpur), which insists, perhaps as an afterthought, that the Mandaikkadu riots in Kanya Kumari district, in which Christian fishermen on March 1, 1982 obstructed the Hindu harijan fishermen and fisherwomen from taking holy bath in the sea near Bhagavathi Amman temple, should be projected not as a communal riot but as a class conflict between the poor fishermen who, by accident, happen to be Christian and the exploiters who happen to be the Hindu followers of the Vivekanand Kendra, Kanya Kumari.[65]

Similarly, an item published in the fortnightly *Christian Monitor* (New Delhi) December 16, 1980 tries to project the large-scale conversion to Christianity in Kanya Kumari district in the past as a part of the struggle of the oppressed people–mainly fishermen against Malayali feudalism and tries to paint the national resolve to establish the Swami Vivekanand Rock Memorial Temple at Kanya Kumari as a revival of Malayali feudalism represented by Malayali landlords and Nadar traders.

To conclude main features of the new church strategy may be summed up as follows:

(a) To break Hindu society from within by exploiting all its weak spots and creating local conflicts.

(b) To involve non-Christian intellectuals in its activities by providing them facilities for research, documentation, publications, seminars and conferences etc.

(c) To seek cooperation of the non-Christian political activists and social workers under the cover of non-religious slogans such as uplift of the poor, liberation of the oppressed and creation of a radical social structure.

(d) To focus their struggle against the forces of nationalism and national integration by forging alliance of Christians, Muslims etc.

(e) To weaken the Centre by fermenting and supporting separatist movements in different parts of the country.

(f) To carve out a Christian dominated territorial chunk in North-East India under the cover of separate tribal identity.

References

1. *Religion and Society* (Quarterly), Bangalore. Vol. XXI, No. 3. 1978; in *Ecumenism in India.* (Ed. M. Zachariah), (I.S.P.C.K., Delhi, 1980), p. 95.

2. Nirad C. Chaudhry: The Catholic Community in India, p. iv-vi; Ecumenism in India, op. cit. p. 96.

3. T. V. Phillip: Church Unity Discussion in India-Some suggestions for Consideration; in Ecumenism in India, op. cit. p. 97.

4. D. B. Forrester: 'Indian Christian Attitudes to Caste in the Twentieth Century' *Indian Church History Review* (Quarterly), Vol, IX, No. 1 (Mysore, June 1975), p. 3.

5. M. Zachariah, *Illustrated Weekly* of *India.* (Bombay) December 23, 1982.

6. George Soraes Prabhu S.J.: Jesus Christ and the Religions and Ideologies of India Today; in Ecumenism in India, op. cit. p. 3.

6a. Neogy Committee Report (Abridged Edition), Delhi, p. 5.

7. *Cf.* Reference 5.

8. National Christian Council Review (NCCR), September, 1971 in Christian Presence in India. (Ed. M, Zachariah), (C. L. S., Madras, 1981) p. 36.

9. NCCR, August 1969; in Christian Presence in India; op. cit. p. 17.

10. D. B. Forrester, *op, cit.* p. 10.

11. Christian Presence in India, op. cit. p. 36.

12. *Ibid.* p. 37.

13. *Ibid.* p. 41.

14. Ecumenism in India, op. cit. p. 9.

15. Christian Presence in India, op. cit. p. 57.

16. John Sadiq: *Adventure in Christian Fellowship.* (I.S.P.C.K., Delhi, 1966), p. 27-28.

17. CISRS Director's Report (1977-79), p. 45.

18. Christian Presence in India, op. cit. p. 16.

19. CISRS Director's Report (1977-79), p. 65.

20. Christian Presence in India, op. cit. p. 13.

21. *Ibid* p. 21.

22. *Ibid.* P. 32-33.
23. *Ibid.* p. 42.
23a. *Ibid.* p. 44.
24. *Ibid.* p. 82-83.
25. CISRS Director's Reports (1977-79), p. 46.
26. Directory of Voluntary Action, (AVARD, Delhi, 1978), pp. 106-107.
27. Christian Presence in India op. cit. p. 83.
28. *Ibid.* p. 75.
28a. *Ibid.* p. 76.
29. CISRS Director's Report (1977-79), p. 47.
29a. *Ibid.* p. 48.
30. Christian Presence in India, op. cit. p. 75-76.
31. *Ibid.* p. 83.
32. Directory of Voluntary Action, *op. cit.* p. 100.
33. CISRS Director's Report (1977-79), p. 52.
34. *Ibid.* p. 55.
35. *Ibid.* p. 56.
36. CISRS Director's Report (1977-79), p. 52.
37. *Ibid.* pp. 128-129.
38. CISRS Director's Report (1977-79), p. 52.
39. *Ibid.* p. 57.
40. *Ibid.* p. 52.
41. Christian Presence in India, op. cit. p. 76.
42. G. Mathew (Ed.), *A Day with Paulo Freire,* (I.S.P.C.K., Delhi, 1980), pp. 89-90.
43. CISRS Director's Report (1977-79), p. 32.
44. *Ibid.* p. 29.
45. *Ibid.* p. 67.
46. *Ibid.* p. 57.
47. *Ibid.* p. 68.
48. *Ibid*, p. 53.
49. *Ibid* p. 70.
50. *Ibid.* p. 44.
51. CCA-URM: Eleventh Committee Meeting, (Hong Kong, February 3-6-1980), *Minutes: National Reports: Biblical Reflections,* p. 48.

52. *Ibid.* p. 51.
53. *From Penang to Bangalore,* (CCA, Singapore, 1981), p. 8.
54. *Ibid.* p. 7.
55. CCA-URM: Eleventh Committee Meeting, *op. cit.* pp. 139-140.
56. *Ibid.* pp. 144-146.
57. Christian Presence in India, op. cit. p. 19-20.
58. John Sadiq, op. cit. p. 44.
59. CCA-URM: Eleventh Committee Meeting, *op cit.* p. 48.
60. *'Political Process and Action Groups in India.'* in *N. C. C. R.* (N.C.C.I. Mysore, November, 1981), p. 602.
61. *Ibid.* p. 606.
62. *Ibid.* p. 607.
63. *NCCR,* December 1981, pp. 692-693.
64. *NCCR,* November 1981, p. 605.
65. *NCCR,* June-July, 1982, p. 384.

19

Hinduism vis-a-vis Christianity and Islam

Ram Swarup

A Delhi based Intellectual and dedicated spiritual Sadhak

Hinduism is different not only from West's materialism in its two varieties, *liberal* and *communist*, but it also differs in some important ways from some other religions and religious value-systems, particularly those of Semitic origin. Here we are referring to Christianity and Islam.

As a way of life which emphasizes spiritual values, Hinduism has several points of contact with cultures that take into account this dimension. In fact, there is quite a strong movement amongst men of goodwill all over the world which says that all religions hold the same truth and all scriptures preach the same thing. They cull passages from different scriptures and prove their point. This is a noble and well-intentioned thought and effort. In a world suffering from so much unnecessary conflict, the truth of unity and harmony has to be emphasized. If a man is the same in his more common sensibilities, he must also be the same in his spiritual ones. If he laughs when he is tickled and pained when he is pricked, he must also be filled with a sense of awe, wonder and holiness in the presence of the profundities and mysteries of life.

But this view-point is not equally shared by all. While this truth comes naturally to a Hindu or Buddhist, it is denied both in theory as well as in practice by Christianity and Islam. They believe that not only are they different, but they are also superior. From the start, they believed that the god they worshipped was superior to the gods of their neighbours and their religion was invested with truth while others wallowed in falsities. As a result, they have developed along missionary and crusading lines. Their God-given task has been to teach the principles of a true religion to a benighted world of idolators, pagans, infidels and devil-worshippers. This view-point may have lost its appeal in certain sections influenced by new trends in thought towards more universalism, but it is still quite popular with the organized churches. Look at the way Islam and Christianity are working in Asian and African countries and draw your conclusions. The more naked methods of good old days may no longer be suitable and may require a different approach, but the old mind is still very much there and we mustn't forget this fact.

There is also another point of a more philosophical import. Even if we admit a fundamental unity between different religions, the differences too cannot be denied and they have to be accounted for. For example, if you study carefully different scriptures like the *Upanishads* and the *Gita* on the one hand and the *Bible* and the *Koran* on the other you find great differences of approach, ethos and temperament. Many times, you feel that these differences are more than differences of idioms and treatment. In fact, you feel that the very worlds of the two scriptures are different. Therefore, to treat these differences and to try to understand them is not without its intellectual and spiritual interest. In fact, to overlook them or slur over them would be an act of intellectual shoddiness.

Read from this angle, we find that the two scriptures are very different in their atmosphere. The scriptures of Semitic inspiration are hortative, admonitory; they urge, they reprove, they enjoin, they warn, they even enforce. There is a note of feverishness in them. But the atmosphere of the Hindu scriptures is unhurried, relaxed and expositional. The first variety seems to goad you; the second one to lead you step by step. The first one is passionate, zealous, the second one calm and detached. The first one plays on your hopes and fears; it threatens you with a hell and promises you a paradise; while the second one aims at opening up your understanding.

There are other differences along the same line. The Hindu approach is speculative, pluralistic, introvert; the Christian and the Islamic approach is extrovert, monistic, dramatic and spectacular. There is Adam and Eve, the forbidden fruit, the devil and the original sin. Then the *only* God sends his *only* son and he pays the ransom for man's original transgression with his blood. Then there is a final day of judgement and a throne surrounded by angels. On this day, some are saved but many more are damned.

There are other differences as well. Christianity and Islam are religions of faith; Hinduism and its powerful offshoot, Buddhism, are religions of *Prajna,* wisdom. The former deal with intensities of feelings, the latter aim at awakening the mind. The former have been religions of piety with a strong tendency to deny reason. The latter are religions of 'understanding', giving due place to reason though it will have to be purified and separated from the dross of desire before it becomes an instrument of a higher life.

Piety lacking in purity degenerates into hypocrisy and faith into narrowness and intolerance, but in their purer states they are adornments of the soul. A simple faith–which is different from a strong, induced belief–has its place and its appeal. It provides certainty in the midst of uncertainty, a cozy niche in a strange, wide world. Therefore, Christianity and Islam have a natural appeal to a certain type.

But those who seek wider pastures of the spirit will have to take recourse to *Buddhi* or reason. True reason, however, will have to have a strong foundation in faith, *Shraddha,* and, passing through *Virya, Smriti* and *Samadhi* must acquire its true status in *prajna.* On the contrary, reason lacking this foundation ends merely in doubts and denials and makes one footloose, spiritually speaking.

In Hinduism, faith is rendered by the world *shraddha,* that which lies hidden in the recesses of the heart; so, faith means faith in the hidden truths of the soul, faith in the unrealized possibilities of the mind. In Christianity and Islam, faith means belief in the established dogmas of the Church, or belief in the external authority of a particular book, or a prophet. Similarly, the word 'reason', too, has different connotations here. In Islam, reason was overpowered by faith from the very start; in Christianity, when eventually it earned some kind of uneasy place, it had to become the handmaid of faith. It was *apologetics.* It was used for proving the truths of the dogmas and for proving the superiority of the Christian religion. In this way, reason was denatured and prostituted. In the West, people had to wage a grim battle against Christianity in order to liberate reason from its shackles. The Islamic world has yet to learn to evaluate its religious dogmas, its history, its Book, its Prophet, his personality and his revelation in the light of reason, both secular as well as spiritual. In short, it has yet to undertake self-introspection.

In Hinduism, reason was not seen in this light. Reason has its own *svadharma,* its own nature, which should be allowed its free play. It should be allowed to question, to investigate, to doubt, to dare, to speculate. Of course, it should also be purified so that it is not at the disposal of one's lower mind, passions, prejudices and preferences and so that, in its higher status, it becomes the instrument of direct seeing, of reflecting reality as it is.

In this respect, Hinduism represents the spirit of the new age in which reason has acquired a new importance and when things will not be taken for granted, and yet when there is also a search for something more deep and meaningful. Hinduism can eminently fulfill the West's religious urge without doing violence to its hard-won possession–rationality. Hinduism can raise both faith as well as reason.

II

There are other very important differences. Christianity and Islam are built round historical personalities; Hinduism round the truths of man's own higher nature. So if there was no Jesus or no Mohammad, there would have been no Christianity and no Islam. But according to the Hindu approach, man's religion does not depend on any such exigency. There is a *dharma* for all times, *Sanatan dharma,* because it lies there always in the soul. It may undergo an eclipse for a time is a result of veiling influences of some other propensities, but it is all the time there, ready to manifest itself whenever the conditions are propitious. Therefore, true religion can neither be borrowed nor lent; one carries one's religions within one self wherever one goes.

According to Semitic religions, God chooses some favourite individual his Son or his Prophet, for his self-revelation and others must accept this revelation second-hand. According to Hinduism, there is no such arbitrariness; God-consciousness is an inherent quality of the soul and God makes himself known to any sincere seeker.

On this point, Christianity even goes further than Islam. It is not satisfied with only an intermediary like Islam; it must have in him also a mediator, a saviour. But whether a messenger or a saviour, his role is central and Christianity and Islam cannot be conceived without this character. In a certain sense, these religions do not deal with God but they deal with God-surrogates, with his only Son, or his last Prophet.

According to Christianity and Islam, God has given his truths finally and once for all through his favourite, intermediary, and these are now deposited in a book. The other revelations and books are either denied or they are considered as merely preparatory: they exist merely to confirm the truths of the new revelation. Subsequent revelations become false or redundant. If they contain anything new or different they are false; if they contain the same things, they are redundant. In either case, they have no right to exist. The Church has even gone further. It has codified and numbered these truths for the convenience of its flock. These truths are there pre-packaged, pre-cooked even pre-digested.

Hinduism deals in no such truths; at any rate, it considers them meaningless. Its truths are truths of man's own deeper being. He has to grow into them. The more he understands himself, the more he understands these truths. According to Hinduism, these truths connote by easily put in verbal formulae, cannot be made into numbered articles of faith. They cannot be easily handed down. One cannot commit them to memory, repeat them, confess them and be considered a good catholic or a good Anglican. The truths Hinduism cares for are received in a different way, through some kind of self-preparation. One has to get ready for them. One has to be *reborn* in order to receive them.

Hinduism also does not teach a God who reveals himself only to a chosen individual, letting others receive their truths from this exclusive channel. It speaks of truths which are revealed wherever there is seeking, purity of aspirations and motives, necessary preparation. It believes that all nations share God's grace. It does not believe that there are pagans and infidels waiting to be converted to a particular system of beliefs and ideas or a race of the damned waiting to be saved. Hinduism respects differences and seeks God's working in different races and peoples.

One can see for oneself that in this kind of approach, there is no place for 'conversion'. True religion can neither be borrowed nor lent. A man carries his religion within himself wherever he goes and he has to be his own lamp. The conversion one experiences at this level is inner and it is very different from the conversions that the countries have known under the aegis of Christianity and Islam. These conversions are political and military acts, acts of aggressive hard sale.

For example, in its own tribals, Hinduism saw God working. It lived happily with them for thousands of years without trying to convert them. If it lent them anything, it also borrowed from them in silent communication. But all this changed with the advent of Christianity. It is working overtime in giving them a sense of sin, a ready-made Saviour and all its other ideological trappings. The missionaries make use of the nation's poverty and their own power as white-men. They offer the tribals temptations. They reward them with cheap terylene pants if they are converted, with motor-bicycles if they help their brothers to be converted, They lend money–say five or ten dollars–on interest, which they know could not be paid back; but the payment of which could be waived off if the debtor accepted Christianity. They have big churches even in places where there are no Christians. On other levels, they run schools and dispensaries and engage in social work. But we must know that social work has now become big business and ominous politics. For itself the West has rejected Christianity, but it is still keeping it for export. The Western friends must realize what they are doing.

What is happening in India is also happening elsewhere. For example, the African people are under the double attack of Christianity and Islam. The attack is economic as well as political. But the cultural attack of monolatory is even more deadly than the political or economic attack. It cuts off the people completely from their roots.

III

There are other differences of appeal and organization also. From the beginning, Christianity and Islam have talked of 'we' and they'. They divide mankind into peoples of faith on one hand, and benighted infidels on the other, people who are saved and people who are damned. They are religions of *umma* or *millat.* Their rejection and hatred of the 'other' is written in capital letters in their doctrines and in the pages of their history. We all know how much part the sword played in the spread of Islam, but that part was equally prominent in the spread of Christianity. There was a time when many good Christians did not regard non-Christians as men at all. That sense is still retained in one of the meanings of a Christian as given in *The World Book Dictionary.* He is defined as "human; not animal". This idea is made still clearer in *Webster's Third New International Dictionary:* a Christian is a "human being, as distinguished from a lower animal." This only indicates their attitude, the way they have thought of themselves and of others. Similarly, Islamic thought divided the world into three sections: 1) the people of faith, which means themselves; 2) people of the Book, which means religions of the Semitic origin; and 3) the rest. The second people were called '*zimmis*', the 'protected ones'. They could still co-exist under certain disabilities as second grade citizens but the option for the third section was 'either Islam or death'. It is another matter that this policy could not always be implemented.

The development is not accidental. A single source of inspiration, a single Sonship or a single Prophethood or a single Book must lead to the concept of an exclusive brotherhood. A privileged revelation must lead to the concept of a chosen people or a chosen Church. The only trouble is that there are too many of them claiming this privileged revelation for themselves or for their teachers. So they have to be denounced as false messiahs, and false prophets. Jesus warned against "many false prophets (that) shall rise". False prophets are not rare and a warning against them is quite in order. But from this, his disciples drew the conclusion that all prophets other than their own master were false. Muhammad, practical in all matters, got his rival claimants eliminated. He got even those murdered who questioned his prophetic claims. Kab son of Ashraf, Asma daughter of Marwan, Abu Afaq, a centenarian, were poets who put their doubts in verse. They were all done to death by practised assassins.

Hinduism, on the other hand, always spoke of 'man'. It did not divide mankind into 'we' and 'they'. Even the word 'Hindu', people of the river 'Sindhu', was given to it by others. It claims no privileged revelation. 'Thou art That', (*Tattvam-asi*) is a universal truth and is open to all who have the necessary seeking and who put in the necessary effort and *tapas.*

This emphasis on privileged revelation leading to the concept of a privileged brotherhood or a chosen church has affected Christianity and Islam in more than one way. It made their morals tribal and their social organization power-oriented. Their organization is eminently suited for outward, political expansion–though the religious dimension is not altogether lacking and it still does bring spiritual solace to their many followers. Their *kalma* and dogmas have been more of battle-cries than confessions of faith. "Allah-o-Akbar" has been heard as often in the battle-field as in the mosques. They ceased being purely spiritual cultures like Hinduism; they became power-structures. These religions grew with political power and their religious functionaries were more than priests. They were officials of the state; or, even when they retained their own separate identity and discipline, they were still part of the same power-establishment.

Christianity and Islam also became theocracies, as we have already observed. The common men were governed by *Mullahs* and priests–church functionaries administering laws claiming a divine origin, taking care of the morals of the people, interpreting the will of God for them. In Hinduism, there is no such theocracy. There is a highly respected *Brahmin* class but their functions are purely priestly. They teach; they preside on such occasions as birth, death, wedding, But the deeper ethos of the Hindus is shaped by saints and religious mendicants and even by the householders who have the reputation, rightly or wrongly, of having 'seen' God. There are no *excathedra* pronouncements, no *fatwas,* no official credo or a list of beliefs formulated by a body of theologians. Hinduism has known no pope, no *khalifa.*

Because of the preponderant role of the clergy and religious officials and intellectual theologians, and also because of the emphasis on faith, Christianity and Islam have been authoritative and fundamentalist. On the contrary, Hinduism, because of the greater role of mysticism and reason in it, is more psycho-experimental. The truths it speaks about are capable of verification by any individual (*Chipassik*, 'come and see', as Lord Buddha says), though the conditions of verification are difficult to fulfill by many individuals. It is also true that Hinduism gives a very high place to *shabda pramana,* to the testimony of those who are in a position to testify, but the truths of Hinduism are still, in the last analysis, a matter of experience, of progressive assimilation and growth. As a result, Hinduism has been more concerned with explaining, examining, investigating, experiencing and with *sadhana*; on the contrary, Christianity in particular has been concerned with dogmatically affirming justifying, apologetically proving and establishing. Islam in its turn refuses to argue. It simply cuts off your head. Discussion, in its view, is merely a waste of breath; it has found that the logic of force is more convincing.

Compassion for all Living Beings: A Cosmic Vision

One more point deserves a special mention. Hinduism has greatly emphasized the value of compassion towards all living beings. We have already said that Hinduism thinks of 'man' and not of a privileged botherhood or church. The fact is that the Hindu vision is cosmic. It extends beyond man to all nature and elements. This vision embodies sound ecological sense as we increasingly realize it. Hinduism does not believe that man is created for domination over the fowls of the earth and fishes of the sea. To say so is nothing but man's egocentricity. Others also have their rights. True, man too has his share in the bounty of nature and he could take out of it according to his need (not greed), after he has contributed to it according to his capacity; but nothing gives him a right to exploit others, to treat them cruelly. Egoistic use of men and nature sets up a process of retribution. In treating the animal-world as soul-less, man himself loses his soul. Cruelty to animals turns into cruelty to-one's own kind. Wide- prevalent vegetarianism amongst the Hindus comes from their compassionate, non-egoistic outlook. It has been their great contribution to the world culture.

Hinduism is the oldest religion which is also still flourishing. It also represents what is truly the best in the new age of reason and universality. This it does precisely because it is not a historical religion, a. child of a particular age. It has something of the eternal, *Sanatan,* in it. It has concerned itself with man's eternal verities, with truths of the awakened soul, truths of which man himself may not be conscious in a particular state or age. It teaches you to live in the eternal while extending your time-vision at the same time. It links you with the transcendental and the eternal, with the cosmic, with humanity, with your own past and future lives. It gives you a sense of continuity, and brings you the message of immortality. It satisfies man's deepest spiritual and ethical urges. It has developed different *yogas* to facilitate growth in a more meaningful, unitive and intuitive life. It is humanist in approach, world-wide in outlook; it fully admits reason; it is both experimental and speculative in its investigation. It is pluralist, compassionate and non-violent in temper. In short, it has all that the man seeks in his deeper being and it is the product of this seeking. All deeper seekers, who turn it for guidance, should find it immensely fulfilling.

20

Conversion or Denationalisation

K.S. SUDERSHAN

Akhil Bharatiya Bauddhik Pramukh,
xRashtriya Svvayamsevak Sangh (R.S.S.)

Expressing surprise at the nation-wide reaction to mass conversion at Meenakshipuram, Sh. Shahabuddin, M. P., remarked: 'Why this hullaballo if a few Harijans got converted to Islam? After all, they are going to remain Indians even as Muslims!" Apparently the remark carries weight and assumes added importance in view of the fact that there was no such stir when, some years ago, Dr. Ambedkar along with lakhs of his followers embraced Buddhism. Rather, it was considered a welcome step if it could really contribute towards eradication of the age-old scourge of untouchability at the social level. If, as is made out, the same goal could be achieved through conversion to Islam also, why should that be objected to? Why should the leaders of all major opposition parties and even the Prime Minister herself have rushed to condemn it?

Before delving deeper into this question, it seems called for to consider an incident. A reporter happened to come across a newly converted child and his father at Meenakshipuram. When the child greeted him in his usual Tamil style saying

Vanakkam, his father rebuked the child telling him that he was no more a Hindu or a Tamil and that he should change over to *Salam-valekum.* When the reporter asked the child his name, he in all his innocence came out instantly 'Shivalingam'. Again his father slapped him saying, "Forget all that. Now you are Mahmud Ghazanavi." Can we, in any way, correlate Shivalingam with Mahmud Ghazanavi? Some other names given to the new converts included those of Afzal Khan and Mohammed Ali Jinnah.

This incident gives birth to many counter questions in relation to Shahabuddin's own question. Why should a religious conversion be followed by complete break off from Tamil language and even Tamil felicitation? Does it mean that with the change of his religion, the child should forget the very language, that he had learnt since his birth, or the stories of Tamil saints like Thiruvalluvar, Alwars and Nayanmars and other great heroes like Chola, Pandyas and Pallavas that had moulded his psyche and had given him his dreams? Does it mean that the Tamil lullabies that used to sooth him into sleep will cease to be his own with the change of his religion? How come that *Vanakkam* became alien and *Salam Valekum* became his own? What wonder, if an incident of this nature which at one stroke converted the whole traditional environment of the child into an alien one, which established his relationship with a foreign invader who had destroyed the holy 'Shivlingain' of Somnath and which makes him take pride in such ignonimous acts as the destruction of Tulja Bhawani temple or the partition of Mother India–should stir the conscience of the whole Hindu society irrespective of caste, community, language and party labels? But, if Syed Shahabuddin and his company counsels us patience in the face of such an incident, does it not put a serious question-mark on the definition of Indianism that he or his fellow travellers carry with them?

Constitutional Citizenship and Nationality

Does Shahabuddin's concept of Indianism stop at the fact of one's living within the geographical boundaries of India? Is it sufficient, according to him, to be a legal citizen of India to become an Indian? A person from any part of world may become a legal citizen of India after fulfilling certain conditions of residence and language and can enjoy all the rights and privileges accruing therefrom. But does he become an Indian national merely by this? There are innumerable Indians who have become citizens of England. But have they become 'Englishmen'? Will the English ever recognize them as the ones belonging to themselves without their becoming Englishmen? Does it not require something else for becoming an Englishman? The same question may be asked in a different way: Is there any difference between the constitutional citizenship and nationality of a country?

Let us, for example, consider some Islamic countries. Can an Indian Muslim, howsoever conversant with Arabic language, well-versed in the holy *Koran* and settled permanently in an Arab country be ever regarded a true Arab national? How is it that the Abdas (black Arabs, whose forefathers were brought as slaves from Africa) have not been accepted as equals in the main-streams of Arab-nationalities? How is it that even after becoming Muslims the Iranians were considered inferior by the Arabs? In consequence, they not only established their separate identity from Sunni Arabs by adopting Shiaism, but also gave an entirely new form to Islam by superimposing on it the Parsee beliefs and philosophy. Sufism is the ultimate culmination of that transformation. Not merely this, they retained their 'non-Islamic' names like Rustom, Sohrab, Jamshed, Behram and continued to observe the non-lslamic festivals like 'Navroz'. And they used the Parsi word 'Khuda' more often than the Arabic 'Allah'. Mustafa Kamal Pasha of Turkey had also objected to the use of the Arabic 'Allah' and ordered the use of the Turkish 'Tari' instead, got the Arabic *Koran* translated into Turkish and insisted on offering the *namaaz* also in Turkish. How did this alienation from the Arabs grow in Turkey? Is it not abundantly clear that, in spite of their concept of 'Umma-Muslima', there is something else that separates the Turks, the Afghans, the Arabs and the Iranians from one another and provides each one of them with a distinct identity? Similarly, in India too that 'something more' could be expected of a person to be an Indian. Therefore, if accepting Islam leads to abandoning that 'something', it would be construed as severing of relationship with Indianism. The question arises: what is that 'something else' and does it in any way contradict one's faith in Islam?

It is this 'something else' that forms the basic foundation of nationality and creates a feeling of oneness amongst the people of a country. Islam, Christianity and Communism have, all in their own ways, tried to bring together their followers under one banner by-passing the national affiliations. But in every case, nationality has proved to be the stronger urge and in fact these 'ideologies' themselves got divided into different streams which became more or less expressions of distinct nationalities Thus Saudi Arabia, Egypt, Turkey, Afghanistan and Indonesia adopted their own forms of Islam: Italy, France, England, Germany and Spain developed different shades of Christianity and Russia, China, Albania, Yugoslavia, Cuba and Vietnam ended up with their own forms of Communism. It is clear that the sentiment of nationality is present in all groups of peoples in a natural way and it cannot be summarily dismissed. It is, therefore, essential to understand more deeply the concept of nationality.

Concept of Nationality

Nationality has been defined by Joseph Mazzini as the 'Individuality of a People'. But, the famous Indian freedom fighter Sh. Bipin Chandra Pal maintained that the idea of 'individuality' born out of ego implies inevitable conflicts and crises. To obviate the probable danger of 'separation' arising out of it, the dogma of 'Fraternity' was added to the earlier two dogmas of 'Equality' and 'Liberty'. Bipin Chandra Pal preferred to describe nationality as the 'Personality of a People'. 'Personality' is deducted from the Latin word 'persona' meaning 'mask'. The function, of a mask is to create a difference in appearance only. Therefore 'personality' implies diversity rather than real contrast or difference. The Indian Philosophy also regards the entire diversity of the universe as illusory and transitory. The sages and seers of this land had long ago realized that God did not create everyone identical:

मुण्डे मुण्डे मतिर्भिन्नाः कुण्डे कुण्डे नवम् पयाः ।
जातो जातो नवाचाराः नवा वाणी मुखे मुखे ॥

(Every brain has its own thinking; every well its new (characteristic) water; every tribe has its own traditions and every mouth has its own speech.)

Indian ideologues also experienced that just as the success of a drama depends on the different characters getting absorbed in their roles, similarly the success of this great drama of the universe lies in all 'persons' playing their assigned roles wholly engrossed in them. But, as in a drama, it is essential for everybody to be aware at a certain level of consciousness that it is a mere drama. And so the great saints of this country invented a way of life accepting the purposiveness of different masks or personalities and preserving the identity of every one of them. However, along with this, realizing the fundamental unity behind these masks and conceiving the oneness of the whole universe, efforts were made to overcome confrontation. A complete methodology of '*samskaras*' was formulated to cast the entire Indian life accordingly. Indian nationalism is the outcome of this effort. The question that arises is: is it possible to maintain the same relationship with this methodology of *samskaras* even after conversion to alien ways of life? To answer this question, it seems necessary to understand this methodology in detail.

Nationality and Universalism

To the great thinkers who had realised that there is one spirit behind the whole universe, the proclamation of *Vasudhaiva Kutumbakam* (the world is a family) was a simple, natural consequence. But for the realisation of this, it was imperative to create a feeling of a family unity, yet preserving the diversity of the universe as well. For this, some experiment had to be made somewhere. When those thinkers exercised their mind for a suitable laboratory for the purpose, they found India, the land situated between the Himalayas and the seas most ideally suited for the experiment. In that age, with scarce means of transport, the choice of such a vast land was an ambitious plan. But they chose it for its uniqueness when compared to the rest of the world. Perhaps, nowhere in the world, such a variety of seasons and soils, animals and birds, fruits and vegetables is to be found as in this land of ours. According to botanists and zoologists, half of the varieties of flora and fauna available in the world are to be found in India. It appears as if it is a miniature world. Where there is such a diversity of soil and climate, it is natural that a large variety of food, style of living and behaviour also prevails. They thought that if in this land, unity could be achieved along with the preservation of the beauty of its diversity, than it would be an ideal worth following for the establishment of *Vasudhaiva Kutumbakam*.

The first step, in this direction, was to inculcate in every heart a feeling of 'oneness', kinship and devotion for this land which is the first condition essential for nationalism. A beginning was made by assigning a meaningful name to it. Dr. Radhakumud Mukherji writes: "It is a well-known doctrine of logic that, when a common name is applied to different things, it is because of some principle of unity which connects them to a system in spite of differences. It was hence a consciousness of unity that made the *rishis* of the old apply a single indivisible appellation to this vast stretch of territory, with parts full of endless varieties and people of many sects speaking many dialects, professing many faiths and many traits of cultures." The deeper the roots of nationalism go in a country, the healthier and stronger is the spirit of nationality. But along with depth the wider the extension of the background, the loftier and nobler is the feeling of the underlying unity.

Emotional Relationship with the Land

It is true that nationalism can survive without a territory, as the soul can exist even without a body; but, just as the soul cannot perceptibly express itself without a body, so also nationalism requires a territory for its effective expression. The secret of survival of national spirit among the Jews, though pushed out of their land for the last 1800 years, is that every Jew living in any part of the world would before going to bed remember his motherland, where Moses preached, 'Makabis' fought battles, Soloman got temples constructed and their ancestors sacrificed their lives. The daily prayer before God that 'their next year may be in Israel' materialised after 1800 years. Their unflinching love for the motherland prepared them for innumerable sacrifices and saved them four times from extinction at the hands of sworn enemies.

The other example is that of Poland, which, passing through many upheavals and frontier-squeezes between 1795 and 1914, almost became a non-entity. But, the feeling: 'We are Poles' again assumed the form of a nation re-born. Today also, even after coming under the Russian subjugation, the aspiration of Liberty for their land has exerted its utmost to throw away the yoke of slavery. Even presently, the soul of the nation is fluttering its wings frantically to be liberated from its cage. The basis of the nationality, however, in both the instances, is an unswerving emotional attachment to a particular land of their own.

Devotion to the Motherland

It is easy for even the ordinary individuals to feel the utility of a small territory for their worldly life and attach themselves emotionally and sentimentally to it. But, to develop such affection for a sub-continent like India was an almost impossible task. It yet is surprising that our thinkers of yester-years through their efforts and foresight made it possible. Love for the motherland in the form of "**three hindi words**:" had already developed during the *Vedic* period. What an affectionate devotion to the motherland has been expressed in the following verse from the 12th chapter of '*Shounak-Samhita*' in '*Atharva Veda*'!

यस्यां पूर्वे पूर्वे जनाविचक्रिरे यस्यां देवा असुरानभ्यवर्तमन।
गवामश्वानां वयश्च विष्ठा भगं वर्चः पृथ्वी नो दधातु ५॥

(Where our ancestors performed great deeds; where gods destroyed demons, O motherland, who gave birth to cows, animals, horses and birds, bless us with prosperity and power.)

Here the endless efforts made by millions of sages and saints through the ages for developing this sublime attachment to the motherland which took roots into the hearts of men are visible. How thousands of dedicated devotees for centuries have been taking the sacred water of the Ganges from Haridwar or Kashi to Rameshwaram, and the water of the sea from Rameshwaram to Gangotri and have been going from our North to the South and from the South to North for anointing the 'Shiva'; or how every three years 'Kumbh' fairs are held respectively at Prayag, Haridwar, Ujjayini and Nasik where from every nook and corner of the country saints, ascetics, devotees, teachers, disciples and followers from every sect, cult and community have been gathering in lakhs is enough of a proof for appreciating the gigantic efforts that the great thinkers of this land have been making to forge the unity and emotional integrity of the country. Dr Radha Kumud Mukherji has rightly written, "It was this supremely Indian institution in fact which served in the past in place of the modern railways and facilities for travel to promote popular movements from place to place and inter-communication between parts to producing a perception of the whole. It allowed no parochial Provincial sense to grow up which might interfere with the growth of the ideas of the geographical unity of the vast motherland, allowed no sense of physical comforts to stand in the way of the sacred duty of intimately loving one's own motherland and softened the severities of the old world travelling by dividing pilgrims' route by holy halting places at short intervals." Feeling pride at the greet efforts made for the unity and integrity of the country Gandhiji also wrote "Our foresighted forefathers established 'Setubandh' in the South, Jagannath in the East and Haridwar in the North–all this was done for pilgrims. Do you know, why? You will agree that they were not ignorant. They knew that God can be worshipped in one's house. They had learnt that their hearts, who have adopted truth, are sacred. But they saw that nature had created India as an indivisible country. So after a conscious deliberation they comprehended that India is a nation. Keeping this in mind they created sacred places throughout the country. Only we, you and many others who consider themselves civilised and feel superior to others, imagine that we are many nations."

Due to the efforts made for centuries, idioms such as 'आसेतु हिमाचल' 'कश्मीर से कन्याकुमारी', 'कच्छ से कामरूप' and 'अटक से कटक' etc. (Himalayas to the ocean', 'Kashmir to Kanyakumari', 'Kutch to Kamroop', 'Attock to Cuttack' etc.) have so impressed the sub-conscious mind of the masses that in the event of an attack on the country, people forgetting their differences of caste, creed or language come forward for the defence of the country. We all experienced this feeling of unity at the time of aggressions by China and Pakistan. Even the DMK leaders like late Sh. Annadurai who had once demanded an independent Tamil Nadu said, "An attack on the Himalayas in an attack on all of us and we will together repel it."

Indivisibility of India

Even foreigners have had a deep realization of the fundamental unity of India. Noted historian Vincent Smith writes:

> 'India undoubtedly possesses a deep fundamental unity far more profound than that produced either by geographical association or political suzerainty. That unity transcends innumerable diversities of blood, colour, language, dress, customs and sects. The most fundamental unity of India is due to the fact that various people of India have given birth to a peculiar civilization and culture entirely different from the rest of the world."

Lord Wavell, in a report to British Parliament, wrote, "God has made it (India) one, you can't divide it, into two". Labour leader Clement Atlee said, "Partition of India is impossible. It is a God-made triangle."

Here a natural question arises as to why this feeling of unity, which impressed even the foreigners, could not pervade Indian Muslims? There are two reasons for this. Firstly the Muslims are devoid of the religious and spiritual foundation on which the whole edifice of devotion to the motherland has been built, because according to Islam it tantamount to idol worship and hence '*Kufr*' and worth rejection. Secondly, they could not give any other basis for developing an unflinching faith in the motherland as Islami '*millat*' does not accept the territorial limits of a country and considers all the Muslims of the world as one community. Sh. M.R.A. Beg says:

> Since Muslims ideologically should have no country, they have in compensation an excessive sense of community. This characteristic effectively bars their assimilation in non-muslim countries and inhibits a practising Muslim being either an internationalist, nationalist or humanist. Islam makes him a trans-national communalist who feels at home only in Muslim majority countries."

Countries with Muslim majority are called '*Darul-Islam*' compared to the non-Muslim countries counted as '*Dar-ul-Harb*' (enemy country) or '*Dar-ul-Aman*' (friendly country). Looking to it, it becomes essential for an Indian Muslim to decide what he considers India. Majority of Indians worship idols and so India is '*Dar-ul-Harb*'. This is not something unnatural, if an ordinary Muslim thinks that way, and this country cannot become an object of devotion till it is converted into '*Dar-ul-Islam*'. If they accept it as '*Dar-ul-Aman*', then the question arises if ever India goes to war with a '*Dar-ul-Islam*' country like Pakistan, which side will a Muslim be to loyal to? Nationalism demands that they should be loyal to India whereas Islamic values impel him to side with '*Dar-ul-Islam*'. This was experienced in 1971 at the time of India-Pak war which resulted in the division of Pakistan and creation of Bangladesh. When the people of East Bengal were suffering under the tyranny of West Pakistan and most of the Indians had sympathy for them, at that time Muslims of India were pained at the very thought of division of Pakistan. Describing the feelings of Muslims in West Bengal, Sh. Hamid Dalvai had written in an article that Islamic thinking has failed to find a solution of the clash of loyalties that every muslim feels for the nation and for Islam in a non-Islamic country and hence conversion to Islam would mean swerving away from national loyalty which is the basis of nationalism of a country.

Through a deep contemplation, the great thinkers infused the idea of a country in this land, spread from the Himalayas to Kanya Kumari, and enunciated the principle of 'unity in diversity', and this is the chief attribute of Indian Nationalism. The first evidence of this culture is the freedom permitted to different forms of worship. All the paths or forms of worship and concepts that limit the selfishness of man and make him liberal and universal are deemed as right. Thus no Indian will ever object if a person practises Islam, Christianity or any other religion provided that it leads him to liberality and universality and provided he also accepts for others the same freedom of worship of the forms prescribed by their faiths and judges them by the same measure whether those paths help them in becoming liberal and universal. "My path is right; yours too is not wrong"; is a maxim fundamental to Indian thinking. Whereas this attitude does not impose restriction on any presentation of realised truth, it does not deny the truth realised by others or the path they follow. Judging with this mentality, wherein all paths are right and lead to Truth, difference in religion has no meaning and a person can choose his own specific path according to his nature and tendency. In such a situation, mass religious conversion is entirely meaningless.

Semitic Exclusiveness

Let us compare this mentality with those of Semitic religions like Islam and Christianity, which proclaim that only their path leads to truth and heaven and the others lead to falsehood and hell. At the time of Eucharistic Congress in 1964 in Bombay when the Pope, for the first time, had come to a non-Christian country, the Chief Priest of India, Cardinal Gracias told with sorrow:

> "It is a matter of grave concern for us that in spite of the efforts made during the last few centuries, only three percent of the population of India could be attracted to embrace Christianity."

The sorrow expressed for the Indians was an outcome of the belief that they are deprived of the form of worship that leads to heaven, and that the paths that are followed in India lead to hell. Whence it was their duty to somehow conduct these unfortunate persons to the only beneficent path. As all the means like explaining, rebuke, cure and beating are deemed as proper for restricting an immature child from committing wrong, if in the same way the ignorant children of India can be brought on the right path through understanding, enlightenment, coercion or force, it is to their benefit. If they think in this manner, there is nothing surprising in it. Whenever Christian missionaries are criticised for this, they accept it with a view that the ignorant children do resist. After all, which child would like to be beaten? At the time of Eucharistic Congress when the masses talked of protesting against the Pope by showing black flags for the religious conversion practised by Christian missionaries, Cardinal Gracious, clearing his position, said to reporters, "Christianity is against no religion". But when one of the reporters asked if he, like a Hindu, could say that all paths were true, he told, "I am selling a particular brand of soap in this market. How can I say that the other brand of soap is as good as mine?" If religion is a saleable commodity, then it is obvious that publicity, advertisement, incentives of commission etc. will also be used in this business. That is why, pointing to it, Mahatma Gandhi has said, "Conversion, now-a-days, has become a matter of business like any other. I remember having read a missionary report saying how much it costs per head to convert and then presenting a budget for the next harvest." There is no need of such a religious conversion in India. The prime need of today is a conversion based on self-purification and self-realisation. But the religious convertors are never guided by the *aim*. Cannot we say to those who want to convert the religions in India, 'Doctor, heal thyself first'?

Convertors to Islam are also not bothered for inner purification. Acceptance of 'Allah' and his prophet is considered more important. In that context an incident relating to Abu Talib, the uncle of Hazrat Mohd. is worth mentioning. He saved the Prophet from various fatal attacks and it was under his patronage that Hazrat Mohd. could succeed in lie publication and expansion of his views. When Abu Talib was on his death bed the followers of Hazrat Mohd. requested him to read '*Kalma*' before death as it would take him to heaven. But he did not agree to leave the faith of his ancestors. So the Muslims believe that he must have been condemned to hell. This is the mentality that assigns hell to a person who throughout his life was indirectly instrumental in the publicity and expansion of Islam, for not reading the *Kalma* i.e. "there is no God other than 'Allah' and Hazrat Mohd. is his prophet." To hope for liberality from people of such a mentality is to expect an unclouded rain. It was this mentality that inspired Maulana Mohd. Ali to remark that, 'Even the most sinful amongst the Muslims is better than Mahatma Gandhi because he believes in Allah and his prophet.'

Such a mentality readily accepts Jinnah, who never said prayers (*Namaz*) and ate pork but does not accept the leadership of Maulana Abul Kalam Azad, a devout Muslim saying prayers five times a day, and a famous expounder of *Quran* because he opposed the formation of Pakistan by supporting the Congress, a party with Hindu majority.

Coexistence Impossible

'Your religion is for you, our religion is for us', 'there is no compulsion or force in matter of religion', *Quran* abounds with such '*Ayats*' on the basis of which it can be proved that Islam is a liberal and extremely tolerant religion. But when we consider the 'Nasikh' and 'Mansukh' context, an altogether different picture emerges. Then are some '*Ayats*' in *Quran* that annul others. When two contradictory '*Ayats*' appear on the same subject, the former '*Ayat*' is considered annulled by the latter. Annuling '*Ayat*' is called 'Nasikh' and the annulled is called 'Mansukh'. A list of 162 annulled '*Ayats*' that Allama Sijuti has given with proof in his book '*Lababan Naqul Ti Asba Ninnajul*' has been reproduced by Sh. Ved Prakash in the first part of his book '*Quran Parichaya*'. Considering these annulled

'*Ayats*', it is difficult to find in *Quran* the '*Ayats*' that preach generosity and mutual tolerance, and if we agree with the following statement of Shri M.R.A. Beg, we would not be unjust. Shri Beg says:

> "However, in spite of all the contradictions, it would seem in the final analysis that neither the *Quran* nor Mohammad advocated humanism or coexistence between Muslims and non-Muslims and that Islam, with all apparatus was conceived and devised as the religion to end all the other religions. This goes against making its adherents (Muslims) popular in India or in any country in which they are in a minority. This also explains why no country in which Muslims are in majority can have a secular constitution and why no practising Muslim can be a Humanist."

There are many incidents in the life of Hazrat Mohammed that tell about his kind and sympathetic heart. Also, many strict decisions that he took were due to the pressing demand of the situation often to save the very existence of this newly formed sect. It is incontrovertible that Hazrat Mohammed had to simultaneously play the roles of a religious preacher, social reformer, commander and judge and executor. These roles in those circumstances were often contradictory to each other. If divine orders received for the performance of these roles are also contradictory, there is nothing surprising in it. But the question arises whether the freedom that was available to Hazrat Mohammed, to think over right and wrong and reach conclusions on that basis, is also available to his heirs? It is true that permission is granted to Islam for 'Izma' (consensus) 'Izihad' (fresh explanation) and 'Kayas' (thinking on the basis of similarity) and it has been used also in certain cases but it is clear that the fear of going far from the original does not permit such a solution which widely differs from previous directives.

Intolerance in the Muslim Psyche

When we find that even slight variations in ideology within Islam like those in its different sects such as 'Shia', 'Sunni', Ahmedia, Wahabi, 'Motzala', 'Bahai' etc. cannot be accepted, it is difficult to believe that mutual tolerance can ever become a part of Islamic thinking. Declaration of Ahmedia sect as non-Muslim in Pakistan for its not accepting Hazrat Mohammed as the last Prophet and the genocide of the followers of the Bahai sect in Iran are fresh to the modern history. Muslims may be compelled to be tolerant in a particular place where they are in minority. But wherever they got the opportunity, they have either tried to convert the followers of other religions or to eliminate them. To rename Shivalingam as Mahmud Gaznavi immediately after his conversion to Islam or to remind of the idol-breaker of Tulja Bhawani or of the person who was responsible for the division of Mother India by naming converts as Afzal

Khan and Jinnah are the products of the same all-destroying, intolerant attitude. This change of attitude that follows the conversion as Muslim is opposed to 'Bhartiyata' and hence to say that 'What difference does it make if one is converted into a Muslim, he will continue to remain Indian' may be constitutionally correct but *ideologically* it is wrong, and since this ideology is the mother of the idea that 'We are one,' this sort of religious conversion is in opposition to Indian Nationalism.

Islamic Culture is alien to India

Islamic culture in its original form is Arabic culture. The total environment of the *Quran* is Arabic, and so whereas Islam is quite natural for Arab Nationalism, the moment it gets transferred to a different environment, it develops contradictions because the culture of every country is inextricably mixed with its environment. The camels, trees, *kabilas* (tribes), their living style, customs and manners which are so natural to the Arab land, become unnatural in Iran, Indonesia, India, China, etc. because the environment and the life based on i is totally different. The description of paradise in the *Quran* as 'Where there is greenery all the year round and the rivers flow perennially' may be highest bliss for an Arab, but such a paradise for a Keralite or Assamese has no great attraction whatsoever. It is also true that the literature of a language is the reflection of the environment and life of that place. And it is correct to accept that the environment described in Indian Languages is different from what is described in the Arabic. Not only that, the traditions, folklores, similes and other figures of speech used in the Arabic literature of the *Quran* are not in harmony with the literatures of other lands and if loyalty to Islam is considered an identification with the whole environment that is found in *Quran*, cessation of relation from the environment that traditional folk lore, similes, plots and figures of speech etc. established through other languages becomes inevitable. It is out of this that the commandments "We are no more Tamils and now say '*Salam Valekum*' and not '*Vanakkam*' spring up. In our day to day dealings it is not easy to severe our relations with the language of the place of birth, but when on mental level it is impressed that this language and the environment, traditions and history expressed through its medium is not ours; using the new language one does not feel oneness with it. Folk-lores, festivals and functions, all that was natural till yesterday becomes alien and worthy of being rejected and destroyed. And if the environment established by the Indian language that joins the people and is the basis of nationality of this country becomes alien, the religious converts lose the sense of belonging.

In spite of Urdu's origin in India, its environment, with a few exceptions, is almost foreign. Urdu was born as a language in the soldier-camps of Muslim kings. It emerged out of necessity of Arab, Persian, Turk,

Afghan and Mughal soldiers in their dealings with the local population. But among the court poets and littérateurs, Arabic and Persian scholars were dominant. At a later date when the number of Muslim converts increased, Urdu literature that was developed to Keep them separate, contained descriptions, less Indian and more of Arab and of Persia, therefore, the Muslim mind that is nurtured on this fails to develop a feeling of belonging with the environment, history folklores of this country and finds itself lost. It can be easily seen in the internal struggle of young Pakistani littérateurs or the revolt of the matured writers of Bangladesh.

After the formation of Pakistan as '*Dar-ul-Islam*', the people of that country were impelled to associate themselves with the local languages and the environment created by them. 'Jiye Sindh' struggle is an outcome of this and its leader G.M. Sayed has very clearly said that Urdu is a language that divides. It divided India, it also divided Pakistan and in future it may divide the rest of Pakistan. But the most surprising incident is that the young generation whose ancestors came from Bihar and Uttar Pradesh appreciated Hindi poem written by Asad Mohd. Khan, which was broadcast from Karachi station of Pakistan Radio. The poem written in praise of Hazrat Mohd. gave birth to a controversy. The causes of controversy were, why is the poem written in Hindi? Why is Hazrat Mohd. compared to Girdhar? Why this relation with the plains of Ganga, Yamuna? The youth had only one reply: "Since we are the products of the plains of Ganga-Yamuna, we are bound to associate with it. What are we to do with Iran or Iraq?"

It may be wrong to say that the Indian Muslims are not impelled by a desire to associate themselves with this land and its environment. But the fear of losing their separate identity once they associate themselves with the environment, language and symbols used in this land pulls them apart from all this This dilemma can be seen in the following two statements of Iqbal when the idea of Pakistan was still not born. Describing India as the loveliest country, he said, "Religion does not teach us to be enemy to each other. We all Indians belong to one country, and India is ours." Here his nationalism is at its peak. But when he says "China and Arab are ours, India is ours; we all Muslims belong to one country and the whole world belongs to us"; then he is swayed by circumscribed trans-national communalism and talks of Pakistan. When this sire of Pakistan found that Pakistan is likely to be created, he said to Mr. Thomson, one of his English friends: "The Pakistan plan would be disastrous to the British Govt., disastrous to the Hindus and disastrous to the Muslim community." Lying on his death bed, he said the same thing with tears in his eyes to Pt. Nehru, when he went to see him during his visit to Pakistan. This dilemma has been expressed by Sh. M.R.A. Beg in the following words:

> "The Muslims dilemma is this. Is it better for Muslims to assimilate and thereby lose their identity or are they bound by Islam to preserve their identity and thereby suffer the mental, physical, social and economic consequences of non-assimilation?"

It is possible that Indian Muslim leadership, dazzled by petro-dollars from Arab countries and lost in day-dreams of converting India into an Islamic state may overlook it as irrelevant talk, but waking to the countrywide reaction irrespective of caste, creed, community or language, delaying the question of assimilation for a longer time would bear no good result. The necessity is for a new Muslim leadership that may say like the twelfth century poet Jallaluddin;

"The marrow from *Koran* have I drawn, And the dry bones into the dogs cast."

Responsibility of the New Muslim Leadership

In a 'Hadish' which Syed Amir Ali referred in his famous book '*The spirit of Islam*', Hazrat Mohd. himself says, "Ye are in an age in which, if ye abandon one tenth of what is ordered, ye shall be ruined. After this, a time will come when he who shall observe one tenth of what is now ordered will be redeemed." The new leadership is to tell what part of '*Quran Sharif*' is eternal; and what, ephemeral. Secondly nationalism is to be presented as an in-controversial outcome of Islamic thought. According to Indian thought the individual, family, caste, society, nation, world and universe are considered successive widening units and no contradiction found in these units. So, it was not compelled to accept universal brotherhood opposed to nationalism. Instead, it was regarded a necessary step towards unity of the world. Not only this, the principle of 'Unity in Diversity' has accepted the uniqueness of each nation as a necessary concomitant to the beauty of the universe and it is through the preservation of this uniqueness that the aim of '*Vasudhaiva Kutumbakam*' is to be achieved. But this coordination or harmony has yet to become a part of Islamic thought. This is a universal experience that feeling of nationalism is more natural and deep. So the question is whether devotion to Bharatmata, respect for the ancestors of this land and unity in diversity and 'loyality to Islam' can be harmonized to the extent that in the event of an invading Islamic country raising the slogan that 'Islam is in danger,' the Indian Muslim suffers no dilemma in sacrificing his life for the defence of the country and is sure that he is behaving according to the dictates of his religion. Every Islamic country has moulded Islam according to its situation. Then why cannot the Indian Muslims do the same? If Iran's Islam is not affected by adopting and respecting the ancestors prior to the advent of Islam, how can Indian Islam be? If an Indonesian Muslim can continue to remain a Muslim even after accepting *Ramayana* and *Mahabharat* as his cultural books, then why does an Indian Muslim fear to do it? If Turkey and Pakistan can remain Muslim even after doing away with polygamy and purdah system, then why does an Indian Muslim fear to do so? So far as preserving a separate identity is concerned, India is the only country which does not destroy anybody's identity. Parsis and Jews, in spite of being in a small minority, continue to retain their identity and have never been the victim of any atrocity. When different tribes have maintained their identity, why should eighty millions of Muslims fear to lose it? Again, in the words of Sh. M.R.A. Beg,

> "Muslims must, therefore, decide whether they are Muslims of the Indian branch of the Muslim-family whose heartland is in West Asia or whether they are Muslim Indians of the Muslim branch of the Indian family which is rooted in the Indian soil."

It is after this decision that one will be able to know whether a person in spite of being a Muslim is an Indian or not. For the present one would say in the words of Dr. Ambedkar, "Conversion to Islam or Christianity will denationalise the depressed classes."

21

The Origin of the Caste System & Advent of the Untouchability

Dr. Surendra Nath Mittal

Reader, Department of Political Science, Allahabad University

The origin of the caste system has been a matter of controversy and as will be seen later, different scholars have advanced different theories in this respect. However, Caste System could hardly be distinguished from *Varna* System as Caste System to a great extent owes its origin to the *Varna*. Therefore, we first take up the origin of the *Varna* System.

The origin of *Varna* System is enshrined in the *Purusha-Sukta*[1] of the *Rigveda*. The *Rishi* says:

"ब्राह्मणोऽस्य मुखम् आसीद्

बाहू राजन्यः कृतः ।

ऊरु तदस्य यद् वैश्यः

पद्भ्यां शूद्रो अजायत ॥

[The man of knowledge (*Brahmana*) was his mouth;

His arms were made the ruling man (*Rajanya*);

His thighs were that which is the man of trade *(Vaishya)*

Out of his feet was born the working man (*Sudra*).]

When oblations were offered to *Purusha* i. e. the Cosmic Being and he was invoked by the deities, the above four divisions came into being.

Thus it is seen that *Vedic* literature recognises the division of society into four categories–the man of knowledge and Dharma *(Brahmin)*, the man of politics and warfare *(Kshatriya)*, the man of trade and industry *(Vaishya)* and the working man *(Sudra)*; but it says that all of them are limbs of the Cosmic Being *(Purusha)* and are respectively the mouth, arms, thighs and feet of *Purusha*. In philosophical language, it means that the above four *Varnas*[2] i.e. the *Sudra*, the *Vaishya*, the *Kshatriya* and the *Brahmin*, though divided by *Guna* (quality) and *Karma* (occupation), are the same in spirit. This is yet another instance of 'many in one' or of social *Advaita* and upholds the principle of unity in diversity.

But some scholars have interpreted this *Sukta* to suggest that the *Varna* system existed right from the beginning of the Universe, while according to the post-*Vedic* literature[3] (the *Mahabharata* and the *Puanas*) there was only one *Varna* in the beginning or there were no *Varnas* in *Satyug*.[4] Since *Mahabharata* ordains that *Vedas (Shruties)* should be interpreted through the texts of history and *Puranas* only[5], it will be proper to conclude that *Varnas* were a later creation.

This entire concept also conforms to the Indian thought tradition, according to which all the important institutions such as the *Varnas*, the *Ashramas*, the family and the state were created at one or the other later date. With regard to *Ashramas* the *Baudhayan Dharmasutra*[6] says "*Acharyas* (are of the view) that there was only one *(Ashrama)* as other *(Ashramas)* do not allow procreation" and adds "Kapil, son of *Prahlad* was an *Asura* and was responsible for this division into four *Ashrams*."\ It is possible that this may not be *Baudhayan's* own view and he might have made a mention of some current belief. As per a story given in *Mahabharata*, the institution of marriage i.e. of family was created by Shwet-Ketu,[7] wherein it has been stated that when his mother deserted his father and eloped with another *Brahmin*, he the angry Shwet-Ketu" prescribed a rule for men and women, that a woman can be only one man's wife. He ordained that the woman who cohabits with a man other than her own husband will be committing a grave sin like that of an abortion, which will result in deep distress. The same will be the fate of the man who flirts with a woman other than his own chaste wife. The origin of the state has been dealt with in *Manusmriti* and *Kautiliya Arthashastra* and in *Mahabharata* in detail. *Manusmriti* says "when people were horrified to see anarchy all around, a king was appointed by the *Prabhu* (i.e. the Almighty or *Prajapati*) for the protection of the people.[8]" *Kautilya* too says that "on being tortured by the

Matsanyaya i.e. anarchy in which the bigger fish swallows the smaller one, people elected Manu as their king".[9] So far as the *Mahabharata* is concerned both these versions are found in a mixed form as given in a story.[10] In ancient times when people were without a king, they destroyed each other just as a weaker and smaller fish was swallowed by a bigger and stronger one...Then those people in distress collectively went to *Prajapati* and said that they would not be able to survive without a king...(Therefore) they requested, "O God ! Bestow us with a king whom we may respect and who may take care of us. Then *Brahmaji* appointed Manu. On getting an assurance from the people, Manu assumed their kingship and he made them to follow their *Dharma*.[11]

All this indicates that the various organs of the Hindu social order did not come into being the very day when Hindu society began its journey. All these were created as and when the necessity arose. Likewise, the *Varna* system must have been devised keeping in view the fact that qualities (good or bad) differ from man to man and therefore it was necessary to allot them functions according to their respective qualities (*Gunas*)[11a] In fact the *Purush Sukta* of *Rigveda* also propounds the same theory although in a different language. According to *Purush Sukta* the mouth of *Purusha* was the *Brahmana* i.e. it was the duty of the *Brahmana* to store the entire thought tradition in his memory and to lay down the rules of *Dharma,* to preach, to impart education and thus to protect the cultural heritage of the country. The arms of the *Purusha* became *Rajanya* i.e. *Kshatriyas* and, therefore, it became their duty to carry arms, to wage wars, to protect the noble and to punish the wicked; in short, to give protection to the people. The thigh or the middle part of the *Purush* was *Vaishya. Atharvaveda* clearly used the word *Madhya* (middle part) in place of *uru* i.e. the thigh. It means that the duty of the *Vaishya* was to produce and acquire all the basic necessities of the society and then to feed all the organs of the society; in short, to perform the role of a producer as well as of a supplier. From the feet of the *Purusha* came forth the *Sudras* which means that just as without the cooperation of the feet all other parts of the body cannot function properly, likewise the *Sudras* too sustain the other three *Varnas* and make them fit for action by extending their cooperation. It is further evident that broadly the *gunas* have been divided into three categories viz. *Satva, Rajas* and *Tamas*–which are symbolised by these three *varnas* i.e. *Brahmana, Kshatriya* and *Sudra. However,* from the functional point of view a fourth *varna,* namely *Vaishya* was also created which is considered to be an admixture of *Rajas* and *Tamas.*

The oldest reference to the later evolution of the *varna* system is found in *Brihadaranyaka Upanishad*[12] wherein it has been stated that originally *Brahma* was all alone; being alone he could not project himself and demonstrate his superhuman faculties to anyone. Therefore, gradually

Kshatriyas, Vaishyas and *Sudras* were created and ultimately to keep them on the right track *Dharma* had to be established.

All such references make it clear that the *Varna* system did not exist since eternity and that it came into being much later out of some necessity. It is rather difficult to fix the date of its origin or to link it with any particular book. Only this much can be said that the caste system was created and organised in a pre-historic period for which we have no evidence. No doubt, some foreign and Indian scholars have said that the origin of *Varnas* took place in the last phase of *Rigvedic* period because *Purush Sukta* is a part of the tenth *mandal* of *Rigveda,* which is said to have been composed much later, and that even if the *Varnas* had originated during the *Rigvedic* period, there was no rigidity pertaining to marriage and profession. Here many questions may be raised. Firstly, whether *Rigveda* is the oldest *Veda*? It may be correct to say that the different *Suktas* and *Mantras* of all the *Vedas* might have been perceived *(darshan)* or heard *(shrawan,* as *Vedas* are called *shruties*) or even composed at different times, can it be said that all the *suktas* and *mantras* of *Rigveda* belong to an earlier period than all the *suktas* and *mantras* of *Yajurveda* and *Atharvaveda*? This question becomes all the more significant because the Indian tradition holds that originally there was only one *Veda*[13] and Vyas divided it into several parts for the purpose of *Yajna.*[14] Secondly, as admitted by the late *Mahamahopadhyaya Shri Pandurang Vaman Kane,*[15] the *Vedas* or the *Vedic* literature do not present systematic compendium of social order or social laws. Moreover, *Rigveda* contains very few rules regarding social order. It will be too much to conclude on the basis of these scanty and scattered references that the *Varna* system did not exist during the whole period of mantra composition.[16] Kane quotes three *Mantras* from the eighth *mandal* of *Rigveda* wherein *Brahma* (*Brahmana*) has been associated with intellect, the *Kshatra* (*Kshatriya*) with men and *wish* (*Vaishyas*) with cattle herding.[17] Here is a clear reference to the intellectual role of the *Brahmin* and the roles of *Kshatriya* and *Vaisya* of protecting man and animal respectively.

The contention that here the *Brahmana, Kshatriya* and *Vaishya* have nothing to do with the *Varna* system does not hold good. In another *mantra* of *Rigveda*[18] there is a mention of different functions of different people such as the performance of *Yajna,* the duty of protection, performance of trade and labour. In yet another *mantra* and that too, belonging to the early portion of *Rigveda,* the *Rishi* says to *Indra,* "O Indra, the follower of a straight path! Will thou make me a cowherd (as per the translation by Pt. Satvalekar), or a king of men or a *Rishi* who enjoys a drink of *Somras* or bestow upon me inexhaustible wealth."[19] This *mantra* also clearly refers to the four *varnas* i.e. *Sudra, Kshatriya, Brahmana and Vaishya.* Haug, the German scholar says,[20] "Recently a theory has been advanced that the *Varna* system is not known to the early portion of the *Vedas,* but this seems to be a hasty conclusion drawn without proper scrutiny of the evidence available". Shri Upendra Nath Ghoshal, giving a brief summary of this whole controversy, says; "The problem of the existence of caste system in *Rigveda* has been a matter of long drawn serious controversy amongst scholars. It has been established by Haug (*Brahma* and *Die Brahmanen*, 1871), Kern *(indische Theorien over de standenverdeeling)* and Ludwig (in his German-translation of *Rigveda* III, 237-43) that there is a reference to Caste System within *Rigveda* itself. It has been stated by Oldenberg *(Das Religion Des Veda,* page 373 etc.) and Geldner (*Vedische studier* 2. 146n.1) is of the view that caste system was fully entrenched during the *Rigvedic* period. This view was strongly opposed by Muir, (*Old Sanskrit Tenets* Vol. I page 239 etc.) and by Zimmer. Recently, the authors of *Vedic Index* after examining the arguments given by Muir and Zimmer have come to the conclusion that during the *Rigveda* period, Caste System was a commonly accepted fact."[21]

Thus it is clear that *Rigveda* too makes a mention of *Varna* System as well as the distribution of professions in accordance with these *Varnas.* The word "*Brahma-putra*" contained in an earlier portion of the *Rigveda,* namely, "Thou chanteth the *Stotras* of *Yajna* just like a *Brahma-putra*"[22] indicates that to some extent, *Varna* had acquired a hereditary character. Similarly, a *Sukta* of *Rigveda* (to a great extent) by prohibiting adultery, in a way, insists on inter-*varna* marriages only.[23] While pointing out to the king *(Kshatriya)* the ill consequences of kidnapping the wife of a *Brahman,* it urges upon him to return her. Keith is also of the view[24] that, "Undoubtedly, during the *Rigvedic* period, the *Purohit* class had assumed hereditary character (i.e. *Varna* by birth)." Two more *mantras* are quoted to support the theory that there was no rigidity in *Varna* system during the *Rigvedic* period. In one of these *mantras*"[24a] the *Rishi* says that he is a composer of *mantras,* while his father is a *vaidya (Bhishag)* and his mother pounds cereals with the help of stones and thus they earn money through different professions. This *mantra* does not make any mention of professions belonging to different *varnas* being practised by the members of the same family because composition of *mantras* and the vocation of a *vaidya* both come within the purview of the duties of a *Brahmin* and pounding cereals is a household job which every mother is supposed to do. The second one is a reference to Devapi and Shantanu where Shantanu has been depicted as a king and Devapi as a *Purohit.* According to a story given in *Nirukta* both of them were the sons of Rishtisena and Shantanu the younger of the two got kingship, When, during the reign of Shantanu a famine broke out, Devapi performed a *yajna* and acted himself as *Purohit.* From this an inference has been drawn that a change in *Varna* was feasible. This fact has been recognised by later *shastras* also. Several instances in support of this fact are available in the historical texts and *puranas,* amongst which

Vishwamitra's episode is too well known but such instances are very rare and are feasible in the case of one out of millions and that too through severe penance.[25] This whole discussion leads us to a conclusion that during the *Rigveda*-period, *Varna* system was an accepted fact, but it is difficult to surmise on the basis of the few social inferences available in it that the *Varna* system had not assumed a hereditary character and that there were no instances of marriage within the *varna*.

Varna and Caste

After having discussed the origin of *varna* system, we can proceed to examine the origin of the caste system. Some persons make a distinction between '*Varna*' and 'Caste'. They are of the view that the division of society into four functional groups is natural as well as justified, but the caste system i.e. division of society into hundreds of small groups on the basis of birth has no justification at all. As the *Varnas* are only four in number, while the castes are innumerable, it is obvious that these two are not the same thing. But let us look at this problem from a different angle. Caste has been defined as a group based on birth. Now the question is whether the four *Varnas* could also be termed as castes? The Indian tradition does not seem to distinguish *Varnas* from Castes because while Vasishta calls a *Sudra* "*Krishna Varna*"[26] (Blask in colour), *Nirukta*[27] calls him as "*Krishna Jatiya*" (Black by birth) almost in the same context, meaning thereby, that the *Varnas* and the Castes are the same. When Apastamba says that if there be any doubt in regard to the *jati* (caste) and character of a person approaching for the study of *Dharma,* it should be verified in the presence of fire, here caste means *Varna.* On one occasion *Yajnavalkya* used the words "*Savarna*" (having the same *varna*) and "*Sajati*" (having the same caste) as synonyms.[28] The rules which have been prescribed by *Manu* and *Yajnavalkya Smritis*[29] with reference, to caste-elevation, have been given by Gautam[30] with reference to change of *Varna.*[31] Similar expressions are found elsewhere also. This means that the ancient Indian thinkers have treated the words "*Varna*" and "Caste" as synonyms. The theories put forth by the Western Scholars namely Ibbetson, Risley, Senart etc. regarding the origin of caste system mainly deal with the origin of the *Varna* system.

Although Ibbetson differentiates between the *Varna* and the Caste, he traces the origin of *Varna* system while dealing with the origin of Caste system. According to him, in the beginning, tribal organisation throughout the world was based upon common descent and similarly the professions were also hereditary, but later on this hereditary system disappeared and was replaced by one based upon personal merit. But in India, the *Brahmanas* with the help of *Kshatriyas* institutionalized this hereditary system. According to Risley, who was later on supported by Mahamahopadhyaya Kane, the word *'Varn'* was originally used to distinguish only two categories: the Aryans and the dark skinned, Dasyus who were later on called *'sudras'*. In his opinion there were three classes amongst Aryans which did not enter into inter-caste marriages. There were several mixed castes and many castes sprang up out of the assimilation of foreign elements into the society. Risley believes that the caste system must have come into force immediately after the entry of Aryans into India because, had it not been so, caste system would not have been so uniformly prevalent throughout India. According to Senart, the factors of exclusiveness in regard to marriage and food, caste Panchayats and expulsion from caste etc. are found in all the Aryan societies such as Romans, Greeks, Persians and Indians. In India all these factors have been traditionalized. Hocart says that in every royal court certain rituals were observed and to meet the requirements of these rituals different people were allotted different functions and in the interest of the purity of the ritual, inter-dining and inter-marriage between these groups was prohibited. According to Slater, caste system was more rigid in South India as compared to North India. Therefore, the caste system must have originated amongst the Dravidians much before the advent of the Aryans. Amongst the Dravidians the professions were hereditary and became the basis of matrimonial relations. With the arrival of Aryans the colour difference added to the rigidity and introduced the element of superiority and inferiority. But, this view is based upon a very debatable Aryan-Race theory.

Hutton is opposed to the view that the caste system was a clever device of the *purohits* to maintain their own superiority. "But this view cannot be accepted. It was not possible to impose such a social institution like that of caste through an administrative fiat alone. Deep rooted and widely prevalent, the caste system does not seem to have been artificially created, rather it must have grown organically". He adds that, "As this system is so deeply entrenched in India and as it does not exist anywhere else, its origin will have to be searched for somewhere in India itself and not outside it." He concludes that the study of certain aboriginal tribes of India shows that the division of professions, restrictions or inter-dining and inter-marriages existed among them also. These tribals believe that anybody violating these prohibitions will only invite disaster for himself. With the advent of Aryans on one hand the element of superiority and inferiority crept into this system and on the other hand the geographical isolation of India as well as the theory of *Karma* etc. further strengthened the caste system. Nesfield does not attribute the origin of caste system to the advent of Aryans in India. Even if the theory of Aryan invasion be accepted, it has not been possible to distinguish between the Aryans and the aboriginals during the last three thousand years, which means that they got completely submerged with the local population. In the opinion of Nesfield, discrimination of castes into high and low on the basis of their professions must have developed with the march of civilization. Human groups following primitive professions such as hunting etc. have been given the lowest berth in the social hierarchy, next to them have been placed those groups who earn their livelihood through professions linked with water, such as fisherman and boatmen etc. Above them were placed the cattle rearing castes such as cowherds and shepherds etc.[32]

A perusal of all these theories about the origin of caste system makes it clear that all these theories are based just on conjecture. But most of the theories admit that the caste system was born out of *varna* system and is nothing but its extended form. A study of the organisational structure of various castes goes to prove that this view is nearer the truth. Various castes such as *Kanya Kubja, Gaur, Saraswat* etc., among *Brahmanas* and *Agrawal* etc. amongst *Vaisyas,* which were born either out of geographical consideration or on the basis of professions, are covered by the *Varna* system. Certain castes such as *Maha-Brahmins* amongst *Brahmins,* wine sellers and carpenters amongst *Vaishyas,* and cobblers etc. amongst *Sudras,* have professional entity. Certain castes are not covered by any *Varna* but their professions are generally earmarked such as trade for *Khatries,* Landlordship or peasantry for *Bhoomihar.* It could be that they belong to *anulom* hybrid castes such as *Khatries* born out of *Kshatriya-Vaishya* Union, as is evident from their names and professions; *Bhoomihars* are a mixture of *Brahmins* and *Kshatriyas* because some of them call themselves as *Brahmins* and some others as *Kshatriyas,* though they may have marital relations amongst themselves. It could be that these castes are the products of the process of assimilation of foreign elements into Indian society. But like the hybrid castes, they have also become an integral part of Indian society. Only a few castes have sectarian origins i.e. they are based upon the forms of worship followed by different sects irrespective of the fact that these sects may have drawn people from different *Varnas,* such as *Bisnois* in Western Uttar Pradesh and *Lingayats* in South India. Therefore it will be proper to say that caste system has originated mainly from the *Varna* system itself. As has been propounded in almost all the Indian Classics[33], in addition to these four *Varnas* there exist several other *Anulom* (castes in which the man belongs to a superior caste and the woman belongs to an inferior caste) and *Pratilom* hybrid caste (in which the man belongs to an inferior caste and the woman belongs to a superior caste). Their professions have also been spelt out. Several scholars have criticized this view saying that the theory regarding the origin of castes[34] is just a speculation and that the theory of hybrid castes has been invented with a view to accommodate several professions as well as to absorb certain groups of a particular area in the *Varna* system or to assimilate foreign tribes in the Indian society. Whatever the fact may be, this much is certain that various castes have been adjusted (branded as hybrid castes) within the frame work of *Varna* system. As is clear from the above description. Therefore, it cannot be accepted that the caste system has a source of origin other than the *Varna* system, as has been spelt out by Nesfield, this system is not a by-product of the advent of the Aryan race and as laid down by Hutton this system was not a result of some shrewd scheme on the part of the priestly class to serve its vested interests. On the contrary, this is based on the need of the society and the quality aspect of different persons.

No Link with Untouchability

This description of the origin of caste system or *Varna* system should not lead to the conclusion that untouchability is in any way related to the *Varna* system or caste system. According to the Indian thinkers, untouchability is linked with the concept of purity which has been advocated throughout. The conclusion which can be drawn out of the *Varna* system or the caste system is that according to Indian sociologists of the past all men are not born equal. They have different qualities. Therefore, their functions, their rights and duties will be based on their qualities. In Indian thought it had been described the theory of merit. Therefore, in the Indian social order there exists not only a distribution of functions for every individual but also there are provisions as to how much respect he will command in the society, what privileges he will enjoy or which hard and fast rules he will have to observe. For instance the *Brahmin* was expected to follow the laws of *Dharma* very religiously and to lead a life of almost self-sacrifice and hardship but at the same time it was impressed upon the society that he should not only be accorded respect but he should be taken care of thoroughly and he should be extended maximum facilities for performance of his duties. On the other hand the binding of the observance of the laws of *Dharma* was relaxed to a great extent in the case of a *Sudra*. There was enough freedom in personal life but he must take care that as an artisan or a labourer he should fulfill the needs of the society and should not behave arrogantly with others. This aspect could be discussed in further details but this is not within the purview of this article. It may also be debated whether it was proper to make birth a basis for the functional division and if at all it was proper, then to what extent. But we will not enter into the controversy here. It would suffice here to say that according to Indian thought men are not equal on the mundane and social levels, because this equality is not visible in practice anywhere. However, it could be added that, untouchability is in no way connected with this inequality and if at all any connection could be traced, it is very indirect.

Whenever we think of untouchability these days, our attention goes only to *Sudras* but according to the ancient *shastras,* the *Sudras* were not untouchables and in practice also at least in Hindi speaking areas no untouchability is observed towards anybody, except scavengers. As far as backward classes like *Ahirs* are concerned, no untouchability was practised with them. We shall deal with this aspect in detail with reference to *Dharma Shastras* at a later stage. But untouchability varies in form and we can have a long list of those with whom dining is prohibited and it includes not only *Sudras* but also typical *Brahmanas* and others e.g. a woman belonging to a so-called high caste is treated as an untouchable in her own family during her period of menstruation.

Contact was completely prohibited with persons who were found guilty of committing any one of the major sins such as murder of a *Brahmin*, abortion, adultery with the wife of a teacher or an elderly relative, theft of gold or other valuables or indulgence in drinking, so much so that contact was not allowed with those who were not prepared to dissociate with these sinners. Untouchability is observed for a certain period at the time of birth or death in a family. Certain commentators and interpreters of *Dharma Shastras* have branded certain sects, inhabitants of particular countries, people of certain tribes and followers of certain professions as untouchables.[35] Besides even touch of impure things is prohibited.[36] Detailed instructions have been given to remove the impurity relating to urination or defecation etc.[37] After defecation the body should be so purified with water and soil as to wipe out all kinds of foul smell and coating. According to *Manu*[37a] there are twelve kinds of excreta in the body namely fat, semen, blood, marrow, urine, feces, impurites from the nose and ears, saliva, and tears which need cleansing. In *Manu smrit*[37b] and *Vishnu Smriti*[37c] elaborate rules for cleaning after defecation are given. According to *Manu,* with soil and water genitals should be washed once, the anus thrice, the left hand ten times and both the hands seven times and according to *Vishnu Dharmasastra* feet should be washed thrice. This number is meant for house-holders only. For *Brahmacharis,* for *Vanprasthis* and for *Sanyasins* it should be two fold, three fold and four fold respectively. Not only impure things but even the impure rivers were to be avoided e.g. rainfed rivers were treated as have having monthly course and bathing in these waters was prohibited.[38] All this leads us to the conclusion that the idea of untouchability, to whatever extent it existed, was not confined only to the *Sudras* but covered several types of peoples and things. Therefore, the basis of untouchability was not caste, rather, the idea of purity–internal as well as external.[39] If any mention of untouchabiliy has been made in relation to certain groups it was because they were considered to be impure or devoid of *Dharma.*

Just as we found it difficult to fix a definite period for the origin of *Varna* or Caste system, so also it is not possible to fix the exact period of the origin of the idea of untouchability in Hindu tradition. We can only say that *Yajur Veda* prohibits touching a woman having menstruation and according to *Taittiriya Brahmanas,* while performing a *Yajna* a woman having monthly course should be kept in isolation.[40] *Aitareya Brahmama*[41] hints that a ten days period of impurity was observed at the time of birth in a family. *Rig Veda* prohibits the use of an impure vessel during *Yajna*[42] *Taittiriya Aranyak, Jaiminiya Brahmana* and *Shatpatha Brahmana* insist upon purification of the body before *yajna* is performed by the sponsor and his wife.[43] So far as the issue of certain castes is concerned, in *Purush Medha* of *Yajurveda pulkas* has been associated with repulsiveness (i.e. he lived in a repulsive manner) and a *chandal* has been associated with the air *(vayu)* i.e. he lived in open and isolated places.[44] Ail this description is indicative. *Gautam Dharma Sutra* and *Manusmriti* clearly say that if a person touches depraved, a *chandal, Sutika* (woman giving birth to a child), *Rajaswala* (a woman having menstruation) and a dead body, he should take a bath and according to Gautam he should take a bath fully dressed.[45] *Manu* adds that one should not sit with a depraved, *chandal, pulkas,* an idiot, a person showing arrogance of richness, an outcast (probably, belonging to the caste lowest in order) a person living on the outskirts of village and according to *Manu* the offspring of a *chandal* male and *nishad* female. *Vedas* should not be recited in the presence of an outcaste, in the opinion of *Bhardwaj, Shrauta sutra* and *Yajnavalkya Smriti.*[47] Any type of association with these people and the study of *Vedas* in their presence is prohibited. But *Yajnavalkya* adds that on touching an outcaste a person is purified by air i.e. automatically.[48] According to *Apastamba Dharma Sutra*[49], one should take a bath after having touched a *chandal,* should converse with a *Brahmin* after having talked with him (a *chandal)* and should gaze at the stars after seeing him. *Yajnavalkya* has prescribed a penalty of 100 *panas* if a *chandal* touches a twice-born deliberately while Vishnu has prescribed physical punishment for the untouchables if they do so.[50] According to Manu, a *chandal* and *swapak* should live outside the village and a person following the lowest profession should live in the cremation ground.[51] During the day time the *chandals* and *swapaks* were required to display certain prescribed insignias and were to maintain separate utensils.[52] This means that mainly, there is only one caste i.e. *chandal* which was considered as untouchable. Contact was prohibited only to some extent with the offspring of a *swapak* and *pulkas* woman as well as persons following the lowest professions because these people had been placed in the category of the depraved and dead. Therefore, the idea of purity seems to be at the root of untouchability.

Generally, a *Sudra* was not treated as untouchable. This is clear from the two laws mentioned by *Apastamba*. According to *Apastamha*, the feet of an *atithi* (guest) should be washed by a *Sudra* and as per the second law the guest should be given the honour of *abhisheka* (sprinkling of water for purification) at the hands of a *Sudra*. *Hiranyakeshi Grihya Sutra* prescribes this rule for *snatakas* (graduates).[53] *Apastamba* also adds that either a clean *Arya* should cook meals for *Vaishwadeva* or a *Sudra* should cook under the supervision of an *Arya*.[54] Both these situations have been mentioned while dealing with the rules maintaining purity. Even partaking of the food offered by a *Sudra* is not totally forbidden which proves that a *Sudra* is not an untouchable. *Apastamba* prohibits food brought by an impure *Sudra* and *Manu*[54] forbids food cooked by a *Sudra* who does not perform *shraddha* etc. *(Pak Yajna, Panch Mahayajana etc)*. *Gautam, Vishnu, Manu, Yajnavalkya* and *Parashar* have allowed the partaking of food offered by the care-takers of animals, plough-men and servants and menial functionaries such as barbers etc. serving the family.

According to *Parashar, Attri* and *Agni Purana* it is permissible to partake *ghee*, oil and eatables fried in these items, milk, curd, *gur*, butter milk, fruits, *sattu* etc. offered by a *Sudra* and according to *Parashar*, food can be taken at *Sudra's* residence in case of emergency which has been recognised by *Manusmriti* also.

Just as many of the *Sudra* castes are not untouchables and untouchability is not related to caste but to external (e.g. *Rajaswala*) and internal (*e.g.Mahapatki*) impurity, similarly the meals are also connected with external and internal purity. Not only was the food offered by a *Sudra* forbidden but there were several others whose meals were to be avoided (*Abhojyanna*) and they are listed in the *Dharmsutras* and *Smritis*.[55] Even certain types of *Brahmins* are included in such lists such as a *Brahmin* neither accepting food from anyone, nor offering food to anyone, accepting food from all without consideration, a person not feeling repentant, one receiving education from his son, abjuring *agnihotra,* performing *agnihotra* prior to his elder brother, selling *soma,* evading self-study and *japa,* unscrupulous *sanyasin,* performing *yajna* for the entire village or for women. According to Kane, the royal *purohit* and astrologer were also included in this list. These lists include not only *Kshatriyas* or government servants but even the king himself, whose food according to *Manu* deprives the partaker of his manhood. It includes other categories of government servants such as a person who executes punishment, a person keeping others captive and who acts as a spy, *Vaishya,* money lender, gold smith etc. A person renting out his house has also been included in this list. Several other types of sinners and defaulters such as a liar, a person indulging in violence, a person committing arson, a poisoner, a thief, an adulterer, a false witness, a depraved, a woman having relations with several persons, a paramour and his mistress, a bachelor indulging in sex act, a person of mean nature– such as cruel, arrogant, ungrateful, tyrant, miser, slanderer, a drunkard, an angry man, a henpecked husband, a son abandoned by his father, a person keeping others in bondage for the recovery of loan, a person not repaying such debt and a convict are listed. Also are included persons having external impurity such as a person living on discarded food, a patient, dog breeder, executioner, a prostitute, a washerman, a *charmakara* (cobbler), wine-seller and other castes.

Apastamba is of the view that in student life one should not accept food from either *Kshatriyas, Vaisyas* or *Sudras* barring *Brahmins* and should also not accept it from the *Brahmins* who do not atone for the sins committed by them. Thus the *Sudra* was one amongst many others including the king, whose food was forbidden, but partaking of food offered by a *Sudra* was not totally forbidden, which means that a *Sudra* was not treated as an untouchable.

Temple-entry and Marriage

So far as the question of temple entry for *Sudras* was concerned it was not prohibited anywhere in the *Dharma Sastras. Bhagwat Purana* says that if the outcastes could get purified only by listening to the glory of God, then how much purification they can earn by the touch of the idols.[56] The *Puranas* contain several stories which describe how the *Sudras* could attain salvation by lighting a lamp and brooming etc. in a *Hari* temple.[57] Moreover *Dharma Shastras* allow the *Sudras* to perform all types of religious rites except *Vedic yajna* which proved that temple entry for them was not prohibited. *Skanda Purana* contains a story of a *Chandali* who despite being a gross sinner observed fast on *Shiv Ratri* in *Shri Gokaran Kshetra* without sleeping in the night and offered *belpatra* to *Shiva.* In this very *Purana* is given the story of one *Paijvan Sudra* who was always engaged in the worship of deities and guests religiously and who during the four months of the rainy season was especially engrossed in the worship of *Lord Vishnu* and was told by *Galav Muni* that all the noble *Sudras* have a right to worship *Shaligram.* Similarly in *Narada Purana* there is a story of a fowler who went to a temple and due to the impact of *Satsanga* and approximites of the idol of God, all his sins were absolved. *Padma Purana* narrates the story of a *Pulkas* who at the time of death was approached by the agents of *Yama* for carrying him but a sage took pity on him and that kindhearted sage came near the *Pulkas* with a *Shaligram* stone in his hand and poured sacred *charnamrat* of Lord *Shaligram* mixed with the leaves of *tulsi* in his mouth and whispered in his ears the name of *Rama,* put the *tulsi* leaves on his forehead and the *Shaligram* stone on his chest.[58] The above description and specially the last story completely demolishes the myth of the untouchability meted out to *Sudras* or of ban on temple-entry.

Now let us think about marriage which is the last cogent factor with regard to untouchability. According to Indian belief *Savarna* marriage is the best type of marriage, next to it *anulom* marriage is allowed. In *anulom* marriage a *Brahmin* can marry girls from all the four *varnas,* a *Kshatriya* can marry from the other three *varnas* (except a *Brahmin* girl), a *Vaishya* can marry girls from two *varnas* and a *Sudra* can marry only with the girl of his own *varna.*[59] *Manu* adds that a *Sudra* bride at the time of marriage holds one end of the dress worn by the bridegroom of a higher *varna.*[60] It may be correct to say that marriage with a *sudra* girl was not considered proper but[61] the permission of such a marriage does prove that *Sudras* were not considered untouchable.[62]

But the fact that untouchability is based on the idea of purity and impurity, does not mean that the *Sudras* enjoy equal status with the other *varnas* in the Indian polity. Indian thought tradition did not believe in the theory of the equality of mankind. It believed that all are not born equal. There is difference between man and man. Therefore, the rights and duties of a *Sudra* are of a different nature. *Sudras* were not expected to follow strictly all the laws of *Dharma,* nor was it obligatory for them to perform the daily rites. *Manusmriti* says that a *Sudra* neither commits any sin by not performing daily rites nor is he eligible for *Upnayana samskar* nor is he entitled to preach *Dharma* nor are the doors of *Dharma* closed to him. A *sudra* who understands *Dharma* and is inclined to follow it and shows an aptitude for leading a noble life, though devoid of the knowledge of *Veda,* was not considered impure but deserved appreciation.[63] *Vishnu Purana* elaborating this point says. "Twice born are first required to study the *Vedas* by observing *Vratas,* then they have to perform a *yajna* in the prescribed way out of the earnings in accordance with their natural profession with honesty, contentment and without greed. Irrelevant talks, undesirable food and improper *yajna* are considered to be damaging for a twice born and therefore they have always to lead a life of austerity. If they do not perform all their duties properly they incur sin. They cannot dine and drink freely. All their movements are restricted i.e. they have to observe certain rules. Therefore, they attain different *lokas* after severe penance while blessed is the *Sudra* who though entitled only to *pakyajna,* attains the desired *lok* by simply attending to the society and as such is more lucky. Therefore, *O Muni* ! He is not bound by any rules with regard to food and drink and there also he is blessed.[64] From the point of view of rights only two things are generally forbidden for a *Sudra,* first, study of *Vedas* i.e. the right to wear the sacred thread and secondly, to perform *Vedic Yajna* (*Srauta Yajna*). While depriving them of the study of *Vedas,* lie knowledge of *Dharma* was made available to them through *Itihas Purana. Vyas* Says, "Through *Mahabharata* I have revealed the meaning of the *Veda* so that a woman as well as a *Sudra* can also acquire the knowledge of *Dharma*." It is also said, "Kind hearted lord *Vyasa* made an arrangement by which persons of lower intelligence can also grasp he meaning of *Vedas*. Since it was difficult for a woman, a *Sudra* and a twice born only in name to understand the *Vedas,* therefore, *Vyas* was kind enough to compose the *Mahabharata* so that people having no aptitude for noble living would also attain salvation.[65] According to *Gautama*, a *sudra* cannot perform a *Vedic yajna* but he is entitled to perform *pak yajna, punch mahayajna* and *Purta dharma*.[66] A *Sudra* is also forbidden to acquire wealth in excess of his need. It is the duty of the person under whom he serves to take care of all his needs.[67] Both these restrictions were imposed probably for the reason, lest a man dominated by *tamas guna* and therefore placed in the *Sudra* category, may ill-treat and impose himself on others as a result of accumulation of wealth and knowledge. Possibly this may be the reason why a harder punishment is prescribed for the *Sudras* in case they ill-treat people of other *varnas* especially the *Brahmanas.* They were to get a comparatively lighter punishment for personal offences such as theft etc.[68]

Therefore, we can draw the conclusion that according to Indian thought tradition in the primitive age i.e. during *Satyug* "when a person on his own used to follow the path of *dharma,* there existed neither regulations nor *varnas,* neither marriage nor state. These institutions came into being due to erosion of *dharma* on the part of some persons in the society.[69] Because of qualitative differences from man to man and for meeting social requirements *varnas* were created due to professional and geographical divisions. As a result of inter mixture of *varnas,* castes came into being which observed rigidity in the matter of profession and marital relations. Different rights and duties were prescribed for these *varnas* on the basis of their aptitudes *(guna)* and capacity (to observe harder rules). *Sudras* were not treated as untouchables and bod relations with them were not totally forbidden. Whatever restrictions had been imposed in this respect were based on ideas of internal as well as external purity Other castes and *varnas* have also been treated as untouchables and inter-dining with several others was also forbidden.

A *Sudra* has always been treated as an integral part of the society. According to the *Vedas* and in the post *Vedic* period too he was considered an integral part of the social order but on the basis of the modern theories and just to appease the present day public opinion, it will be wrong to say that in the beginning there was no distinction based on *varnas* and there was no rigidity about those distinctions and that it was a later development. Formerly the *Sudras* were treated as equals; they also had the right to change their *varnas* whenever they so desired, but later on the practice was discontinued.

References

1. 10/90.
2. Unpublished thesis; *Artha Shastra Tradition* by Ambadutt Pant.
3. *Mahabharata*, Shanti Parva, ch. 188, Gita Press.
4. *Vayu Purana*, Sanskriti Sansthan, Bareilley Edition, Chapter 56.
5. 1/1/267-68.
6. 2/6/29-30.
7. 1/123.
8. 7/3.
9. 1/13/5.
10. 12/67/17-32.
11. For another story of this type see *Mahabharata* 12/59.

11a. चातुवर्ण्यं मया सृष्टं गुणकर्म विभागशः। (भगवद् गीता ४/१३)

12. 1/4/11-15.
13. *Narada Purana* 1/1/41.
14. *Mahabharata* 1/60/5.
15. P. V. Kane, *History of Dharmashastra*, Vol. I, pp. 4 &7.
16. 1st half of the said portion, p. 28.
17. 35/16-18.
18. 1/113/6.
19. 3/43/5.
20. Quoted from *the Origin & Growth of Caste in India* (Part I), p. 32 by Nripendra Kumar Dutt.
21. *History of Hindu Public Life*, p. 7 Text 8.
22. 2/43/2.
23. 10/109.
24. *Religion & Philosophy of the Veda* (Part I), p. 270.

24a. 9/112/3.

25. Surendra Mittal: *Samaj aur Rajya: Bharatiya Vichar*, p. 106-107.
26. 18/17-18.
27. 12/13.
28. 1/90.
29. Manu 10/64: Yajna 1/96.
30. 4/18.

31. P. V. Kane's *History of Dharamshastra,* pp. 55 & 61.
32. Views of Ibbetson, Risley and Nesfield from the *Census Report* of Russel and the views of Hocart and Slator from "*Caste in India*" by Hutton.
33. Gautam 4/14-17, Baudhayan 1/9/2-15, Vasistha 18/1-10, Vishnu 16, Manu 10/7-56, VajnaValkya 1/91/95, Mahabharata 13/48/1-33, Kautilya 3/7/20-38, Aushnas-Smriti Complete, Apastamba 2/2/6, Agnipuran – 151.
34. For example, *Kautilya Arthashastra* by Kangle, Part 3, pp. 146-147: *India of Vedic Kalpasutras*, pp. 115-116.
35. *History of Dharmasastra* by Kane, Part II, 1st half, p. 169.
36. As the liquor pot, *Atrismriti* 60-61.
37. Gautam 1/45-46, Vashistha 3/48, Manu 5/126 and Yajna, 1/17, Vishnu 60/24.

37a. 5/134-35, 37 b. 5/136-7, 37 c. 60/25-8.

38. *History of Dharmasastra* by Kane, Part II, 1st half, p. 66.
39. Vide author's book "*Samaj Aur Rajya: Bharatiya Vichar*" p. 91-92.
40. *Taitiriya Samhita* 2/5/1/5-6, *Taitirya Brahmana* 3/7/1.
41. 33/2.
42. 5/76/2.
43. *Taitirya Aranyak* 3/5, *Jaiminiya* 3/8/3-11, *Shatpath* 7/1.
44. *Vajasaneyi Samhita* 30/17, 21.
45. Gautam 4/28, Manu 5/85.
46. 4/79.
47. Bharad, 11/22/12, Yajna, 1/148.
48. 1/197.
49. 2/2/8-9.
50. Yajna 2/234, Vishnu 5/104.
51. 10/36, 51.
52. 10/52, 55.
53. 1/12/18 - 20; 2/6/9-10.
54. 2/3/1-8.
55. Apastamba 1/18-19, Gautam 17/17-18, Manu 4/205-20 Yajna, 1/160-65 etc.
56. 10/70/43.
57. *Skanda*, Brahm Khanda 3/15-16, 4/3 *Padma Purana,* Patal Khanda 20, *Narada Purana* 1/1/37.
58. Author's book "*Samaj Aur Rajya: Bharatiya Vichar*" p. 126-127.
59. Baudhayan 1/8/2 Vasistha 1/24-25, Vishnu 24/1-4 Manu 3/13, Yajna, 1/57.

60. 3/44.

61. Vasistha 1/26-27, Vishnu 26/5-6, Manu 3/15-19, Yajya 1/57.

62. *History of Dharma Shastra* by Kane regarding untouchability.

63. Manu 10/126-27.

64. 6/2/19-24.

65. *Bhagwat Purana* 1/4/29, 24-25.

66. Gautam 10/54, 66-67.

67. Manu 10/129, Gautam 10/60-61, 63.

68. Gautam 21/12-14, Manu 8/337-38.

69. In this respect it seems that there is an astonishing similarity between Indian thought and Marxian thought. According to Marx also, all people were equal in the primitive stage, there was no marriage and state system. All lived collectively in communes (primitive communism). He believed in the four stages of History like four *yugas* and accepted that after the fourth stage (capitalism) communism will appear again just as *Satyug* follows *Kalyug* once more. The only difference is that in Marx's view this transformation is a materialistic and economic one i.e. with the change in mode of production, human nature also gets changed, while according to Indian thought the basis of this change is spiritual i.e. these changes are caused by gradual degeneration of character and erosion of religious values.

22

The Depressed Classes

LALA LAJPAT RAI

Originally published in The Modern Review, *Calcutta, July, 1909*

There can be no denying the fact that the rigidity of the Hindu caste system is the bane of Hindu society. It is a great barrier in the way of the social and national progress of Hindus. It confronts them at every step and slackens the speed with which, otherwise, the nation would climb up to the heights of national solidarity. The condition of the "low" castes, sometimes described as "*untouchables*", at other times as the "*depressed classes,*" is nothing short of disgraceful. It is a disgrace to our humanity, our sense of justice, and our feeling of social affinity. It is useless to hope for any solidarity so long as the depressed classes continue to be so low in the social scale as they are. The intellectual and moral status of the community as a whole cannot be appreciably raised without the co-operation of all the classes forming the community. So then, as there are classes amongst us who are untouchable by the so-called superior classes, because of their having been born of certain parents, the moral and intellectual elevation of the community as a whole can only proceed by slow, very slow, degrees. The condition of the depressed classes is a standing blot on our social organisation, and we must remove that blot if we are really desirous of securing the efficiency of our social organism. All the parts of whole must be raised, not necessarily to the same level but to a level from which they can, by their individual efforts, talents and achievements, rise to the highest possible position within the reach of the member of the social organism.

The present arrangement is a cruel and unjust arrangement. Besides, it is both economically and politically unsound. A community which allows so much valuable human material to rot in a state of utter depression and helplessness, cannot be said to be economically wise. As to the political danger involved by the continuance of these classes in their present condition, one need only look at the arguments advanced by our friends of the Muslim League in support of their contention for a larger representation on the Legislative Councils than they are entitled to by virtue of their numerical strength. Quite ignoring the fact that they are as much affected by these classes as the Hindus, they make it a point to say that in counting the Hindu for the purposes of representation the untouchables enumerated with them should be excluded. Whatever may be the value of this argument for the purpose for which it is used here can be no doubt that the existence of these classes in their present deplorable condition is a menace to the power and influence of the Hindu community. The line of argument adopted by our Muslim friends and by some missionary critics of the Reforms Scheme ought to open the eyes of the Hindus to the absolute necessity and urgency of raising the social status of their fellow-religionists, called and known as the members of the depressed classes. Thus from every point of view, whether that of humanity, justice or fair-play, or that of self-interest, it is the bounden duty of the so called high-caste Hindus to give a helping hand to their brothers of the "low castes" and raise them socially as well as intellectually. We are living in a democratic age. The tendencies of democracy are towards the levelling down of all inequalities.

That there are forces working amongst us which will sooner or later demolish all artificial barriers due to accidents of birth between man and man, is patent to all far-sighted people. Under any circumstances then, the day of the depressed classes is bound to come. If so, would i not be wise to take time by the forelock, and to take in hand, in all willingness, what other forces, which are not in our control, must perforce bring about? I say this not because I have the least doubt about the shocking injustice involved in the existing arrangements, but because it is perfectly legitimate to point out the moral of our neglecting to do what is right, and by the weight of that moral to ask people to avoid the evil consequences of letting the forces of nature to have their own revenge. Morality requires that we should take to the work of elevating the depressed classes out of a sheer sense of justice and humanity regardless of any outside considerations. But to appeal in the name of expediency, when the latter strengthens the demands of morality and humanity, involves no breach of principle, and we may very well point out that the communal interest of the Hindus also lies that way. There are agencies at work which are doing their best to remove these Hindus from the pale of Hinduism, which, bereft of these classes, might live, but only as an exhausted frame. The classes themselves are anxious to remain Hindus even though the latter may not promise them the fullest social privileges which they may be in a position to obtain by change of religion. The only thing for Hinduism to do is to meet them half way at once and remove at least the principal grounds of their depression. The least that we can do without delay is to make the untouchables touchable and take away the sting out of their names. Hindu who is not prepared to do even this is an enemy to the community, however unconscious he may be of the great injury he is causing it thereby. I confess, we, the educated Hindus, are not doing our duty in the matter honestly and manfully. Most of our time and energies are employed in agitating for trivial political rights, the good of which can at best be remote, to the neglect of questions upon the right solution of which depends our immediate safety as a nation. I am only repeating what I have already said times out of number that the work of nation-building must be begun from below. The nation that has to be built up lives in huts and not in palaces. Legislative Councils principally composed of the latter are not likely to be the best instruments of building the nation from below. I say this without in any way disparaging the agitation to obtain more legislative powers. But I cannot help saying that to me there seems to be a lack of proportion in the importance that is being attached to a scheme which for the present at least altogether ignores the masses as well as the lower middle classes.

II

In educated circles there seems to be fairly practical unanimity as to the inherent injustice and monstrosity of the existing system; nay, even further, there seems to be an agreement as to the desirability of taking steps to elevate the moral, material and social condition of the caste system. What stand in the way of progress in this direction, however, is the prejudice of the illiterate and the apathy of the educated classes. The former are wanting in that broad outlook on human affairs without which the consciousness of a sense of corporate social responsibility is slow to awaken, the latter lack in that backbone without which it is impossible to bring about changes which look radical but the absence of which blocks the avenues that lead to national consciousness and national solidarity.

For the latter purpose what is required is fairness and humanity at least, if not perfect equality in the relations of the different units that compose the social organism.

At the present moment the greatest strength of the Hindus consists in their number. It is true that intellectually and educationally, in trade and commerce, in brain and body, in mind and muscles, in the arts of peace and war, they are second to none. But in their numerical strength lies that power which is not shared by any other community in this country. This numerical strength, however, may easily be converted into the chief source of their weakness if not properly organised for national purposes. At first sight the Hindus look a heterogeneous mass of untidy humanity without any ties to bind them to one another. Their lack of homogeneity is their curse. To an outsider they seem to agree in nothing. Caste and inter-caste jealousies block the way to progress. The energies which should be spent in bringing about solidarity are being spent in rearing up individuality in the different social units which make up the community. The *Brahman*, the *Khatri*, the *Baniya*, the *Kayastha*, the *Rajput*, the *Jat*; among *Brahmans* the *Gaur*, the *Sanadhya*, the *Nagar*, the *Kanaujia*; &c &c. are all dominated by separatist tendencies. Their collective ambition moves in the circumscribed circle of their own little group, which gives a sectional or rather only a sub-sectional colour to their patriotism or nationalism, but what is even worse is their attitude towards the lower classes and the latter's attempt to retaliate. The former's denial of equal or any opportunities of worship to the latter in their temples or shrines is a standing disgrace to the good name of Hinduism. The so much boasted of tolerance of the Hindus disappears, the moment that tolerance is demanded by the classes lower in the social scale. The high-caste Hindus of the present day, men who have received their education under Western ideals, are often heard to speak with pride of the spirit of toleration possessed and shown by Hinduism towards other religions and other communities, but a critic may very well say that this toleration is the offspring of fear or greed. You dare not be uncivil or unkind to Mohammedans or Christians because they can make matters unpleasant for you, but you are insolent towards your own people, whom you think you can defy without any fear of retaliation. The consequences are plain and can be seen even running. The Hindus are going down in numbers. Your insolence towards the lower classes of Hindus is being repaid by the latter running their back on you. Mohammedanism and Christianity are extending their arms to embrace them and indications are not wanting of the readiness of the lower classes of Hindus to accept the hospitality of non-Hindu religions and social systems. Why, the reason is obvious. As a Hindu you won't touch him; you would not let him sit on the same carpet with you, you would not offer him water in your cups, you would not accept water or food touched by him; you would not let him enter your temples, in fact you would not treat him like a human being. The moment, however, he becomes a Mohammedan or a Christian, without even giving up his ancestral occupation, you are all smiles to him, you welcome him to your home; and have no objection at times to offer him drink and food in your utensils etc. It is a deep-rooted sentiment that has so far prevented the depressed classes of Hindus from deserting Hinduism *en-masse* Sentiments are, however, melting away before the matter-of-fact civilization of the West. The time does not seem to be very distant when sentiment will cease to control the desire of the depressed classes to better their social position, if it cannot be had otherwise than by a change of faith. There are circumstances and causes in the environments of these c asses which are working with effect to bring about that consummation and if the Hindus want to avoid that catastrophe, it is time that they subordinated there caste-pride to the exigencies of the situation and took time by the forelock.

III

Commenting on the figures of the Census of 1901, giving the respective strength of the three principal religions of India, Sir H. Risley remarks:

"During the ten years preceding the census of 1901, the Mohammedans increased by 9 per cent, and the Christians by nearly 28 per cent. Hinduism is the dominant religion of India; in all its developments it is intimately associated with caste, and the two sets of factors, the social and the religious, can hardly be considered apart. The two rival creeds, Christianity and Islam, for Buddhism may be left out of account, avowedly reject the principle of caste, and have been affected by its influence solely through their contact with Hinduism. So long as Hinduism shows no decline from its present strength, caste will preserve its ancient reign, and nothing short of a great accession of strength to either Islam or Christianity can materially modify the social and religious future of India. Are there any signs of a tendency in this direction? Can the figures of the last census be regarded as in any sense the forerunners of an Islamic or Christian revival which will threaten the citadel of Hinduism or will Hinduism hold its own in the future as it has done through the long ages of the past?

"The statistics of the last census show that during a decade of famine the Mohammedans in India increased by nine per cent. No doubt these proportions affected by the fact that the famines were most severe in those parts of the country where the Mohammedans are relatively least numerous, but in the fertile and wealthy region of Eastern Bengal, which has never been touched by real famine, though people on small fixed incomes suffer from high prices, their rate of increase was 12.3 per cent, or nearly double that of the Hindus. The figures illustrating the proportion of children tell a similar tale, and indicate that in that part of India the Mohammedans are not only more enterprising and therefore better off than their Hindu neighbours, but also more prolific and more careful of their offspring."

Sir H. Risley then explains the reasons for these conditions, with some of which we are not directly concerned just now. One of the causes contributing to the increase in the number of Mohammedans is said to be conversions to Islam, about which he remarks:

"Conversions from Hinduism to Islam must also contribute in some degree to the relatively more rapid growth of the Mohammedan population. Here no appeal to statistics is possible, but a number of specific instances of such changes of religion were extracted by Mr. Gait, C.I.E., from the reports of Hindu and Mohammedan gentlemen in 24 Districts and published as Appendix II to the Bengal Census Report of 1901. The motives assigned in various cases–names and particulars are usually given–may be grouped somewhat as follows:

1. Genuine religious conviction of the purity and simplicity of Islam, derived from study of the Mohammedan scriptures or from the preaching of the *Maulvies* who go round the villages.
2. The growing desire on the part of lower Hindu castes to improve their social position leads individuals among them to embrace a creed which seems to offer them a fair chance in life. *Malis, Kahars, Gowalas, Napits, Kans, Baildars* and other castes of similar status furnish numerous illustrations of this tendency.
3. Causes connected with taboos on food and drink and with various caste misdemeanors have also to be taken into account. Hindus in sickness and distress are tended by Mohammedans and take food and water from their hands; the caste excommunicates them and they join the ranks of a more merciful faith.

It is needless to observe that none of these causes, nor all of them taken together, exercise an influence wide and potent enough to bring about a great Islamic revival in India. The day of conversions *en masse* has passed, and there are no signs of its return. Nevertheless certain tendencies are discernible which may add materially to the number of individual conversions. On the one hand, the Mohammedans may raise their standard of education, they may organize and consolidate their influence, they may establish their claim to larger representation in the Legislative Councils and in Government service, and they may thus come to play in Indian public life a part more worthy of the history and traditions of their faith. On the other hand, the spread of English education among the middle and lower ranks of the Hindus may lead to a revolt against the intolerance of the higher castes, and in particular against their virtual monopoly of place and power.

In Southern India whole castes have been known to become Mohammedans because the *Brahmans* would not allow them to enter

Hindu temples and compelled them to worship outside. It is conceivable that other parts of India will someday realize that for the low-born Hindu the shortest road to success in life, whether at the bar or at the public service, may lie through the portals of Islam.

Faithful to its earliest traditions, Christianity in India has from the first devoted itself to the poor and lowly, and its most conspicuous successes have been attained among the Animists and the depressed of Hinduism. To the Animist haunted by a crowd of greedy and malevolent demons ever thirsty for blood, like the ghosts that flocked round Ulysses, Christianity opens a new world of love and hope, To the Pariah, the Mahar, the Dher and a host of other helots, it promises release from the most searching and relentless form of social tyranny–the tyranny of caste; it offers them independence, self-respect, education, advancement, a new life in an organised and progressive society. "These People", says Mr. Francis, writing of the pariahs of the South, "have little to lose by forsaking the creed of their fore-fathers. As long as they remain Hindus they are daily and hourly made to feel that they are of commoner day than their neighbours. Any attempts which they may make to educate themselves or their children are actively discouraged by the classes above them; castes-restrictions prevent them from quitting the toilsome, uncertain and undignified means of subsistence to which custom has condemned them, and taking to a handicraft or a trade; they are snubbed and repressed on all public occasions; are refused admission even to the temples of their gods and can hope for no more helpful partner of their joys and sorrows than the unkempt and unhandy maiden of the paracheri with her very primitive notions of comfort and cleanliness. But once a youth from among these people becomes Christian his whole horizon changes. He is as carefully educated as if he was a *Brahman*; he is put in the way of learning a trade or obtaining an appointment as a clerk; he is treated with kindness and even familiarity by missionaries who belong to the ruling race (! !); he takes an equal part with his elders and betters in the services of the church; and in due time he can choose from among the neat-handed girls of the Mission a wife skilled in domestic matters and even endowed with some little learning. Now-a-days active persecution of converts to Christianity is rare. So those who hearken to its teaching have no martyr's crown to wear, and sheltered, as they often are, in a compound round the missionary's bungalow, it matters little to its adherents if their neighbours look askance upon them. The remarkable growth in the numbers of the native Christians thus largely proceeds from the natural and laudable discontent with their lot which possesses the lower classes of the Hindus, and so well do the converts as a class use their opportunities that the community is earning for itself a constantly improving position in the public estimation."

Making a sufficient allowance for the Padri's anxiety to paint thick–Hinduism black and the chances afforded by conversion to Christianity bright–there remains enough to put the thoughtful Hindu to shame. We do not mind those cases of apostasy from Hinduism where the change of religion results from a change of religious convictions, but we have every reason to be ashamed of those conversions that are the direct result of our insolence and inhumanities towards the so-called lower classes. It is high time that our indifference to the lot of the depressed classes ceased and we gave them a new start in social life.

These quotations should leave no doubt in the mind of any Hindu as to the urgency and importance of the question of improving the lot of the depressed classes and of raising their social status. I am of opinion that the matter should be taken in hand in each province by influential provincial committees composed of men of provincial reputation. Depressed classes missions for smaller area should be organised under the guidance and control of these committees and the work pushed through with earnestness and zeal. The sympathies of young men should be enlisted, from whom eventually some may be inclined to make it their life-work. The subject has an important bearing on famine relief and the development of home industries, from which point of view I intend to discuss it in another article.

—Cited from '*Writings and Speeches*', Vol. 1 (pp. 166-176).

VIVEKANAND'S CALL FOR ACTION

The Caste-system is opposed to the religion of the *Vedanta*. Caste is a social custom, and all our great preachers have tried to break it down. From Buddhism downwards, every sect has preached against caste, and every time it has only riveted the chains. Caste is simply the outgrowth of the political institutions of India; it is a hereditary trade guild. Trade competition with Europe has broken caste more than my teaching.[1] In religion there is no caste; caste is simply a social custom.[2]

Modern caste distinction is a barrier to India's progress. It narrows, restricts, separates. It will crumble before the advance of ideas.[3]

The peasant, the shoemaker, the sweeper, and such other lower classes of India have much greater capacity for work and self-reliance than you. They have been silently working through long ages, and producing the entire wealth of the land, without a word of complaint.[4]

Never mind if they have not read a few books like you, if they have not acquired your tailor-made civilization. What do these matter? But they are the backbone of a nation in all countries. If these lower classes stop work, where will you get your food, clothing from? If the sweepers of

Calcutta stop work for a day, it creates a panic; and if they strike for three days, the whole town will be depopulated by the outbreak of epidemics. If the labourers stop work, your supply of food and clothes also stops. And you regard them as low class people and vaunt about your own culture.[5]

Who will bring light to them–who will travel from door to door bringing education to them? Let these people be your God–think of them, work for them, pray for them incessantly–the Lord will show you the way. Him call *mahatman* (great soul) whose heart bleeds for the poor, otherwise he is a *duratman* (wicked soul). Let us unite our wills in continued prayer for their good. We may die unknown, unpitied, unbewailed, without accomplishing anything, but not one thought will be lost. It will take effect, sooner or later. My heart is too full to express my feelings; you know it, you can imagine it. So long as he millions live in hunger and ignorance, I hold every man a traitor, who having been educated at their expense, pays not the least heed to them; I call those men, who strut about in their finery, having got all their money by grinding the poor, wretches so long as they do not do anything for those two hundred millions who are now no better than hungry savages![6]

Cited from Swami Vivekananda: *Caste. Culture and Socialism,* (Calcutta, 1979).

23

Ambedkar's Journey to Mass Conversion

Bhagwan Das

Born in an 'untouchable' family in Himachal Pradesh; embraced Buddhism in February 1957; Founder Chairman, Ambedkar Mission Society; Chairman, All India Samata Sainik Dal founded by Dr. Baba Saheb Ambedkar; Regional Secretary, Indian Buddhist Council; Director, Asian Centre for Human Rights; Member Executive, World Conference on Religion and Peace (Indian Committee); Author of many books and practising lawyer in Delhi

Dr. Bhim Rao Ambedkar was born in an 'untouchable' family of Maharashtra. His father was employed as a *Subedar* in the Bombay Presidency Army of East India Company. *Subedar* was the highest rank that an Indian in British Army could attain in the last decades of the eighteenth century. The family was by no means poor nor in the army cantonments did Ambedkar experience any discrimination, being the son of a Junior Commissioned Army Officer. Outside the cantonment the life was different. As a young boy he was shocked when he could not hire a bullock cart to take him to his father's house. After de-mobilisation his father was employed as a Treasurer. In civil life they experienced a lot of humiliation and harassment at the hands of the upper caste

Hindus. Ever after his return from United States of America and England, loaded with degrees in many disciplines, when he was appointed as a high ranking officer in Baroda *Darbar* he was insulted by the menial servants in his office who rolled the carpet before him for fear of pollution and threw files at his table from a distance. In spite of his higher rank, outstanding education and impressive personality, he could not hire a house in the city of Baroda. Even the Manager of a Parsee *Dharamsala*, where he was staying, drove him out and threatened to assault him. When he set up legal practice in Bombay High Court, no solicitor was ready to work with an 'untouchable' barrister. These bitter experiences left many a scar on his sensitive mind. The story of Moses, the prophet of Jews, was being repeated here.

Dr. Ambedkar was a religious man. Like most Untouchable and *Shudra* families, his father was also an admirer of Saints. Saints, many of them born among the Untouchables, sang the praises of Krishna, Rama, Vithal etc., labouring under the belief that they were the saviors of the poor and the low. Saints throughout the world were prophets, rebellious and ridiculed learning because the learned had oppressed and exploited the poor people.

Ambedkar's Early Views

Dr. Ambedkar quite naturally protested against this treatment meted out to him and his people throughout the Presidency. But he did not blame Hindu religion for this inhumanity and indignities heaped on him by the caste Hindus. His letter-pad had the image of Bhawani and the words 'Jai Bhawani' printed underneath on the left hand corner of every sheet. He used to pray according to Hindu customs as it was done in affluent *Mahar* families in imitation of the caste Hindus.

Owing to the harassment and oppression of Untouchables many of them were renouncing Hinduism and embracing Christianity. In other parts they were becoming increasingly restless. In Kerala the Untouchables had launched an agitation at Vaikom for the right to walk or the road some fifty yards away from the temple, which under the existing law and practice they were not allowed to use. Depressed Classes in Bombay had been agitating for equality and justice and asking for a share in services, especially police. A Depressed Classes Conference was organised and Dr. Ambedkar, who had recently returned from England, was invited to address the people. He spoke against conversion of Untouchables to other religions, as a means of removing disabilities. He stressed self-improvement, unity and organization as the road to better life for the Untouchables. He said, "If we remain Hindus as we are, then the Aryan religion will be preserved in this country. On the other hand if we become Muslims, then there will be a predominance of that foreign culture in

India. If this were not so, the *Brahmans* would not have been ready to offer *Satyagraha* for the Untouchable class at Vaikom".[1]

From a perusal of his paper written in Columbia University, which was published in 1916-17 under the title 'Caste in India', it appears, that he had studied the origin and mechanism of caste system very thoroughly but until then he had not lost faith in the Hindu reformers who were trying to remove some of the cobwebs from Indian life.

But the events and the role of the Hindu leaders and hypocrisy of Hindu life disillusioned him very soon. Untouchables were not allowed to draw water from tanks in many towns of Bombay Presidency. Mahad agitation (1927) led by Dr. Ambedkar and the court case in respect of Chowdhar Tank were the first struggles which united the Untouchables under the leadership of Dr. Ambedkar. *Manusmriti,* the law book of Manu, which had influenced the behaviour of Hindus very much, was publicly burnt and thus started a rebellion against Hinduism. The first Round Table Conference was held in London in 1930. Dr. Ambedkar was invited to represent the Untouchables and he spoke forcefully about the plight of the Untouchables and the apathetic attitude of the Government. In the Second Round Table Conference, Gandhiji attended the Conference as the sole representative of the Untouchables. It appears he had been writing very much in his papers and addressing many meetings but had not been reading much, for he believed that Dr. Ambedkar who was championing the cause of Untouchables was perhaps a Maharashtrian *Brahmin*. Gandhiji claimed to represent all–Hindus, Moslems and the Depressed Classes. He went even so far as to say that Dr. Ambedkar does not represent the Untouchables. On the question of separate representation to Untouchables Gandhi stubbornly opposed the demand of the Untouchables, His apprehension was that by this step Untouchables would be separated from Hindu community and that would weaken Hinduism.

Poona Pact

After coming back to India, Gandhi went on fast-unto-death to deprive the Untouchables of the right to elect their own representatives which they were granted under the Communal Award (1932) granted by the British Government in response to their request, since the Indian delegates had failed to arrive at a decision in respect of the minorities. To save Gandhiji's life a compromise agreement was signed by Dr. Ambedkar and other Hindu leaders, which is popularly known as Poona Pact. Under the Communal Award, Untouchables were granted 78 seats with a right to elect their own candidates and also the right to vote in the general seats. Under this pact they were granted 148 seats with 18% reservation in the Central legislature, but the right to elect their own candidates was withdrawn. In its place a very expensive and complicated method was adopted. The final election rested in the hands of the majority community. Dr. Ambedkar approached Gandhiji proposing a change in view of the expenses and practical difficulties but the latter declined his suggestion saying that the arrangement envisaged in the Poona Pact was the best one.

Atrocities, social boycotts and persecution of Untouchables continued in the country side. Hindus would write articles, deliver lengthy speeches, pass very convincing and heartening resolutions in their Conferences, stage inter-dining *tamashas* but failed to translate their pious thoughts into action. The result was that the Untouchables began to lose faith in Hinduism; many even renounced Hinduism to embrace other religions.

Gandhiji, the greatest leader born among the Hindus after Shankaracharya, was keener on strengthening Hinduism than on striking at the roots of the evil of caste. He wanted to remove Untouchability but glorified *Varnashram Dharma* which he considered an ideal and divine system based on division of labour. He could not afford to antagonise Hindus, especially the trading communities who provided funds for his political activities, nor did he want to touch the problem of caste, for caste sustained Hinduism to a great extent.

Dr. Ambedkar did not believe that the problem of Untouchability and discrimination could be solved through legislation or by getting representation in the legislature. Speaking in the Hindu Conference held at Bombay on the 25th September, 1932 (the Poona Pact was signed on the 24th September at Yervada), Dr. Ambedkar warned the Hindus of the likely developments:

> "I do not believe that the joint electorates are going to be the final solution for the problem of absorbing the Depressed Classes in the Hindu Community. Any electoral arrangement, I believe, cannot be a solution of the larger social problem. It requires more than any political arrangement, and I hope that it would be possible for you to go beyond this political arrangement that we are making today and devise ways and means whereby it would be possible for the Depressed Classes not only to be part and parcel of the Hindu community but also to occupy an honourable position, a position of equality of status in the community."

Concluding he said:

> "So long as the Depressed Classes were an ignorant lot, not imbued with a sense of self respect, it was possible for them to accept the social status that was given to them by Hindu laws, but as they get education they will begin to smart under these social laws and there is a great danger of their seceding from the Hindu

society. I beg of you to bear that in mind and hope that you will do the needful in the matter."[2]

Yeola Conference (1935)

Untouchables were holding conferences in different parts of India. Rao Bahadur M.C. Raja was in the Hindu camp. A conference of the Untouchables was held at Yeola, a town in the district of Nasik. Thousands of people had come to attend the meeting which was held in the afternoon of 13th October 1935. Shocking news of atrocities were being received from all parts of India in the office of Dr. Ambedkar. At that time he was working as Principal of a Law College but devoted considerable time towards the service of his people. Yeola meeting was addressed by many leaders of the Untouchables. They were more anxious to hear their beloved leader, Dr. Ambedkar. In his presidential address he spoke about the difficulties of his people, and discriminatory treatment meted out to them in all spheres of life. Finally, he announced that he had decided to renounce Hinduism for good and embrace some other religion which promised equality.

> In a voice charged with anguish and sorrow he said "It grieved me very much to state how tyrannical caste-Hindus thwarted our attempts throughout the country to obtain our rights as members of the Hindu community."

Referring to the Kalaram Temple agitation and Ram Rath Yatra agitation, he said:

> "I realize now that the time, money and efforts spent over these matters have come to nought. I believe that the time has come to make a decision in the matter and settle the question of our future. The disabilities we have suffered and the indignities we had to put up with were the result of our being the members of the Hindu community. Will it not be better for us to leave that fold and embrace a new faith that would give us an equal status, a secure position and rightful treatment? I advise you to sever your connection with Hinduism and to embrace any other religion. But in doing so, be careful in choosing the new faith and see that equality of treatment, status and opportunities will be guaranteed to you unreservedly."[3]

An Undelivered Presidential Address

During the same period he had been invited to a Conference of the *Jat Pat Todak Mandal*, an organisation of the Arya Samajists of Punjab. On reading the Yeola Declaration about renunciation of Hinduism in newspapers, the organisers got panicky. They sent an office bearer of the organisation to obtain an advance copy of the lecture prepared by

Dr. Ambedkar. Dr. Ambedkar declined the invitation to preside at their Conference and got his Address printed at his cost. In his undelivered Presidential Address, he reiterated his earlier stand to renounce Hinduism.

In the concluding part of this speech Dr. Ambedkar had written:

> "......these views are the views of a man, who has been no tool of power, nor flatterer of greatness. They come from one, almost the whole of whose public exertion has been one continuous struggle for liberty for the poor and for the oppressed and whose only reward has been a continuous shower of calumny and abuse from national journals and national leaders, for no other reason except that I refused to join with them in performing the miracle–I will not say trick–of liberating the oppressed with the gold of the tyrant and raising the poor with the cash of the rich. All this may not be enough to commend my views. I think they are not likely to alter yours. But whether they do or do not, the responsibility is entirely yours. You must make your efforts to uproot caste, if not in my way, then in your way. *I* am sorry, I will not be with you. I have decided to change."[4]

This last sentence the Mandal desired to be deleted for fear of offending the Hindus, especially the Arya Samajists in the Punjab but how could Dr. Ambedkar sacrifice his prerogative as President of the Conference to say whatever he wanted and considered relevant?

If some people believed that perhaps Dr. Ambedkar had made the declaration at Yeola on the spur of a moment, there was now no doubt left in the minds of such people in regard to his determination to renounce his religion.

Kavitha Incident

Gandhiji attributed his decision to the incident at Kavitha, a village in Gujarat where two untouchable boys had been admitted to a Government school and the villagers belonging to Garassia caste–a land holding caste of Gujarat–were forcing the parents to withdraw their children because they could not suffer to have their children sit in the same class with the lowly untouchable boys. The Untouchables of the village were also adamant not to withdraw the boys. The Garassias used coercive measures and enforced a boycott forbidding the shopkeepers to sell victuals, obstructing their entry in the locality and not allowing their cattle to graze in the village land. The boycott and harassment continued for more than two weeks and finally the high caste villagers poured kerosene in the wells so as to deprive them of the drinking water. It was the month of June, the hottest month of the summer and this was the torture of the worst kind which could be inflicted on poor, innocent Untouchable women, children and men of the village.

The brutality and the inhumanity of the Hindus of Kavitha did not shock the conscience of the Hindus, but the fear of losing the Untouchables as a result of call given by Dr. Ambedkar sent tremors far and wide in the whole Hindu world. Same kind of "dramas", which were enacted during the four days of Gandhiji's fast it Yerwada in September 1932, began to be enacted again to woo the Untouchables and dissuade them from following the advice of Dr. Ambedkar. Hindus condemned this call for conversion and exhorted the Untouchables not to forsake Hindu religion which is the religion of their ancestors. Hindu leaders approached Dr. Ambedkar also and appealed to him not to change his religion.

Hindus always sing praises of their religion and consider their religion to be the best religion of the world. Sarvapalli Radhakrishnan, the greater philosopher who rose to be the President of India, wrote:

"Though people of different races and cultures have been pouring in India from the dawn of history, Hinduism has been able to maintain its supremacy and even the proselytising creeds backed by political power have not been able to coerce the large majority of Hindus to their views. The Hindu culture possesses some other more forceful currents."[5]

Hinduism: Two Views

Gandhiji also held similar views about Hinduism. In fact, he was the greatest Hindu religious leader born after Shankaracharya. According to Gandhi:

> ".....there is something in Hinduism that has kept it alive up till now. It has witnessed the fall of Babylonian, Syrian, Persian and Egyptian civilizations. Cast a look around you. Where is Rome and where is Greece? Can you find today anywhere the Italy of Gibbons or rather the ancient Rome, for Rome was Italy? Go to Greece, where is the world famous Attic civilisation? Then come to India, let you go through the most ancient records and then look around you and you would be constrained to say, 'Yes, I see here ancient India still living."[6]

Baba Saheb Ambedkar was not impressed by this boastful talk about the glory and greatness of Hinduism, which had driven millions of its people to the sub-human level of animals. Dr. Amedkar judged this civilisation in a different manner:

> "......the question is not whether a community lives or dies. The question is on what plane does it live. There are different modes of survival. But ail are not equally honourable. For an individual, as for a society, there is a gulf between merely living and living worthily. To fight in the battle and Jive in glory is one mode. To beat a retreat, to surrender and to live the life of a captive is also a

> mode of survival. It is useless for a Hindu to take comfort in this fact that he and his people have survived. What he must consider is what is the quality of their survival."[7]

The more he studied Hinduism and saw its functioning, the more hardened his views about Hinduism became.

Hinduism had kept millions of it people ignorant. Education was the monopoly of the *Brahmins* who also performed priestly duties. Owing to division of caste there was no mobility upward. They deliberately kept millions of people illiterate and ignorant. Poverty was imposed on the majority of the people. In later period, the Saints misguided by *Brahmin* leaders further worsened the situation by glorifying poverty and condemning the intellectuals because the educated classes had been exploiting the poor. Society was fragmented. The result was slavery stretching over thousands of years. Inequality and poverty gave rise to disparities in all the spheres of life. Hinduism introduced the dogma of, what Dr. Ambedkar called, 'graded inequality'.

> "This graded inequality is not accidental or incidental. It is the religion of Hinduism", he wrote describing the causes for lack of unity in Hindu society, "The graded inequality is the official doctrine of Hinduism. It is sacred and no Hindu can think of doing away with it. The Hindu communal majority, with its religion of graded inequality is, therefore, not a passing phase. It is a permanent fact and a menace forever."

Hinduism-a blasphemy

From the point of view of the Untouchables the history of social life of Hinduism is nothing but the history of treachery and deception, bunkum and blasphemy, exploitation and oppression, fallacies and hypocricy. The Hindus have not only deprived the Untouchables of the fruits of their labour but also tried to falsify their history. They have tried to rob them of their tradition and history. Just to prove the veracity of caste system and theory of incarnation and rebirth, they branded almost all the saints born among the Untouchables as bastards or illegitimate sons of philandering *Brahmins*, since any acknowledgement of their greatness and nobility of character coupled with the acquisition of wisdom and knowledge would have been tantamount to refutation of the theory of caste and supremacy of *Brahmins*. Valmiki, they said, was a scion of a *Brahmin* family but was spoilt in the company of the low caste people. Tiruvalluvar was an abandoned *Brahmin* child found in a bush and brought up by untouchables. Kabir was not born in a family of untouchable weaver but was the son of a *Brahmin* found by a weaver. Ravidas was not born among the *Chamars* but an illegitimate child found and brought up by a *Chamar* family. They did not end up there. "Immediately after his birth", they wrote, "he refused to suck has mother's breast for fear of pollution because he was a *Brahmin* in past birth".

Hindus did not spare even Dr. Ambedkar. A whispering campaign was started to malign and degrade him in the eyes of his people. *Brahmins* in Maharashtra started the rumour that Ambedkar, the leader of the Untouchables, was the illegitimate son of a Maratha ruler. The Sikhs in their zeal to convert Ambedkar to their way of thinking and to coerce him to embrace Sikhism, even wanted to use it as a threat. The Russian Scholars guided or misguided by their Communist comrades in India went a step further and wrote in the Contemporary History of India that Dr. Ambedkar was the illegitimate son of a Maharaja. In view of such facts, no wonder Dr. Ambedkar held that "The Hindu civilization…..could hardly be called a civilization. It is a diabolical contrivance to suppress and enslave humanity. Its proper name should be infamy".

Dr. Ambedkar saw no hope for the Untouchables in Hinduism. In view of the teachings of the *Shastras* any reform would be superfluous and temporary. At best a few more new castes could be added thus adding to the burden and misery of those sitting at the lowest rung of the ladder.

Gandhi, the defender of Caste System

Gandhi, the greatest Hindu leader, who spoke authoritatively about Hinduism, further convinced Dr. Ambedkar that conversion was the only way to escape the tyranny of Hinduism. Gandhi's writings, couched in the Mahatmaic language, added fuel to the fire and instead of alleviating the suffering of the people added to their misery. We give below a few extract from gardhis writings during the crucial period preceding the Yeola announcement made on 13th October, 1935.

"As a reformer of Hinduism, I want to restore the ancient *Varnashrama Dharma* to its pristine purity. *Varnashrama* lays down the functions and duties of various classes according to their special aptitude and gifts and has nothing to do with questions of marriage and food and drink."[8]

"Belief in and practice of *Varnashrama Dharma* may be said to be the distinguishing characteristics of Hindu *Dharma*. I regard myself a *Sanatani* Hindu, because I try, to the best of my ability, to obey eternal precepts of the faith as embodied in *shastras* as I understand them."[9]

"Both the *Brahmin* and *Shudra* who forsake their *Swadharma* are fallen. In their fallen state, they belong to no *Varna.* They can repair their mistakes by resuming *Swadharma,* their own calling.[10]

"In my opinion, it is not the caste that has made us what we are. It was our greed and disregard of essential virtues which enslaved us. I believe that caste has saved Hinduism from disintegration…..I am certainly against any attempt at destroying the fundamental divisions. The caste system is not based on inequality, there is no question of inferiority; and so far as there is any such question arising, the tendency should undoubtedly be checked. But there appears to be no valid reason for ending the system because of its abuse."[11]

They give us some inkling of the views of Gandhiji, who was the greatest Hindu-leader of the twentieth century. Untouchables who were the worst sufferers under caste system could not accept these views as correct. Such views only convinced them that there was something wrong with Hinduism. The real enemy was not the poor ignorant Hindu but his religion.

When Dr. Ambedkar declared at Yeola that he would renounce Hinduism, Gandhiji thought it was owing to the Kavitha incident that he had decided to change his religion. Dr. Ambedkar retorted by saying,

> "Let none think that I have done this in a huff or as a matter of wrath against the treatment meted out to the Depressed Classes at the village of Kavitha or any other place. It is a deeply deliberated decision. I agree with Mr. Gandhi that religion is necessary, but I do not agree that man must keep to his ancestral religion, even if he finds that religion repugnant to his notions, the sort of the religion he needs, as the standard for the regulation of his own conduct and as a source of inspiration for his advancement and well-being. My only advice is that Mr. Gandhi should allow the Depressed Classes to chalk out their own line of action. *Kavitha Does Not Represent an Isolated Incident.*"[12]

Meanwhile, leaders of many religions approached Dr. Ambedkar and tried to persuade him to accept their respective religions. Christians expected conversions at a scale larger than they had ever had in India. Some missionaries approached their headquarters in England for making provision for larger funds. Some leaders of the Church, who did not favour mass conversions, also had a second thought. Muslims in Bombay approached Dr. Ambedkar and a Youth organisation invited Mr. Khalid Latif Gauba, a Mohammedan lawyer, son of Lala Harikishan Lal Gauba, a famous Minister of North West Frontier to persuade Dr. Ambedkar to embrace Islam. Meanwhile Thiya community in Kerala decided to renounce Hinduism. They invited Dr. Ambedkar to address their conference. Many of them embraced Christianity. Some embraced Islam and some fifty members of Thiya community embraced Sikhism. Sikhs offered to set up a college for the benefit of the Schedules Castes in B0ombay to coax Dr. Ambedkar. He sent his nephew and an assistant to Punjab to see how Sikhism is practised. Like many outsiders Dr. Ambedkar believed that Sikhism is a better religion. In one of his speeches he showered praises on Sikhism saying that Sikhs did not believe in caste and untouchability and allowed everybody to enter their *Gurudwaras*.

In the Hindu Mahasabha Conference which was held immediately after this sensational declaration, Hindu leaders condemned his move for conversion. Dr. Kurtkoti, Shankaracharya of *Karveer* supported the move but advised the Untouchables to embrace Sikhism for he did not find much difference between the Sikhs and Hindus. Sikhs fought for the defence and protection of cow and *Brahmin* and Hinduism in general, was his argument.

But other Hindu leaders including Madan Mohan Malaviya and prominent leaders from Punjab did not favour conversion to Sikhism. They intensified their propaganda to keep the Untouchables within the Hindu fold. Gandhiji, who had asked the Sikh leaders to close their community kitchen during Vaikom agitation since removal of untouchability was the internal affair of the Hindu society and Sikhs should not meddle with it, also did not favour conversion of Untouchables to Sikhism.

It is understood on good authority that his Highness the Maharaja of Patiala had offered Ministership to Dr. Ambedkar but he declined the offer. His Exalted Highness the Nizam of Hyderabad was the richest ruler of a state in India. In ordinary life Nizam was parsimonious where expenditure was concerned, but it is understood he offered 4 crores of rupees to Dr. Ambedkar for organising the conversion of whole of the Untouchable population to Islam.

Sikhs were most persistent and they collected money to help the Scheduled Castes. They saw the prospects of becoming the third largest community in India if Dr. Ambedkar embraced Sikhism and advised his followers to embrace Sikhism. Dr. Moonje, the leader of Maha Sabha prevailed upon Dr. Ambedkar to issue a statement in favour of conversion to Sikhism which was prematurely leaked out by Rao Bahadur M. C. Rajah and given wide publicity by national press. Master Tara Singh, leader of the Sikhs, gave a statement in Kerala expressing the difficulties of the Sikhs,

> "......the Sikhs themselves are a comparatively poor people on point of finances. They are not in a position to offer allurement of material benefit to the converts nor would they do so even if they could. Such benefits degrade the giver and the taker. We want people, who after studying Sikhism and the world, feel the will and the urge. We would like people to stand on their own legs. Nor do we want people who will come over simply out of the hatred for or a negative attitude towards Hinduism or, for that matter, towards any religion. The people cannot rise by mere conversion"

A Delegation from Egypt

During one of the Depressed Classes Conferences, held in 1936, a

Moslem scholar from *Al-Azhar*, a Moslem university in Egypt, was also present. He became impressed and, as a good Moslem, saw the prospects of converting a large number of Untouchables to Islam. After few days a meeting was held in the *Al-Azhar* University and they decided to send a delegation to study the situation in India. A letter was addressed to Sir Mohammed Iqbal in Punjab who gave a reply stating that the conversion affected only some southern states and language would be a great difficulty.

Al-Azhar however sent a delegation consisting of five scholars including Prof. Sheikh Ibrahim-el-Gibali, Sheikh Abdel-Wahab-en Naggiar, Sheikh Prof. Mohammed el Adani, Prof. Mohammad Habib, Professor of History in the Theology Faculty and Mohammed Salah-el-Din en Naggiar, son of Sheikh Abdel-Wahab-en Naggiar who worked as the secretary and coordinator. It was stated that the Mission had no fixed or limited programme, its object was to study the situation of the Depressed Classes; to see what *Al-Azhar*, as a cultural and religious institution could do to lead the Untouchables to Islam; to approach, if possible, the leaders of the Depressed Classes and to remove the controversies existing among the leaders of different rites bringing concord among them.

After the Mission landed in India and after the ritual of garlanding and feasting was over, they had discussions with the Moslem leaders. The object of the Mission was declared to be different from what was originally announced. The statement said, "The purpose of the mission to India was to establish relations of mutual acquaintance between Egyptian and Indian Moslems." This was done with a view to avoid hostilities between Hindus and Moslems.

The Egyptian Mission visited many cities in India and submitted a report to the University.[13] A very elaborate programme was drawn up. The text of the report is given below:

Recommendations:

1. If the *Al Azhar* should see fit to undertake any direct work it would be founding the centres for the spread of Islamic Culture and of the message of Islam (in accordance with the scheme attached to the report) in the following places: a Centre in the province of Kerala in the south west of the Deccan, and a centre in the province of Surat in the State of Bombay; a Centre in the province of Dhakka in Little Bengal and a Centre in the province of Rangoon in Burma and a Centre in the Central Provinces.

2. If this should be decided on, it would be advisable to get in touch with Professor Ghulam Bahig Nirang to come to an agreement with him regarding the establishment of these Centres; and likewise, if it should

be desired to expand this work, it would be advisable to establish a Central Administration for it in Lahore which would become the point of contact for those various centres with each other and in turn with *Al-Azhar*.

3. In case *Al-Azhar* felt that it should guard against the difficulties that may conceivably arise, should it decide to send missions under the name of preaching (*Tabligh*), the Mission is of the opinion that in that case *Al Azhar* should send a number of its men to preach Islamic Culture charging them at the same time to get in touch with existing preaching societies and direct them.

Moreover, *Al Azhar* should undertake the following: it should accept as students in *Al Azhar* five outcaste students holding the Matriculation certificate to complete their studies and to specialise in preaching and guidance. It should give financial assistance to the Association of the *Ulema* at Lucknow in return for their receiving twenty out-caste boys in the name of *Al Azhar* to complete their religious education; and give assistance to the Islamic Society at Nagpur in return for its opening new classes for out-caste boys and give assistance to the '*Anjuman*' for preaching of Islam at Ampala on condition that the money given be applied to the preaching of Islam among the outcastes of the Province of Kerala."[13]

It is not known whether the Moslem organisations mentioned above pursued the matter or the rising tide of politics diverted their attention from religious conversion to political power through elections. But it did result in changing the attitude of the Mohammedans towards the Untouchables. In many villages Hindu landlords committed atrocities on the untouchables. Police dominated by the Hindus did not protect the Untouchables and did not even care to register their complaints. Now the Moslems became more sympathetic towards the Untouchables. In administration wherever there was conflict between the Hindus and the Untouchables they helped the Untouchables. Consequently, many among the Untouchables embraced Islam.

Hindu reaction to Conversion Threat

The declaration regarding renunciation of Hinduism was made on the 13th October, 1935 at Yeola. The final decision as to which religion should be embraced was not taken. The matter began to be debated in many quarters. Hindus were agitated because the age-old slaves who provided cheap labour and whom Hinduism had enslaved and incapacitated mentally and physically had challenged the authority of their religion and under the leadership of a charismatic leader, endowed with many virtues like learning, knowledge, character, courage and vision, had threatened to renounce their religion. With their migration to other religions Hindus were to lose their political strength. Mass conversion would affect them economically also. While remaining within the Hindu fold the Untouchables remained disunited, subservient and exploitable, conversion would give them unity. While remaining Hindu, they had no friends. After conversion they would have friends and allies. Moneylender, trader, merchant, priest–all would suffer. So they all combined to make propaganda and to use all possible means to keep them within the Hindu fold and to maintain the status quo. But Ambedkar like Thycidydes believed, "It may be in your interest to be our masters; but how it can be in our interest to be your slaves?"

While Hindus were persuading Dr. Ambedkar to give up his decision to change his religion, they started vigorous propaganda among the Untouchables against conversion. They were appealing the orthodox to accept Untouchables as their brethren and asking them to open the doors of their temples to the Untouchables. At the same time they were encouraging the Untouchables to adopt Hindu customs' etc. so as to keep them away from Moslems and Christians.

Hindus were also staging dramas like 'inter-caste dinners' simply to befool the poor innocent Untouchables in the cities. Many among them after partaking the food prepared or served by the Untouchables either performed purificatory ceremonies or rushed to the Ganga for washing away the sin of pollution contracted through the touch of untouchables.

Dr. Ambedkar with his meager resources was carrying on lie propaganda among the Untouchables. Many conferences were held in different parts of India to discuss the problem. Christians and Mohammedan missionaries were approaching Ambedkar and his people. The Hindus–both Arya Samajists and *Sanatanists* and their organisations like the Indian National Congress and Hindu *Maha Sabha* were also approaching the Untouchables and dissuading them not to change their religion. Ambedkar had thrown a bomb-shell and shocked the Hindus. His views had reached where otherwise they would not have reached at all, had he spoken only a soft or reformatory language, because us tally national papers did not give publicity to his views.

Mahar Conference at Bombay

Meanwhile, it was decided that a conference would be held where final decision would be taken. A conference was held at Bombay on 31st May, 1936. It was not the Depressed Classes Conference but only a conference of the Mahars. Mahars from all parts of India–Hyderabad, Central Provinces and Berar, Bombay Presidency, Mysore etc.–assembled in Bombay. In this conference two major decisions were taken. One was to renounce Hinduism and the other was not to fellow Hindu customs or observes Hindu festivals etc. The following resolution was passed:

"The Conference of the Mahar community in the Bombay Presidency after thorough consideration declares:

a. that a change of religion is the only remedy for the Mahar community to obtain equality;

b. assures Dr. B.R. Ambedkar, their accredited leader, that the Mahar community is prepared to change its religion *en masse*"

c. urges on the Mahar community, as a preliminary step towards the change of religion, to refrain henceforth from worshipping Hindu deities, to put a stop to observance of Hindu festivals and to put a stop to visiting Hindu holy places."

The decision to embrace any religion was deferred indefinitely. This part of the speech was not given much publicity by the national press. The reason why he called only the Mahars was because he thought that approaching his own caste in the matter of conversion was a better method to ascertain their views than approaching individuals. Christians had learnt, particularly in Hyderabad, that the people in India especially those belonging to lower castes embraced Christianity not individually but in groups. After considerable thought Dr. Ambedkar had rejected Christianity and Islam for mass conversion of his people. In a statement which was prepared by him in consultation with Dr. B.S. Moonje of Hindu *Mahasabha* and which was prematurely released by Rao Bahadur M.C. Rajah, partly to malign Ambedkar and partly to become popular with Hindu leaders, Dr. Ambedkar had given reasons for not accepting Islam for which he had great admiration.

Which Religion to Choose

"Islam" he wrote, "seems to give the Depressed Classes all they need. Financially, the resources behind Islam are boundless. Socially, the Mohammedans are spread all over India. There are Mohammedans in every province and they can take care of new converts from the Depressed Classes and render them all help. Politically the Depressed Classes will get all the rights which Mohammedans are entitled to."

The same reasons held good for Christianity notwithstanding the discriminatory treatment meted out to the Untouchable converts in Southern India and the number of the adherent of this religion being very small. But Ambedkar believed that the European and American Christians would help the new converts. Sikhism appealed to him more than any other religion because by embracing Sikhism the Untouchables did not forsake the Indian culture. Sikhs however, needed financial help from the Hindus for converting the Untouchables because, in spite of the existence of some Sikh states in Northern India, the community had few rich men at that time. By adopting Sikhism the Untouchables were also not likely to lose their political rights which they had recently won under the Communal Award and the Poona Pact.

There were other reasons too, which he did not let be known to the Untouchables or to members of the other communities but which are important and were to a great measure responsible for deferring the decision for indefinite period. He knew his strength and the weaknesses of his people. Majority of them was illiterate and ignorant. He had no funds and no infra-structure to carry out such a gigantic programme of conversion of millions of people. Moreover the decision would have adversely effected the elections which were due to be held in February, 1937. One significant reason was the fear of eruption of violence which the mass conversion of Untouchables could result in. This could result in annihilation of innocent people in the rural areas as well as in the cities. In an interview with the editor of a Jewish paper Dr. Ambedkar referred to this eventuality. Hartman, Editor of *Zion's Herald* pointed out,

> "You are not strong enough yet to announce a decision? If you compromise with the Hindus, all is lost. If you choose Mohammedanism, the Hindus will crush you. If you go Christian, both the Hindus and the Moslems will be on your back."

'Exactly', confirmed Dr. Ambedkar, "We are not ready yet."

Adoption of Buddhism (1956)

Final decision was announced some time in 1951 and the final step was taken on the 14th October, 1956, twenty one years after the Yeola declaration. Ambedkar chose Buddhism and formally renounced Hinduism and embraced Buddhism along with many lakhs of his followers at Nagpur on 14th October, J956. Although bulk of the followers belonged to the Mahar caste of Maharashtra, yet many thousands of hem living in other states also took a decision to renounce Hinduism. In the 1951 Census the population of the Buddhists in India was 1,41,126 only. In 1961, five years after the greatest religious conversion of history, it rose to 32,06,142, showing an increase of 3128.69 percent. In subsequent census taken in 1971 (38,74,942) the growth rate was 19.01% as against the growth rate of Hindus (23.71%), Muslims (30.84%), Christians (32.60%), and Sikhs (32.28%).

The mass conversion of Untouchables to Buddhism did not shock the Hindus very much and they did not feel perturbed. Hindu *Mahasabha* leader V.D. Savarkar commented, "Instead of taking a long jump, Dr. Ambedkar has taken only a high jump." Conversion to Buddhism was not likely to do much harm to Hinduism but the Hindus saw a danger in it.

The Buddhism preached by Dr. Ambedkar was different from the

Buddhism which was being practised in the Buddhist countries. It was based on the orthodox Buddhism as preached by Lord Buddha. The traditional Buddhists could not influence its progress because of being in small minority. Their population was barely 200,000.

Hindus could see the seeds of separatism in Buddhism which the followers of Dr. Ambedkar had embraced. The twenty two oaths which he prescribed for conversion of Untouchables to Buddhism were striking at the very roots of Hinduism.

Hindu reaction to his conversion to Buddhism was not very violent. The usual comments, 'conversion is no solution', 'it is not likely to do any good to the Untouchables' etc., were passed by the Hindu leaders and leader-writers in the newspapers. 53 days after the mass conversion, Baba Saheb Ambedkar passed away at Delhi. Opponents of Buddhism took a sigh of relief believing that the movement would die a natural death. But men and women in larger numbers congregated in the conference organised by the Buddhist organisation founded by Dr. Ambedkar and other organisations which took birth immediately thereafter. The movement is spreading slowly but steadily. Hundreds of local organisations have cropped up and are working for the propagation of Buddhism in almost all states of India.

The Central Government immediately issued orders that the concessions admissible to the Scheduled Castes, as members of Hindu and Sikh religions would not be permissible if they embraced Buddhism. After results of 1961 Census became available, Government again issued a circular asking Scheduled Caste employees whether they had embraced any religion other than Sikhism. Such enquiries are being made more frequently now. Bureaucracy is dominated by the orthodox Hindus who make use of their powers to check conversion of Untouchables to Buddhism by holding out the threat to withdraw the concessions like reservation in services, educational institutions, grant of scholarships and other aids etc.

In spite of these coercive measures and discriminatory attitude towards Buddhism, the number of Buddhists is showing a reasonable increase. □

References

1. Ambedkar's Speech on Vaikom Satyagraha.
2. Pyarey Lal: *The Epic Fast*, pp. 190-191.
3. *Times of India* dt. 16 Oct. 1935, cited in Thus Spoke Ambedkar Vol. IV p. 108.
4. Ambedkar: *Speeches and Writings* Vol. I (published by Education Department, Government of Maharashtra, 1979) p. 80.
5. Hindu View of Life.

6. *Young India* 24th. Nov., 1927.
7. Ambedkar: *Annihilation of Caste* in Speeches and Writings, Vol. I. p. 66.
8. *Harijan*. Aug. 24, 1934.
9. *Harijan*, Sept. 28, 1934.
10. *Harijan*, Sept. 28, 1934.
11. *Young India*, Dec. 8, 1920.
12. *Times of India* November 17, 1935.
13. Oriente Moderno, Nov. 1936.
    Al Balagh dated 15th Dec. 1936.

Dr. Ambedkar's Statement in 1948

Muslims not Friends of Harijans

"Notwithstanding the gloomy prospect for the scheduled castes who are in India, I would like to tell the scheduled castes who happen today to be impounded inside Pakistan to come over to India by such means as may be available to them. The Congress Party has weakened the political safeguards necessary for the scheduled castes under the new Constitution to such an extent as to make them worse than useless. Nonetheless, our numbers are so great that if we are well organized, we cannot fail to influence the Government of the day, no matter who are in charge of it, even if we have no safeguards. I, therefore, suggest to those who are in Pakistan to come over to India.

"The second thing I want to say is that it would be fatal for the scheduled castes whether in Pakistan or in Hyderabad, to put their faith in Muslims or the Muslim League. It has become a habit with the scheduled castes to look upon the Muslims as friends simply because they dislike Hindus. This is a mistaken view. The Muslims wanted the support of the scheduled castes but they never gave their support to the scheduled castes. Mr. Jinnah was all the time playing a double game. He was very insistent that the scheduled castes were a separate entity when it suited him, but when it did not suit him he insisted with emphasis that they were Hindus. The Muslims and the Muslim League, charged as they were with the passion to make the Muslims a governing class as quickly as possible, will never give consideration to the claims of the scheduled castes. This I speak from experience.

"As regards conversion to Islam, I ask all the scheduled castes not to succumb to it as an easy way of escape. I cannot say that they should die rather than be converted. What I say is that they must look upon it as a last resort forced upon them by violence. And even to those who are converted by force and violence, I say that they must not regard themselves as lost to the fold forever. Fortunately for us we are not hampered by the rules of the Hindu *Shastras* according to which once a convert always a convert. To all those who are forcibly convened I pledge my word that if they wish to come back I shall see that they are received back into the fold and treated as brethren in the same manner in which they were treated before conversion.

"To the scheduled castes of Hyderabad I want to say that they should under no circumstances side with the Nizam and Anjuman-e-Ittehad-Muslimin. Whatever the tyranny and oppression which the Hindus practise on us, it must not wrap our vision and swerve us from our duty. The scheduled castes need freedom and their whole movement has been one of freedom. That being so, they cannot support the Nizam."

Dalit Movement in Karnataka
Rajshekhar Shetty

24

Gandhi and Conversion-Issue

PROF K.N. VASWANI

Director, Gandhi Society, Delhi;
formerly Editor, Collected Works of Mahatma Gandhi;
Vice-President, Vivekanand Kendra, Kanya Kumari

Gandhiji looked at the issue of religious conversion, strictly, from a spiritual angle. He believed that all religions were equally true and could lead to the spiritual salvation of their respective adherents, if their basic tenets were followed with pure and sincere hearts. Expressing this view point, he wrote:

> "I believe that there is no such thing as conversion from one faith to another in the accepted sense of the term. It is a highly personal matter for the individual and his God. I may not have any design upon my neighbour as to his faith, which I must honour even as I honour my own. For, I regard all the great religions of the world as true at any rate for the people professing them, as mine is true for me."[1]

Gandhiji elaborated this idea even more clearly, eloquently and beautifully during a discussion with the members of the Council of International Federation, who met in a Convention for three days at Sabarmati Ashram. Among them were Christians, Hindus, a Parsi and a Muslim;

including Shri C.F. Andrews, Prof. P.A. Wadia (a Zoroastrian) and also some Americans, an English, a Swiss, a Russian and a Swede. During the discussion, Gandhiji expressed himself thus:

> "I came to the conclusion long ago, after prayerful search and study and discussion with as many people as I could meet, that all religions were true and also had some error in them, and that whilst I hold by my own, I shall also hold others as dear as Hinduism, from which it logically follows that we should all be as dear as our nearest kith and kin and that we should make no distinction between them. So we can only pray, if we are Hindus, not that a Christian should become a Hindu, or if we are Mussulmans, not that a Hindu or Christian should become a Mussalman, nor should we ever secretly pray that anyone should be converted, but our inmost prayer should be that a Hindu should be a better Hindu, a Mussulman a better Mussulman and a Christian a better Christian. This is the fundamental truth of fellowship. If, however there is any suspicion in your minds that only one religion is true and others false, you must reject that doctrine.....I plead for utter truthfulness. If we do not feel for the other religions as we feel for our own, we had better disband ourselves for we do not want a wishy-washy toleration. My doctrine of toleration does not include toleration of evil, though it does the toleration of the evil-minded.....I would not only not try to convert but would not even secretly pray that anyone should embrace my faith...I would take an illustration from the physical world, and explain what I mean. If I want to hand a rose to you there is definite movement. But if I want to transmit its scent, I do so without any movement. The rose transmits its own scent without a movement. Let us rise a step higher and we can understand that spiritual experiences are self-active. The joy of spiritual experience, if it is real joy, boundless joy, will spread itself without the vehicle of speech. God is a self-acting force. Let God work His way."[2]

All Religions are Equal

Mahadev Desai reports a dialogue between Gandhiji and missionaries in which, Gandhiji said: "My trouble is that the missionary friends do not bring to their work a purely humanitarian spirit. Their object is to add more numbers to their fold". At this, a missionary asked if he would say the same thing about a Christian who embraces Hinduism. Gandhiji replied:

> "I would. Here is Mira Behn. I would have her find all the spiritual comfort she needs from Christianity, and should not dream of converting her to Hinduism even if she wanted to do so. Today

it is the case of a grown-up woman like her, tomorrow it may be that of a European child trusted to my care by a friend. Take the case of Khan Saheb's daughter entrusted to my care by the father. I should jealously educate her in her faith and should strive my utmost against her being lured away from it, if ever she was so inclined. I have had the privilege of having children and grown-up persons of other Mussalmans, Parsis or Jews by their contact with me."[3]

Gandhiji had arrived at this faith in the equality of all religions after a long chain of personal experiences. Recounting such experiences, he once said:

"There was a time when I was wavering between Hinduism and Christianity. When I recovered my balance of mind, I felt that to me salvation was possible only through the Hindu religion and my faith in Hinduism grew deeper and more enlightened."[4]

In fact, Gandhiji had personally passed through efforts made by his Christian friends for his conversion to Christianity. Narrating this experience in his address before the Christian missionaries at Y.W.C.A. in Calcutta, he said:

"There was even a time in my life when a very sincere and intimate friend of mine, a great and good Quaker, had designs on me *(laughter)*. He thought that I was too good not to become a Christian. I was sorry to have disappointed him.....

"I must tell you in all humility that Hinduism, as I know it entirely satisfies my soul, fills my whole being, and I find a solace in the *Bhagwad Gita* and *Upanishads* that I miss even in the Sermon on the Mount. Not that I do not prize the ideal presented therein, not that some of the precious teachings in the Sermon on the Mount have not left a deep impression upon me, but I must confess to you that when doubts haunt me, when disappointment stares me on the face, and when I see not one ray of light on the horizon, I turn to the *Bhagwad Gita* and find a verse to comfort me, and I immediately begin to smile in the midst of overwhelming sorrow."[5]

It was through his deeper understanding of Hinduism that Gandhiji developed an attitude of equal respect towards all religious faiths. In 1933, when Jawaharlal Nehru, out of his wrong notion of secularism, was not able to appreciate Gandhiji's announcement for commencing an unconditional and irrevocable fast for 21 days in connection with Harijan movement, Gandhiji wrote to him from Yerwada Jail on May 2, 1933:

"The Harijan movement is too big for mere intellectual effort. There is nothing so bad (as untouchability) in the world. And yet

> I cannot leave religion and, therefore, Hinduism. My life would be a burden to me, if Hinduism failed me. I love Christianity, Islam and many other faiths through Hinduism. Take it away and nothing remains for me. But, then, I cannot tolerate it with untouchability–the high and low belief. Fortunately, Hinduism contains a sovereign remedy for the evil. I have applied the remedy. I want you to feel, if you can, that it is well if I survive the fast and well also if the body dissolved in spite of the effort to live."[6]

For Gandhiji, *Hinduism was an all-inclusive religion.* Therefore, professing himself to be a devout and *Sanatani* Hindu, he could attract to his *Ashram* quite a large number of Indian and foreign Christian disciples, notably J.C. & Bharatan Kumarappas, Mira Behn and Sarala Behn, C.F. Andrews and others to name a few, as well as some Muslim devotees like Khan Abdul Gaffar Khan. He never tried to influence their religious faith. In a reply to a letter from Rajkumari Amrit Kaur, who was one of his many Christian disciples, which he published under the caption: "A Christian Letter", Gandhiji made his position very clear:

> "There is in Hinduism room enough for Jesus, as there is for Mahomed, Zoroaster and Moses. For me the different religions are beautiful flowers from the same garden, or they are branches of the same majestic tree. Therefore, they are equally true, though being received and interpreted through human instruments equally imperfect. It is impossible for me to reconcile myself to the idea of conversion after the style that goes on in India and elsewhere today. It is an error which is perhaps the greatest impediment to the world's progress towards peace. 'Wairing creeds' is a blasphemous expression. And it fitly describes the state of things in India, the mother–as I believe her to be–of Religion or religions. If she is truly the mother, the motherhood is on trial. Why should a Christian want to convert a Hindu to Christianity and vice-versa? Why should he not be satisfied if the Hindu is a good or godly man? If the morals of a man is a matter of no concern, the form of worship in a particular manner in a church, a mosque or a temple is an empty formula, it may even be a hindrance to individual or social growth, and insistence on a particular form or repetition of a creed may be a patent cause of violent quarrels leading to bloodshed and ending in utter disbelief in Religion i.e. God Himself."[7]

Differences with Shaukat Ali

Having adopted this position, how could Gandhiji reconcile to the idea of conversion? Long back in 1924-25, Gandhiji had chosen to part company with his second lieutenant in the Khilafat agitation, Maulana Shaukat Ali on the issue of forcible conversion of Hindus to Islam in Kohat (NWFP) during the riots in September, 1924. On the basis of an on-the-spot study Gandhiji got convinced that one of the main causes which precipitated the riots on 9th September 1924, was "the resentment felt by the Musalmans over the resentment felt in their turn by the Hindus over the conversions (so-called in my opinion) of Hindus–men and married women, and consequent steps taken by them, the Hindus..."[8] This fact disclosed the wide divergence of views between him and M. Shaukat Ali, who had also accompanied him for the enquiry. Gandhiji in a letter dated Feb. 23, 1925, conveyed his differences to Shaukat Ali:

> "I cannot treat the conversions as lightly as you seem to do. In my opinion the Khilafatists have greatly neglected their duly and *Maulvi* Ahmed Gul certainly betrayed the trust reposed in him..."[9]

In his Report on Kohat riots, condemning strongly these forcible conversions, Gandhiji wrote:

"But the most important assurance that should be given is, that in future no conversions are to take place except in the presence of the elders of the communities and except in the case of those who understand the full meaning of what they are doing ; and if such conversions are attempted they should receive no recognition.....I am unable to conceive genuine conversions on the Frontier where Hindus live purely for purpose of gain and where they, a hopeless minority untrained in the use of arms, live in the midst of an overwhelming majority who are, moreover, by far their superiors in bodily strength and use of arms. The temptation for a weak man in such circumstances to embrace Islam for worldly gain is irresistible..."[10]

> As far back as 1927, he made it clear: "After much prayerful study of the Hindu *Shastras*, I have come to the conclusion that there is no room in them for conversions such as they have in Islam and Christianity. I am also certain on a prayerful reading of the *Quran* that there is no warrant for the *tabligh* that is being promoted today."[11]

Fight against Untouchability

As a devout Hindu, Gandhiji must have adopted this position of *Sarva-Dharma-Samabhav* and non-Conversion for himself, but he was not living in a vacuum or acting in isolation. He and the Hindu society were faced with the most aggressive proselytising faiths in Islam and Christianity. The Christian missionaries backed by foreign money and British administration were dreaming of converting the whole of India to Christianity, while the Muslim fanatics, with an organised muscle power at their back, were trying frantically to wean away weaker sections of the Hindu society into the fold of Islam. Face to face with this double menace, the Hindu society was badly divided within itself because of a degenerated and rigid caste system impregnated with the stinking evil of high and low leading to social untouchability. A very large segment of the Hindu society called 'Depressed Classes' or "Untouchables" was forced to suffer a sub-human living under this cruel caste system for many centuries and was craving for a better living and social equality. Quite naturally, both these expansionist religions decided to exploit this internal weakness of the Hindu society and selected these weaker sections as their main target for conversion.

Within a few years of his arrival in India in 1915, Gandhiji seemed to have realized the gravity of this situation. During his tours all over India, he established direct rapport with all sections of the society, and gradually evolved a multifaceted strategy of action:

a. To generate a powerful social reform movement within the Hindu society for the emancipation of the Depressed Classes. While stoutly defending the theoretical basis of the original *Varna Vyvastha* Gandhiji rejected its present degenerated form based upon the high and low belief and a feeling of untouchabilily, and

b. to carry on a face to face dialogue with the leaders of the proselytising religions i.e. Christianity and Islam.

In November 1920, while he was deeply engrossed with the Non-Cooperation movement against the British Government, he inaugurated the Gujarat Rashtriya Vidyapeeth, established and run by staunch Gandhians. The Vidyapeeth resolved to admit the depressed class children on its rolls which came as a shock to the orthodox Hindu opinion in Gujarat and elsewhere. A fierce debate ensued for many months in Gujarat on this issue. Gandhi was personally attacked by papers like *Gujarati* and at some places he was even harassed. But instead of getting cowed down by this hostility, Gandhiji made the social and educational emancipation of Depressed Classes an integral part of the constructive programme, officially adopted by the Congress Working Committee at Bardoli in February 1922. The famous Bardoli Resolution laid down the following programme in this direction:

> "To organize the Depressed Classes for a better life, to improve their social, mental and moral condition, to induce them to send their children to national schools and to provide for them the ordinary facilities which the other citizens enjoy."[11]

In 1921, Gandhiji tried to delink the so-called low and unclean professions such as scavenging and cobbling from the caste basis and, thus, to knock out its offshoot–untouchability.[12] He exhorted the upper caste Hindus to take to these professions, and at least to fulfill their own scavenging requirements with their own hands. In this direction, he presented his own example by taking to scavenging and made it an integral part of his *Ashram* life. Similarly, Gandhiji gave his attention to the opening of drinking water-wells and temples to members of the Depressed Classes and to the removal of other disabilities imposed upon them by the Caste-system. In 1923, with Gandhiji's inspiration. Congress officially invited the cooperation of Hindu Maha Sabha also in its battle against untouchability and for the emancipation of the Depressed Classes.

Fast Against Communal Award

Perhaps, shaken by this powerful social reform movement within the Hindu society, the British imperialists hatched a conspiracy to break Hindu society into two parts by extending their old game of granting separate electorate to the Depressed Classes also, under British Prime Minister's Communal Award of 1932. History bears testimony that had Gandhi not staked his life by undertaking a fast unto death against this pernicious Award, the Hindu society would have faced the worst type of disintegration from within and the imperialist game of 'divide and rule' would have succeeded completely. But Gandhiji defeated this imperialist conspiracy by exerting his moral force, generated through his historic fast unto death, which resulted in the famous Poona Pact. Gandhiji broke his fast only after the British Prime Minister accepted the Poona Pact signed on 24th September, 1932 and the Hindu leaders took a pledge to carry an all-out fight against the evil of untouchability.

In a way, Poona Pact marks the beginning of a second phase in Gandhiji's efforts towards Hindu social reform. Determined to translate the pledge for the removal of untouchability and the emancipation of the Depressed Classes taken by the Hindu Conference at Bombay on Sept. 25, 1932, i.e. next day of the signing of Poona Pact, Gandhiji, while still imprisoned in Yerwada Jail, made up his mind to launch a more vigorous anti-untouchability movement. Immediately after the breaking of his fast on Sept. 26, 1932, Gandhiji announced through a press statement:

"The sacrificial fire lit shall not be put out as long as there is the slightest trace of untouchability still left in Hinduism."[13]

Harijans, not Untouchables

In pursuance of the 25th Sept, resolution, an all-India Anti-untouchability League was formed on 30th Sept. 1932. But due to severe restrictions imposed by the British Govt. on Gandhiji he was not able to contribute anything directly to anti-untouchability campaign from the jail till the removal of these restrictions on 4th November, 1932. Between 4th and 26th November, 1932, Gandhiji issued nine statements, one after the other, from jail about the problems of untouchability and emancipation of the Depressed Classes. One important thing to note in these statements is that from second statement onward Gandhiji started using the word Harijan for the 'untouchables' or 'Depressed Classes'. It contributed a lot to the bridging of the psychological gulf which the use of a derogatory word like 'untouchable' had created. It relieved the so-called untouchables of their inferiority complex and instilled in them a new sense of self-confidence. Explaining the background of the term 'Harijan', Gandhiji wrote:

"It is not a name of my own coining. Some years ago, several 'untouchable' correspondents complained that I used the word '*asprishya*' in the pages of Navjivan. 'Asprishya' means literally 'untouchable'. I then, invited them to suggest a better name and one of the untouchable correspondents suggested an adoption of the name "*Harijan*" on the strength of its having been used by the first poet saint of Gujarat."[14]

The term 'Harijan' having been sufficiently popularised through his continuous writings, on Gandhiji's suggestion, the name of all India Anti-untouchability League was also changed to Harijan Sevak Sangh on 9th December and in February, 1933 Gandhiji renamed his weekly periodicals also as '*Harijan*' in English and '*Harijan Sevak*' in Hindi.

In the beginning of 1933, Gandhiji got two private bills introduced in the Central Legislative Assembly, one for abolition of untouchability by law and second for the right of temple-entry to Harijans. Gradually, the battle against untouchability seems to have become his first priority over all other activities. In order to revolutionize the Hindu mind and heart on the vital issue of untouchability, Gandhiji announced from jail to begin a self-purification List for 21 days on 8th May, 1933 onwards. The government got nervous and released him on the very first day of his fast but even after release he continued it up to 29th May at Poona. In August, 1933 Gandhiji was arrested again and lodged in Yervada jail. Gandhiji had to go on hunger-strike on August 16 against the Government refusal to permit him to carry on his Harijan work. His condition became serious and when his life was thought to be in danger, he was released unconditionally. On Sept. 4, he made an announcement that during the entire period up to August 1934, he would devote himself to Harijan upliftment only. September 24 was observed as Harijan Day and a pledge for removal of untouchability was taken in public meetings all over the country On November 7, Gandhiji started his all-India Harijan tour. During this whirlwind tour he visited Harijan colonies, addressed public meetings, collected Harijan Fund and aroused nation's conscience against untouchability. But his march was not very smooth. At many places, he had to face the wrath of orthodox opinion among Hindus. At the end of his Harijan tour, Gandhiji decided to retire from Congress membership and to dedicate himself wholeheartedly to the task of Harijan uplift and village development.

Gandhiji and Dr. Ambedkar

While Gandhiji was busy in building up a powerful nationwide social reform movement within the Hindu society for Harijan upliftment and removal of untouchability, Dr. Ambedker, the leader of a section of Harijans, threw a bombshell in Indian public life on 13th Oct., 1935 by exhorting Harijans to get converted *en masse* to any other religion outside Hinduism. This advice, commonly known a Yeola Declaration, gave a new fillip to the race for proselytisation of Hindu Harijans, which had been going on for long between Islam and Christianity in India. This time, unfortunately, Sikhism also joined this race. They all started wooing Dr. Ambedker and offered him different allurements to mobilise wholesale conversion of 40 million Harijans to the religion of the highest bidder.

Gandhiji reacted immediately to this bombshell. On one hand, he entered into a public debate with Dr. Ambedkar and, on the other, he admonished Christian and Muslim leaders to desist from this unseemly race for conversion. In his first public reaction to Dr. Ambedker's threat, Gandhiji made an earnest appeal through Associated Press:

> "I can understand the anger of a high-souled and highly educated person like Dr. Ambedkar over atrocities such as were committed in Kavitha and other villages. But religion is not like a house or a cloak which can be changed at will. It is a more integral part of one's self than that of one's body. Religion is the tie that binds one to one's Creator, and whilst the body perishes as it has to, religion persists even after death. Dr. Ambedkar has faith in God. I would urge him to assuage his wrath and to reconsider the position and examine his ancestral religion on its own merits, and not through the weakness of its unfaithful followers. Lastly, I am convinced that a change of faith by him and those who passed the resolution, will not serve the cause which they have at heart, for the millions of unsophisticated, illiterate Harijans will not listen to him and the others when they have disowned their ancestral faith, especially, when it is remembered that their lives for good or evil are intertwined with those of the caste-Hindus."[15]

Conversion: No Solution

In fact, Gandhiji had always held the view that conversion to any other religion was no remedy of the problem of 'uutouchablity'. As far back as 1920, he had written:

"A remedy suggested to 'untouchables' is rejection of Hinduism and wholesale conversion to Islam or Christianity and if a change of religion could be justified for worldly betterment, I would advise it without hesitation. But religion is a matter of the heart. No physical inconvenience can warrant abandonment of one's own religion. If the inhuman treatment of the *Panchmas* were a part of Hinduism, its rejection would be a permanent duty both for them and for those like me who would not make a fetish even of religion and condone every evil in its sacred name. But I believe that untouchability is no part of Hinduism. It is rather its excrescence to be removed by every effort. And there is quite an army of Hindu reformers who have set their heart upon ridding Hinduism of this blot. Conversion, therefore, I hold, no remedy whatsoever."[16]

And again in 1940 at the end of twenty years of his Herculean efforts for removal of untouchability, he reiterated the same view in reply to a question from a Muslim, who asked:

"If the object of the Congress in the liquidation of untouchability is to give Harijans a status of equality with the rest, is this not achieved by their conversion to Islam? Why does the Independence Pledge allocate the programme of the removal of untouchability to Hindus only? Does this not show that the Congress is anxious to maintain a Hindu majority and, therefore, denies to the Mussalmans their right of conversion?" Gandhiji's reply was:

"Liquidation of untouchability cannot be attained by the conversion of untouchables to Islam or any other religion. For, it is the so called caste Hindu who has to rid himself of the sin of untouchability. He can wash away the stain only by doing justice, however tardy, to the outcaste. You will thus see why Muslims are not invited by the Congress to share the burden with the Hindus. They have committed no sin against the untouchables. I cannot prevent you from looking at a simple but necessary social reform as a political dodge to maintain a majority. Tens of thousands of Hindus who are doing penance have not thought of majority. All they want is to do justice to those whom, under the guise of religion, caste. Hindus have reduced to a state worse than slavery."[17]

But now he was faced with a situation in which an eminent Hindu leader like Dr. Ambedkar had threatened a mass conversion of Harijans outside Hinduism. Naturally, his announcement gladdened the hearts of those who had been angling for conversions in India's troubled waters for long. Faced with this situation, Gandhiji turned his attention to the religious enthusiasts who were vying with each other to reap the coming windfall of mass conversions. Addressing them Gandhiji wrote in Harijan dated 22nd Aug, 1936:

> "If the leaders of different religions in India ceased to compete with one another in enticing Harijans into their fold, it would be well for this unfortunate country. I have the profound conviction that those who are engaged in the competition are not serving the cause of Religion. By looking at it in terms of politics or economics they reduce the religious values, whereas (he proper thing would be to estimate politics and every other thing in terms of religion."[18]

Missionary Propaganda Challenged

Various Christian missionary organisations were so much enthusiased by Ambedkar's threat of conversion outside Hinduism, that they started big fund collection drives in European countries by presenting a false picture of mass conversion in India. Gandhiji taking note of a report published in *The Church Times* of 16th Oct. 1936 and giving the details of a meeting of Christian denominations held in London under the president-ship of the Archbishop of Canterbury, wrote in *Harijan* dated 19th Dec. 1936:

"I have rarely seen so much exaggeration in so little space. A reader ignorant of conditions in India would conclude that the figures relate to the conversions due to the movement led by Dr. Ambedkar... Where are "the multitudes in India who marvel" at the transformation in the lives of "four and a half millions of the depressed classes?" I am one of the multitude having practically travelled more than half a dozen times all over India and have not seen any transformation on the scale described by Dr. Picket and certainly none of recent date. I have had the privilege of addressing meetings of Indian Christians who have appeared to me to be no better than their (Hindu) fellows. Indeed, the taint of untouchability persists in spite of the nominal change of faith as far as the social status is concerned."[19]

Then Gandhiji took note of a pamphlet published by the Church Missionary Society of England, appealing for "an emergency fund of £ 25,000 to enable extra grants to be made during the next five years to those areas where this big movement is taking place." Interspersed with sub-headings as, "Who is Ambedkar?" and "What Does India Say to Dr. Ambedkar's Advice?" the pamphlet said, "Recent news in the papers has attracted widespread attention to the untouchables of India. We have read of great conferences of outcaste peoples who have decided to break away from Hinduism. We are, therefore, compelled to examine more closely what is happening in India and to see how far we are reaping the harvest which has come." Overplaying Ambedkar's threat and undermining Gandhiji's anti-untouchability drive, it wrote:

"There is no doubt that there have been important repercussions all over India from the conference of untouchables. Mr. Gandhi had previously carried on a campaign for the removal of untouchability, but he has signally failed because he clung to the Hindu system which has been the cause of the trouble."

Gandhiji, writing in *Harijan* dated 26th December, 1936, point by point, punctured the exaggerations and falsehoods packed in this small pamphlet:

"The exaggeration of Bishop Pickett, with which I had the misfortune of dealing last week, are beaten perhaps by those contained in this appeal… ..I am utterly unconscious of the 'signal failure.' I have not clung to the Hindu system which has been the cause of the trouble. On the contrary, I have rejected that which has been the cause of the trouble, namely untouchability. And I have not abandoned the campaign as suggested in the quotation."[20]

Impact of Harijan Movement

The reality as reported by Mahadev Desai in January, 1938, was that the progress of the anti-untouchability campaign had disturbed some of 'our Missionary friends'. He wrote, "Gandhiji has had letters from some of them, and a friend discussing the matter with Gandhiji the other day, summed it up this way: "Your campaign is taking away popularity from the Missionaries." To this Gandhiji replied:

> "I see what you mean, but I do not know why it should disturb them. We are not traders trenching on one another's province... Why should Missionaries complain, if I open a school which is more liked by Harijans than theirs? Is it not natural?"[21]

In fact, Gandhiji at the time of launching his second phase of anti-untouchability campaign under the auspices of *Harijan Sewak Sangh* had openly invited the Christian missionaries to join hands with Hindu reformers in this sacred task. Addressing a Christian audience at the Leonard Theological College, Jubbulpore on 7th Dec. 1933, Gandhiji had said:

> "Having made these introductory remarks, it is easy for me to cell you on what terms you can give your assistance to the anti-untouchability movement. You should work in co-operation with, and if I may say it, in subordination to the Society that has been formed for suppression and eradication of untouchability, namely, the Servants of Untouchable Society (renamed *Harijan Sewak Sangh*) That is to say, you should put your talents at the disposal of the society. I don't mean *metallic,* talents. These have to come from those who have to make repentance and reparation."

And, then, warning against proselytisation, he said:

"......But there is also the wrong way, you may choose to work independently. You may have conversion of Harijans to Christianity. You may see in the movement a chance for propaganda. If you work among the Harijans with such an aim, you can see that the very end we have in view will be frustrated. If you believe that Hinduism is a gift, not of God but of Satan, quite clearly you cannot accept my terms. You and I would be dishonest if we did not make clear to one another what we stand for."[22]

Gandhiji's sincere appeal fell on deaf ears and except a few patriotic Christian individuals, all Christian organisations kept away from Harijan uplift movement as they saw in it a setback to their conversion plans. Given this background, Dr. Ambedkar's threat for mass conversion appeared to them a God-sent opportunity and they immediately jumped upon it to catch it by the forelock. The Bishop of Dornacal issued an *Open letter to the Depressed classes in India* offering them many baits for conversion. A Christian Conference was held at Lucknow which, welcoming the statement of Dr. Ambedkar, invited Harijans to join Christianity. Bishop Pickett's speech in London and a pamphlet published by the London Missionary Society, which have already been alluded, provide some samples of the propaganda which was unleashed by various Missionary Societies in Europe.

Gandhi–Missionary Dialogue

Gandhiji's ever-alert eyes took note of all these hectic activities through the columns of his weekly *Harijan*. Not stopping here, he entered into a direct dialogue with responsible Christian leaders of different denominations on this issue. During all these dialogues Gandhiji stressed the following points:

a. Why this sudden concern about the redemption of Harijans only? Why, instead of extending a helping hand to the social reform movement within Hinduism, Dr. Ambedkar's threat was being blown up out of all proportions?

b. Why instead of appealing to reason or soul, poor and illiterate Harijans arc being approached with worldly promises?

c. Why false and exaggerated propaganda is being carried on to attract foreign money in the name of evangelisation?

d. How can the conversion achieved through such unethical means be called religious in true sense?

Commenting on a letter written by one General Booth, leader of a Missionary body named Salvation Army, to his son, in which was said,

"The social work is the bait, but it is salvation that is the hook that lands the fish", Gandhiji wrote in *Harijan*:

> "Of course, what is true of the Army is more or less true of all Christian Missions. Their social work is undertaken not for its own sake but as an aid to the *salvation* of those who receive social service."[23]

Social Service, a Bait for Conversion

When a Christian Missionary Dr. Ceresol visited him at Sevagram, Gandhiji made him confess this aspect of the Missionary method. Gandhiji told him:

"Whilst you give the medical help you expect the reward in the shape of your patients becoming Christians." Dr. Ceresol admitted, "Yes, the reward is expected. Otherwise, there are many other places in the world which need our service. But instead of going there we came here."

Gandhiji clinched. "There is the kink. At the back of your mind there is not pure service for its sake, but the result of service in the shape of many people coming to the Christian fold."[24]

Gandhiji was very forthright in his condemnation of religious conversions brought about through material inducements. Much earlier he had written:

> "I hold that proselytising under the clock of humanitarian work, is, to say the least, unhealthy..........Conversions have now-a-days become a matter of business, like any other. I remember having read a missionary report saying how much it cost per head to convert and then presenting a budget for the next harvest."[25]

Gandhiji felt so much exasperated with these methods of the Missionaries that he refused to give his autograph on a photograph to a Polish research student during his visit to Sevagram, when he told Gandhiji that the proceeds of the sale of this photograph world go to help a school run by Catholic Fathers. Returning the photograph Gandhiji said, "Ah, that is a different story. You do not expect me to support the Fathers in their mission of conversion? You know what they do?" And then he told him in a couple of minutes the story of the so-called conversion in the vicinity of Tiruchengadu, the desecration and demolition of a Hindu temple and so on. Getting emotional Gandhiji opened out before that stranger the deep wound that the recent conversion of his perverted son Harilal to Islam had inflicted on his soul. Referring to his open letter addressed, '*To My Numerous Muslim Friends*' published in *Harijan* dated 2nd June, 1936 Gandhiji said in a voice full of pain:

"Have you read what I have written on my son's so-called conversion to Islam? If he had become a Muslim from a pure and contrite heart, I should have no quarrel with him. But those who had helped him to embrace Islam and are enthusing over his apostasy simply exploited his weaknesses. They are no true representatives of Islam. My letter to the Muslims, I tell you was written with my pen dipped in my heart's blood, Similarly there is no redeeming feature about the Tiruchengadu conversion I have spoken to you about."[26]

Why Harijans? Why not me?

When Dr. Crane, a distinguished clergyman from America came to meet Gandhiji at Sevagram and asked him, "What do you say to the attempt to convert?" Gandhiji's immediate reply was:

"I strongly resent these overtures to utterly ignorant men. I can perhaps understand overtures made to me, as indeed they are being made. For they can reason with me and I can reason with them. But I certainly resent the overtures made to Harijans. When a Christian preacher goes and says that Jesus was the only begotten son of God, he will give him a blank stare. Then he holds out all kinds of inducements which debase Christianity."[27]

Gandhiji poured out the agony of his heart when Deenbandhu Charles Andrews visited him at Sevagram after a prolonged absence from India. When Charles Andrews tried to know from Gandhiji his reaction to the present attitude of missionaries, Gandhiji in an anguished tone said:

"Their behaviour has been as bad as that of the rest who are in the held to add to own their numbers. What pains one is their frantic attempt to exploit the weakness of Harijans. If they said, 'Hinduism is a diabolical religion and you come to us', I should understand. But they dangle earthly paradises in front of them and make promises to them which they never keep. When in Bangalore a deputation of Indian Christians came to me with a number of resolutions which they thought would please me, I said to them 'This is no matter for bargain. You must say definitely that this is a matter to be settled by the Hindus themselves. Where is the sense of talking of sudden awakening of spiritual hunger among the untouchables and then trying to exploit a particular situation?' The poor Harijans have no mind, no intelligence, no sense of difference between God and no-God.".

And then, referring to undue importance being given to Dr. Ambedkar's pronouncements, Gandhiji said:

> "It is absurd for a single individual to talk of taking all the Harijans with himself. Are they all bricks that they can be moved from one structure to another? If Christian Missions here want to play the game, and for that matter Musalmans and others, they should have no such idea as that of adding to their ranks whilst a great reform in Hinduism is going on."

Andrews, supporting Gandhiji's observations, said:

> "I said in Australia that all talk of Dr. Ambedkar and his followers was not in terms of religion, and I said also that it was cruelty to bargain with unsophisticated people like the Harijans as they are in most parts of India."[27a]

Dialogue with Missionary Leader

It is interesting to note that while this public debate on the question of conversion was going on in India, 71 years old Dr. John Mott, Chairman of the International Missionary Council, descended upon India because, according to Mahadev Desai, "he had in mind what the Christians believed to be an unprecedented ferment among the "untouchables" in India and he came with a desire to *help.*" Realizing the force of Gandhiji's personality in Indian public life, Dr. Mott came all the way to see him at Sevagram in November, 1936. Opening the dialogue[27b] with Gandhiji, Dr. Mott said:

> "I am Chairman of the International Missionary Council which combines 300 Missionary societies in the world. I have on my desk reports of these societies and I can say that their interest in the untouchables is deepening. I should be interested if you would feel free to tell me, where, if anywhere, the Missionaries have gone along wrong lines."

Without mincing any words, Gandhiji replied:

"I cannot help saying that the activities of the Missionaries in this connection have hurt me. They with the Musalmans and the Sikhs came forward as soon as Dr. Ambedkar threw the bombshell and gave it an importance out of all proportion to the weight it carried, and then ensued a rivalry between these organisations. I could understand the Muslim organisations doing this, as Hindus and Muslims have been quarrelling. The Sikh intervention is an enigma. But the Christian Mission claims to be a purely spiritual effort. It hurt me to find Christian bodies vying with the Muslims and Sikhs in trying to add to the numbers of their fold. It seemed to me an ugly performance and travesty of religion. They even proceeded to enter into secret conclaves with Dr. Ambedkar. I should have understood and appreciated your prayers for the Harijans, but instead you made an appeal to those who had not even the mind and intelligence to understand what you talked; they have certainly not the intelligence to distinguish between Jesus and Muhammad and Nanak and so on."

Here Dr. Mott disclosed that "in the secular papers it had got abroad that Dr. Ambedkar could hand over 50 million people to those who were prepared to accept them. I had sensed that it might mean a tremendous disservice. The most trustworthy leaders of Protestant Missionary forces would give what you have said great heed...... Tell us what we can wisely do and what we cannot wisely do." Upon this Gandliiji said, "So far as this desire of Dr. Ambedkar is concerned, you can look at the whole movement with utter calmness and indifference."

Gandhiji snubs Dr. Mott

Then Gandhiji made a pointed reference to the Christian Conference held at Lucknow. Dr. Mott declared it to be unauthoritative. But he did not mean complete Christian withdrawal from the game of conversion and therefore, asked Gandhiji, "But must we not serve them?"

Gandhiji replied, "Of course, you will, but not make conversion the price of your service."

Dr. Mott, "I agree that we ought to serve them whether they become Christian or not."

Welcoming this, Gandhiji said, "If Christians want to associate themselves with this reform movement, they should do so without any idea of conversion."

Dr. Mott continued his prodding. He asked Gandhiji, "Apart from the unseemly competition, should they not preach the Gospel with reference to its acceptance? Because, the whole Christian religion is the religion of sharing our life, and how can we share without supplementing our lives with words?" Gandhiji could immediately see through his mind and quipped, "Then what they (Christian missionaries–Ed.) are doing in Travancore is correct? There may be a difference of degree in what you say and what they are doing, but there is not difference of quality. If you must share it with the Harijans, why don't you share it with me, Thakkar Bappa and Mahadev? Why should you go to the 'untouchables' and try to exploit this upheaval? Why not come to us instead?" Here Gandhiji compared the then state of Harijan education and understanding with that of a cow.

After a few days of Dr. Mott's visit, Mr. Basil Mathew, who happened to be Dr. Mott's biographer also, came to see Gandhiji and drew Gandhiji's attention to Archbishop of Canterbury's speech at the Central Hall, Westminster.

Gandhiji said,

"I am convinced that, if Christian Missions will sincerely play the game, no matter what may be their policy under normal circumstances, they must withdraw from the indecent competition to convert the Harijans. Whatever the Archbishop of Canterbury and others may say, what is done here in India in the name of Christianity is wholly different from what they say. There are others in the field also but as a devotee of truth I say that if there is any difference between their methods, it is one of degree and not of kind. I know of representatives of different religions standing on the same platform and vying with one another to catch the Harijan's ear. To dignify this movement with the name of spiritual hunger is a travesty of truth."

Then referring to his long conversation with Dr. Mott, Gandhiji told Mr. Basil Mathew,

"Arguing on the highest plane I said to Dr. Mott, if they wanted to convert Harijans had they not better begin to convert me? I am a trifle more intelligent than they and therefore more receptive to the influences of reason that could be brought to bear upon me. But to approach the *pulayas* and *pariahs* with their palsied hands and paralysed intelligence is no Christianity. No, whilst our reform movement is going on, all religious minded people would say: Rather than obstruct their work, let us support them in their work."[28]

Harijans and Cows

Unable to counter Gandhiji's arguments on any other ground, the missionary circles jumped upon to exploit Gandhiji's analogy of Harijans with cows *vis-a-vis* Christian presentation. Without appreciating the reality of Indian situation, a virulent propaganda was let loose against Gandhiji that he had no regard for Harijans and treated them at par with animals. This propaganda was carried on in all Christian countries including America. Letters of protest and anxiety started pouring to Gandhiji from abroad. But he stood his ground firmly. Replying to his well-wishers as well as critics, Gandhiji wrote in Harijan,

"I hold that my comparison was as innocuous as it was appropriate. It was innocuous because of the unique place the cow occupies in India. It was appropriate because in the matter of presentation of Christianity the ordinary, Harijan can no more take it in than the cow."

To an American missionary sister, who was very critical of Gandhiji's attitude, he replied,

"My attitude is not 'superficial' as she will have it to be. Whatever it is, it is based on deep experience and observation dependent net on a day's or even a years' contact, but on close contact for years with tens of thousands of India's masses, not as a superior being but feeling as one of them."[29]

He made it clear that "the discussion related to the present condition, not to future possibility."[30]

"That, after a long course of training, Harijans can have their intelligence developed in a manner a cow's cannot, is irrelevant to the present discussion."[31]

Harijan Reality of Thirties

And who can say that Gandhiji was not reflecting the Indian reality of his days very correctly? During his many intensive all India tours, he had seen that reality face to face. He had seen the sub-human conditions steeped in illiteracy, ignorance and poverty, in which the vast multitude of Indian population called Harijans were forced to live in those days. Gandhiji's description of that reality may appear to be repulsive to our conscience today when, as a result of manifold expansion of educational infrastructure and creation of special opportunities for Harijans through Reservation Policy during the last 36 years of Independence, the percentage of education among Harijans has gone up several times of that in the thirties. But even today, if we compare the low level of education, both quantitatively and qualitatively amongst Harijans with that of the other sections of Indian society (See the news items captioned 'Reserved for square pegs in round holes' published in *The Statesman*, New Delhi, dated 5th Nov. 1983–Ed.), we can very well imagine the abject conditions which might have prevailed in the thirties, when this dialogue between Gandhiji and the Christian missionaries was taking place. The number of literates among Harijans was microscopically small in those days. It was this hard reality which Gandhiji had seen face to face and to which he was again and again alluding in his debate on the conversion issue.

Of course, Gandhiji held the Hindu society solely responsible for this pitiable plight to which the millions of Harijan brethren were reduced and therefore he wanted the *savarna* Hindus alone to do penance for the sin of their forefathers by sincerely striving for the upliftment of Harijan masses. On his own part, ever since 1920, he had been doing his utmost towards the opening of more and more educational opportunities to the Harijans and fight against untouchability.

But what he objected to was that the preachers of other religions were trying to exploit this educational backwardness of the Harijans by converting them to their own religion through material inducements. Therefore strongly defending his comparison of Harijans with cows in the given situation, Gandhiji wrote:

"Presentation, with a view to conversion, of a faith other than one's own, can only necessarily be through an appeal to the intellect or the stomach or both. I do maintain that the vast mass of Harijans, and for that matter Indian humanity, cannot understand tin presentation of Christianity, and that generally speaking their conversion wherever it has taken place has not been a spiritual act in any sense of the term. They are conversions for convenience. And I have had overwhelming corroboration of the truth during my frequent and extensive wanderings."[32]

Referring to Christian concern for the plight of Harijans, he said:

"One could understand the attack on untouchability and many other errors that have crept into Hindu life. And if they would help us to get rid of the admitted abuses and purify our religion, they would do helpful constructive work, which would be gratefully accepted. But so far as one can understand the present effort, it is to uproot Hinduism from the very foundation and replace it by another faith."[33] and further,

"I assert that it is a travesty of religion to seek to uproot from the Harijans' simple minds such faith as they have in their ancestral religion and to transfer allegiance to another, even though that other may be as good as and equal to the original in quality. Though all soils have the same predominant characteristics, we know that the same seeds do not fare equally well in all soils."[34]

Conversion leads to Denationalisation

Here, the Swadeshi spirit in Gandhiji was reacting to the denationalising effect of religious conversions in India. Long back, addressing a Christian audience, he had said:

"As I wander about throughout the length and breadth if India, I see many Christian Indians ashamed of their birth, certainly of their ancestral religion, and of their ancestral dress. The aping of Europeans on the part of Anglo-Indians is bad enough, but the aping of them by Indian converts is a violence done to their country and shall I say, even to their new religion."[35]

Because, he said:

"Conversion must not mean denationalisation. Conversion should mean a definite giving up of the evil of the old, adoption of all the good of the new and a scrupulous avoidance of everything evil in the new. Conversion, therefore, should mean a life of greater dedication to one's own country, greater surrender to God, greater self-purification." And then he asked them pointedly:

> "Is it not truly deplorable that many Christian Indians discard their own mother tongue, bring up their children only to speak in English? Do they not thereby completely cut themselves adrift from the nation in whose midst they have to live? But they may answer in self-defence that many Hindus and even Mussulmans have become denationalized. The *Tu Quoque* argument serves no useful purpose."

Harijan Leaders support Gandhiji

Gandhiji's assessment that Ambedkar's conversion threat had a very limited appeal and it was being blown up out of all proportions was confirmed by the statements issued by many other influential leaders of the Depressed Classes in those days. Mr. Balu, the famous cricketer and the leader of a large section of the Depressed Classes of Bombay Presidency, Rai Bahadur R. Srinivasan, M.L.C., Rai Sahab Y. L. Muniswami, M.L.C., Rao Sahab L. C. Guruswamy Ex. M.L.C., Dr. Ram Prashad, Dr. Solanki, M.L.C. and others expressed strong disapproval of the Yeola Resolution. All these leaders were greatly impressed by the sincere efforts made by Mahatma Gandhi for the removal of untouchability and upliftment of the Depressed Classes. Rai Bahadur M.C. Rajah, President, All India Depressed Classes Association, in a very strong statement issued on 12th November, 1935, opposing Dr. Ambedkar's call for conversion paid glowing tributes to the efforts made by Mahatma Gandhi. He said,

> "The Congress under the inspiration of Mahatma Gandhi has taken up the question of the removal of untouchability and the Hindu Mahasabha has followed suit. It is our duty to help them in their endeavor and not to throw obstacles in their way." Pointing to Ambedkar's limited following, Rajah said, "It should be noted that this conference is only a district conference."[36]

And then, challenging Ambedkar's bonafides, Rajah pointedly asked, "Did he ever take part in social and religious reform movements in Hindu Society before coming to the conclusion that Hinduism is unreformable, before taking upon himself the responsibility of advising seventy millions of people to change their religion?"

Referring to Dr. Ambedker's dubious role with regard to the Temple Entry Bill and Untouchability Abolition Bill, pending before the Central Legislative Assembly, Rajah said,

> "Did not the chief opposer to these bills and the stout champion of the *Sanatan Dharma*, Raja Bahadur, G. Krishnamachariar call to his aid the President of the Conference (Dr. Ambedkar–Ed.) and declared that he (Dr. Ambedkar–Ed.) did not want temple entry ?...Is it not a fact that he (Dr. Ambedkar) opposed Mahatma

> Gandhi when he placed religious reform before the economic? There is Mr. C.F. Andrews testifying to this fact in an interview granted to the Manchester Guardian."[37]

Another Depressed Classes leader, Sh. Ganesh Akkaji Gavai, Member of the Legislative Council, Central Provinces and Berar in his statement said:

"Admittedly, there is untouchability and inequality in the Hindu society, but at the same time, it cannot be denied that prominent leaders like Mahatma Gandhi are struggling for the removal of untouchability and inequality and their efforts are proving to be fruitful. If Dr. Ambedkar is so keen about the removal of these disparities quickly he must obtain some magical wand for these leaders."[38]

Charging Dr. Ambedkar of changing his views and line of action many times during the first five or six years of his public life, Gavai said, "And this conversion is not for the sake of 'conviction' but for some personal convenience". As to the impact of Dr. Ambedkar's call for conversion upon Harijans, Gavai clearly said, "you need not think that this declaration is likely to create a great stir among the Depressed Classes."[39]

In view of all these developments, the Christian leaders thought it wise to withdraw from the game of mass conversion. Fourteen top Christian leaders issued a joint statement in early 1937, announcing their retreat from this competition. This statement also took note of the deep and wide impact made by Gandhiji's efforts upon the Depressed classes. It said:

> "We believe that the process of absorption of the Depressed and Backward classes into the Hindu community, in which a serious beginning has been made, is likely to confer on the present generation of the Depressed and Backward Classes immediate benefits on a large scale which the Church will not be able to give to the whole community.

"We are of the opinion that with the political privileges which the Indian Constitution and the Poona Pact have conferred on these classes, with the special educational and other advantages provided in many Indian provinces for their exclusive uplift, and with this great gesture of friendliness which the Caste Hindus have shown them, they will not have same dissatisfaction with Hinduism which often times led them to gravitate towards Christianity or Islam. *Therefore we are unable to share the hope that the present upheaval is going to result in an influx of the Depressed and Backward Classes into the Christian Church in the phenomenal measure in which, it is said, it is going to happen.*"[40]

From the above, it is evident that this was simply a face-saving device in face of a hopeless situation. Naturally, Gandhiji wanted to welcome this statement but his piercing eyes did not fail to note that at the tail-end of the statement was contained an assertion in the name of Karachi Congress Resolution, of "the right not only to profess and practise, but also to *propagate*" their religion to illiterate Harijans. Commenting on this part of the statement, Gandhiji wrote in *Harijan*:

"The purpose of the manifesto is not to condemn unequivocally the method of converting the illiterate and the ignorant but to assert the *right of preaching* the gospel to the millions of Harijans...... Men and women do not seek the fellowship of the Christian Church. Poor Harijans are not better than the others...When the missionary of another religion goes to them he goes like any vendor of goods. He has no special spiritual merit that will distinguish him from those to whom he goes. He does, however, possess material goods which he promises to those who will come to his fold." Gandhiji added, as if to hit the nail right on the head, "Then mark, the *duty* of Christian Church in India turns into a *right!* Now when duty becomes a right it ceases to be *duty*...... In the spiritual sphere, there is no such thing as a *right*."[41]

Ban on Proselytising

In fact, continuous use of immoral methods for enticing the poor and backward sections of the Hindu society to Christian fold and the subsequent denationalising effect of Conversion, had led Gandhiji to favour a legal ban on the missionary activities in India, much before the controversy started by Ambedker's Yeola statement. Gandhiji had made his position clear in this regard when a Christian lady missionary asked him, "Would you prevent missionaries coming to India in order to baptize?" Gandhiji's reply was:

> "Who am I to prevent them? If I had power and could legislate, I shall certainly stop all proselytising... In Hindu households the advent of a missionary has meant the disruption of the family, coming in the wake of change of dress, manners, language, food and drink."

When the lady, in an effort to defend the missionary position, asked, "Is it not the old concept you are referring to? No such thing is now associated with proselytisation", Gandhiji silenced her with his most up to date information:

> "You talk of the conception being no longer there. Only the other day a missionary descended on a famine area with money in his pocket, distributed it among the famine-stricken, converted thorn to his fold, took charge of their temple, and demolished it. This is outrageous."[42]

Perhaps to extract Gandhiji's approval for the continuation of missionary propaganda in India, the missionary further asked him, "You have objected to Christian propaganda on the ground that Harijans are illiterate and ignorant; what would you say of propaganda amongst non-Harijans?" Gandhi's frank reply was:

> "I have the same objection, because the vast mass of people of India would not understand the pros and cons of Christianity better than a cow. I repeat this simile in spite of the fact that it has been objected to......[42a]

Home coming of converts

Having received first-hand information about large number of such shameful incidents of conversion through fraud and force, how could Gandhiji accept them as genuine religious conversions? Therefore, replying to the following four questions sent to him by a correspondent:

"1. Hindus who once renounced their faith for some reason or other and joined Islam or Christianity, sincerely repent and want to come back. Should we re-convert them or not? You may take the instance of your own son, Harilal.

2. Lakhs of the Depressed Class people in South India, as you know have joined Christianity wholesale. Some of them, since the Travancore Durbar's Declaration and the popularity of the Harijan movement, feel it worthwhile to readopt their ancestral faith. What would you advise about them?

3. A Hindu was made to join another faith for certain material considerations. After some time he feels disillusioned and comes and knocks at our door. Shall we welcome him or not?

4. Young Hindu boys and girls are often taken hold of by Christian missionaries and converted. At some places Muslims are also making use of their orphanages for this purpose. What should we do, when these boys and girls, either alone or with their guardians, approach us for *Shuddhi* ?"

Gandhiji, in his inimitable style, answered:

> These, or such questions have been asked and answered before now in these columns in some shape or other. I do not need to answer each separately. In my opinion, they are not examples of real heart conversions. If a person, through fear, compulsion, starvation, or for material gain or consideration, goes over to another faith, it is a misnomer to call it conversion. Most cases of mass conversion, of which we have heard so much during the past two years, have been to my mind false coin. Real conversion springs from the heart and at the prompting of God, not of a stranger. The voice of God can always be distinguished from the

voice of man. The hypothetical cases coined by my correspondent are, so far as I can see, not cases of conversion. I would, therefore, unhesitatingly readmit to the Hindu fold all such repentant without ado, certainly without any *Shuddhi*. *Shuddhi* is not applicable to such cases. And, as I believe in the equality of all the great religions of the earth, I regard no man as polluted because he has forsaken the branch on which he was sitting and gone over to another of the same tree. If he comes back to the original branch, he deserves to be welcomed and not told that he had committed a sin by reason of his having forsaken the family to which he belonged. In so far as he may be deemed to have erred, he has sufficiently purged himself of it when he repents of the error and retraces his step.[43]

When asked "Won't you object to a Harijan-*sevak* attending a voluntary *shuddhi* ceremony of this character? Gandhiji replied:

"I see no objection to his attending such a ceremony, but let him be clear that *shuddhi* is no part of the Harijan *Sevak Sangh's* programme and also he should be sure that the man wanting to be reconverted was doing so absolutely freely and without the offer of any inducement. The question is: Are you convinced of the down-right sincerity of the man wanting to be reconverted? If you are, do everything to befriend him."[44]

In 1939, an American missionary, took strong exception to some congressmen encouraging the reconversion of Indian Christians to Hinduism. He wrote to Gandhiji, "Your friend, the late Prime minister (C. Rajagopalachari–Ed.) of Madras sent a wire of congratulation to Christians who became Hindus. Is that being neutral? And just the other day, here near Bombay in Thana District, when about fifty hill-people returned to Hinduism, the leaders in making them Hindus were the Congress leaders of Thana District. So, this plainly shows that the Congress leaders favour Hinduism." To this accusation, Gandhiji's reply was:

"I am not aware what Shri Rajagopalachari said. He is well able to take care of himself.....But I should see nothing wrong in Hindus congratulating those who having left them may return to their fold. I think that the Christians of free America would rejoice at the return to their ancestral Christianity of Americans of the slums if there are any in America–temporarily calling themselves Hindus under the influence of a plausible Hindu missionary. I have already complained of the methods adopted by some missionaries to wean ignorant people from the religion of their forefathers. It is one thing to preach one's religion to whomsoever may choose to adopt it, another to entice masses. And if those thus enticed, or being undeceived, go back to then old love, their return will give natural joy to those whom they had forsaken."[45]

As late as 1942, when somebody asked Gandhiji, "You oppose all conversion without conviction? But are you not inconsistent? You profess equal respect for all religions, why then worry about how the conversion is brought about?"

Gandhiji's bold reply was:

"Conversion without conviction is a mere change and not conversion, which is a revolution in one's life. You too seem to forget that equal respect implies respect for my own faith as much as for yours or any other neighbours. My respect for my own faith forbids my being indifferent to my children abandoning their parents' faith without conviction. And I should have little respect for you if you led my children astray by making all kinds of worldly promises in which matters of the spirit had no play."[46]

Barter Mentality

While Gandhiji felt deeply concerned about the enticing of illiterate and innocent Harijans into the net of religious conversion, he had no sympathy for those educated persons who deliberately tried to use the threat of conversion for bargaining some personal material gains for themselves.

When some cases of this type were brought to his notice, he drew public attention to them:

"Dr. Ambedkar's threat has had its repercussions on such Harijans too, who are at all literate and are able to read newspapers. They have begun to approach Hindu institutions or reformers with a demand for posts, scholarships, or the like, accompanying it with the statement that the writer might in the event of refusal, be obliged to change to another faith and having been offered on behalf of the representatives of that faith."[47]

Strongly disapproving this barter-mentality, he appealed:

"Without a doubt these threats are a portent and a matter of grave concern to those who care at all for the religion of their forefathers. But it will not be served by coining to terms with those who have lost faith in Hinduism or for that matter, in any religion. Religion is not a matter of barter. It does not lend itself to purchase in any shape or form. Or if such an expression can be used in connection with things of the spirit, religion can only be purchased with one's own blood. I would, therefore, plead with enlightened Harijans for their own sake not to seek material betterment under threat of conversion."

A Prophetic Warning

At the same time he cautioned Hindu social reformers that,

"The course before *Savarnas* is, therefore, on the one hand, rot to interfere with Harijans wishing to leave the Hindu fold, by trying to keep them within it by the offer of bribes in the shape of finding employment or scholarships, and on the other hand, to insist on full justice being done to Harijans in every walk of life. Indeed, reformers should anticipate the Harijans' requirements and not wait till they begin to complain."[48]

This caution was followed by his prophetic warning,

"Hinduism is passing through a fiery ordeal. It will perish not through individual conversions, not even through mass conversions, but it will perish because of the sinful denial by the so-called *Savarna* Hindus of elementary justice to Harijans. Every threat of conversion is, therefore, a warning to the *Savarnas* that if they do not wake up in time, it may be too late."

Recent events have proved how prophetic he was and hew careless and short-sighted the Hindu society has been so far.

References

1. *Harijan*, 30.1.37.
2. *Young India*, 19.1.28.
3. *Harijan*, 27.6.36.
4. *Young India*, 27.4.21.
5. *Young India*, 22.9.21.
6. Bunch of old Letters, Ed. Nehru, p. 113, II Edition, Bombay, 1960.
7. *Harijan*, 30.1.37.
8. *Collected Works*, Vol. 26, p. 338.
9. *Ibid.* p. 191.
10. *Young India*, 26.3.25.
11. c.f. Ambedkar ; What Congress and Gandhi have Done to the Untouchables, (Bombay, 1946), p. 70.
12. *Navjivan* (Gujarati), 5.4.21, Speech at Ahmedabad, 13.4.21.
13. *Mahatma Gandhi: A Chronology*, Pub. Divn., Delhi, 1977, p. 137.
14. Tendulkar: *Mahatma* Vol. III, p. 192.
15. *Times of India*, 16.10.35.
16. *Young India*, 27.10.20, p. 3.
17. *Harijan*, 20.4.40.

18. Gandhi: Christian Missions, Ahmedabad, July 1960, p. 52.
19. *Harijan*, 19.12.36.
20. *Harijan*, 26.12.36.
21. *Harijan*, 25.1.35.
22. *Harijan*, 15.12.33.
23. *Harijan*, 12.6.37.
24. *Harijan*, 18.7.36.
25. *Young India*, 24.9.31.
26. *Harijan*, 27.6.36.
27. *Harijan*, 6.3.37
27a. *Harijan*, 28.11.36.
27b. *Harijan*, 19.12.36.
28. *Harijan*, 5.12.36.
29. *Harijan*, 12.6.37.
30. *Harijan*, 13.3.37.
31. *Harijan*, 9.1.37.
32. *Harijan*, 12.6.37.
33. *Harijan*, 13.3.37.
34. *Ibid.*
35. *Young India*, 20.8.25.
36. Bhagwan Das: *Thus Spoke Ambedkar*, Vol. 4, p. 278.
37. *Ibid.*
38. *Ibid.* p. 309.
39. *Ibid.* p. 308.
40. Gandhi: Ch. Missions, p. 78.
41. *Harijan*, 3.4.37.
42. *Harijan*, 11.5.35.
42a. *Harijan*, 17.4.37.
43. *Harijan*, 25.9.37.
44. *Harijan*, 4.7.36.
45. *Harijan*, 30.12.39.
46. *Harijan*, 29.3.42.
47. *Harijan*, 21.3.36.
48. *Ibid.*

DOCUMENT

Gandhiji on Conversion of his Son

In May, 1936 Gandhiji's eldest son Harilal Gandhi accepted Islam and became Abdullah Gandhi. Gandhiji poured out the agony of his heart in an open letter addressed "To my numerous Muslim friends" which was released to Press from Bangalore on June 2, and published in *Harijan* dated June 6, 1936. It is being reproduced here–Ed.

"The newspapers report that about a fortnight ago my eldest son Harilal, now nearing fifty years, accepted Islam and that on Friday last 29th May in the midst of a large congregation in the Jumma Musjid at Bombay, he was permitted to announce his acceptance amid great acclamation and that, after his speech was finished, he was besieged by his admirers who vied with one another to shake hands with him. If this acceptance was from the heart and free from any worldly considerations, I should have no quarrel. For, I believe Islam to be as true a religion as my own.

"But I have the gravest doubt about this acceptance being from the heart or free from selfish considerations. Everyone who knows my son Harilal, knows that he has been for years addicted to the drink evil and has been in the habit of visiting houses of ill fame. For some years, he has been living on the charity of friends who have helped him unstintingly. He is indebted to some Pathans from whom he had borrowed on heavy interest. Up to only recently he was in dread of his life from his Pathan creditors in Bombay. Now he is the hero of the hour in that city. He had a most devoted wife who forgave his many sins including his unfaithfulness. He has three grown-up children, two daughters and one son, whom he ceased to support long ago.

"Not many weeks ago he wrote to the Press complaining against Hindus–not Hinduism, and threatening to go over to Christianity or Islam. The language of the letter showed quite clearly that he would go over to the highest bidder. That letter had the desired effect. Through the good offices of one Hindu councillor, he got a job in Nagpur Municipality. And he came out with another letter to the Press about recalling the first and declaring emphatic adherence to his ancestral faith.

"But, as events have proved, his pecuniary ambition was not satisfied and in order to satisfy that ambition, he has embraced Islam. There are other facts which are known to me and which strengthen my inference.

"When I was in Nagpur in April last, he had come to see me and his mother, and he told me how he was amused by the attentions that were being paid to him by missionaries of rival faiths. God can work wonders. He has been known to have changed the stoniest hearts and turned the sinners into saints, as it were, in a moment. Nothing will please me better than to find that during the Nagpur meeting and the Friday announcement he had repented of the past and had suddenly become a changed man, having shed the drink habit and sexual lust.

"But the press reports give no such evidence. He still delights in sensation and in good living. If he had changed, he would have written to me to gladden my heart. All my children have had the greatest freedom of thought and action. They have been taught to regard all religions with the same respect that they paid to their own. Harilal knew that if he had told me that he had found the key to a right life and peace in Islam, I would have put no obstacle in his path. But no one of us, including his son, now twenty-four years old, and who is with me, knew anything about the event till we saw the announcement in the press.

"My views on Islam are well known to the Musalmans, who are reported to have enthused over my son's profession. A brotherhood of Islam has telegraphed to me thus: 'Expect, like your son, you–a truth seeker–to embrace Islam, truest religion of world.'

"I must confess that all this has hurt me. I sense no religious spirit behind this demonstration. I feel that those who are responsible for Harilal's acceptance of Islam did not take the most ordinary precautions they ought to have in a case of this kind. Harilal's apostasy is no loss to Hinduism and his admission to Islam a source of weakness to it, if, as I apprehend, he remains the same wreck that he was before.

"Surely conversion is a matter between man and his Maker who alone knows His creature's hearts. And conversion without a clean heart is, in my opinion, a denial of God and religion. Conversion without cleanness of heart can only be a matter for sorrow, not joy, to a godly person.

"My object in addressing these lines to numerous Muslim friends is to ask them to examine Harilal in the light of his immediate past and if they find that his conversion is a soulless matter, to tell so plainly and disown him and, if they discover sincerity in him, to see that he is protected against temptations, so that his sincerity results in his becoming a god-fearing member of society. Let them know that excessive indulgence has softened his brain and undermined his sense of right and wrong, truth and falsehood. I do not mind whether he is known as Abdulla or Harilal, if by adopting one name for the other he becomes a true devotee of God, which both the names mean."

25

Shuddhi Movement: A Brief Survey

Dr. Ravindra V. Ramdas

Director (Research), Brihan Bharatiya Samaj, Bombay

Mahamahopadhyaya Dr. P.V. Kane notes in his *History of Dharmasastra,*

> "One important matter dealt with by a few of the *smritis* and some of the digests is the re-admission into the Hindu fold of those who were converted by force or by invading Mlechchhas. In view of the fact that *Manu VIII, 169, Vishnu Dh. S. Vii 6-7, Yajnavalkya* S. 11-89 declare that what is given by force, what is enjoyed by force and what is caused to be written by force and all transactions whatsoever that arc brought about by force are void and to fulfil the burning desire of many people forcibly converted in times of disturbances to return to the Hindu fold and to the religion of their forefathers, the movement, now called *Shuddhi* should be encouraged by all interested in the well-being and stability of Hindu Society."[1] Kane suggests it is better to call this return by the name '*Paravartana.*'[2] A model but brief rite for

the *paravavtana* of those who were forcibly converted or even for those who voluntarily left the Hindu fold but want to return to it is given by Kane in the Appendix.[3]

In ancient times such people appear to have been taken into the Hindu fold by the performance of *Vratyastoma*.[4] The same *prayoga* with suitable changes may be employed taking into the Hindu fold anyone who was not born a Hindu or was converted to some other religion.

Not only was there re-admission of those that were converted, but non Hindu tribes such as Yavanas, Kiratas, Sakas were absorbed into the Hindu fold and were induced to adopt the practices of Hindus. A Greek ambassador of King Antalikita (Antialkidas) named Heliodora, son of Diya (Dion), was accredited to the court of King Bhagabhadra, called himself Bhagavata and raised a column in honour of Vasudeva in 2nd century B.C.[5]

Shuddhi in Medieval Period

The Muslim invaders were aggressive proselytisers; with the consequence that instead of Muslims being converted to Hinduism, many Hindus became Muhammadans. However, Hinduism began to tide over this crisis by reclaiming most of the Hindus that were being converted to Islam. *Shuddhi* was prescribed by the sage Devala, who was staying on the banks of the Sindhu. The ascetics and saints approached him and questioned him on the concept of *Shuddhi* which is a word used in the *Smriti* itself. The *Devala Smriti* enjoined expiation of Hindus, who having touched or remained together for a long time with the *Mlechchhas* became impure. The composition of *Devela Smriti* dates to the 10th century A.D. *Devala Smriti* expressly lays down that everybody, male or female, healthy or diseased, shall perform a purificatory rite, if he or she is from eleven to eighty years old.[6] The Muslim historians attest to this reconversion of the converts. "The people of India had returned to idolatry except those of Kosa."[7] Al-beruni refers to the return of the Hindu slaves in Muslim countries to their own country and religion.[8]

> Deva Raya of Vijayanagar in 1398-99, says *Tawarikh Farishtah,* invaded the territory of his Muslim neighbour. He was defeated in the struggle that ensued and 2000 *Brahman* girls were made captives by the army of Firoz Shah Bahamani. This compelled the Rajah to sue for peace as the *Brahman* demanded that their girls be restored to them from their Muslim captors. A treaty was signed and the girls were released. Evidently the *Brahman* girls polluted by the touch of the Mohammedans were taken back into the Hindu fold.[9]

During the southern expedition of Mohammed Tughlaq, two Hindu chieftains Harihar and Bukka were taken to Delhi as prisoners and were converted to Islam. But under the inspiration of Vidyaranya Swami, they returned to south, got reconverted to Hinduism and founded the mighty Vijaynagar Empire in 1336, which successfully resisted the Muslim expansionism in the south up to the fateful battle of Talicotta in 1565.

Devala Smriti considers also the cases of women who have been raped by the *Mlechchhas* and have even conceived. Vijnaneshwara in his commentary on *Yajnavalkya Smriti* quotes verses from many *Smritis* to show that a woman can be taken back into the caste even if she is raped by *Chandala, Pukkasa* or *Mlechchha.*[10] Thus till the beginning of 12th century A.D., the time when Vijnaneshwara lived and wrote, it was considered to be a correct procedure, both in North and South India, to purify a woman abducted by a *Mlechchha.*

Prof. T.L.Vasvani notes in his chapter "Call of the Flute" of the '*Ancient Murli*',

> "Krishnabhakti transformed the life of a great scholar and logician Chaitanya. Krishnabhakti became a life giving religion to thousands of Hindus. And even Moslems came under the spell. Some very moving songs about Krishna and Radha were composed by a Muslim disciple who called himself Chaitanyadas. Chaitanya's enthusiasm to spread the message of the Murli was boundless. Dabir Khan and Mallik were Hindu converts to Islam. They learnt Arabic under Syed Fakir-uddin. Shri Chaitanya brought them back into Hindu society gave them Hindu names Santan, Rupa and initiated them into Vaishnava Faith. This Santan became an honoured apostle of Sri Krishna's message. So we read of a moslem named Chaitanyadas who was brought into the Hindu fold by Chaitanya's followers. The message of the flute made a new Bengal."[11]

Bhavishya Purana mentions that the disciples of Swami Ramananda reached Ayodhya, and brought back thousands of converts to Islam back to the Hindu-fold. It says:

कृत्वा विलोमं तं मंत्रं वैष्णवास्तानकारयत् ॥

भाले त्रिशूलचिह्नं च श्वेतरक्तं तदाऽभवत् ।

कंठे च तुलसीमाला जिह्वा राममयी कृता ॥

म्लेच्छास्ते वैष्णवाश्चासन रामानन्द प्रभावतः ।

आर्याश्च वैष्णवाः मुख्या अयोध्याया बभूविरे ॥

—भविष्य पुराण, प्रकरण 421[12]

The Portuguese also witnessed the reconversion of the Christians to Hinduism on the west coast of India. Dr. Gerson du Cunha notes,

"But amidst their great successes, fame and opulence the members of the Society of Jesus in Bassein (Vasai) were not quite happy. Their wily rivals, the *Brahmans*, were constantly instigating their converts to recant and return to their ancestral faith. Many were the expedients resorted to for this purpose, but the most irritating to the Jesus priests was the annual jubilee of general baptism in the water of the sea or the rivers. This general bathing took place once a year in the last quarter of the moon in the month of August *(Gokula Ashtami)*.

"The *Brahmans* used to impress on the mind of the new Christians that a bath in the river on such festive occasion in the Hindu calender was far more efficient to purify one's sins and all the lustrations even of Christians' purgatory. The priests of the Church of the name of Jesus, provoked by such blasphemous language, tried at first to prevent the sacred ablutions of the Hindus by planting Crosses all along the banks of the Bassein creek down to the Thane river and even as far as Bombay. But nothing would stop the jubiliar baptism, as the Hindus shifted yearly from one place to another."[13]

In a treaty concluded with the Portuguese in the beginning of the year 1667, it was demanded by the Mughal Emperor that the orphans of the subjects of the Mughal King, though they may be Hindus or Mohammedans, should not be converted to Christianity by force.[14]

Shivaji Resorts to Shuddhi

It appears that the authorities of Goa on the pain of banishment had prohibited the exercise of any other religion, except Roman Catholic Christianity in their territory. Shivaji led an army against the Portuguese for their fanatic policy of religious intolerance.

"Shivaji, deeply resenting their rigour, on 19th November, 667 invaded the precincts of Bardese, not far distance from Goa and there cut off the heads of four *padres* that refused to return Marathas of his own persuasion, they having cancelled the destruction of all that were opinionated as themselves which terrified the Viceroy that he was forced to revoke his fierce and severe edict. Shivaji burnt and destroyed all the country and carried away 150 lacs of pagodas."[15]

A treaty of peace was immediately concluded between the Portuguese and Shivaji on 5th December 1667.

Chhatrapati Shivaji did not tolerate the oppression or injustice of one religious group over the others, which is amply revealed by the stern warning he gave to Jesuit Missionaries at Vasai who had confiscated the properties of Hindu orphans there. The Portuguese authorities compelled the Jesuit Missionaries to restore the properties to the original heirs.[16]

The reconversion of Netaji Palkar to Hinduism by Chhatrapati on 19th June, 1676, has been referred to in Jedhe Shakavali. It is interesting to note the English also did not fail to note this event of great importance.

"Sevagee has lately returned to him a subtle fellow by name Netaji who had been 10 years in the Mogul Court, turned Muslin, but now remade a Hindu."[17]

Dayanand and Arya Samaj

Swami Dayananda, the founder of the Arya Samaj heralded a new era by giving '*Shuddhi*' a prominent place in the programme of Arya Samaj. According to Harbilas Sarda, one of his biographers, Dayananda himself is usually credited with the first Arya Samaj reconversion. During his second visit to Amritsar, Dayananda persuaded Khada Singh, a Christian convert, to abandon his new faith and join the Samaj. Dayananda made the first convert from Islam at Dehradun.[18]

Kenneth William Jones in his unpublished Ph. D. dissertation on "*The Arya Samaj in Punjab: A study of Social Reformation and Religious Revivalism 1877-1902*", submitted to the Berkley University of California in 1966, notes:

> "The Arya Samaj added a new and extremely significant dimension to the Hindu Religion. Hinduism became a *pracharak dharma,* a conversion-religion. No longer did the Hindu community face threats of conversion empty handed. *Shuddhi* provided the capacity for defence and offense. Aryan efforts to proselytize, convert, educate and reform were supported by a variety of modern and traditional techniques...The Samaj stood boldly in defence of Hinduism, but only in its Aryan interpretation.[19]

In 1920, large number of Hindus who had been forcibly converted to Islam by the rebellious Moplahs in Kerala were brought back to Hindu fold through *Shuddhi.*

Sikh Support to Shuddhi Movement

As early as 1917, Gajanan Bhaskar Vaidya founded *Hindu Missionary Society* in Bombay and between 1917 and 1924 brought back 121 converts back to the Hindu fold.[20]

The close working of Arya Samaj and the Hindu groups is indicated in the following excerpts taken from the *Shuddhi Vyavastha:* "On August 30, 1922, *Kshatriya Upakarni Mahasabha* decided at Kashi under the presidentship of Raja Sir Ramphal Singh to take back Hindu Rajputs, who at one time or another turned Muslims. Until December 31, 1927, *Bharatiya Hindu Suddhi Sabha* had reclaimed one lakh sixty three thousand (i.e. 1,63,000).[21]

Various other organizations which sanctioned the *Shuddhi* included the *Vidvat Parishad* of Kashi, the *Bharat Dharma Mahamandala*, the *Bengal Brahmana Sabha*, the *Hindu Mahasabha*, the *Maharashtra Hindu Dharma Parishad* etc. Members of Sikh organizations also supported *Shuddhi* for the Malkana Rajputs. Bhai Kartar Singh and Baba Fateh Singh pleaded for the *Shuddhi* of the Malkanas. Not only did the Sikh support the idea of *Shuddhi*, but they offered protection from violent Muslim reaction. Lal Singh Akali, Secretary, *Punjab Khalsa Sabha, Samoondari*, Lyallpur wrote:

> "The Muslims are agitated over the *Shuddhi* of Malkanas and are threatening the Hindus, but Sikhs would not tolerate any persecution of the Hindus.[22]

Swami Shraddhanand became a martyr in the cause of *Shuddhi* on December 23rd, 1926.

Savarkar and Hindu Mahasabha

The *Shuddhi* or the reconversion movement was initiated by Veer Savarkar during his deportation for life in the Cellular jail in the Andaman Islands. A number of Hindu prisoners were allured to embrace Islam by the Pathan warders. Savarkar along with Bhai Paramananda and Ashutosh Lahiri not only put a stop to any conversions to Islam but also brought back to Hindu fold those who were earlier converted.

Under Savarkar's guidance the *Ratnagiri Hindu Sabha* from the middle of 1926 onwards reconverted several persons to the Hindu fold through prescribed religious ceremonies. The most difficult problem which arose after these reconversions was how and where to arrange the marriages of the *Shuddhikritas*. The *Ratnagiri Hindu Sabha* got two reconverted girls married to two Hindu youths and Savarkar himself performed their marriage rites. During Savarkar's internment at Ratnagiri about two hundred persons were saved from the ditches of non-Hindu forces. The Muslims and the Missionaries lodged complaints against Savarkar with the District Magistrates, who happened to be a Muslim, charging Savarkar with creating communal disharmony and tension in the district. Savarkar told the District Magistrate if the reconversion movement created tension why should the conversion movement be not considered so? He emphasised that if at all anybody was to be held responsible for the tension, the missionaries and the *moulavies* should be held so because they had started the conversion movement first. Reconversion followed only afterwards.[23]

In November 1924, during Savarkar's stay in Bombay, Shaukat Ali came and met him. Shaukat Ali praised Savarkar for his patriotism and sacrifice but expressed his dissatisfaction at Savarkar's *Hindu Sangathan* ideology and wished that it should be stopped. Thereupon Savarkar asked Shaukat Ali to stop his Khilafat Movement first. Shaukat Ali replied that the Khilafat Movement was the breath of his nostrils. Savarkar told him that as long as there were separate organisations of the Muslims and the Movement of conversion *(Tabligha)* was carried on by them so long the movement for *Hindu Sangathan* and *Shuddhi* would go unabated Shaukat Ali told Savarkar that the Muslims were agitated and were against his *Hindu Sangathan*. Savarkar replied with equal force that where the mighty British Raj failed to browbeat him, a handful of Muslims armed with knives would not succeed.[24]

Masurkar Maharaj Carries Shuddhi to Goa

Swami Vinayak Maharaj Masurkar founded *Masurashram* on 1st August 1920 with the object of reviving and rehabilitating the glory of Hindu religion. His work of getting back into the Hindu *Dharma* thousands of Hindus converted to Islam and Christianity can be only paralleled with that of Swami Shradhananda in this sphere.

Swami Vinayak Maharaj toured the districts of Goa during 1927-28 then under the Portuguese rule. He found thousands of converted Hindu ready to join their ancestral *Dharma*. Swamiji and his disciples visited a number of villages and assured the people complete rehabilitation in the Hindu society on their return to the Hindu fold. It was indeed a shock to the Catholic Church and the Portuguese Government when on 26th February 1928 Swami Masurkar arranged a Public performance of mass reconversion of over 1,000 Goan Christians on the territory of Goa itself.[25]

The Catholic Church and the Portuguese Authorities tried to intimidate and threaten those who wanted to return to Hinduism but to no avail. The Portuguese Government arrested prominent workers of Swami Vinayak Maharaj. The Portuguese Viceroy was flooded with hundreds of telegrams of protest from prominent organisations and personalities in India. Shapurji Saklatwala, a member of the House of Commons and who is claimed to be leftist by communists, raised the issue on the floor of the House. The Portuguese authorities had to release the arrested *Swamis*. A delegation led by Dr. B.S. Munje, N.C. Kelkar, Siddheshwar Sastri Chitrav met the Portuguese Viceroy on 26th May 1928. The Portuguese Viceroy assured the delegation that the Government would not interfere if the converted Christians wanted to join Hinduism.[26]

The Mass re-conversions had a far-reaching effect on the domestic and international politics. Firstly, it suddenly transformed the Hindu minority into majority in Goa. Secondly, it paved the way for further re-conversions, the discontented people openly and willingly coming forward to renounce the alien religion which was forced upon their ancestors. The Catholic Church got its first and rudest shock in as much as its four hundred years of proselytizing activities had been shaken within a few years from their foundation and its dream of making Goa a Christian land had been completely shattered.[27]

After his astounding success in Goa, Swami Vinayak Maharaj Masurkar turned his attention to the several "Muslim" petty-states in the Satpura mountains such as Kathi, Bhagdari, Gangtha and others. These were originally Rajput States established by Rajput princes during the Muslim invasions in the North. They were an eyesore to the British Government, So the British Collectors and Missionaries, especially by introducing wholesale alcoholism, tried to win them over to Christianity but were unsuccessful. However, *Mullahs* and *Moulavis* were successful in getting the rulers converted to Islam and with them a large majority of the population. In the year 1935, Shri Masurkar Maharaj stayed in the mountain jungles for a long period, personally contacting the 'Muslim' rulers and the people and influencing them by his personality and approach, awakened in them a pride for their Rajput ancestry. Finally, he could prevail upon them to return to the Hindu fold. It was a formidable task and after a good deal of persuation, Shri Musurkar Maharaj overcame all the seemingly insurmountable difficulties and the rulers one after the other bowed down to the Maharaj and came back to Hinduism. A Hanuman temple was built up in each one of these states at the hands of its r dors.[28]

The work of Vinayak Maharaj Masurkar is being carried on with equal vigour by late *Brahmachari* Dattamurthi and presently by *Brahmachari* Vishwanathji of Masurashram, Goregaon, Bombay who have brought thousands of converts to Islam and Christianity back to the Hindu fold.

Gandhiji's Son Converts and Reconverts

Gandhi's son Harilal embraced Islam in May 1936. Harilal had announced his acceptance of Islam in the Jumma Masjid, Bombay, amidst great acclamation. Gandhi issued a statement from Bangalore on 2nd June 1936 concerning his son. Gandhi said if this acceptance was from the heart and free from any worldly considerations, he should have no quarrel with it but he had the gravest doubt about his acceptance of Islam. As regard his conversion, it was said that he went over to the highest bidder. Harilal, who took the name of Abdullah was fined in Madras in September for being drunk in a public place. For some days he continued to preach Islam. However, he came to his senses and re-adopted Hinduism at a function organised by Arya Samaj in Bombay in the second week of November, 1936.[29]

In Independent India

During the British rule, the leaders of India were engaged in the freedom struggle of their motherland. India achieved freedom but the country was partitioned. It was expected that after Independence the proselytising activities of the Muslim and the Christian missionaries would stop. However, in 'secular' India, they got a free hand and their activities increased to the detriment of the national interests.

The Malaviya Report brought to light details of negative activities of the missionaries in the eastern states. Niyogi Report (The Report of the Christian Missionary Activities Inquiry Committee 1956) brought forth valuable data and evidence about their nefarious activities.

The organization *Hindu Dharma Prasarak Mandal* was formed in Bombay in 1960 with *Acharya Baba* L. R. Kulkarni as the President and Shri Anandrao D. Bhende as the Secretary. During 1961 and 1971 with the efforts of *Baba* Kulkarni, the organization brought back 1,600 Christian converts to the Hindu fold from their centre at Talasari in Thane District of Maharashtra State, where the Christian Mission was very active converting Hindus to Christianity.[30]

After the birth of *Vishwa Hindu Parishad* in 1964, the reconversion movement has gained new momentum and orientation under the name *Paravartan*. As this *Paravartan* movement launched by *Vishwa Hindu Parishad* represents the most powerful phase of the reconversion movement, it needs a separate and detailed treatment, which is not possible here and may be left for future.

References

1. Kane P.V. *History of Dharmasastra,* Vol. IV, 1953, p. 118.
2. *Ibid.*
3. *Ibid.* pp. 828-830.
4. Kane P.V. *op. cit.* p. 118.
5. *JBBRAS,* Vol. 23, p. 104.
6. Bhandarkar D.R. *Some Aspects of Indian Culture,* 1940, p. 67.
7. Elliot's *History* of *India,* Vol. 1, p. 126.
8. Sachau's *Alberuni's India,* Vol. II, pp. 162-3.
9. Brigg's trans. Vol. II. pp. 374-5.
10. Commentary on *Yajnavalkaya Smriti,* Chapter III, V, 265.
11. Kshirsagar S.D., *Shri Dasbodha Masik,* Gomantak Shuddhi Number, Shaka 1853, p. 69.
12. *Ibid.* p. 61.
13. Cunha Gerson da; *The Origin of Bombay,* p. 17.
14. Indian Historical Records Commissioner, Vol. IX, pp. 114-6.
15. E.F. 1665-67, p. 286, 30th Nov. 1667.

16. B.P. Unav, Vol. 7, pp. 1,3 ,O.C. 4139.
17. Rajapur to Surat, 24th July 1676, F.R. Surat, Vol. 89, pp. 60-61.
18. Seunarine J.F. *Reconversion to Hinduism through Suddhi,* 1977, p. 32.
19. *Ibid.* p. 33 Kenneth W. Jones' thesis has been published in a modified form under the title "*Arya Dharma: Hindu Consciousness in 19th century Punjab.*" (Manohar, Delhi, 1976)
20. Dale, S.R.: *Maharashtra Hindu Sabhechya Karyacha Itihasa,* 1975, p. 2.
21. Swami Chidanand Sanyasi: '*Suddhi Vyavastha*' 1928, pp. 12-13.
22. *Ibid.* p. 85.
23. Keer Dhanajay; *Veer Savarkar,* 1966, p. 180.
24. *Ibid.* pp. 168-169.
25. Kshirsagar S.D: *Gomanatak Shuddhi Number,* Chapter IV, p. 1.
26. *Ibid.* p. 56-57.
27. *Masurashram Patrika* 1974, p. 21.
28. *Ibid.* p. 22.
29. Keer Dhanajay; *Mahatma Gandhi,* 1973, p. 622.
30. The Hindu Dharma Prasarak Mandal, Report for Shaka 1902, p. 6.

26

Hindu Renaissance

(A Brief Survey of the Hindu Responses to the Major Internal and External Challenges facing the Hindu Society)

H.V. Sheshadri

An Eminent Social Organiser of the South: Thinker and Writer

The present wave of Hindu Resurgence sweeping over the entire length and breadth of the land is directed towards meeting the challenges facing the society on both the fronts–the internal as well as the external. Of the two, the first is, of course, more basic and important. It concerns the weaker and neglected sections of the society. And even among these, the *Vanvasi* or *Janjatis* (tribals) and the so-called Harijans have begun receiving urgent attention from the missionaries of Hindu Renaissance. The problems of each of these two groups have their own peculiar ramifications–psychological, social, political and economic. Intrigues by foreign powers under religious garbs have added a new dimension to the problems.

Opening a New Vista for Vanvasis

The *Vanvasis* and *Girivasis,* totalling about 5 crores in number, residing in jungles and hills are geographically secluded. However, the geographical impediment had not deterred our saints and religious preachers in the past from carrying to them the message of *Sanatana Dharma.* Acharya Shankar Dev, for example, had moved extensively among them in the North Eastern region and set up satras *(mutts)* for their enlightenment. The fact that their religious convictions are, in essence, the same is of the rest of Hindus, and the popularity that *Ramayana* and other ancient epics enjoy among them, only confirm their intrinsic cultural identity with the Hindu mainstream.

However, after the advent of the British, *Vanvasis* or *Janajatis* were made a special target of their 'divide and rule' policy. Tribal areas were marked out as no-entry-zones, especially to the Hindu religious and social workers, by declaring them 'Protected Areas'. It was 'protected' in the sense that Christians missionaries were afforded protection to carry on conversion without let or hindrance! The *Vanvasis* were declared 'animist' having no religion worth the name. Their devotion to their ancestral faith was sought to be sabotaged by hook or crook. Their emotional bones with Bharat and her cultural life-springs were sought to be snapped and in its place. Western-oriented Christianity planted. The converted *Vanavasis* were further instigated by the foreign missionaries to consider themselves as separate from Bharat, having independent tribal nationalities of their own. The fact that the anti-Bharat insurgency being witnessed in North East is a direct result of this foreign machination is too well known to need elaboration here.

In the North-East

The *Janjati* community in the North East is divided into 182 tribes within itself. The tribes speak different dialects, live in different surroundings and face different problems.

The '*Bharatiya Jana Jati Sanskritik Manch*' (Indian Tribal Cultural Forum) has come into existence to tackle both these types of isolation– that from the rest of Bharat and between themselves. Even while trying to pull down these barriers, the Forum, in line with the spirit of 'unity in diversity' of *Bharatiya* culture, has encouraged the formation of a separate tribal body for each tribe to deal with its own peculiar problems, maintain and refurbish its own religious practices and popularise its traditional literature. The last mentioned programme has been found very effective in loosening the octopus-like grip of Christian missionary propaganda. At present, the Bible, translated into the local tribal languages using the Roman script, is taught to the *Janajatis* in all their educational institutions. In Government institutions, the *Janajatis* receive only secular education. With the result, the *Janajatis* have been totally cut off from the very soul of their ancestral faith. The void created in their hearts by the absence of any faith whatsoever, makes them fall an easy prey to Christian proselytisers.

Shri Onderson Mawari, author of scholarly books on the Khasi faith, is one of the leading figures of the I.T.C. Forum. Through his books and speeches, the Khasis are becoming increasingly conscious and proud of their glorious past. The atmosphere of growing awareness of their pristine spiritual and cultural values has drawn a number of Christian Khasis back to their ancestral Khasi faith.

As a result of the various endeavors of the Forum a healthy resurgence is visible among Nagas also. With the renowned and revered *Rani* Guidinliu taking the lead, the three main branches among the Nagas–the Neimi, the Rengmei and the Jeliong are coming together in a common movement for their religions rejuvenation called 'Hareka', i.e. 'the pure faith' The 'Hareka' Conference organised in January 1981 with the inspiration and support of the I.T.C. Forum proved to be historic and unprecedented, The 3-day Conference was attended by more than two thousand Naga delegates drawn from 81 villages of the three states of Assam, Nagaland and Manipur. Some of the delegates had to walk six days at a stretch to reach Kokairam–the Naga village where the Conference was held. Besides being the first Naga religious conference, this was the first occasion when the Khasi religious leaders mingled with their Naga brethren and recognised the common spiritual bonds between themselves.

In Arunachal Pradesh it is Shri Turn Pak Ete who has taken the initiative. He has resigned his lucrative Government job and dedicated himself for bringing out the excellence hidden in the religious literature of his Adi Tribe. The coming up of the Adi Research Centre is the fruit of his devoted labours. The Karbi tribals have begun to receive new light on their ancestral *Vaishnav* faith through *Lakhimon Sangh.* Needless to say, all these healthy trends have been set in motion by the incessant efforts of the I.T.C. Forum. The Bodos in plains have started celebrating their traditional BATHO POOJA in increasing numbers and enthusiasm.

The non-*Janajati* sections of Hindus in the Assam plains too have started responding to the call of the Forum. This new trend promises to provide the urgently needed vital link between the two and set at naught the sinister designs of the missionaries to set one against the other. True, while some of the *Vanavasi* groups have no hesitation to call themselves Hindus, the others are still hesitant to do so. But eve n the latter frankly acknowledge that among the *Bharatiya* faiths, the 'Hindu' faith is like their 'elder sister'. *'Seng Khasi'* in one its issues wrote "During the British regime every one of the European writers had sought to project a worst type of distorted and vulgar picture of the North- Eastern region. They never uttered a single good word about the tolerant, generous attitude of the Hindus. The attitude of Hindu *Dharma* towards our Khasi faith has been more than motherly". The last sentence, indeed, highlights the degree of emotional integration achieved by the I.T.C. Forum and an inspiring measure of its success. This was also reflected in the significant expression of U. Hipson Roy at a Conference at Lakhimpur organised by the Forum, "Partition of Assam was a blunder. While politics divided us, culture shall unite us."

The Nagas in the N.C. Hills districts are divided into two religious groups–the Hindu and the Christian. The general practice among the *Janajatis* is to call all the indigenous faith as Hindu as distinct from foreign faiths such as the Christian. The Khasis, however, do not call themselves Hindu. However, a revealing incident occurred when Onderson Mawari was on his way to the *Hareka* (Hindu Naga) conference. He was asked whether he was a Christian Khasi, or a Hindu Khasi. Mawri introduced himself as a Hindu Khasi, in order to denote that he was following the indigenous Khasi faith and that he was not a Christian Khasi. How beautifully this incident signifies the fact that the all-embracing term to signify all that is indigenous in this country is Hindu and that it forms the common unifying thread for them all !

Another significant fact is this. It is Hindi–though it be a smattering–which is understood by most of the illiterate members of *Janajatis,* and not English. So Hindi promises to become the natural link language between the various groups in place of English which is being forced down their throats by the Governmental agencies and the missionaries. Once Hindi comes in, Devanagari script too is bound to become popular for their dialects replacing the Roman script. Very recently, the Dimasas and the Jemi Nagas have adopted Devanagari for their scripts.

There is an interesting example of how the all-embracing Hindu viewpoint is able to appeal to the *Janajatis* and dispel the misconceptions indoctrinated into their minds by the British propagandists. The celebrated Naga Freedom fighter *Rani* Guidinliu was invited to participate in the historic World Hindu Meet at Prayag, organised by the *Vishwa Hindu Parishad* in January 1979. She was surprised that she 'an animist and not a Hindu' was being invited to a Hindu conference. She pleaded her inability. The *Parishad* workers explained that worshipping animals, birds and trees finds respectable place in the traditions of Hindu *Dharma*. They gave a number of examples to elucidate how the Hindu looks upon all these objects as various manifestations of the One Absolute and Immanent Godhead. This basic viewpoint appealed to the *Rani* immensely. She came to the conference along with her Naga disciples and gave an inspiring address.

After attending that Conference, a new spark of self-respect is lit up among the *Janajatis* who had come from the Khasi and Jayantia hill areas of Assam. They said "Day in and day out, intrigues are afoot to convert us to Christianity. All sorts of pressure-tactics are being resorted to. Allurements are held out. But now that we have seen so vast a Hindu fraternity standing solidly by us, we are filled with confidence that we can stand on our own and never fall a prey to conversion. This is our solemn pledge."

A press correspondent from Shillong, who was specially invited to the conference, also expressed himself in a similar vein: "We had been experiencing all these years that we were an isolated lot, living in some far-off and neglected corners of the land, uncared for and not even remembered by anyone else. But the present experience has opened a new vista for us. We now feel that we are as much part and parcel of this great Hindu Nation and inheritors of this holy and noble Hindu *Dharma* as others."

As a result, the assertion of the voice of Hindu tribals in public life is gaining momentum. The dominating Christian influence which was being taken for granted so long is now being resented and even challenged. In Meghalaya, Christians who are just 46% of population, command a majority in the Assembly and the Government administration. Having cornered the lion's share in educational and economic facilities available for the *Janajatis* they have come to dominate political, social, cultural, educational etc., activities of the State. On the Christmas Day, the Government Offices and even the Assembly Building used to be illuminated as if Meghalaya was a Christian State. In 1979 the Hindu tribals bestirred themselves and submitted a memorandum to their Chief Minister objecting to this practice as being against the secular nature of our Constitution. Copies of the same were sent to the Prime Minister and the Central Home Minister also. The effect was visible the very next year. The Meghalaya Government issued a circular to all Government Offices that no Government buildings shall in future be used for religious celebrations.

The fascinating, "Students' Experience in Inter-State Living", project organised by the *Akhil Bharatiya Vidyarthi Parishad* has furnished one more convincing experience to *the janajatis* of the North East. As one of the many items included in that project, 30 students from different parts of the North East Region were invited for a pilgrimage of Southern Bharat in 1980. At every place, apart from the top men in the educational and literary field, lecturers and students joined to extend to them a most warm welcome. Even more than the felicitation in Universities, they were deeply touched by the regard and affection showered on them by the women folk who welcomed them to their homes like their own kith and kin and served them with various types of Southern delicacies.

The one thing which astonished the Khasi students, especially, was the extraordinary interest displayed by one and all to understand the special features of Khasi faith and Khasi tradition. However, they felt equally ashamed in not being able to satisfy their curiosity. For, they had been tutored by the Christian missionaries and had never bothered to know all such 'oldish and outdated' things. Now, after their Southern trip, they felt the glow of their identity. They turned to the *Seng Khasi* to learn about their heritage. The *Seng Khasi* which was till now a 'religious institution for the old and the orthodox', has now become 'young and dynamic', with youngmen and women enthusiastically thronging to its programmes.

The Poorvanchal Hindu Conference at Gauhati on February 19-22, 1982 turned a new page in the history of Assam with the Hindus from the plains, rubbing shoulders with representatives of over 20 tribal groups, and has given a tremendous boost to the process of national integration going on silently in the N.E. region.

The positive response that the nationalist Hindu appeal is evoking even in areas infested with insurgency is something remarkable. There are elements among insurgents also who sincerely wish well of the work of Hindu missionaries. The school run by the latter at Manipur, with a strength of 800, is the biggest in the state. Once, when a couple of insurgents happened to meet some persons running the school, they told "Well, we are not opposed to your project. In fact, we do want our children to grow in such a healthy and noble atmosphere."

Then, there is the amazing experience of a worker of *Vanavasi Kalyan Ashram* of Silchar in Cachor district who had gone on a visit to Mizoram to survey the conditions of *Janajatis* there. At a village, notorious for its rebel activities, the local Christian tribals surrounded him and began closely questioning him about his background, the nature of the *Kalyan Ashram* work, his intention in coming over there, etc. The worker obviously felt himself in the soup. And when one of them invited him to his house, his apprehensions became even more graver. Being in no position to say 'no', he quietly followed him. Inside the house, the *vanavasi* brought him a drink. The worker now felt that it might well be his 'last drink'! However, his fears soon gave way to intense relief and happiness when the host took out Rs. 500 and offered him, saying, "Please take this for your noble work. But I feel you have come to us too late. You should have come here 30 years earlier."

Of course, the *Kalyan Ashram* worker knew that it was never too late!

The remarkable response the Hindu appeal is able to evoke from the *Janajatis* lies in the realisation rapidly dawning upon them that their tribal identity is safe only within the Hindu fold. Conversion to Christianity cuts it at the roots and sucks them into a nameless, faceless imitation of Western habits and tastes. Their age-old values are not only obliterated but despised. It is this shocking realisation that is making even the converted *Janajatis* sit up and think.

A couple of year back, a Naga cultural delegation headed by a Minister had visited America. They were Christians. At every place they were asked to describe the special Naga traditions, their significance and so on. When they replied that they were now converted Christians and had given up those indigenous customs, the Americans were shocked, "What if you have changed your faith? Have you ceased to be Nagas?" they asked accusingly. After his return to Bharat, the leader remarked that if they had to command respect in the eyes of the outside world they had to perforce stick to their ancestral Naga traditions.

In Madhya Pradesh, Maharashtra etc.

The Vanavasi Kalyan Ashram of Jashpur in Madhya Pradesh has been making pioneering efforts in many directions for the total uplift and enlightenment of the *Vanavasi* brothers and sisters. Here also, the innate appeal of the Hindu traditions is able to work miracles. The *Ashram* was founded in 1952 by Shri Balasaheb Deshpande. Shri Deshpande who was in Government Service in the Tribal Welfare Deptt. resigned his job with a view to playing a more purposeful and effective role in the *Vanavasi* field and took to the legal profession. The first large scale religious awakening was carried out in 1963, starting from the *Govardhana Pooja* of *Deepavali* right up to *Ramanavami.* Scores of religious programmes were carried out. *Harikathas* about great religious and national leaders, sermons by saints and *sadhus,* opening of *Ramayna Mandalis,* discourses on *Romayana,* participation of a number of *Bhajan Mandalis* from the surrounding places in *Ramanavami* celebrations at Jespur–all these wafted waves of unprecedented religious fervor among the *Vanavasis.* The inauguration of the *Ashram* Building in the presence of Revered Shri Gurujee Golwalkar and the Raja of Jashpur was attended by over 10,000 *Vanavasis.* The residential schools and hostels for the *Vanavasis* are not merely the centres of academic education. They instil also the noble Hindu ideals into their young minds.

Indala Pooja–the worship of Indra is the most popular festival for the *Bhils.* Three branches of the *Kadamba* tree are worshipped as representing *Ganesh, Indra* and *Dewa Anna Deva.* The ceremonial worship is made even more thrilling by all the men and women folk dancing in devotional rupture round the three symbols. Their traditional belief that Indra Deva–the God of rains will be pleased by this oblation and bring down rains actually came to pass after the worship in Mavali village on 21-12-80. That day also witnessed a unique programme–the urban elite from cities like Bhopal, Indore and Sendhwa mingling with their *Vanavasi* brothers in their feast. Several new temples have been built and many old ones renovated. Quite a few *sadhus* and *sanyasins* have volunteered to serve the *Vanavasis.*

How massively the *Vanavasis* respond to the religious appeal was evidenced during the four-day (8-11, Dec. 1982) tour of Swami Sathyamitrananda Giri in the Jashpur area. 32,000 *Vanavasis* drawn from 250 villages assembled at Jashpur Nagar to receive his blessings. The prince of Jashpur, Rajakumar Dilip Sinh, was present to welcome the Swami and join in the community feast. At Samarvara, the *Vanavasi* saint, Shri Rameswara Prasad, Gadhara Guru, the founder of *Sanatana Sant Samaj* and the *Guru* of 80,000 strong Kavar tribe, joined Swami Satyamitranandji. The two km-long procession of 15,000 people was joined by Sri Larang Soi, ex-Central Minister, in their songs and dance. The spell of traditional *Dharmagurus* over even the converted Christians could be seen in the presence of 5000 men and women from among them, who had come to listen to the two Hindu saints.

Yajnas and *Yagas* particularly fascinate the *Vanavasis* and they participate in them with great religious fervor. *Vanavasis* are encouraged to come and offer in person their oblations into the sacrificial f re, just as other Hindus. This simple ceremony at once instils in them a sense of religious dignity and social equality. The students in the *Vanavasi* hostels move out during the *Ramanavami* Celebrations to new *Vanavasi* areas carrying the message of Hindu brotherhood. In Madhya Pradesh this religious awakening has resulted in 1,200 *Vanavasi* Christians returning to their parental Hindu fold. Similar activities on the religious front have been started practically in all the provinces.

Apart from the religious awakening, *Samskara Kendras* (character molding centres) have been started in a number of places, especially for the children and women. Vices like drinking and gambling have perceptibly come down in quite a few such places. Functions like *Raksha Bandhan* afford an opportunity for bringing together the various groups among *Vanavasis* and also for the intermingling of the urban gentry with them. Schools, Student-Hostels and Reading Rooms are also coming up.

In places where medical aid is badly needed, free dispensaries and hospitals are being opened. The full-fledged hospital at Muttil, in Wynad district of Kerala is one such. With Dr. Dhananjaya Sakhadev, MBBS, from Nagpur as its dynamic Resident Medical Officer, the service centre is growing rapidly. The Indian Coffee Board has been its foremost generous donor for the last three years.

On the economic front too, village and cottage industries are being started. Training centres for *Ambar charkha,* tailoring and bee-keeping are being opened. The *Chakrapad Ashram* founded by Sri Lakshmananand Saraswati in Phoolvani District of Orissa has been spearheading these activities. In Rajasthan, the *Vanavasi Kalyana Parishad* has pioneered Grain Bank, Blood Bank, Medicine Bank in Udaipur, Banswada, and

Jhalawada. In Talasari, (Thana District, Maharashtra), Sri Madhava Rao Kane has devoted himself fully to this task since 1967. The student Hostel run both for boys and girls among the *Vanavasis* are model institutions, both in terms of affording vocational training and instilling moral values and national character. Many of them are sent for training in poultry, tailoring, carpentry and electrician's courses at Kalyan. Some of them have undergone a special course in Agriculture and Horticulture also. A few of these students now hold high Government posts. The work of religious awakening is also receiving a remarkable response. 192 villages of the five *taluks* surrounding Talasari with a population of over 50000 have come under this wholesome influence. In terms of reconversion too, this influence is markedly felt. So far, over 5,000 *Vanavasis* who had embraced Christianity have come back to the Hindu fold.

The successful experiment at Talasari is striking in one more respect. The five *Taluks*–Pahlghad, Jowhar, Makhada, Talasari and Wade–are all entirely *Vanavasi* areas. A rebellion engineered in those areas some years back had attracted the notice of the entire province. The *R.S.S.* and *Vishwa Hindu Parishad* workers look it up as a challenge, and had started work on a positive basis for the all-round uplift of the *vanavasis* in the economic, educational, social, cultural and religious fields. *Hindu Seva Sangha* has arranged for 6 hand-lift pumps for irrigation in the villages. *Sahyadri Adivasi Seva Sangha* is another Center in the Mokhada *Tenshil* near Nasik. *Gopal Ganesh Dandekar Pratishthan*, Bhiwandi, *Rugnopachara kendra* at Virar in Vasai *Taluk*, *Maharashtra Gopalana Samiti* are some of the other institutions which have pioneered service to the *Vanavasis* in various fields.

Bihar Area

Bihar is another province where the *Kalyan Ashram* work is making rapid headway. The *Ashram's* constructive activities in several fields of *Vanavasi* life together with the efficient handling of the Government scheme, 'Food for Work' has immensely endeared its workers to the *Vanavasis.* Here, too, over 5,000 of the converted *Vanavasis* have enthusiastically responded to the call of their mother-faith over the last one year and embraced Hinduism.

An inspiring feature of the *Vanavasi Kalyan Ashram* mission is that 248 full-time workers–56 of them from amongst the *Vanavasis* themselves have volunteered to take up various responsibilities in several provinces.

So far, out of a total 175 *Vanavasi* districts in the country, 91 districts and 4,155 *vanavasi* villages out of about 50,000 have been brought into active contact with the *Kalyana Ashram* work. A total of 303 centres are busy running 75 Students Hostels, 118 free medical-aid centres, (some of them full-fledged hospitals), 102 schools of various grades, 37 centres for vocational training and economic relief.

However the real success of the *Kalyan Ashram* work is not to be measured in these figures and statistics: it lies in the spirit which informs all those activities. Just last year, Sri Roy, after his visit to the *Vanavasi Kalyan Ashram* centres in Madhya Pradesh, feelingly remarked "It is here that we feel completely satisfied and above all, our head and heart elevated." Roy had in these few words indicated how the *Ashram* had realised what Pandit Nehru had stated long back: "The core of tribal problems was not to make available to them schools, hospitals, graingolas, and such other schemes for the so-called developmental programmes, but was to understand these people, make them understand us and create a bond of affection and understanding between us."

Finally, a word about the insistence on the use of the word *Vanavasi* instead of *Adivasi*–a usage emphasised by the British to make it appear as if they alone are the original inhabitants of Bharat and the rest are all settlers or aggressors. The mischief is now being recognised by all unbiased persons. Dr. Harekrishna Mehtab, after participating in the *Kalyan Ashram* programme in Orissa said "Yes, your usage of '*Vanavasi*' is the correct one. The world *Adivasi* is misleading and divisive."

The process has just started. The blending of *nagaravasis, gramavasis* and *vanavasis*–all into *Bharatvasis* is gathering momentum day by lay. As a result, religious perversion and anti-national instigation of the *Vanavasis* by foreign agencies, as also their cruel exploitation by the Government officials and private contractors is bound to breath its last. And one of the greatest achievements of the Hindu Renaissance would be when all the *vanavasis,* including those who had left their ancestral fold for the time being, will contribute their own unique note to the grand spiritual symphony of Bharat.

Effacing 'Untouchability'

The other crucial challenge namely 'untouchability', does not stem from geographical seclusion. The *Harijans,* on the other hand, are spread out all over the country and in all the cities and towns and practically all the villages. This obnoxious practice has not been sanctioned by the ancient *Dharma* of the Hindus and has been allowed to go on for long, masquerading as a religious injunction. The present Hindu Resurgence has directed its fire against this dangerous perversion of *Dharma* as well.

More than ten years ago all the various Hindu *mathadhipatis* (Heads of the various religious orders) assembled at the Vishva Hindu Conference at Udupi in 1969, declared with one voice that untouchability has absolutely no scriptural sanction. They ordained that all Hindus should thereafter behave with one another as equals. Any feeling of high or low, touchable and untouchable, in our social and religious intercourse is a sinful *adharma.* In September 1981, the leading *Mathadhipatis* in Karnataka took one more revolutionary step. They came forward to give *mantra deeksha* (initiation), which was till now reserved for their own followers, to all Hindus, including Harijans. They also declared their *mutts* open to all Hindus, including Harijans, and sanctioned equal rights to all in matters of *pooja, tirtha* and *Prasad* (Ritual worship, consecrated water and food offerings). The various *mathadhipatis*, till now looked upon merely as heads of their respective Sects, are gradually attaining the enlarged stature of Hindu *mathadhipatis*. Scores of *mathadhipatis* and *sanyasins* are following up these resolutions in practice as well. They have started moving and mixing with the *Harijans* in their *mohallas*, visiting their houses, worshipping in their temples and partaking of the *prasad*.

During the Poorvanchal Hindu Conference at Gauhati, Assam, in 1982 Vibhudesh Tirtha Swamiji of Admar *Mutt*, Udupi, stayed with a fisherman. The Swamiji carried out the *mutt's* time honoured daily worship in his house and distributed *prasad* to the entire fishermen community. No wonder they were so overwhelmed that they felt that "God himself came to them in the form of Swamiji."

The visit of Sankaracharya of Dwaraka Peeth to Harijan localities in Jammu, in the wake of the Hindu Unity Conference in Jammu (1981) and of several saints and *Mahants* to Harijan localities after the historic *Dharma Sammelan* in Amritsar in March, 1983 have furnished the much needed religious sanction to the movement of social integration in those areas.

Even the most orthodox religious heads have, after their visits to such localities, come back overwhelmed with the religious fervor of our neglected brethren. The visit of a *Sanyasi* or a *Mathadhipati* becomes a big religious festivity for them. The lanes are cleaned, watered and decorated with *Rangoli;* men, women and children bathe and dress up as if for a worship. Ladies offer *Aarti*. After visiting such slums in several places, the Pejawar Swamiji of Udupi said, "In no other locality do I find such utter devotion, such simplicity of faith, as I had there. It is indeed an inspiring lesson in religious faith for others."

The Admar Swamiji of Udupi mused in the Conference of the religious *Mathadhipatis* held in September last at Bangalore, "The depth of faith and devotion amongst our Harijan brothers is beyond compare. In fact, I feel a touch of holiness when they clasp my feet. When I move among the rich and die aristocratic, their pomp and show nauseates me. However, the sin that sticks to me in such an atmosphere of hypocrisy is washed clear whenever I visit the lowly huts of our Harijan brothers."

This is truly one of the most remarkable features of the present Hindu upsurge. For the first time in the history of our social reforms, the traditional *mathadhipatis* too have joined hands. They have also thrown open the till now forbidden portals of *Vedas* and other sacred scriptures to all those who were deprived of the same so far. One month training camps at Narikombu in Dakshina Kannada Dist. and Hariharpura in Chickmangalur distt. in Karnataka for teaching *Vedas* being conducted under the guidance of Pejawar Swamiji are attended by all sections of Hindus, including Harijans. A full-fledged six-year *Vedic* cum agricultural training course also has been initiated at Narikombu, thanks to the dedicated efforts of the local *RSS Sanghachalak*, Sri Krishna Somayai, who has personally spent over Rupees 2 lacs for the purpose.

Training for the Harijan *archakas* (priests) in the *Vedic* tradition was organised by the Kanchi Shankaracharya in Kerala 2 years ago. A similar camp was organised last year at Tirupathi by the *Vishwa Hindu Parishad* under the auspices of *Tirupati-Tirumala Devasthanam Board* for 100 participants. The programme conducted in Karnataka in May, 1983 under the patronage of the Adi Chunchanagiri *Mathadheesh* in the precincts of the *Mutt* itself, trained 60 such *archakas.*

In such camps is witnessed the deep rooted faith in the *Vedas* among such sections who have been deprived of its learning since millennia. In recent decades, especially this deprivation has begun hurting them seriously. Their sense of dignity and devotion to *Dharma* has received a humiliating shock. The British diplomacy of 'divide and rule' had added fuel to the fire and roused passions of the deprived sections against the religiously privileged. However, this hatred did not result in resentment against the sacred scriptures themselves. Their faith and adoration for them have remained undiluted, which speaks eloquently for the innate fund of noble *samskaras* preserved by them over the past centuries. The conducting of 'Speak Sanskrit' camps in Harijan localities initiated by the *Hindu Seva Pratishthan*, Bangalore, has also helped to inject into their minds a sense of cultural dignity and oneness with the rest of the society.

All this is nothing short of a major socio-religious revolution. Barriers, thousands of years old, are being pulled down. Inequalities and a sense of high and low, bred in the name of *dharma,* are being ironed out. Discrimination and injustice born out of these distortions are being discarded. The true meaning of *dharma* is gradually dawning on the people. The principle of social integration implied in *dharma*, but forgotten for too long, is being re-established. No *Smritikaras* (Hindu law givers) who could recognise the timely responses necessary to meet the new challenges had come up over the last one thousand years. Now, all over the country such saints and sages have arisen, trumpeting the birth of a new Hindu *Smriti*, epitomised in the short mantra '*Hindavaha sodarah sarve*' (all Hindus are brothers to each other).

This is undoubtedly an outstanding feature of the present Hindu Renaissance. It is entirely positive and enduring in its content, and is in tune with the glorious tradition of self-reformation and self-rejuvenation which is the key to the immortality of our *dharma* and *samaj* (society).

Apart from the massive Hindu awakening, a silent intermingling of the other castes with their Harijan brothers is taking place in thousands of places in the form of daily *shakhas* (training centres) of the *Rashtriya Swayamsevak Sangh.* It is in the crucible of the *R.S.S. shakha* that all such vicious disparities like 'touchable' and 'untouchable', high and low etc., are dissolved into one harmonious social whole. Even the residue of one's own caste consciousness does not remain. It is this miracle which Gandhiji witnessed in the Wardha Youth Camp of the *R.S.S.* in 1934 and exclaimed that there was not a shadow of untouchability in the *R.S.S.*

The Hindu people at large have come to recognise this unique achievement of the *Sangh*; this confidence has now spread to the Harijan sections also. The experience of *R.S.S.* workers during the *Jana Jagarana* Campaign of 1980 and also the *Raksha Bandhan* Campaigns in recent years have given ample proof of this.

Kailashnagar in Mysore, for instance, is a backward locality. When the *R.S.S.* workers were moving from house to house, tying *Rakhis* to the residents there, a lady accosted them and invited them to her hut. When they went inside, she waved *Aarti* (waving of lamps before Gods) for them and applied *Tilak* on their foreheads. When offered the *Rakhi,* she smiled and said, "That is not the right procedure, and she tied *Rakhis* to the wrists of all of them and then offered them sweets. When the *Swayamsevaks* stretched their hands to receive it, she said, ''No, open your mouths" and put the sweets into their mouths saying "This is how *Raksha Bandhan* has to be observed."

At a small place in Shimoga Distt. as it was raining, the *Raksha Bandhan* function was arranged in a spacious house. The *Swayamsevaks* had just assembled. Just then a *swayamsevak* (who happened to be from the Harijan community) reached there. The head of the household noticed him and objected to his entry into the house. The *Karyavaha* (*R.S.S.* secretary) did not enter into any argument with the elderly gentleman. He quietly decided to hold the function outside in the rains, saying that it was against the tenets of the *R.S.S.* to exclude any Hindu from a *Sangha* programme. The *Swayamasevak* however came forward with a request to be allowed to sit outside, till the conclusion of the function because it was unbearable for him to see all his *Swayamsevak* brothers get drenched in the downpour, for his sake. The *Karyavaha,* though unwilling, acceded to his request. At the close of the function, the elderly person who had listened to the talk and observed the holy atmosphere became a totally changed person. He came out, affectionately put his hands on that *Swayamsevak's* shoulders, brought him inside, tied the *Rakhi* and offered light refreshments to one and all.

In Tamilnadu *Samabandi (Sahapankti*) feasts were arranged by the Govt., (in the wake of Meenakshipuram episode) in 5,000 temples, to dispel the disparities between Harijans and other Hindus. However, at many places the Harijans would not turn up thinking that it was just an official hoax. It was only after the *Swayamsevaks* took the initiative that they came and the programmes became successful. The *Mathadhipaties* and *Sanyasins* of various sects there have come out of their cosy shells. Leaders of all castes and sects 'touchables' and 'untouchable' have begun gathering together in Hindu Unity Conferences. Oneness and harmony is becoming the stirring theme of their invocations. Religious and social leaders have begun visiting their neglected brethren. They enquire after their problems, and offer immediate relief. Most important of all, they refurbish their faith in their ancestral *Dharma*. The Hindu renaissance wave is indeed catching on.

The secret of success achieved by the *Sangha Shakhas* lies in its *mantra* of '*Hindu Sanghatan*' The whole and sole emphasis in thought, word and deed, on 'Hindu Oneness' without ever referring to one's caste, creed, or sect, at once kindles the spirit of brotherhood amongst one and all. A spirit of equality, love and respect is spontaneously created. While the Harijans and other neglected sections thereby overcome their inferiority complex, the other castes too get cleansed of their superiority.

There is an instance of Tamilnadu in the Madappally village of N. Arcot Dist. The evening *RSS shakha* was going on. A local DK leader came there and wanted to distribute sweets to the *Swayamsevaks*. The *Swayamsevaks* were naturally surprised, even puzzled. However, after the *Shakha* was over, the *Karyavaha* asked the *Swayamsevaks* to assemble. The DK man explained ; "Well, I have been observing your activities for a number of days and I feel the dream of our great founder E.V.R is being fulfilled here. As a mark of my joy and appreciation I have come to offer sweets to you all." Looking at the astonished faces of the *Swayamsevaks* the DK man continued. "Well, E.V.R founded the DK to abolish caste and create a casteless society. But now in Tamilnadu we find hatred and enmity growing between one caste and another. And DK itself is afflicted severely with that disease and is cracking up. But here I have been seeing before my own eyes, children of the *Agraharam* (*Brahmin* locality) mingling and playing with the slum children, as if they are of one family. This was the sight which our E.V.R dreamed to realise."

The *Samskars* (good habits) inculcated among the children in the city-slums by the *Swayamsevaks* through various social and educational centres are having a most welcome effect on the entire locality. The healthy moral habits cultivated in the children are influencing the parents as well. In Delhi, a N.S.S. (National Service Scheme) man reached one such tutorial centre in a slum on a scheduled visit. However, the local person in charge of the classes would not open the class-room. He requested the gentleman to return. Subsequently, he explained that the NSS man had arrived there with a cigarette in his mouth and he did not want such bad examples to be set before his children. It must be remembered that, that person in-charge is a resident of the same slum, infested with vices like drinking, gambling etc. But now the moral instincts of these slum-dwellers are being awakened and they would not like their children to come in contact with any of the vices, not even smoking.

The efforts of the Hindu missionaries in reviving the social aspect of our *dharma* are also bearing remarkable fruits. The involvement of religious heads in social service activities, especially among the worker sections, is on the increase. The *Hindu Seva Pratisthan* has, over the last three years of its existence, trained and pressed into service over 80 full-time missionaries in fields such as educational, medical, economic, moral etc. It has as its *Kulapati* the head of Pejawar *Mutt*, Udupi.

Meeting challenge of Conversion

The external challenge to Hindu Society stems mainly from conversion and allied activities of fanatic Islamic and Christian agencies. The most potent factor, of course, in putting the Hindu Society on the alert against conversion is the *RSS*. The *RSS* is fast developing as the rallying point for all Hindu forces in checkmating the inroads of proselytisers among the weaker sections of Hindus. The wave of mass conversions to Islam triggered off by Meenakshipuram episode was effectively neutralised by the prompt and timely initiative taken by the *RSS*. The Hindu Unity and Resurgence Conferences, the *padayatra* of *RSS* and *Vishwa Hindu Parishad* workers, visits to Harijan localities of the *Mathadhipatis* like Sri Pejawar Swamiji, Madurai Adheenam, and Ramdasar Swamiji of Malayasia, joint tours of Hindu leaders belonging to various castes and sects–all these helped to rouse the Hindu conscience. Sri Shankaracharya of Kanchi also blessed these efforts. As a result, the Hindu Society in general and the Harijan and other backward sections in particular got their faith in Hindu *Dharma* re-charged. They felt confident of facing the machinations of proselytising agencies. On the much trumpeted first anniversary of Meenakshipuram conversions, the Islamic agents had declared that the entire remaining body of Hindus in Meenakshipuram would embrace Islam. But the plan totally flopped. They could not convert even a single Hindu.

Same is the experience in Kerala too. Conversions mostly to Christianity, is now possible only in far-off hilly regions like Wynad and Idukki districts. Elsewhere in Kerala the *RSS* has, through its closely knit branches, brought within its fold even the weaker sections. As such the conversion process has lost much of its force.

The immediate provocation for the Christian religious heads of Kanyakumari District for taking an aggressive posture against the Hindus in general and *RSS* in particular is also due to this very factor. The fast-spreading *Shakhas* of *RSS* coupled with the general Hindu awakening generated by the Hindu Unity and Resurgence Conference in Nagercoil last year (1981), has delivered a severe blow to their conversion plans. On the other hand, for the first time Christian families in Kanyakumari and Kerala have started trickling back into the Hindu fold.

The *Peethadhipatis* have also come forward to warn people of the dangerous social and national implications of conversion. They have now come out of the 1000 year old delusion that conversion is a personal affair, and that it did not matter even if one changed one's faith into Islam or Christianity. So far the general mass of people, as also the political and social leaders of Hindu Society, who normally took their commands in religious matters from such *Dharmagurus,* had also remained a mute witness to the one-way traffic from the Hindu fold to Islamic and Christian ones. But now the active participation of religious heads in the campaign against conversion has proved to be one of the most potent factors in strengthening the defences of Hindu society against the onslaughts of alien faiths.

One of the major reasons for the conversion of certain section of Hindus in Tamilnadu has been the uprooting of their faith in our *Dharma* by the Dravida Kazagam protaganists under the garb of rationalism. The fact that the activists of D.K. and D.M.K. were themselves the first to fall victim to the lure and had taken a leading part in mass conversions is an evidence in point. However, now, the *Jnana Ratham* project launched by the *VHP* is proving an extremely effective antidote to this anti-religious campaign. Lord Muruga installed in the *Ratham* by the Kanchi Shankaracharya and the Pejawar *Mathadheesh* is being taken to the Harijan localities all over Tamilnadu. The wave of religious fervor the *Ratham* is generating is sweeping clean all the anti-religious propaganda and is taking within its fold even the staunch DK and DMK element.

The conversions in Tamilnadu have shaken up the Tamilnadu Hindus to the truth of their basic Hindu social identity. They are steadily realising that the separatist Dravidian doctrine could not help protect either their social identity from the invasion of alien faiths or even their so-called Dravidian identity. For, the converted Muslims no more remained 'Dravidian'. Their culture, social customs, historical memories etc., had all been obliterated. As in a flash, the Hindus there are realising that it is only the invoking of the 'Hindu' spirit that will safeguard all that they hold precious in their tradition. This is precisely the reason why even the one-time DK, DMK and AIADMK activists are now turning into active sympathisers and workers of the Hindu renaissance movement. As some of them told the present writer, "The Hindu spark was there in our hearts too, but it was covered by the ashes of political propaganda. But now, after our contact with *RSS*, the ashes have been blown away. We now realise that it is our first duty to protect our Hindu *Dharma* and Hindu society. That is our foremost loyalty; our political loyalties come only later."

Our *Dharmacharyas* have taken one more revolutionary step *vis-a-vis* the challenge of conversion and have cried a halt to the 1000-year-old suicidal practice of banning reconversion into the Hindu fold of the once converted. History bears painful testimony to the tragic consequences of this suicidal practice in the past which had resulted in continuous swelling of anti-Hindu ranks at the cost of the Hindu Society. The loss of areas like Afghanistan and recently the creation of Pakistan stand as glaring evidence to this ruinous approach.

However, our religious heads are now openly coming forward to take back our lost brothers and sisters. A new *mantra, 'Na Hindurpatito bhavet'* 'a Hindu shall never be a fallen man' has now gone forth heralding the birth of a new *Smriti*. This has gone a long way in projecting the right religious perspective with regard to its social and national aspects. In 1981, Pejawar Swamiji was personally present to receive and bless the 1000 and odd Christians in Belthangady *Taluk* in Karnataka who decided to come back to the Hindu fold, thanks to the efforts of *Nagarika Seva Samiti* which has undertaken a number of projects for the social and economic betterment of the Harijans and *Girijans* of the *Taluk*. Having been reassured of religious sanction, the leaders in various walks of Hindu life are also coming forward to call back their lost brothers and sisters in their respective areas. In response to this call more than 4,000 mostly Christians and some Muslims in Andhra, 5000 *Vanavasi* Christians in Bihar and 8000 Muslims in Rajasthan have come back to the parental fold over the last one year.

In conclusion

This silent social transformation, of reform, rejuvenation and reclamation' now fast becoming a general Hindu Renaissance movement promises to do away, root and branch, with the internal schisms and neutralise the external challenges, and thus fulfill the aspiration of scores of our past social reformers and religious and national leaders who had striven all their life in this direction.

Index

B

C

I

J

L

M

Z